INTERMEDIATE LOAN

THIS ITEM MAY BE BORROWED F...

ONE WEEK ONLY

INTERMEDIATE LOANS ARE IN HE...
PLEASE RETURN OR...
To re... ...OGN...

KT-549-355

...CHILDREN IN BRITAIN

essential information

WITHDRAWN

UNIVERSITY COLLEGE CHICHESTER LIBRARIES

AUTHOR:
RUTTER

WS 2184519 0

TITLE:
SUPPORTING

CLASS NO:
371·8 RUT

DATE:
OCT. 2001

SUBJECT: TES

SUPPORTING REFUGEE CHILDREN IN 21st CENTURY BRITAIN
a compendium of essential information

Jill Rutter

National Education Advisor, Refugee Council

Trentham Books

Stoke on Trent, UK and Sterling, USA

Trentham Books Limited

Westview House	22883 Quicksilver Drive
734 London Road	Sterling
Oakhill	VA 20166-2012
Stoke on Trent	USA
Staffordshire	
England ST4 5NP	

© 2001 Jill Rutter

All rights reserved. No part of this publication may be reproduced or transmitted in any form or by any means, electronic or mechanical including photocopying, recording or any information storage or retrieval system, without prior permission in writing from the publishers.

First published 2001

British Library Cataloguing-in-Publication Data
A catalogue record for this book is available from the British Library

ISBN 1 85856 185 X

Designed and typeset by Trentham Print Design Ltd., Chester.
Printed and bound in Great Britain by Biddles Ltd
www.biddles.co.uk

Contents

Acknowledgements • vii

PART ONE: Being a Refugee in the UK • 1

Chapter One
Who Are Refugees? • 3

Chapter Two
Refugees in the UK • 13

Chapter Three
The Rights and Entitlements of Asylum-Seekers and Refugees • 33

Chapter Four
The Reception, Settlement and Integration of Asylum-Seekers
and Refugees in the UK • 51

PART TWO: Refugees in Schools • 67

Chapter Five
Towards an Education Policy for Refugee Students • 69

Chapter Six
A Warm Welcome: Admission and Induction • 89

Chapter Seven
Supporting Children Whose First Language is not English • 94

Chapter Eight
Home Language Maintenance and Development • 109

Chapter Nine
The Psychological and Emotional Needs of Refugee Children • 121

Chapter Ten
Challenging Racism and Xenophobia in Schools • 135

Chapter Eleven
Home and Community Links • 145

Chapter Twelve
Unaccompanied Refugee Children • 149

Chapter Thirteen
Meeting the Needs of 14-19 Year Old Students • 161

Chapter Fourteen
Early Years Provision • 169

PART THREE: Refugee Groups in the UK • 181

Terminology • 289

Bibliography • 291

Organisations • 301

Index • 305

Acknowledgements

During the last twelve years I have participated in many in-service training sessions run by schools and LEAs. This book attempts to summarise and extend the issues raised by teachers. I could not have written it without the contributions of those who have attended these sessions: students, teachers, advisers and refugees themselves. My thanks goes to the many people who have helped and inspired me.

Others have made comments on the text or provided me with material. I would like to thank Sasha Acimovic, Alison Fenney, Richard Lumley, Deng Yai, Judith Dennis and other colleagues in the National Policy and Development Team of the Refugee Council. Peter Marsden and Vije, both of the Refugee Council, deserve thanks for their comments. Mike Young and Imran Hussein of the Refugee Council deserve thanks for use of their own published material, as does Robert Oswald for helping me with my editor's corrections. Nina Chodha (Salusbury World), Tina Hyder (Save the Children), Janie Robertson and Susanne Martin (Enfield Under Fives Home School Liaison Service), Maggie Hewitt and Jeanette Redding (Hackney LEA), Sheila Melzak (Medical Foundation for the Care of Victims of Torture), Bill Bolloten and Tim Spafford (Newham Refugee Support Team), Giles Diggle (CIRCLE, Gloucestershire LEA), Albanian Youth Action, Hakim Mohamoud, the Minority Rights Group, Louise Williamson, Sheila Kasbova, Joe Flynn, Sue Mayo and Leah Thorne have also provided me with ideas and written material or comments.

Many work colleagues have given me support and friendship while I have been writing this book. They include all those in the National Policy and Development Team and colleagues in the Fundraising Team at the Refugee Council. Thanks also to Richard Williams, Crispin Jones and staff at Daisies Nursery.

I would also like to thank my editor Gillian Klein and John Stipling and all at Trentham Print Design for their work.

My family deserves special thanks: my parents for always being there for me. Guy, my husband, for continued love and friendship and for putting up with all those absences. Since writing the first edition of the book I have had two children who bring new happiness every day. It is for them, Emil and Isador Pilavsky, that I dedicate this book

PART ONE
Being a Refugee in the UK

1

Who Are Refugees?

We drove from Jaffna to Colombo by car and then took a plane to Singapore. We arrived in Singapore and stayed there for one week. It wasn't only us, there were plenty of people. They wanted to go to Germany and all different countries. They all lived in our hotel.

We stayed in our hotel for one week. The agents arranged all that. My dad gave money to them. And they gave us food and stuff.

And then we arrived in Bombay. From there I think it was Africa. And we stayed for two years because we had all these problems with passports and everything. The agents were messing us around and they lied to us, so we stayed there for two years. We stayed in a big house and we had to cook. We had no money but sometimes my Dad sent money to us.

Two men died there. They got sick with malaria, many people get sick there. All sorts of people came to the house, Sri Lankans to go to Germany, to Britain, to France and other places. Mum was angry with the agents because we were going to come to Britain straight away from Colombo, but the agents made us stay in Africa for a long time.

There were six or seven rooms upstairs and downstairs in the house. Downstairs it was a big place and we could play there. I know some children because I stayed for two years and I got some friends. But I couldn't go to school.

Then I came to Holland and from Holland I came to Germany, Germany to France and it's a long story! This was all because of the agents as well. We spent a lot of money because of the agents.

I stayed in Germany for six months. We stayed with Auntie which was nice. From Germany I went to France in my uncle's car. Then we stayed on my uncle's house in France for about a week. We left France in my uncle's car and went to Dover. I didn't have a passport of my own, so I had to dress up as a girl! I had to dress up as a girl so when they asked for a passport we showed a girl's passport and we came through. I was wearing a hat. My sisters, they were laughing at me.

My Dad was in Britain, so that's why we came to Britain you see. He was over here before us and had live in England for about six years.

We arrived in the morning about six. It was a Sunday. My dad, he was at home. He was different from before. He was very different and felt like a stranger to me.

It took two or three years to reach England. That is why I was late starting my education. It was hard on me at school. I was in Year Two in Jaffna and I was in Year Five in London.

I don't think about all of this anymore, but if I do, it's really strange and horrible.

Arjun, a Tamil refugee from Sri Lanka

Some 18 million people are asylum-seekers and refugees today. Many others are living in refugee-like situations. The migration of refugees is a growing challenge to governments, NGOs and international agencies. Even in the UK the numbers of refugees has increased substantially since the late 1980s. Almost every English local education authority (LEA) now has refugee pupils attending its schools. About 4.5 per cent of the school population in Greater London are refugee children, something that could not have been predicted 15 years ago.

The word refugee is now part of everyday vocabulary. But it does have a precise legal meaning. A person with refugee status is defined someone who has fled from his or her home country or is unable to return to it 'owing to a well founded fear of being persecuted for reasons of race, religion, nationality, membership of a particular social group or political opinion'. An asylum-seeker is a person who has crossed an international border in search of safety, and refugee status, in another country. In the UK asylum-seekers are people who are awaiting a Home Office decision as to whether they can remain.

The definition of refugees is taken from the 1951 UN Convention and 1967 UN Protocol Relating to the Status of Refugees, international law, now signed by 137 states including the UK. These two legal instruments enshrine the rights of asylum-seekers and refugees, preventing them being returned to countries where they fear persecution.

Other international laws can be invoked to protect asylum-seekers and refugees. The European Convention on Human Rights (now incorporated into the Human Rights Act) has been used by some immigration lawyers as it contains commitments preventing the return of people to countries where they would be subject to 'cruel or degrading treatment'.

The Organisation of African Unity has broadened the definition of refugees to include people compelled to leave their home countries by 'external aggression or domination' or 'by events seriously undermining public order'. In African countries protection is thus afforded to large groups of people who are living in generally dangerous or unstable conditions, for example because there is a civil war in their home countries. European countries are not so generous: an increasing number of people who have fled war are being refused refugee status, even when the conflict is of an ethnic or religious nature.

In addition to asylum-seekers and those with refugee status, at least 27 million other people are living in refugee-like situations. About 25 million people are internally displaced, having fled from their homes but not crossed an international border. Others may be 'de facto refugees'. They may have fled from their countries and be living in host countries with other forms of immigration status such as temporary residence permits, or they may be living in the host country without the correct documentation. The main populations of refugees and internally displaced people are shown on page 10-11.

The UN High Commissioner for Refugees (UNHCR) is the organisation responsible for ensuring that the humanitarian principles outlined in the 1951 UN Convention and 1967 UN Protocol Relating to the Status of Refugees are observed by contracting states. The UNHCR began operations in 1951. The headquarters are in Geneva, Switzerland, and it has offices in more than 120 countries. It is funded by donations from individual countries, and has three separate responsibilities

– the legal protection of refugees and asylum-seekers, ensuring that they would not be returned to danger

– working with other organisations to ensure that aid reaches refugees

– working for long-term solutions for refugees, which may include repatriation or resettlement.

UNHCR's annual budget increased substantially in the 1990s because greater funding was given by western governments to work with refugees and internally displaced people in or near their countries of origin. The work of UNHCR in Bosnia is an example of this: here UNHCR was working with internally displaced people, outside its official mandate. Some critics of UNHCR believe there may be a conflict of interests in this approach, as extra funding has been given because western governments want refugees kept in their regions of origin. This may not always be in the best interests of the refugees themselves.

Persecution

Persecution takes many forms and people are forced to flee for many different reasons. Some people flee after long periods of political activity, others simply run away because they are frightened. The type, intensity and duration of persecution obviously influences how individuals and families psychologically cope and attempt to rebuild their lives in new countries.

The majority of the world's refugees have fled from war, escaping fighting, aerial attacks and the deliberate terrorisation of civilian populations. Today over 85 per cent of warfare's casualties are among civilians – conflicts rarely involve just the active combatants. In January 2000 some 32 conflicts continued to claim casualties and produce refugees. These can be 'total' or 'high intensity' wars as experienced by those living in Kosova, Chechnya, Angola, Congo (Zaire) and Sri Lanka, where civilian populations may be shelled and bombed. Other conflicts only involve small arms – guerrillas using secondhand AK47s or lightly armed regular armies on counter-insurgency missions. Conflicts raging in Burundi and Colombia are typical of this type of warfare, which usually has severe long term psychological effects on a population.

In other parts of the world persecution can mean the denial of the right to a chosen way of life: denial of the right to peaceful political organisation, or being denied religious or sexual freedom. Those who defy such rulings risk intimidation, losing their jobs, arrest, torture or execution. In 1998 Amnesty International concluded that torture and the beating of detainees and prisoners occurred in 92 countries. Torture is a method of political control, usually part of that state's mechanism for controlling dissent. A torturer may require specific information, but torture is also a way of inducing fear in a larger population. In some countries children are tortured. It seems likely that most people who are tortured do not survive the experience. Those who do often suffer acute, chronic or long term physical and psychological damage.

Traumatic experiences

Refugee children in British schools will have had widely varied exposure to traumatic events. A small number will have no direct experience of persecution. Perhaps they were abroad when conditions in the home country changed, or their families may have been able to protect them from direct experience of conflict and persecution. Other children are kidnapped and tortured, some witness the killing of parents, siblings and friends, some are separated from their parents or spend protracted periods of time in refugee camps. Some children come under direct fire while others watch the conflict on television. Not to be underestimated is the effect of poverty as a stressor.

The greater the duration and intensity of traumatic and stressful experiences, the greater the likelihood that a child will suffer from a psychiatric disorder. That child's healing mechanisms will not be able to overcome such events. Recent research in the Lebanon, Central America and South East Asia has attempted to quantify the traumatic experiences of childhoods disrupted by war and persecution (see for example Maksoud 1992). The findings may make shocking reading for those of us who have grown up in western Europe and are testimony to the resilience of most children.

Mona Maksoud attempted to assess war trauma in Lebanese children. She distributed a questionnaire to the parents of 2,200 children aged between three and 16 years in Greater Beirut. The sample was selected to be representative of class, gender and religion. Parents were asked to report on the traumatic events experienced by their children. The results are shown below.

Of these children,

> 90.3% had been exposed to shelling or combat
> 68.4% had been forcibly displaced from home
> 54.5% had experienced grave shortages of food, water and other necessities
> 50.3% had witnessed violent acts such as murder
> 26% had lost family and/or friends

21.3% had become separated from their families
5.9% had been injured
3.5% were the victims of violent acts such as arrest, detention and torture
0.2% were forced to join militia.

In the Lebanese conflict, older children, boys and children from poorer families were more likely to have experienced multiple traumatic events; a richer family was more likely to have had the resources to send their children to a safer part of the country. Assessments of the experiences of refugee children from central America and Cambodia show that a similar proportion of children had experienced warfare, the loss of family and friends and extreme poverty.

Flight

Most of the world's refugees are from poor countries and flee to neighbouring states; over 80 per cent live in poor countries, and only seven per cent in western Europe. But to whatever destination a refugee flees, flight is a time of enormous stress. During flight, fears of discovery, arrest, violence, return and family separation are common.

The decision to flee can be planned over a period of days or weeks, or a refugee may be forced to leave home on the spur of the moment. Those who had some time to prepare for exile may cope more readily with future events than refugees who did not anticipate their flight.

Desperate refugees use all available means to escape from danger. Almost all asylum-seekers who arrive in Britain have faced long and exhausting journeys: living in hiding or walking for days through deserts or mountains are usual experiences. Almost all Vietnamese refugees in the UK have made perilous journeys in small boats to Hong Kong and other south east Asian countries – journeys in which at least 10 per cent of refugees perished from dehydration, drowning or pirate attack. Some Somalis, Algerians, Kurds, among other nationalities, may have made perilous sea journeys in the flight to safety.

Most refugees have little choice in their destinations. Trafficking routes and the availability of flights to London are major factors in determining the arrival of refugees in the UK. The few who have more time to plan their journeys have more choice as to their eventual destination. Fluency in English, having made previous visits to this country, or having friends and relatives in the UK can all influence the choice of destination. Recent research shows that the existence of a community in the UK and the English language are much greater pull factors to a potential asylum-seeker than are benefit levels.

Since the mid-1990s a greater proportion of asylum-seekers have arrived in the UK as clandestine entrants: in lorries and containers or as stowaways. The increasingly tight border security in Europe, and the difficulty of entering legally, will have driven refugees to arrive as clandestine entrants. The involvement of organised crime in the trafficking of people is another factor behind the increased numbers of asylum-seekers who arrive clandestinely.

Some asylum-seekers hide themselves in trucks or make their own arrangements with drivers. Police generally refer to this group as being *smuggled* into the UK. Other asylum-seekers may use organised *trafficking* gangs. They may have paid criminal gangs large sums of money to bring them from their country of origin. The trafficking of asylum-seekers has increased during the last five years.

Most refugees and many community organisations are unwilling to talk about methods of clandestine entry for fear of jeopardising routes to safety for other compatriots. Evidence collected by the Refugee Council and published in a report on trafficking indicated that the cost of securing passage to the UK is high (Refugee Council, 1998). In 1999 Kosovar refugees were being charged £3,000-£5,000 per family. Not only is clandestine entry a costly way of finding safety, it is also dangerous. In December 1999 three Iraqi Kurdish children aged two, three and four froze to death in a refrigerated lorry while being smuggled into Greece.

Much negative press coverage has surrounded asylum-seekers' use of trafficking gangs to secure entry to the UK. Almost all asylum-seekers who arrive this way are labelled 'bogus', irrespective of the strength of their case. In any lorry or container which arrives with a human cargo there will be those who have a well-founded fear of persecution and those who do not. As the trafficking gangs do not distinguish between genuine refugees and others, one consequence of increased human trafficking is that more migrants without a genuine claim to asylum will arrive in the UK. This fact needs to be acknowledged by Government policy makers as well as the media.

Life in refugee camps

Some groups of refugees have spent time in camps for refugees or displaced people before arriving in Britain. Almost all Vietnamese refugees living in the UK have come via camps in Hong Kong or other south east Asian countries. Some Somalis, Eritreans, Ethiopians, Kurds, Afghans, Kosovars and Bosnians may also have lived in refugee camps. Conditions are stressful and possibly unsafe. Accommodation is usually overcrowded. Circumstances vary, but throughout the world refugee camps have many things in common

- camps are often located in border areas where refugees are sometimes at risk of attack and bombardment by the government from which they have fled

- refugees in camps are often deliberately segregated from local people, to prevent them from integrating into local society and becoming permanent migrants

- refugee camps are usually overcrowded

- domestic violence and family conflicts are more prevalent

- women and girls are more likely to be raped in a refugee camp than in outside society

- food, clean water and adequate shelter are not always in plentiful supply, and malnutrition is common

- many refugee camps lack adequate sanitation

- malnutrition, combined with inadequate sanitation and overcrowding, result in high mortality in refugee camps

- refugees often have limited access to schooling, further education, training, employment and leisure activities

- refugees who live in camps rarely have the opportunity to develop the skills they will need for resettlement or return to their home country

- refugees rarely participate in decision making processes in camps and are usually dependent on the benevolence of camps officials and the host government. This can lead to people feeling that they have no control over their lives

- most refugees have little idea when they will be able to leave the camp.

Life in a refugee camp is at best a life in limbo. Refugees, both adults and children, can also be exposed to conditions as distressing as those from which they fled: rape, organised violence and shelling. Consequently, the mental health of refugees in camps deteriorates over time, regardless of other factors – a consideration that should be used to lobby for permanent solutions to refugee migrations.

In the UK, refugees do not live in camps. However, a growing number of asylum-seekers are now housed in reception centres and private hotels that act as *de facto* reception centres. Conditions found in refugee camps, such as feelings of hopelessness and a lack of control over events, may also manifest themselves in reception centres and hotels. Whether in a camp or a hotel, it is good practice to try and involve refugees in planning and decision making processes.

Arrival

Gaining entry to western European countries has become increasingly difficult. Since the mid-1980s legislative and policy changes have been enacted that are designed to keep refugees out of 'fortress Europe'. These changes are described in greater detail in Chapter Two, but in summary comprise of

- barriers, such as visa requirements, that prevent asylum-seekers gaining entry to western Europe

- restrictions to asylum-seekers' social rights, in the belief that this will deter arrivals

- an increase in the proportions of asylum-seekers refused refugee status or other forms of residence rights in western Europe.

All these factors may place increased stresses on already traumatised people. At worst they present an impenetrable obstacle to refuge.

Refugees and Internally Displaced People, January 2001

Sources: UNHCR, The Global Internal Displaced Project Database, the US Committee for Refugees and the Refugee Council

In January 2001 there were approximately 18 million asylum-seekers and refugees and a further 25 million internally displaced people. The numbers of refugees includes those not recognised by UNHCR, but living in refugee-like circumstances. The numbers of internally displaced people are often open to dispute, as it is difficult to estimate their numbers when many are inaccessible to outside monitors and providers of aid.

Afghanistan	2,600,000 refugees	600,000 internally displaced people
Algeria	50,000 refugees	100,000 internally displaced people
Angola	350,000 refugees	2,300,000 internally displaced people
Armenia	190,000 refugees	44,000 internally displaced people
Azerbaijan	230,000 refugees	570,000 internally displaced people
Bhutan	125,000 refugees	
Bosnia	300,000 refugees	830,000 internally displaced people
Burma	350,000 refugees	up to one million internally displaced people
Burundi	310,000 refugees	800,000 internally displaced people
Chad	15,000 refugees	
Colombia	100,000 refugees	1,900,000 internally displaced people
Congo-Brazzaville	50,000 refugees	800,000 internally displaced people
Democratic Republic of Congo	260,000 refugees	1,300,000 internally displaced people
Croatia	340,000 refugees	60,000 internally displaced people
Eritrea	320,000 refugees	750,000 internally displaced people
Ethiopia	40,000 refugees	270,000 internally displaced people
Georgia	41,000 refugees	300,000 internally displaced people
Ghana	10,000 refugees	20,000 internally displaced people
Guinea-Bissau	5,000 refugees	200,000 internally displaced people
Haiti	15,000 refugees	
India	15,000 refugees	500,000 internally displaced people
Indonesia (including East Timor)	120,000 refugees	1,200,000 internally displaced people
Iran	75,000 refugees	
Iraq (includes Kurds)	580,000 refugees	up to one million internally displaced people
Kenya	5,000 refugees	200,000 internally displaced people
Kosovars	100,000 refugees	330,000 internally displaced people
Lebanon		450,000 internally displaced people
Liberia	250,000 refugees	75,000 internally displaced people
Mauritania	45,000 refugees	

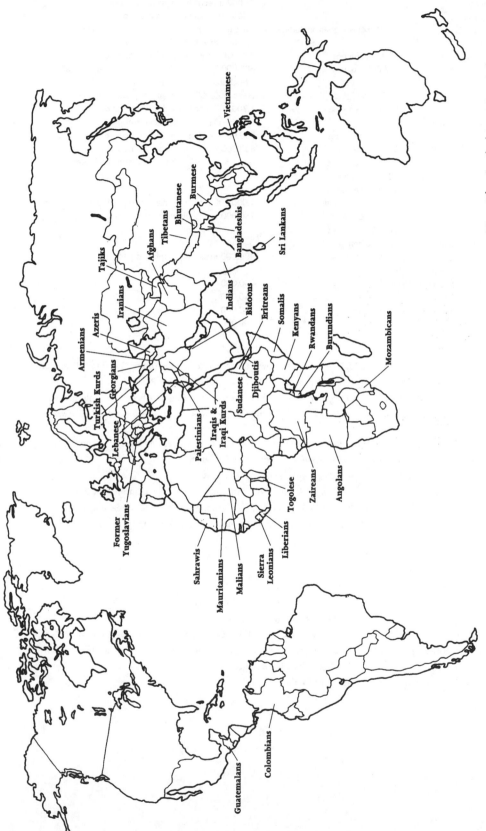

Source: Refugee Council and Amnesty International

Mexico		21,000 internally displaced people
Nigeria		3,000 internally displaced people
Palestinians		4,900,000 refugees, including over one million not registered with UNRWA
Peru		250,000 internally displaced people
Philippines	45,000 refugees	800,000 internally displaced people
Russia	25,000 refugees	600,000 internally displaced people including Chechens
Rwanda	35,000 refugees	up to 500,000 internally displaced people
Sierra Leone	660,000 refugees	1,200,000 internally displaced people
Solomon Islands		32,000 internally displaced people
Somalia	425,000 refugees	350,000 internally displaced people
Sri Lanka	520,000 refugees	800,000 internally displaced people
Sudan	420,000 refugees	up to four million internally displaced people
Tajikistan	60,000 refugees	
Tibetans	135,000 refugees	
Turkey	up to 400,000 refugees	1,000,000 internally displaced people, mostly Kurds
Uganda	30,000 refugees	750,000 internally displaced people
Vietnam	280,000 refugees	
Western Sahara	165,000 refugees	
Federal Republic of Yugoslavia (excluding Kosova)	50,000 refugees	400,000 internally displaced people
Stateless Biharis in Bangaldesh		240,000
Stateless Kurds in Syria		150,000
Stateless Bidoons in Kuwait and Iraq		250,000
Stateless Tartars in the Ukraine		100,000

Bibliography

Bloch, A and Levy, C. (eds) (2000) *Refugees, Citizenship and Social Policy in Europe*, London: Macmillan

Goodwin-Gill G. (1996) *The Refugee in International Law*, Oxford; Clarendon Press

Hathaway, J. (eds) (1997) *Reconceiving International Refugee Law*, The Hague: Kluwer Law International

Maksoud, M. (1992) 'Assessing War Trauma in Children: a case study of Lebanese children' in *Journal of Refugee Studies*, Vol 5 (1)

Nicolson, F. and Twomey, P. (2000) *Refugee Rights and Realities*, Cambridge: Cambridge University Press

Refugee Council (1998) *The Cost of Survival*, London: Refugee Council

UNHCR (2000) *The State of the World's Refugees*, Geneva: UNHCR

US Committee for Refugees (2000) *Refugee Report 1999*, Washington DC: US Committee for Refugees

Vevstad, V. (1998) *Refugee Protection: a European Challenge*, Oslo: Norwegian Refugee Council

Zetter, R. (1991) 'Labelling Refugees: forming and transforming a bureaucratic identity' in *Journal of Refugee Studies*, Vol 4 (1).

Useful Web Sites include

www.amnesty.org	Amnesty International
www.cre.gov.uk	The Commission for Racial Equality
www.drc.dk	The Danish Refugee Council
www.ecre.org	A legal web site of the European Council for Refugees and Exiles
www.homeoffice.gov.uk/ind	The Immigration and Nationality Directorate of the Home Office
www.refugees.org	US Committee for Refugees
www.refugeecouncil.org.uk	Refugee Council
www.unhcr.ch	UNHCR

2

Refugees in the UK

The following chapter looks at refugee legislation and policy in the UK from an historical perspective and includes an analysis of recent asylum legislation.

Refugees: a long history

The arrival of refugees in the UK is not a recent phenomenon. The first written evidence dates back to the 12th century, with the arrival of Armenian merchants fleeing Ottoman persecution. Table One gives an historical overview of refugee communities in the UK up to the present. The first large scale movement of refugees to the UK was that of the Huguenots and other Protestants fleeing France and the Netherlands. They were met with a varied response. Although the churches and Government were sympathetic, the Huguenots were the targets of anti-French sentiment. Workers in the clothing and textile industry also felt their livelihoods were threatened and there were anti-refugee riots in 1675 and 1681. Undoubtedly, the Huguenots and other Protestant refugees contributed enormously to economic life in this country and a large proportion of the white population of southern and eastern England are sure to have Huguenot ancestors.

At the end of the 19th century Jews fleeing oppression in the Russian Empire, Romania and Austrian Galicia started arriving in the UK. Despite their experiences of persecution, there has been reticence among some authorities to see them as refugees. The settlement of this group is well documented (see, for example, Kushner and Knox, 1999), as is the UK's response. The first modern immigration laws were passed in 1905 after a period of agitation led by some sectors of the media and conservative political figures including the avowedly anti-alien Major-General Evans Gordon of the British Brothers League. The Aliens Act 1905 was passed to limit the entry of poor immigrants.

A warmer welcome was afforded to the 250,000 Belgian refugees who arrived during the First World War, perhaps because of the fate that Belgium had suffered at the hands of the invading German army. During early 1915 some 4,000-5,000 Belgian refugees were arriving in the UK every week. The Local Government Board provided transport and temporary accommodation for the refugees,

Table 1: Refugees in the UK

Country of origin	Main dates of entry	Numbers
Protestant refugees from the Spanish Netherlands and France	1560-1700	150,000
Jews from Poland, Russia, Austria and Romania	1880-1914	200,000
Belgians	1914-1918	250,000
Germany, Austria and Czechoslovakia	1933-1939	56,000
Basque refugee children	1937	4,000
Poland	1939-1950	250,000
Other European refugees from the Nazis	1940-1945	100,000
Czechoslovakia, Hungary and Romania	1945-1950	50,000
Hungary	1956	17,000
Czechoslovakia	1968	5,000
Uganda	1972-	42,000
Chile	1973-79	3,000
Ethiopia and Eritrea	1973-	23,000
Cyprus	1974	24,000
Vietnam	1975-1992	24,000
Iran	1978-	28,000
Afghanistan	1979-	18,000
Iraq	1980-	23,000
Ghana	1982-1996	17,000
Sri Lanka (Tamils)	1983-	46,000
Pakistan	1984-	6,000
Somalia	1988-	120,000
Turkey (Kurds)	1989-	38,000
Congo (Zaire)	1989-	23,000
Sudan	1989-	6,500
Angola	1990-	16,000
Bosnia	1992-1996	9,000
Sierra Leone	1993-	10,000
Kenya	1994-	9,000
Algeria	1994-	7,000
Nigeria	1994-	28,000
Kosova	1995-	29,000
Colombia	1996-	8,000
Eastern European Roma	1992-	11,000

Sources: Kushner and Knox, 1999; Holmes, 1991 and Home Office Asylum Statistics, 1988-1999.

who were later moved to more permanent housing outside London. Local refugee committees were set up by volunteers, providing practical assistance. Local resentment to the refugees was rare, except in London where there were anti-Belgian riots in Fulham in 1916. By then the Belgians had started to return home – in the 1921 census less than 10,000 Belgian nationals were recorded.

The interwar period saw few refugees settle in the UK and the passage of further anti-alien legislation in 1919 and 1920. The Aliens Order 1920 gave the Home Secretary almost unlimited power to determine immigration policy.

In 1937 some 3,889 Basque refugee children were brought unaccompanied to the UK, having fled war-torn Spain. Although they were warmly welcomed, the settlement of these children was badly organised and inhumane. Their evacuation and settlement was run by the Basque Children's Committee, a grouping of voluntary sector organisations. Children were first housed in a tented camp near Southampton where there was little by way of organised education. They were later moved on to more permanent 'colonies' – hostels run by organisations such as the Salvation Army, Quakers, the Roman Catholic churches and the trade unions. The conditions in some of the hostels were poor: bad food, strong discipline and a lack of love. There remain long-standing criticisms of the quality of the education the Basque children received. Most had only religious instruction and the occasional English lesson. Only a few attended local state schools or Roman Catholic private schools, with less than one per cent progressing on to university.

During the period 1933-1939 some 56,000 refugees from Germany, Austria and Czechoslovakia settled in the UK. Using similar methods to today, the Home Office erected many barriers to prevent the entry of refugees escaping Nazi Germany, including the requirement for visas. The responsibility for supporting the refugees fell to Jewish and Quaker charities. Most of the refugees were Jewish and their numbers included nearly 10,000 unaccompanied children who arrived on the *Kindertransporte* or children's transport. While there is a great deal of published testimony about the experiences of these children, there has been scant academic research about their educational experiences or psychological adaption.

Polish refugees are the largest refugee group to have settled in the UK. Very few of the 250,000 refugees who arrived in the UK came directly. The many waves of migration include

–   some 2,000 arrivals in 1939 who fled after the Nazi invasion of Poland

–   the escape of 30,000 Polish servicemen, led by General Sikorski, who in 1940 fled from France, the country of first exile

- 101,000 displaced Poles who found themselves in refugee camps in the British sector of post-war Germany

- General Anders' army and dependent civilians

- some 14,000 European Volunteer Workers who arrived between 1946 and 1949 from displaced persons camps in western Europe

- minority groups such as Polish Jews and Ukrainians from eastern Poland

- some 1,500 people who fled the post-war communist government.

General Anders' army mostly comprised Poles who, in 1939, found themselves under Soviet occupation, In a move to suppress all Polish identity, one million Poles were deported eastwards, to Siberia. But in 1941, after Germany invaded the Soviet Union, the latter allowed the Polish Government in Exile to organise an army to fight on the side of the Allies. The journey of General Anders' army from Siberia is an extraordinary trek. About 222,000 Poles, led by Wladislaw Anders, left the Soviet Union for Iran in 1942: 180,000 soldiers and 40,000 civilians including 20,000 children. After walking to Tehran the army made its way to Baghdad, Jerusalem and Cairo. At the end of the journey, able-bodied men and some women were organised into the Polish Second Corps who fought alongside the Allies in Italy. The children who survived the journey were sent to refugee camps throughout the British Empire, including in India and Kenya.

During the Second World War, practical aid to the Polish refugees was offered by non-governmental organisations. Education policy was determined by the Education Department of the Polish Government in Exile, which ran separate Polish schools and a Polish university. After 1945, and the derecognition of the Polish Government in Exile, responsibility for supporting the Polish refugees passed to the British Government, which set up the Interim Treasury Committee. This administered the Polish Resettlement Corps and other functions such as Polish education in the UK.

Some 91,000 Polish adults were enrolled in the Polish Resettlement Corps. They were first housed in army camps and other types of temporary accommodation such as National Assistance Board hostels. Here adults received rudimentary English teaching and some vocational training. The refugees were then allocated to an employer to carry out work of national importance. Refugees were dispersed all over the UK, but dispersal was employment-led, unlike later groups of refugees such as Ugandan Asians, Vietnamese, Bosnians and Kosovars whose dispersal was housing-led and caused high levels of unemployment and secondary migration.

Polish refugee children were the last group of refugees to be encouraged to receive an education separate from the British mainstream. Between 1940 and the mid-1950s nearly half of all Polish children received some or all of their education in separate Polish schools. The proportions of Polish children enrolled in separate education increased between 1945 and 1947, as more Polish primary schools were organised in National Assistance Board hostels. The self-identification of some of the parents who had chosen to remain in the UK was another factor that supported this separatism. As supporters of General Anders, some saw themselves as part of a state in exile that would one day return home triumphantly. Integration into the mainstream of British society, including mainstream education, was subservient to maintaining Polish culture.

Teachers in some of the Polish schools began to articulate familiar concerns: some children had had overwhelmingly traumatic past experiences and were finding it difficult to cope. There were also concerns about children's lack of contact with native speakers of English and about the educational experiences of those who arrived late in their educational careers.

One educational legacy of this period are Polish supplementary schools. In 1975 the Linguistic Minorities Project reported that some 88 Polish language supplementary schools were operating, mostly organised by the Polish parishes in the UK. Another legacy of this time is the Refugee Council. Its predecessor – the British Council for Aid to Refugees (BCAR) – was founded in 1950, as a result of a Government request to provide better coordinated services for refugees. The founding of BCAR was a key policy shift: prime responsibility for settling refugees was handed from central government to the charitable sector. But charities have little control of central and local government policy and funding, making it difficult to achieve coordinated support for refugees.

The Hungarians

The next major refugee group to arrive in the UK were Hungarians who fled after the Hungarian Uprising was crushed in November 1956. After the Red Army moved into Hungary, deposing the government of Imre Nagy, some 3,000 people were killed and more than 200,000 people fled as refugees. Some 21,451 entered the UK in 1956 and 1957, via refugee camps in Austria.

The Hungarians, like all refugee groups, were a diverse 'community'. Their numbers included Jews, Roma and other minorities. There were over 400 unaccompanied children among those allowed to come to the UK and the Hungarian exodus included people from a wide range of occupational backgrounds. The Home Office invited two agencies to settle Hungarian refugees: some 3,500 people were supported by the National Coal Board, the remainder by BCAR. Large reception hostels were opened, with refugees being moved on to second line hostels, mostly in Government buildings. Once they found work they moved to more permanent housing. Children were generally integrated into mainstream schools and the public were generally welcoming.

The Czechs and the Ugandan Asians

The BCAR estimated that some 5,000 Czech refuges settled in the UK, following the invasion of Czechoslovakia by the armies of the Warsaw Pact countries in August 1968. This group included students already studying in the UK who did not want to return home and about 3,000 new arrivals. Most were not initially recognised as refugees either by UNHCR or the British Government. Instead they were granted visas and permission to work and the children were mostly integrated into mainstream state schools.

Five years later, some 29,000 Ugandan Asians expelled by Idi Amin arrived in the UK. Not strictly refugees, most held British travel documents. There was a policy shift: the Government accepted full responsibility for settling the Ugandan Asians and set up the Ugandan Resettlement Board as part of the Home Office. Sixteen reception centres were opened. After a period of time in the reception centre, the refugees were moved to their own housing, often found with the help of the Uganda Resettlement Board. There was a deliberate attempt to disperse the Ugandans throughout the UK, although over one third ended up living in Greater London. The Home Office identified certain areas of the UK as 'no-go areas' for Ugandan Asians: areas of high unemployment, bad housing and large ethnic minority communities but despite attempts to keep them away some 62 per cent ended up living in 'no-go areas.'

Educationally, Ugandan Asian children settled well into school, although some older children faced difficulties continuing their studies. There were reports of teenage pupils being denied school places. The other major problem impacting on Ugandan Asian children was malnutrition. A report published in 1974 by the Community Relations Council indicated that most of these schoolchildren were not eating the full range of school food, because they were unfamiliar with it, or because no *halal* food was available. Although similar nutritional studies have not been repeated with other refugee groups, this finding calls into question the nutritional status of refugee children today.

The Chileans

Some 3,000 Chileans were accepted for settlement in the UK between 1974 and 1979. After the military coup of 1973 nearly nine per cent of Chile's population fled as refugees, mostly to other Latin American countries. A small number sought sanctuary in western Europe and in 1974 the British Government agreed to accept 3,000 Chileans as part of a government programme sub-contracted to BCAR and the World University Service. That the government of the time was Labour and that there was a great deal of labour movement solidarity towards the Chilean refugees undoubtedly prompted the setting up of this programme.

Visas were granted to Chileans who were accepted to come to the UK. Once here, they were granted refugee status and moved to six reception centres and then to move-on accommodation. This housing was located using the services of 'Refugee Reception Committees' – volunteers – who went to look for housing. The high level of trade union and labour party involvement in most of these committees meant that Chileans were found housing in parts of the UK where the labour movement was strong. The exodus comprised of families and single people in about equal numbers, with an overrepresentation of professionals. Unemployment was the most important long term area of concern among these refugees; children's education was not identified as a major problem. About 30 per cent of all Chilean refugees returned to Chile after 1990. The availability of employment on return appears to be the most important influence on the decision to return.

The Chileans were the first refugee group in the UK about whom there was research on gender issues. Diana Kay, in *Chileans in Exile* (1987), concludes that

• There is major bias towards men as informants on refugee issues. This factor is important for those working with refugee children: in some communities children's issues are seen as a woman's responsibility.

• Gender roles within refugee communities show considerable differences. Among Chilean refugees there were many professional women, influenced by the sexual revolution of the 1960s, as well as women who were forced to conform to more traditional gender roles.

• Family dynamics, including the roles within marriage, can change in exile. A husband might resent his wife for learning English more quickly than he.

Other refugee groups in the UK, 1970-1985

Some 24,000 Vietnamese were admitted to the UK between 1979 and 1992, as part of four different Government quotas. They were initially housed in reception centres, then dispersed to their own accommodation, often in areas where unemployment was high – leading to major secondary migration (Robinson, 1989). Another cause of secondary migration was that the First Vietnamese programme, running from 1979-1984, moved refuges into places where they were isolated.

Before the 1980s most refugees arriving in the UK were from eastern Europe, but by the late 1970s new refugee groups began arriving from Asian and African countries. They included Iranians (an estimated 20,000 by 1983), Eritreans and Ethiopians, Iraqis and Sri Lankan Tamils. By the early 1980s about 90 per cent of asylum-seekers and refugees were living in Greater London. It was not until early 1999 that there was any significant movement of refugees out of Greater London and the South East.

Much can be learned from historical studies into the settlement of refugees. Most importantly, compulsory dispersal, unless employment-led, appears to be unsuccessful, with households moving on to find jobs and to be near their own community. There is a lack of transmission of knowledge about the settlement of refugees from one wave of migration to another. Few useful findings drawn from work with Vietnamese and Ugandan Asian refugees have been applied by those working with refugees today.

Modern refugee policy: closing the door

From the mid-1980s onwards European and British asylum policy has converged and moved towards a course of action where greater and greater hurdles have been put in front of the would-be asylum-seeker: fortress Europe has emerged. At the same time, the asylum-seeker has been transformed into a convenient political scapegoat.

European restrictions on primary immigration did not start in the mid-1980s. In the UK, the first major restrictions on post-war immigration came with the Commonwealth Immigration Act 1962, which introduced a work voucher scheme for potential Commonwealth immigrants. Over the next twenty years further legislative barriers made primary immigration more and more difficult. Measures such as the Immigration Act 1971 and the British Nationality Act 1981 attracted wide criticism as discriminating against Britain's black and ethnic minority communities.

Until 1985, asylum-seekers faced few restrictions. But since then they have increasingly been viewed as another group of primary immigrants, and hence people to be kept out. Legislative and policy changes have been enacted to effect this aim. Recent asylum legislation and policy changes are summarised in Table Two. At the same time, asylum-seekers have been attacked in the media and by some politicians. They are being labelled as bogus before having the chance to put their case. The media assault on refugees accelerated after 1996, when the responsibility for supporting destitute asylum-seekers passed to local authorities.

The scapegoating of asylum-seekers has undoubtedly contributed to increased racism and xenophobia, including violent attacks on refugees. Even in school playgrounds the words 'bogus' and 'scrounger' have been used to taunt refugee children. But the response to racism has been not to punish the offender but to blame the victims. Many politicians, too, are using the rise of racism as a means of justifying restrictive asylum policy. Good race relations, it is argued, depends on keeping down refugee numbers.

The British Government has developed a four-pronged approach in changing asylum policy, namely

- barriers that prevent asylum-seekers arriving in the UK

- deterrent measures that make settlement in the UK more difficult

- tightening the criteria by which the Home Office judges an asylum application

- a democratic deficit in immigration and asylum practices, with greater emphasis on immigration rules and on secretive attempts at the European harmonisation of asylum practices.

Table Two outlines the main legislative and policy changes in the UK. At the same time there has been very little coordination and planning at central government level to promote the successful settlement and integration of those refugees allowed to remain in the UK.

Table 2: Asylum legislation and policy changes in the UK 1987-2000	
1987	Immigration (Carriers' Liability) Act fines airlines and shipping companies for transporting passengers who do not have the correct documentation.
1987	Social Security Regulations change, restricting asylum-seekers' allowances to 90 per cent of income support.
1989	Visas are introduced for Turkish nationals after Kurdish asylum-seekers start arriving in the UK.
1990	Visas are introduced for Ugandans.
1992	Visas are introduced for Bosnian nationals at the height of the war.
1993	Asylum and Immigration (Appeals) Act restricts access to social housing for asylum-seekers and introduces fingerprinting.
1994	Visas are introduced for Sierra Leonean asylum-seekers.
1996	The Asylum and Immigration Act stops welfare benefits for in-country asylum applicants and further restricts their access to social housing. The Act also introduces tough checks on employers.
1997	Visas introduced for Colombian nationals
1998	White Paper on Immigration and Asylum outlines most of the measures in the 1999 Act.
1999	Immigration and Asylum Act.

Barriers

The simplest way of keeping asylum-seekers out of any country is to impose a visa requirement for nationals of that country. For an endangered person this can present a formidable obstacle. To obtain a visa, a valid passport is needed, but this may have to be sought from a government, often the very authority from which the person fears persecution. Even if an endangered person has a valid passport, obtaining a visa can be fraught with problems. The journey to the embassy may be perilous, and the visit may be interpreted as evidence of dissent. The customary wait for the issue of a visa may be dangerous in itself. A visa may also be refused. The UK has repeatedly imposed visa requirements when refugee claims from a particular country have increased: on Sri Lankans in 1985, on Ghanaians in 1986, on Turkish nationals in 1989, on Ugandans in 1991 and on citizens of Bosnia-Hercegovina, Serbia, Macedonia and Montenegro in 1992, on Colombians in 1997 and so on. Consequently an endangered person must either try and board an aircraft without passport and visa, or obtain forged travel documents. In Bangkok, Madras, Ankara, Nairobi and other cities 'travel agents' extort money from desperate refugees, in return for tickets and forged travel documents. At the time of writing, hundreds of young Tamil men are marooned in slum hotels in Bangkok waiting for their families to find money for forged documents.

Visa requirements have been coupled with the passage of the Immigration (Carriers' Liability) Act 1987 and the Immigration and Asylum Act 1999. This legislation fines airlines and other carriers £2,000 per passenger transported without the correct travel documents. It has resulted in airline staff and lorry drivers taking over the responsibility for immigration control, without training or scrutiny. Since 1998, the Government has placed growing numbers of Airline Liaison Officers in overseas airports. These are special immigration officers stationed in overseas countries whose job it is to stop passengers with invalid documents from travelling. The Refugee Council believes that pre-entry controls, such as visa requirements and Airline Liaison Officers, should not be operated in countries where serious human rights violations are occurring, as this can effectively trap refugees.

Entry to the UK can also be barred at the port. The crudest method of doing this is summary ejection. Potential asylum-seekers are excluded at the port of entry before they can make their asylum application. This contravenes international and national legislation, but nonetheless such illegal expulsions happen. In 1989 over 100 Turkish Kurds were returned to Turkey before they could make asylum applications. Other cases never come to light.

The new 'fast track procedures', introduced in the Asylum and Immigration (Appeals) Act 1993 and refined in the Asylum and Immigration Act 1996 and the Immigration and Asylum Act 1999 also mean that certain asylum-seekers are effectively barred from entering the UK. Asylum-seekers whose cases are judged at a port of entry to be 'without foundation' can be refused and detained. Their rights of appeal are limited, usually to the Special Immigration Adjudicator only.

The main reason that asylum-seekers' applications are judged to be without foundation is that they have come from or travelled through a safe third country. If an asylum-seeker has passed through another EU country and does not have immediate family in the UK, there are procedures under the 1990 Dublin Convention (and in future under the Treaty of Amsterdam), to remove an asylum-seeker to another EU country. The Immigration and Asylum Act 1999 extended the concept of safe third country by listing other countries such as Canada, USA, Norway and Switzerland as 'safe'. Asylum-seekers entering the UK via these countries and applying at the port of entry will go into the fast-track procedure.

Deterrent measures

The British Government has also introduced legislative and policy changes restricting asylum-seekers' social rights, which are seen by refugee agencies to be a deliberate attempt to deter potential asylum-seekers. The Refugee Council believes that the use of detention, the restriction of rights to welfare benefits, housing and education are deliberate deterrents targeted at asylum-seekers.

Asylum-seekers are liable to detention, in immigration detention centres, prisons and in police cells. On any day in 1999 over 800 asylum-seekers were so detained – and their numbers included children. The UK detains more asylum-seekers than any other western European country.

Some detainees may have been imprisoned in their home countries. For such people detention is a time of great anxiety. People suffer flashbacks, reminding them of their original imprisonment. The fear of return is intense. The unnecessary trauma caused by detention has been highlighted by Stephen Tumin, HM Inspector of Prisons. There have been four suicides since 1990. Self-harm and hunger strikes are regular occurrences.

Asylum-seekers face severe restrictions to their welfare entitlements in most EU countries. In 1987 income support regulations were changed so that asylum-seekers could only claim 90 per cent of the personal allowances of income support. Further changes were implemented in 1996, when the Asylum and Immigration Act 1996 prevented some groups of asylum-seekers from accessing income support.

In 1996 only asylum-seekers who applied at the port of entry were allowed to claim income support. All 'in-country' applicants (see pages 33 and 36) and those asylum-seekers appealing against a negative decision lost access to benefits. Instead, they became the responsibility of local authority social services departments. Families with children were supported under the provisions of the Children Act 1989 and given a cash allowance and some form of temporary accommodation. Those asylum-seekers without children were supported under the provisions of the National Assistance Act 1948 (in Scotland the Children Act (Scotland) and the Social Work (Scotland) Act 1968). This required social services departments to provide sustenance, warmth and shelter – in practice food vouchers redeemable in a single designated supermarket and temporary accommodation. In England and Wales case law deemed that giving asylum-seekers a cash allowance was illegal.

What resulted was a chaotic system detrimental to both the asylum-seekers and local government. Asylum-seekers were left cashless and unable to purchase items such as bus fares, books, clothing and shoes, second hand goods and even the cheapest forms of entertainment such as a cup of coffee. Local authorities were not fully compensated by central government for the services they provided for destitute asylum-seekers. The latter grew increasingly unpopular with some local authority officers and councillors. Some of the less scrupulous councils briefed the press. Headlines such as 'Influx of refugees costing thousands' (*Kettering Evening Telegraph*, 7th August 1998) 'Old Folk's Home to be hostel for refugees' (*Harrow Leader*, 16th July 1998) became commonplace. The involvement of the local press, as well as most of the national tabloids, un-doubtedly created greater public hostility to refugees, and ultimately to greater racial violence.

Further restrictions to social support came into effect on 3rd April 2000 when the new support arrangements of the Immigration and Asylum Act 1999 were implemented. These are described in Chapter Three.

Asylum-seekers' rights to public housing have also been limited by recent legislation. The Asylum and Immigration (Appeals) Act 1993, the Housing Act 1996 and the Asylum and Immigration Act 1996 restricted asylum-seekers' access to social housing. From 1993 asylum-seekers accepted as homeless by a local authority could only be housed in temporary accommodation and from 1996 were barred from a housing waiting list. The new support system intro-duced in 2000 means that any asylum-seeker supported by the National Asylum Support Service can only be housed in allocated accommodation which could be anywhere in the UK. Anyone who refuses that offer of accommodation will lose all support.

These discriminatory measure causes great hardship for many newly-arrived people. Deterrent measures do not prevent desperate people from fleeing – the European Commission has recently described deterrent measures as unworkable (Communication on Asylum and Immigration, February 1994). But deterrent measures do make the lives of asylum-seekers already in the UK much more dif-ficult. They prevent them from rebuilding their lives and integrating into British society.

The tightening of substantive criteria
To be deemed a refugee a person has to prove that he or she 'has a well-founded fear of being persecuted for reasons of race, religion, nationality, membership of

a particular social group or political opinion' (1951 UN Convention Relating to the Status of Refugees). Although the UNHCR has a comprehensive handbook on determining asylum cases, there are no internationally agreed standards for deciding who falls within the UN definition. Instead, individual governments choose their own criteria. This varies from country to country, and depends on policies made by politicians. A country's criteria for determining asylum may also be secret.

Since the mid 1980s the criteria for gaining full refugee status have tightened across western Europe. Proportionally fewer asylum-seekers are now granted full refugee status, and many more are refused.

Table 3: UK asylum applications and categories of decisions, by percentage, 1987-2000

Year	Asylum Applications	Refugee Status as percentages	ELR	Refusal
1987	4,256	11	63	26
1988	3,998	23	58	19
1989	11,640	32	55	13
1990	26,205	23	60	17
1991	44,840	10	44	46
1992	24,605	6	80	14
1993	22,370	9	64	27
1994	32,830	5	21	74
1995	43,965	5	19	76
1996	29,640	6	14	80
1997	32,500	13	11	76
1998	46,015	17	12	71
1999	71,160	42	12	46
2000	76,040	10	12	78

Alongside asylum legislation sits a great deal of secondary legislation. This includes Regulations governing the new asylum support system and the Immigration Rules. The latter are statutory instruments which decide, in practice, whether and how a person can enter or stay in the UK. The Immigration Act 1971 gave the Home Secretary the power to make and change Immigration Rules without needing to change the law. Changes are simply presented to Parliament – which may or may not debate them. Parliament cannot amend Immigration Rules but can only accept or reject them.

Fortress Europe

Barriers and social deterrents are also being enacted at European level. Within Europe the steady rise in the number of people seeking asylum, coupled with the

The Immigration and Asylum Act 1999: what it means to asylum-seekers

The Immigration and Asylum Act received Royal Assent in November 1999 and will be implemented in stages. This legislation is a mixture of barriers and social deterrents. It was passed amid mounting chaos in the asylum process (a backlog of 100,000 cases) and increased public hostility to asylum-seekers and refugees. The new legislation was meant to reform the asylum system, making it 'fairer, faster and firmer'. While it may be firmer, the opinion of many refugee groups is that the Immigration and Asylum Act 1999 denies the human rights of asylum-seekers and fails to deliver a credible and ordered asylum system.

Part One of the Act introduces changes in immigration controls. **Section 4** of the Act give the Home Secretary powers to impose residence restrictions on asylum-seekers, including curfews and accommodation in designated hostels. Ministers have said that this power will be used to prevent public order problems,

Section 11 and 12 of Part One provides for the more rapid removal of asylum-seekers who have travelled via EU member states. Under the 1990 Dublin Convention and Asylum and Immigration Act 1996, certain conditions had to be met before the Home Secretary could remove an asylum-seeker to another EU member state. As long as removal does not breech the Human Rights Act 1998, these conditions no longer have to be met.

Section 15 of Part One allows immigration officers to give directions to remove an asylum-seeker from the UK while his/her claim is being processed, although removal or deportation orders cannot be carried out until an asylum-seeker has been informed of a decision about their case. This means that immigration officers may now prepare removal directions and deportation orders in advance of a decision on an asylum claim.

Section 28 extends criminal legislation, making it an offence for asylum-seekers to enter the UK or remain illegally using 'deception'. As many asylum-seekers are forced to use forged documents in order to reach safety, this puts asylum-seekers at risk of a criminal prosecution. Although a landmark legal case now allows asylum-seekers to plead Article 31 of the 1951 UN Convention Relating to the Status of Refugees as a defence against this type of prosecution, there is still a real danger that asylum-seekers will be prosecuted under this section because of inadequate legal representation.

Part Two of the Immigration and Asylum Act deals with penalties for carrying clandestine entrants to the UK and replaces the Immigration (Carriers Liability) Act 1987. Sections 32-37 and 30 extend carriers' sanctions (a fine of £2,000 per head imposed on any international carriers such as an airline or shipping company) to cover all road passenger vehicles, as well as airlines, ships and international rail services. For those carriers who fail to pay the new civil penalty, there is now the power to impound and sell vehicles until the fine is paid.

Section 41 requires that transit passengers obtain transit visas before travelling to the UK – another obstacle for asylum-seekers.

Part Three of the Immigration and Asylum Act introduces change to the way that asylum-seekers can be detained. All detained asylum-seekers should receive a bail hearing about a week after being detained and asylum-seekers will have a new, general right to be released on bail. Bail hearings will be heard by a magistrate or a special adjudicator and can be held in detention centres. Although the introduction of routine bail hearings for detained asylum-seekers is welcome, there is still no time limit set on asylum detention in the UK.

Part Four of the Immigration and Asylum Act 1999 introduces change to the asylum appeals system. While retaining the present two tier system for asylum appeals, where an appeal is heard first by a Special Adjudicator and then by an Immigration Appeals Tribunal, issues of why asylum has been refused can now be raised at the same time as why a person should not be removed from the UK – a 'one stop' appeals system.

Part Four also abolishes the 'white list' of designated countries where nationals of these states are deemed to have no serious risk of persecution and are refused asylum straight away. Although the official abolition of the white list is welcome, the Home Office has introduced a back door white list. Asylum-seekers from Albania, the Czech Republic, Poland, Romania, the Baltic States, Kenya and India who apply for asylum at Dover may well be detained and told their claim for asylum is unfounded. Part Four of the Immigration and Asylum Act also retains a wide range of other reasons under which an asylum application can be 'certified' – that is refused immediately and only allowed limited appeal rights. Additionally some asylum-seekers will lose all rights of appeal. For example, adjudicators are will be given the power to dismiss appeals without considering their merits and hearing oral evidence. Asylum-seekers refused and removed to a safe third country will continue only to have a right of appeal once removed from the UK.

Section 79 of Part Four introduces a new fine on appellants and their legal representatives when appeals to Immigration Appeals Tribunal are judged to have 'no merit'.

Part Five of the Immigration and Asylum Act 1999 introduces a scheme to regulate immigration advisers. **Section 83, 84 and 85** provide for the appointment of a new Immigration Services Commissioner to regulate the provision of immigration advice and set standards for the profession. Anyone offering immigration advice will have to register with the Immigration Services Commissoner, unless they are already registered as a solicitor or barrister. A new Immigration Services Tribunal will hear cases against inadequate or unscrupulous immigration advisers. However, where an asylum-seeker's case has been damaged by bad advice, there is no power to reopen an appeal or to change an asylum decision.

Part Six of the Immigration and Asylum Act 1999 introduce major changes in the way that asylum-seekers are supported in the UK. **Sections 94-127 of Part Six**

– removes the right to benefits from all asylum-seekers
– removes the rights of asylum-seekers to social housing, some community care

services and support under the National Assistance Act 1948 and the Children Act 1989 (and complementary legislation in Scotland)

— sets up a new support system administered by the National Asylum Support Service within the Home Office.

The support will consist of vouchers and a cash allowance and accommodation (if needed). Asylum-seekers can apply for a support-only package if they have somewhere to live. Asylum-seekers who refuse an offer of accommodation will not be offered an alternative and will lose their vouchers and cash allowance. Part Six also provides for accommodation to be offered by local authorities and housing associations throughout the UK and gives the Home Secretary power to require that local authorities and housing associations provide housing to be used in the new support system.

Unaccompanied asylum-seeking children are excluded from the new support system and remain the responsibility of local authority social services departments under the provisions of the Children Act.

Part Seven of the Immigration and Asylum Act extends the powers of immigration officers. These sections give immigration officers the powers to enter premises, search and arrest people suspected of committing immigration offences – similar powers to those already granted to the police. Part Seven also gives immigration officers the power to use 'reasonable force' to carry out their duties and to conduct intimate personal searches.

Refugee agencies have strongly opposed the above extensions of power. Unlike the police force, the Immigration Service is not subject to oversight by an independent authority with the power to investigate complaints. Within Part Seven, there are also sections which provide for fingerprinting and the subsequent destruction of fingerprint records.

Part Eight deals with the management of detention centres and detainees. Statutory rules will be introduced that will govern the management of detention centres, as well as rules about the duties of detention centre staff.

The Schedules (accompanying legislation) of the Immigration and Asylum Act 1999 include legal provision for ensuring that asylum-seeking children supported by NASS and local authorities receive free school meals. Section 117 of Schedule 14 of the Immigration and Asylum Act 1999 repeals Section 512 (3) of the Education Act 1996. It obliges the LEA in which a child attends school to provide free school meals for that child, as the LEA would for a child whose family is on income support.

For children in Scottish schools, Section 74 of Schedule 14 repeals Section 53 of the Education (Scotland) Act 1980, also obliging the local authority to provide free school meals for asylum-seeking children supported by NASS.

impending abolition of the EU's internal borders has, in the last 15 years, prompted a vigorous political debate on refugee policy. A harmonised approach is emerging. But there are concerns that the harmonisation of policy is reducing the rights of asylum-seekers and refugees, and preventing desperate people from finding sanctuary in Europe.

Individual EU member states are changing national legislation, with countries copying each other's restrictive practices. The process of harmonisation is being speeded by the workings of the Council of Ministers of the EU and its associated civil servants.

At the time of writing not subject to parliamentary scrutiny. Rather, they were part of the EU's Third Pillar.

Table 4: Asylum applications in the Europe Union 2000	
Austria	18,234
Belgium	42,691
Denmark	10,077
Finland	2,848
France	38,588
Germany	78,764
Greece	3,004
Ireland	10,920
Italy	33,360 (1999 figure)
Luxembourg	585
Netherlands	43,892
Portugal	202
Spain	7,037
Sweden	16,368
UK	76,040
Source: UNHCR	

European Union structures

The European Union is founded on three pillars: the European Community institutions, common foreign and security policy and common justice and home affairs policy.

The central core pillar is now known as the European Community (EC). The European Commission and the European Parliament are EC institutions. The term European Community correctly describes actions undertaken within this pillar. This central pillar is flanked by a Second Pillar of common foreign and security policy and a Third Pillar of cooperation in the fields of justice and home affairs. These two pillars are now outside the formal framework of the European Community. Actions taken are, therefore, not subject to European Community law. In a sentence: these two pillars provide for intergovernmental cooperation.

In the past, asylum policy has been determined by intergovernmental co-operation – part of the Third Pillar of the European Union. There are, however, provisions within the treaty of Amsterdam (Article K9), which allow for asylum policy to be transferred to First Pillar – the European Community institutions – within a five year period (by 2002). This would give the European Parliament the right to be consulted on key proposals of the Steering Group on Immigration and Asylum. After asylum policy is transferred to the First Pillar, the European Court of Justice is also granted additional powers over decisions made by the Council of Ministers. The Treaty of Amsterdam also brings the Schengen Agreement within the First Pillar. All the above make for greater judicial and parliamentary supervision and democracy. But the current trend is to resist democracy; it is easier to determine asylum policy in secret.

Key agreements and future work of the Schengen group and the Steering Group on Immigration and Asylum include

1990 The Schengen Agreement. When implemented in 1994 the Schengen Agreement
– increased policing of external borders of Schengen countries
– opened borders between the Schengen states (although some borders have later been closed, often after the entry of certain groups of asylum-seekers)
– harmonised national visa policies of the Schengen countries
– harmonised carrier sanctions
– orchestrated rules by which asylum-seekers will have one chance of applying for asylum in a Schengen state
– enforced a uniform Schengen visa
– compiled a computerised database called the Schengen Information System holding information on criminals, asylum-seekers and visitors to Schengen states.

1990 Dublin Convention
This determines which EU state is responsible for hearing an asylum application. Like the Schengen Agreement, it means that an asylum-seeker can only have his or her case heard in one EU member state. The Dublin Convention may be superceded by a new Treaty, as it has been seen to have failed.

1992 Treaty on European Union (Maastricht Treaty)
This empowered justice and home affairs ministers to establish a framework for European-wide asylum policy.

The future

Asylum legislation and policy will continue to change, at a national and European level. The latest changes mooted in 2001 by EU governments are an attack on the 1951 UN Convention Relating to the Status of Refugees itself. EU governments, led by the UK are presently examining proposals that

1992 Edinburgh Declaration

This proposed that EU states work towards a harmonised system of dealing with asylum cases judged to be unfounded, with most asylum-seekers who have travelled through safe third countries being rejected.

1997 Treaty of Amsterdam

This provided for asylum policy to be brought within the oversight of European Community institutions (the First Pillar) after a five year transitional period. It also brought the Schengen Agreement within the First Pillar. Much greater harmonisation of EU asylum policy was envisaged, but the UK and Ireland were granted permission to determine their own asylum policy. The Treaty of Amsterdam also set an agenda for the Steering Group on Immigration and Asylum. During the five year transitional period, it is intended that the EU, via the Steering Group on Asylum and Immigration, works towards

1. Harmonisation of the substantive criteria of asylum. EU member states will attempt to harmonise what they interpret as 'a well founded fear of being persecuted' and to harmonise asylum procedures.

2. Draw up new criteria for deciding which member state is responsible for hearing asylum applications, in reality new procedures to replace the 1990 Dublin Convention.

3. Develop minimum standards for the reception of asylum-seekers, including things such as more harmonised approaches to providing benefits and housing.

4. Develop minimum standards for the provision of temporary protection in emergency situations (harmonised standards for refugee groups like the Bosnians and Kosovars who were granted temporary leave to remain in many European Union countries rather than full refugee status).

5. Common procedures at external EU borders.

6. Develop systems for the greater sharing of responsibility for asylum-seekers across the EU.

7. Develop more effective ways of combating illegal immigration and the trafficking of people.

8. Compile a European database to collate information (such as fingerprints) of third country nationals entering the EU.

- categorise countries into 'low', 'medium' and 'high risk' countries, with the idea of rejecting all asylum applications from low risk countries

- will enable applications for refugee settlement to be made overseas from, for example, refugee camps. This will enable European governments to pick and choose refugees

- giving greater aid to poor countries that host large number of refugees, to encourage refugees to remain in their regions of origin.

Most refugee and human rights agencies believe that European governments and the Steering group on Immigration and Asylum are cutting a broad swathe through the humanitarian principals of the 1951 UN Convention Relating to the Status of Refugees. Genuine asylum-seekers are being prevented from reaching safety. Europe is host to just 7 per cent of the world's refugees and displaced people. If affluent nations cannot share responsibility for victims of conflict and human rights abuse, one cannot expect the world's poorest nations to continue to provide sanctuary to refugees.

Bibliography

Bell, A. (1996) *Only for Three Months: The Basque Children in Exile*, Norwich: Mousehole Press

Berghahn, M. (1984) *German Jewish Refugees in Britain*, London: Macmillan

Chan, C. and Christie, K. (1995) 'Past, Present and Future: the Indochinese Refugee Experience Twenty Years Later' in *Journal of Refugee Studies* Vol 8 No 1 pp 75-94

Darke, D. (1999) *The Leaves Have Lost their Trees: the long term effect of a refugee childhood on ten German Jewish children*, York: William Sessions

Danish Refugee Council (2000) *The Legal and Social Conditions for Refugees in Europe*, Copenhagen, Danish Refugee Council

Duke, K. and Marshall, T. (1995) *Vietnamese Refugees since 1982*, London: HMSO

Ethnic Communities Oral History Project (1992) *The Ship of Hope*, London: Ethnic Communities Oral History Project

Gershon, K. (Ed) (1989) *We Came as Children*, London and Basingstoke: Papermac/Macmillan

Grant, W. (1985) 'Insider and Outsider Pressure Groups,' *Social Studies Review*, September 1985

Holmes, C. (1988) *John Bulls Island: Immigration and British Society 1871-1971*, London: Macmillan

Home Office (1984) *Race relations and Immigration Sub-Committee Session 1984-85: Refugees*, London: HMSO

Home Office Research and Statistics Department (1993) *Asylum Statistics, UK 1985-92*, London: Government Statistical Service

Isaacs, S. ed (1941) *The Cambridge Evacuation Survey*, London: Methuen

Kay, D. (1987) *Chileans in Exile: Private Struggles, Public Lives*, London: Macmillan

Kay, D. and Miles, R. (1988) 'Refugees or Migrant Workers? The Case of the European Volunteer Workers in Britain (1946-1951)' in *Journal of Refugee Studies* Vol 1 No 3/4 pp 214-236

Knox, K. (1997) *Credit to the Nation: a study of refugees in the UK*, London: Refugee Council

Kunz, E. (1985) *The Hungarians in Australia*, Melbourne: Australian Ethnic Heritage Series

Kushner, T. and Knox. K. (1999) *Refugees in an Age Genocide*, London: Frank Cass

Landau, R. (1992) *The Nazi Holocaust*, London: I B Tauris

Legarreta, D. (1984) *The Guernica Generation: Basque Refugee Children of the Spanish Civil War*, Reno, Nevada: University of Nevada Press

Marrus, M. (1985) *The Unwanted: European Refugees in the Twentieth Century*, Oxford: OUP

Peters, J. (1985) *A Family From Flanders*, London: Collins

Refugee Council (1989) *Asylum Statistics 1980-1988*, London: Refugee Council

Refugee Council (1990) *Vietnamese Refugee Reception and Settlement 1979-88*, London, Refugee Council

Refugee Council (1991) *At Risk: Refugees and the Convention forty years on*, London: Refugee Council

Refugee Council (1997) *Asylum Statistics 1986-1996*, London: Refugee Council

Robinson, V. (1989) *The Geography of Vietnamese Secondary Migration in the UK*, Warwick: Centre for Research in Ethnic Relations

Srinavasan, S. (1995) 'An Overview of Research into Refugee Groups in Britain During the 1900s' in Delle Donne, M. (Ed) *Avenues to Integration: refugees in contemporary Europe*, Naples: Ipermedium

Sword, K. (1989) *The Formation of the Polish Community in UK*, London: School of Slavonic Studies, University of London

Turner, B. (1990) *And the Policeman Smiled*, London: Bloomsbury

Valtonen, K. (1994) 'The Adaption of Vietnamese Refugees in Finland' in *Journal of Refugee Studies*, Vol 7 No 1 pp 63-78

Vevstad, V. (1998) *Refugee protection: a European Challenge*, Oslo: The Norwegian Refugee Council

Wicks, B. (1989) *The Day They Took the Children*, London: Bloomsbury

World University Service (UK) (1974) *Reception and Resettlement of Refugees from Chile*, London: WUS (UK)

3

The Rights and Entitlements of Asylum-Seekers and Refugees

This chapter outlines the process of applying for asylum in the UK and describes the rights and entitlements of asylum-seekers and refugees.

The asylum process

The term asylum-seeker refers to someone who has fled from his or her home country and has made an application for political asylum to the Home Office. Quite often one asylum application is made per family unit, where a family arrives in the UK together. (Family separation during persecution and flight is also common and many families do not arrive in the UK at the same time.) Immigration officers employed by the Integrated Casework Directorate of the Immigration and Nationality Directorate of the Home Office process asylum applications.

Almost all asylum-seekers make their applications on or after arrival in the UK. It is very rare for someone to make a claim for asylum before reaching the UK. Occasionally, however, groups of people will be recognised as vulnerable and in need of protection before they come to the UK and granted permission to enter. Some 24,000 Vietnamese refugees and 3,000 Chileans were granted refugee status by the British government and then evacuated to the UK as part of UK Government Programmes. More recently, quotas of 2,500 Bosnians and 4,400 Kosovar Albanians were brought to the UK in Government Programmes. Neither Bosnians or Kosovars were granted refugee status; instead they were initially granted one year's leave to remain in the UK.

An asylum application can be made at the port of entry, or 'in-country'. At present about half of all asylum-seekers apply for asylum at the port of entry, usually Heathrow Airport, Gatwick Airport or Dover. Those who make in-country applications include asylum-seekers who entered the UK legally, but perhaps did not know what to do when they first arrived or perhaps were anxious about applying for asylum at an airport. People who have entered the UK clandestinely, or remained unlawfully after their leave to remain has expired may also apply for asylum 'in-country'.

There is little special provision for unaccompanied asylum-seeking children and immigration officers receive no special training in dealing with children's asylum cases. However, unaccompanied asylum-seeking children are seldom required to present themselves for interview.

Throughout the asylum process, good quality legal representation is essential. Unfortunately, good immigration lawyers are in short supply, especially outside Greater London and other big multi-ethnic areas. Many asylum-seekers end up being represented by inexperienced lawyers and advisers or those who have no interest or commitment to asylum-seekers. Other asylum-seekers may have no legal representation at all. Some agencies offer free legal advice; these are listed in Part Four. It is also important that asylum-seekers inform the Home Office of any change of address. All correspondence with the Home Office should be sent by recorded delivery post, and copies should be kept of any letters.

At the time of writing the procedure for applying for asylum is in the process of change, with the Home Office piloting new forms and procedures with the aim of speeding up the time it takes for a decision to be made on an asylum application.

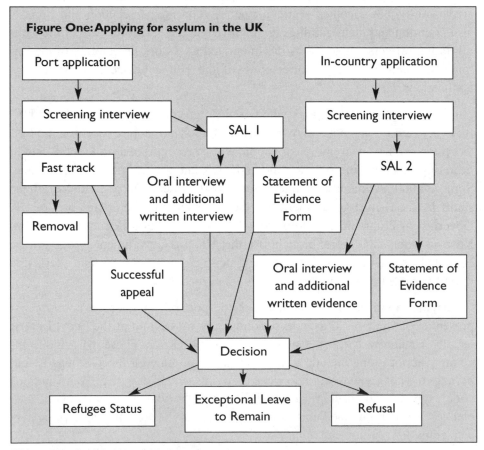

Figure One: Applying for asylum in the UK

SAL = Standard Acknowledgment Letter

Port applications

Asylum-seekers are usually given an initial screening interview by immigration officers at the port of entry. During this interview, asylum-seekers (apart from very young children) are fingerprinted. The screening interview is also meant to establish whether an asylum-seeker has a legitimate claim to asylum or not. Those judged to have no legitimate claim, deemed 'a manifestly unfounded application' enter a fast track procedure and can be detained (see Figure One). Removed from the UK can be rapid – within nine days of arrival.

The main reason that asylum-seekers enter the fast track procedure is that they have passed through a safe third country, prior to arrival in the UK. If an asylum-seeker has passed through another EU country and does not have immediate family in the UK there are procedures under the 1990 Dublin Convention, to remove an asylum-seeker to another EU country. The Immigration and Asylum Act 1999 extended the concept of safe third country by listing other countries such as Canada, USA, Norway and Switzerland as 'safe'. Asylum-seekers entering the UK via these countries and applying at the port of entry may go into the fast-track procedure.

After the initial screening interview asylum-seekers who apply at the port of entry are given a form acknowledging their asylum application. This is called a Standard Acknowledgment Letter (for port applicants it is abbreviated as SAL1). This form gives the names and dates of birth of asylum-seekers and their immediate family. Photographs of the asylum-seekers and his or her dependants are also included. The SAL is an extremely important document, as it is often the only record of identity and date of birth. Asylum-seekers will use the SAL to secure access to financial support. Asylum-seeking parents may also use this document when enrolling their children at school.

As well as the initial screening interview those asylum-seekers who do not enter the fast track process may be given a longer interview when they first arrive, in which they have to explain the persecution they suffered in their home countries. The evidence given in this interview is used to make a decision on an asylum case. The Refugee Council has concerns about asylum-seekers who are interviewed very soon after arrival, as they may not have legal representation or advice and may well be jet-lagged.

After this detailed interview, asylum-seekers are given five working days in which to submit any additional evidence to back up an asylum claim. The evidence they submitted at the port of entry is sent by e-mail to the headquarters of the Integrated Casework Directorate of the Immigration and Nationality Directorate of the Home Office. This is based in Croydon. A decision is made and conveyed to immigration officers at the port. Then the asylum-seeker is invited back for a further interview and given the decision.

Not all asylum-seekers are given a lengthy interview when they first arrive. After the screening interview some asylum-seekers are given a form called a Statement of Evidence Form to complete. In this they have to describe the persecution they faced in their home country. Secondary evidence such as a statement from Amnesty International or a medical report to show torture can be attached to the Statement of Evidence Form. The latter form has to be returned to the Integrated Casework Directorate within a tight deadline, presently 10 working days after the initial screening interview. Some asylum-seekers who receive the Statement of Evidence Form are also required to attend an interview with immigration officers. Eventually, on the basis of written and oral evidence an asylum decision is made.

In-country applications

There is no fast track process for those asylum-seekers who apply for asylum after entry to the UK. In most other ways, the asylum process is similar. Asylum-seekers attend a screening interview, where they are fingerprinted. A Standard Acknowledgment Letter, known as SAL2 is then issued to all asylum-seekers who have attended the screening interview.

After the screening interview some asylum-seekers are invited for an oral interview. It is here that an asylum-seeker has to prove persecution. Other asylum-seekers are given the Statement of Evidence Form to complete. Some asylum-seekers who receive the Statement of Evidence Form are also required to attend an interview with immigration officers. Eventually, on the basis of written and oral evidence an asylum decision is made.

Decisions

After giving evidence to the Integrated Casework Directorate of the Home Office – either in the Statement of Evidence Form, or in oral interview or both, an asylum-seeker then waits for a decision on the case. The Home Office may make a decision rapidly, perhaps within a month or so of arrival. Other asylum-seekers may wait many months or years. At the time of writing, families with children were receiving rapid decisions on their cases, while those without children waited longer. The Home Office has also recently outlined proposals for people who have very strong claims to refugee status to receive fast decisions. But at present many asylum-seekers face a long wait which can be a difficult period. One asylum-seeker described this uncertainty as *'the worst problem – you don't know when you will receive a decision or what that decision will be – and that uncertainty acts as a barrier to employment and training. All you can do is stay at home and stare at the walls'*.

But a decision will eventually be made. Where an asylum-seeker has dependants, the decision given to the principal applicant applies to the whole family.

For example, if a child's father is given full refugee status, this decision applies to a spouse and any dependent children.

If an asylum-seeker is judged to have 'a well-founded fear of being persecuted for reasons of race, religion, nationality, membership of a particular social group or political opinion' (1951 UN Convention Relating to the Status of Refugees), he or she will be granted full refugee status. But there is no internationally accepted definition of what constitutes a well-founded fear of persecution. Instead the interpretation of the UN Convention varies between different countries. In order to try to overcome this subjectivity, the UNHCR has prepared a book describing the interpretation of the UN Convention and Protocol. This is called the Handbook on Procedure and Criteria for Determining Refugee Status. Its principles are accepted by the Home Office.

To be granted refugee status in the UK a person has to show with '*serious possibility*' or '*reasonable likelihood*' that he or she is likely to suffer persecution in the home country. There must be threats to life or freedom, or an accumulation of discriminations and dangers that amount to persecution. Someone granted refugee status must be endangered individually, though the reason for this may be membership of a particular group. People are not normally given refugee status if they a fleeing a generally unstable or dangerous condition, for example if there is a civil war in their home country.

To be given refugee status a person also has to prove that he or she is being persecuted for reasons of race, religion, nationality, membership of a particular social group or political opinion. The UN Convention does not recognise persecution on grounds of gender or sexuality, although some lawyers argue that lesbians and gay men form a social group.

When a person is granted refugee status they have certain entitlements, which are outlined on pages 42-45. Most importantly, those with refugee status can remain in the UK for as long as they need.

The Home Office has another immigration status that throughout the 1980s and 1990s was granted to a much larger proportion of asylum-seekers who were allowed to remain in the UK. This status is called 'Exceptional Leave to Remain' (ELR). It is outside the provisions of the Immigration Rules and is granted at the discretion of the Home Secretary for 'humane and administrative reasons'. People – such as a gay man fleeing Iran – whose persecution falls outside the terms of the UN Convention are often granted ELR. People who are escaping civil war, and for whom return would be dangerous are often granted ELR. The Home Office has also granted ELR to certain groups of people who are forced to stay in Britain because of changing events in their home country. Chinese citizens who entered the UK before 4 June 1989 (Tiannamen Square massacre) were given ELR as a group. ELR can also be given for personal and compassionate reasons. Since 1998, some asylum-seekers who have had to wait unduly long for a decision on their case (sometimes as long as eight years) have been given ELR, in a Home Office exercise to clear the huge backlog of asylum cases.

ELR does not afford the same rights as full refugee status. It is not a permanent status, and has to be renewed at intervals, usually of one year and then three years. Although rare, there are cases of extensions to ELR being refused. After four years, indefinite leave to remain in the UK may be granted (permanent settlement). A person with ELR is not entitled to UN travel documents, and does not have the same rights to family reunion and education. Critics of Government asylum policy argue that ELR is now being granted to people who 15 years ago would have been granted refugee status. They argue that as ELR does not afford the same rights, its widespread use is a deliberate deterrent measure.

As asylum-seeker may also have his or her case refused. He or she may be subjected to the fast track procedures described above, and refused. Those who travel through a safe third country or have come from a particular country are likely to go through the fast track process.

Asylum-seekers may also be refused on the basis of their oral and written evidence. Asylum-seekers may also be refused because

- they have failed to attend an interview, failed to provide additional evidence to support an asylum application, or failed to submit the Statement of Evidence Form.

- their case is weak or badly prepared.

- their case lacks credibility, with the Home Office not believing a story. Asylum-seekers who arrive with false documents or destroy passports and tickets may be not be believed. Anyone who applies for asylum after being refused permission to enter as a visitor or a student is also not likely to be believed.

- asylum-seekers who could have fled to another part of their own country where they would be safe are also likely to be refused.

- an asylum-seeker with strong links with another country may be refused asylum in the UK. Jewish asylum-seekers, for example, would be expected to seek protection in Israel.

People who have committed crimes against humanity will not be granted asylum as the 1951 UN Convention Relating to the Status of Refugees excludes them from being considered a refugee.

Little information exists on what happens to asylum-seekers who are refused refugee status or ELR. Some appeal and may or may not be able to stay. Others leave the UK voluntarily. Other people are issued with removal or deportation orders. And some people 'disappear', joining a substantial number of other people living in Britain without the correct documentation. Demographers estimate that there are between 200,000 and 500,000 people living in Britain without the correct immigration documentation, including many children and young people.

Appeals

Asylum-seekers whose cases are refused have a right of appeal before being removed or deported from the UK. Appeals are first heard by the Immigration Appeals Authority, a quasi-independent body within the Lord Chancellor's department. The legal framework governing appeals is outlined in the Immigration Act 1971, as well as the 1993, 1996 and 1999 asylum legislation. The process is complex and asylum-seekers need good legal representation to stand a chance of winning an appeal. There are very strict time limits. Any asylum-seeker who has been refused should be referred to the Refugee Legal Centre or to an immigration lawyer immediately. Access to good quality legal advice is essential for appeals, as this can make the difference between winning and losing. At present some 10-20 per cent of appeals are successful.

There are two types of appeal: Certified Appeals and full appeals. The appeals process takes place in stages. Appeals are first lodged with the Appeals Adjudicator. Before the Adjudicator hears the case, it will be reviewed at a pre-hearing review. Sometimes an appeal is dismissed at such a review. If the appeal to the Adjudicator is unsuccessful and it is not a Certified Appeal, a further appeal can be made to an Immigration Appeals Tribunal. Some asylum appeals can go further: to a Court of Appeal on points of law.

Certified appeals or fast track appeals

Those asylum-seekers who enter the fast track process and whose case is judged to be without foundation have very limited rights of appeal. Their cases are judged to be Certified by the Home Secretary which in practice means that they can only appeal to the Appeals Adjudicator. Other asylum-seekers can be told that their application for asylum is Certified. The Home Office lists seven cases where an appeal may be Certified. These include

- people who entered the UK with false travel documents and failed to declare this or provide an explanation for using false documents

- cases from countries where human rights condition may have improved and where the reasons for seeking asylum no longer apply

- cases where an asylum application was made after a visa is refused or a deportation order is served

*   applications deemed to be fraudulent or 'vexatious'.

Critics of Government asylum policy believe that the conditions for Certification are so wide that they could apply to almost everyone. Any asylum-seeker whose case is Certified has very tight deadlines in which to give notice that he or she wants to appeal.

Full appeals

Asylum-seekers whose applications are refused but not Certified have fuller rights of appeal. They first lodge an appeal with the Appeals Adjudicator. If this is unsuccessful, a further appeal can be lodged with an Immigration Appeals Tribunal. This is a panel of three people, which after October 2000 will be presided over by a High Court judge. The Immigration Appeals Tribunal makes a recommendation to the Home Secretary, although the latter is not obliged to enact it.

Removals

Since 1996 a greater number of asylum-seekers have been removed or deported from the UK at the end of an appeals process. This trend is likely to continue as it is the Government's stated intention to increase removals. The process of removal or deportation is complicated and likely to change in the near future, with almost all refused asylum-seekers being removed rather than deported from the UK. It is vital for asylum-seekers faced with removal or deportation to get legal representation through a good lawyer or the Refugee Legal Centre.

A child's welfare is considered before removal or deportation. Unaccompanied children have to have a country of origin report prepared before removal. The report is meant to assess the conditions faced by a child if returned, in particular if there is an appropriate person to care for that child. No unaccompanied children have been removed from the UK in the period 1997- September 2000. The Home Office states that it will not generally remove children who have seven years continuous residence in the UK, unless their parents have a 'poor immigration history'. Children for whom removal may put their health at risk or face severe hardship will also generally not be removed or deported. In any appeal to the Home Office, it is important to stress the compassionate reasons that a child should be allowed to stay in the UK. Even after all avenues of appeal seem exhausted, people can still get permission to remain.

A teacher's role in supporting children going through appeals and threatened removal

Teachers working with significant numbers of asylum-seeking and refugee children may well be teaching pupils who are going through the asylum appeal process or even fighting removal. There is much a sympathetic teacher can do to support children in these circumstances, including

- giving the family moral support

- trying to see if the family has got a good legal representative

- helping the family gather compassionate evidence, particularly about their children.

Access to good quality legal advice is essential for a family. At present asylum-seekers receive legal help (legal aid) to enable them to make an asylum application although a person does not get this aid for representation at appeal (the only options are self representation, the Refugee Legal Centre, Asylum Aid or a lawyer who will offer services for free). But despite legal help many asylum-seekers are represented by poor quality legal advisers, or outside the big cities, have no access to lawyers or immigration advisers.

Poor quality legal advice is of concern to refugee agencies. In future, immigration advisers will have to be registered before they can provide immigration advice for a profit. But this requirement does not apply to lawyers. Many asylum-seekers do not know that they can change lawyers, or they feel they might be punished for doing so.

A good lawyer or legal adviser should have a thorough knowledge of asylum law. He or she also needs to be a good communicator and be competent in using interpreters, interviewing people with traumatic past experiences and be skilled in interviewing children. A good lawyer will keep clients informed of all developments in their cases.

The new support system for asylum-seekers

On 3rd April 2000 the National Asylum Support Service, a new Home Office department, came into operation. Its function is to provide housing and financial support for asylum-seekers. Thereafter new asylum-seekers no longer have access to benefits provided by the Benefits Agency. New asylum-seekers who need accommodation will also be housed throughout the UK in an attempt to move asylum-seekers away from London and the South East.

This far-reaching change in the way that asylum-seekers are supported has not come unannounced. As described on page 21, asylum-seekers have had restricted rights to income support since 1987. Further changes were implemented in 1996, when the Asylum and Immigration Act 1996 prevented some groups of asylum-seekers from accessing income support, allowing only asylum-seekers who applied at the port of entry to claim income support. All 'in-country' applicants and those asylum-seekers appealing against a negative decision lost access to benefits. Instead asylum-seekers became the responsibility of local authority social services departments. Families with children were supported under the provisions of the Children Act 1989 and given a cash allowance and some form of temporary accommodation. Those asylum-seekers without children were sup-

The rights of asylum-seekers and refugees

A person's immigration status may affect their rights in the UK including educational rights. The following table summarises a person's rights according to their immigration status.

	Asylum-Seeker	Exceptional Leave to Remain (ELR)	Refugee Status
Rights to Stay	Until a decision is reached on the asylum application and all appeals are exhausted.	Initially a person is given one year's ELR. This can be renewed, usually for three years. After four years a person with ELR can apply for permanent residence in the UK. After one year of permanent residence a person may apply for British nationality, providing other criteria are met.	A refugee is granted permanent residence in the UK at the same time refugee status is granted.
Overseas Travel	An asylum-seeker may not leave the UK until his or her case is determined.	People with ELR and refugee status are free to travel providing they have the correct documentation.	
Travel Documents	None.	People with ELR are expected to maintain the validity of their own passports. If this is impossible the Home Office will sometimes issue a British travel document, providing the person can show that he or she made every attempt to renew their own passport.	People with refugee status are not permitted to travel on their national passports. Instead if a person wishes to travel he or she must apply for a UN Convention Travel Document (CTD). Giving the protection of UNHCR, it offers the right to travel world wide, apart from the refugee's country of origin. Holders of a CTD must comply with immigration and visa requirements of the countries to which they want to travel. A person wanting a CTD should apply to the Travel Document Section, Home Office, Lunar House, Wellesley Road, Croydon. There is usually a long wait before documents are issued.

	Asylum-Seeker	Exceptional Leave to Remain (ELR)	Refugee Status
Family Reunion	Not permitted.	After four years of ELR.	Yes, for immediate family.
Healthcare	Asylum-seekers, people with ELR and full refugees status are entitled to the same healthcare provision as other UK residents. Their entitlements are outlined in Health Circular (82) 15, circulated by the Department of Health.		
Work	Asylum-seekers are initially not allowed to work. After six months the principal asylum applicant may request permission to work from the Home Office. It then issues a form called GEN 25 which states that the person has permission to work.	Full rights to work.	Full rights to work.
Welfare Benefits	90 per cent income support if application was lodged at port before 3.4.2000. No new asylum-seeker has any rights to benefits and is now assisted by the National Asylum Support Service.	Full rights to income support and other benefits.	Full rights to income support and other benefits.
Social Housing	No rights to housing under UK homelessness legislation. Provided by NASS if needed.	Full rights to housing under homelessness legislation.	Full rights to social housing.

Asylum-Seeker	Exceptional Leave to Remain (ELR)	Refugee Status
Support for Unaccompanied Children aged 0-18 years		
Provided by social services departments under the provisions of the Children Act 1989.		
Early Years Provision		
Full rights.	Full rights.	Full Rights.
Schools for 5-16s		
Full rights for all asylum-seekers, those with ELR and Refugee Status. Parents are obliged to send their children to school in all parts of the UK.		
Free School Meals		
NASS supported children and those supported by local authorities have a right to free school meals. In England and Wales this is outlined in Section 117 of Schedule 14 of the Immigration and Asylum Act 1999. In Scotland this is outlined in Section 74 of Schedule 14 of the Immigration and Asylum Act 1999.	As for other children on income support.	As for other children on income support
The Education of 16-18 Year Old Students in the School Sector		
Education is free for school students between 16 and 18, irrespective of immigration status. But between 16 and 18 students are only accepted into a school at the discretion of the head teacher and LEA.		
Fees in Further and Higher Education		
An asylum-seeker is theoretically as an overseas student for fees and awards. This means asylum-seekers may have to find considerable sums of money to pay for fees for full time courses. In FE colleges asylum-	People with ELR are also treated as home students for the purposes of applying for tuition fees at all levels of education. This is outlined in the Education (Fees and Awards) Regulations 1994, as amended.	Refugee are treated as home students for the purposes of applying for tuition fees at all levels of education. This is outlined in the Education (Fees and Awards) Regulations 1994, as amended

Asylum-Seeker	Exceptional Leave to Remain (ELR)	Refugee Status
seekers on benefits or vouchers may study on part-time courses at a concessionary rate. Many FE colleges also allow 16-19 year olds to study for free.

Student Support in FE and HE

Overseas student, therefore no entitlement to a grant or loan. | People with ELR must fulfil three years ordinary residence in the UK before they qualify for a grant and loan. Eligibility for discretionary awards is determined by individual LEAs. This is outlined in the Education (Fees and Awards) Regulations 1994, as amended. | If accepted on a designated course a refugee is entitled to a mandatory maintenance grant and loan. If a refugee is already studying before refugee status is granted he or she can apply to an LEA for a mandatory grant for subsequent terms. This is outlined in the Education (Fees and Awards) Regulations 1994, as amended. Refugees may also apply for discretionary awards. Some LEAs, however, require refugees to have lived in an area for a certain time before giving a discretionary award.

A refugee also has the right to claim income support and study on a full-time EAL course for up to nine months, providing he or she starts the course within twelve months of arriving in the UK. |

ported under the provisions of the National Assistance Act 1948 (In Scotland the Children Act (Scotland) and the Social Work (Scotland) Act 1968). This required social services departments to provide sustenance, warmth and shelter, in practice food vouchers, redeemable in a single designated supermarket, and temporary accommodation. Case law deemed that giving asylum-seekers a cash allowance was illegal in England (although not in Scotland).

By 1997, there was a shortage of hostel type accommodation in Greater London. London local authorities began to move asylum-seekers out of the capital, often to seaside towns. Cashless, unsupported and with nothing to do, these asylum-seekers were a visible group who attracted more adverse media coverage.

Due to growing public hostility and concerted lobbying from local authorities, the Government was forced to take back responsibility for them. Rather than restore benefits, the Immigration and Asylum Act 1999 has introduced a new support system for asylum-seekers, which most refugee agencies believe is beset with problems and will condemn asylum-seekers to high levels of stress and isolation.

Since September 2000 *all* new asylum-seekers who need support and housing enter a new Home Office support system administered by the National Asylum Support Service (NASS). They receive vouchers and a cash allowance of £10 per person per week. The vouchers, printed by a company called Sodexho, will be posted to the asylum-seeker's home address and can be redeemed only at named retail outlets. A cash chitty, exchangeable at a post office, will also be posted. People with nowhere to stay will be dispersed out of London, to NASS-commissioned housing in the new regional Asylum Consortia areas . Any asylum-seeker refusing dispersal will lose all access to support and housing. Local authorities in England, Scotland and Wales have been grouping themselves into regional Asylum Consortia, in readiness to receive asylum-seekers dispersed by NASS. The regional Asylum Consortia are

> Greater London (providing housing only for asylum-seekers with
> exceptional needs)
> the South East
> South Central
> the South West
> Eastern
> the East Midlands
> the West Midlands
> the North West
> the North East
> Yorkshire and Humberside
> Scotland
> Wales

Most Regional Asylum Consortia employ project staff. Their role is to work with NASS to identify public sector accommodation for asylum-seekers and to plan and coordinate services for asylum-seekers. Within each consortium some accommodation will be provided by local authorities and some by private landlords.

The housing provided should meet certain criteria laid out in tender documents and is meant to be furnished and heated. Water, gas and electricity will be paid. Public sector housing providers and private landlords are meant to direct families to schools and LEA services, but in reality few of the latter do so.

Refugee Action, the Refugee Council and the Scottish Refugee Council have been funded by the Home Office to provide advice services, called One Stop Shops, in the new dispersed areas.

Unaccompanied asylum-seeking children will not be supported by the NASS scheme, but will remain the responsibility of local authority social services departments under the provisions of the Children Act 1989.

If an asylum-seekers receives a positive decision on his or her application, that asylum-seeker becomes eligible for benefits and is free to move anywhere in the UK. Provided the asylum-seeker has not lived in a particular local authority for more than six months (and has a local connection under homelessness legislation) that person is also free to apply for social housing anywhere in the UK.

The Interim Support Scheme

Many local authorities are still supporting asylum-seekers. There are people who applied between 1996 and summer 2000 and had no access to income support. This group are being assisted by local authorities as part of the 'Interim Support Scheme'. In practice this group are provided with vouchers and dispersed out of London too.

Hard cases

Some people will no longer be entitled to any form of statutory support in the UK. These are so-called 'hard cases': people who have been refused asylum, have exhausted all avenues of appeal, but have yet to be removed from the UK. They include asylum-seekers without the valid documentation that allows them to be returned and asylum-seekers from countries from where the UK has suspended deportations. Families deemed hard cases are supported by local authorities under the provisions of the Immigration and Asylum Act 1999. A Home Office grant exists for supporting adults without children who are deemed hard cases.

The effects on children of the NASS scheme

Child care and refugee agencies have highlighted the following concerns about the NASS support scheme.

Stigmatisation: Many asylum-seekers report hostility when they exchange their vouchers at shops. And children who have no toys, television or smart clothes will feel stigmatised, at a time in their life they are most sensitive to peer pressure.

Poverty: The NASS scheme is meant to provide essential living needs only, at a level of 70 per cent of income support for adults and 100 per cent for children. Living in a virtually cashless support system will excluded them from many things that everyone else regards as essential: bus fares, haircuts, secondhand good and anything not provided by retail outlets that accept vouchers, toys, television, comics, books, ice cream. Vouchers are meant to be spent within one month of issue. This makes it difficult for asylum-seekers to save for clothes and new shoes. Any parent who needs to travel by bus to accompany a young child to school will find this journey, made 20 times a week, to be impossible to make without cash.

Isolation: Many asylum-seekers are being sent to areas that have no existing refugee communities and report loneliness and isolation, rendering them far more psychologically vulnerable. Excluding the big metropolitan areas such as Birmingham and Manchester, there are unlikely to be refugee community organisations in most new areas of dispersal.

Vulnerability to racial attack: Despite the Home Office guidance on the choice of accommodation, many asylum-seekers will end up being housed in areas where there are few other people from visible ethnic minorities. Some areas will inevitably be places of existing tension and high unemployment. Given the hostile attitudes of much local and national print media towards asylum-seekers, the Refugee Council believes that some groups will be very vulnerable to racial abuse and racial attack.

Reception centres and large hotels: Large hostels/hotels may be particularly unsuitable for asylum-seeking children. They are institutional and no substitute for family housing. Yet much of the planned accommodation for NASS is in hostels and hotels, particularly that offered by the private sector. Such accommodation also has a major effect on local primary schools and local GP surgeries – a small number of schools may receive a comparatively high number of asylum-seeking pupils who soon move on.

Social exclusion in London: In late 2000 an estimated 70 per cent of single adults and 30 per cent of families opted not be dispersed in the interim support system, or left their areas of dispersal within a few weeks of arrival. It is presumed that these families moved back to join compatriots in London and are likely to be living in overcrowded accommodation in the capital. This trend will continue.

Mobility: Asylum-seekers who do opt for NASS support may well choose to move on after receiving positive decisions. Schools who receive large numbers of asylum-seeking children may experience high levels of pupil mobility and this affects all children in the school, not just asylum-seekers.

School and LEA responses to dispersed asylum-seekers

Despite the punitive nature of the new asylum support system, there is still a great deal that LEAs and schools can do to ensure that asylum-seeking chidlren have a positive educational experience. LEAs and schools need to consider the following:

- What plans has the LEA made in advance of children dispersed by NASS or local authorities arriving? Do schools have access to interpreters?

- Who is the named person in the LEA who will receive information from NASS of school-aged children dispersed to the LEA?

- Are LEA staff and schools aware of asylum-seeking children's rights to education and free school meals?

- Have schools received information from the LEA informing them of the arrival of asylum-seeking children and of good practice to help children settle and learn?

- Does the bid made to the DfEE for the Ethnic Minority Achievement Grant reflect the needs of newly arrived asylum-seeking pupils?

- Can the LEA lobby NASS to ensure that large hostels and hotels are not used to house families?

- Do asylum-seeking children have access to school uniform grants?

- Can schools keep stocks of nearly new school uniform, winter clothes and sports equipment for children who will not have the means to buy such equipment?

- Can schools help families set up systems to share the responsibility of accompanying children to school on public transport?

- Are schools aware of local charities that may have toys and clothes for asylum-seeking children?

Bibliography

Joint Council for the Welfare of Immigrants (1999) *Immigration, nationaity and refugee law handbook*, London: JCWI

Refugee Council (2000) *Immigration and Asylum Act 1999: a briefing*, London: Refugee Council

World University Service (2000) *Refugee Education Handbook*, London: World University Service.

The Refugee Council's Information Service provides provides a regular up-to-date service about asylum-seekers and refugees' rights and entitlements.

4

The Reception, Settlement and Integration of Asylum-Seekers and Refugees in the UK

Education is vital for refugees: it helps adults and children rebuild their lives. But it is only one component of their settlement and integration in the UK and many other agencies have to respond to their needs. This chapter examines the role of agencies other than education in the settlement and integration of asylum-seekers and refugees in the UK, focussing on the particular needs of families with children.

Researchers into refugee matters describe different phases in the settlement of asylum-seekers and refugees. After persecution and flight, asylum-seekers who ultimately arrive in the UK will pass through

- the arrival stage, where they may experience exhaustion but also elation at having reached safety

- the reception phase, where they may be accommodated in a hostel or another form of temporary housing. Here they may experience disorientation and feel they are losing control. They will also experience the uncertainty of waiting for a decision on their cases.

- settlement and integration for those who are permitted to remain in the UK.

Refugee and human rights agencies aim to promote humane reception polices for asylum-seekers, to minimise stress felt by them. A further aim of humane reception is to lay the ground for the successful integration of those remaining in the UK – with integration being defined as a process that *'prevents the social marginalisation of refugees, by removing legal, cultural and linguistic obstacles and ensuring that refugees are empowered to make positive decisions on their future and benefit fully from available opportunities'*. (From *The Development of a Refugee Settlement Policy in the UK* (Refugee Council, 1997)).

Central government and the reception, settlement and integration of asylum-seekers and refugees

Clearly central government should play the lead role in promoting British reception, settlement and integration policy, as well as allocating resources. Different government departments have different roles in this process, but the government departments most closely involved with asylum-seekers and refugees are

- *The Home Office* – the Integrated Casework Division of the Immigration and Nationality Directorate (IND) of the Home Office processes asylum applications and appeals, while the National Asylum Support Service (NASS) is also part of IND. The Home Office also has lead responsibility for race relations and funds a small number of refugee organisations. Other Home Office responsibilities affect asylum-seekers and refugees, notably policing.

- *The Foreign and Commonwealth Office* contributes towards the human rights assessments that form the basis for judging asylum cases. The Foreign and Commonwealth Office is also involved in the coordination of overseas aspects of any evacuation programme, such as the 1999 Kosovan programme.

- *The Department of Health* has responsibility for the healthcare of asylum-seekers and refugees. It also guides the work of local authority social services departments. The Department of Health's Social Services Inspectorate coodinates a multi-agency working group on unaccompanied refugee children.

- *The Department for Education and Employment* has responsibility for educational and work related issues. There is a dedicated refugee education team within this department.

- *The Lord Chancellor's Office* heads the legal profession and has ultimate responsibility for the Immigration Appellate.

Other central government departments are also involved in the reception and settlement of asylum-seekers and refugees, for example the Department for the Environment, Transport and the Regions and the Cabinet Office.

The Commission for Racial Equality (CRE), a government body, has a specific legal duties to eliminate unlawful discrimination and promote good race relations. These legal duties laid down in the Race Relations Act (1976 and the Race Relations (Amendment) Act 2000) have major impact on the well-being of refugees.

---

1. The Refugee Integration Strategy also acknowledges that the integration of refugee children starts on arrival and affirms their entitlement to mainstream schooling (*Home Office*, 2000).

Although there were inter-department working groups that planned for the arrival and settlement of groups such as the Bosnian and Kosovan Programme Evacuees, during most of the 1990s interdepartmental communication on refugees issues was poor. The Government intends to redress this. It has recently published a Refugee Integration Strategy and will set up a Refugee Integration Forum, although this will largely involve policy discussion on only those who have been granted refugee status or ELR.[1]

The Asylum Consortia

The regional asylum consortia, although primarily concerned with the operation of the NASS support system, also have a role to play in planning services for asylum-seekers and refugees. This role should involve assessing needs, identifying gaps in services and allocating small amounts of financial resources. The work of regional asylum consortia is meant to be guided by regional reference groups comprising members co-opted from local authorities, the police, health authorities and refugee agencies. Some asylum consortia have set up sub-groups looking at issues such as education or healthcare.

Local government

Asylum-seekers placed in a given area will require a diverse range of services to support them from arrival to integration and some of these services are the clear responsibility of local authorities. Such services include

- emergency planning

- move-on accommodation for those with refugee status and ELR who can be housed under homelessness legislation.

- the processing of Housing Benefit claims for refugees and those with ELR.

- provision of social care to unaccompanied asylum-seeking and refugee children, as defined under the Children Act 1989 and Children (Leaving Care) Act 2000.

- social care obligations to all asylum-seekers and refugees under the provisions of the Mental Health Act 1983, the NHS and Community Care Act 1988 and also other social care provision to support elderly, disabled or vulnerable refugees.

- child protection and child care obligations for all asylum-seeking and refugee children under the provisions of the Children Act 1989.

- access to leisure facilities, libraries and arts facilities

- funding of refugee community organsations and other refugee support agencies working in a particular locality

- funding of refugee community schools

- the education of refugee children

- community education and lifelong learning

- interpreting and translation services.

Case Study: The Bayswater Family Centre, a multi-service support project

The Bayswater Family Centre is a joint venture between NCH Action for Children, Parkside Health Authority and City of Westminster social services. Its client group are families in temporary accommodation, the majority of whom are asylum-seekers. It is based in central London and most of its clients are living in overcrowded hotel accommodation.

Bayswater Family Centre offers a daily drop-in service for parents, a part-time crèche, supervised play for young children and a wide range of other support services. The Centre helps families meet some of their most basic physical needs. It is also a place where families can meet other parents and build up informal social networks that are missing for so many homeless asylum-seeking families. The early years provision in the Bayswater Family Centre is also designed to be stimulating and to help prepare young children for school. More specifically the Bayswater Family Centre offers the following services:

— *cooking and laundry facilities for families*

— *secondhand clothes and baby equipment*

— *a supervised play that children can use while their parents are cooking for relaxing*

— *a twice weekly crèche*

— *other pre-school sessions for refugee children which concentrate on the acquisition of English*

— *school vacation activities for older children*

— *a social worker who can support individual families*

— *advice and advocacy on housing entitlement, welfare rights, immigration and so on*

— *help with GP registration*

— *health advice*

— *outreach visits to hotels*

— *counselling through a wide range of languages*

— *other therapies such as an art therapy group and therapeutic massage*

— *English language classes*

— *careers advice*

The Bayswater Family Centre is recognised as providing a model of good practice in the provision of multi-agency support for homeless asylum-seekers. Different agencies work together effectively and the Bayswater Family Centre has a formalised notification system operating with health visitors, social services and housing departments. But above all, the Bayswater Centre offers a warm and welcoming environment for group of clients who have multiple and complex needs.

Many local authorities now have local authority based multi-agency asylum-seeker and refugee working groups, in order to plan services for these groups. Their brief varies: some limit their role to asylum-seekers; others plan the support of both asylum-seekers and refugees. Some multi-agency working groups include a membership from other statutory and voluntary sector services, others limit themselves to local authority personnel. Some multi-agency groups have conducted research or developed policy (see for example, *Refugees in Haringey*). It is worth a school finding out about local multi-agency groups.

Leisure, libraries and the arts

It is important to ensure that asylum-seekers and refugees have equal access to leisure and library services and that the arts are used imaginatively, to help refugees settle and to communicate their experiences to the wider world. Although most local authority sports and leisure facilities have concessionary fees, even these may be too expensive for asylum-seekers supported by NASS who lack cash – perhaps necessitating a review of pricing policy, particularly in areas supporting large numbers of asylum-seekers. It is also good practice to monitor the use of leisure facilities, by ethnic and national group, as well as gender. Many refugee groups are under-represented in their use of sports and leisure facilities and are not reached by health promotion projects. If monitoring highlights under-use, it is essential to conduct further research and outreach among refugee communities. Perhaps women-only sessions are needed, for example.

There are an increasing number of arts projects working with refugees or about refugee issues, including a number of refugee-led arts projects. These projects use the arts in different ways

- some showcase the work of refugee artists

- a number of projects use art, music, writing and drama therapeutically, to help refugees reflect on their experiences and settle (see Chapter Nine)

- the arts can also be used to communicate refugees' experiences to the majority community and thus help lessen racism.

London Arts has recently brought together organisations and individuals involved in refugee arts through a series of 'artists exchange days'. This networking has been further developed through, a newsletter, *Passages*. Two further organisations have been set up to bring refugee artists together: Artists in Exile and INK Refugee Writers.

Interpreting

Access to good interpreting services are especially important for newly-arrived refugees and for institutions such as schools and LEAs to secure pupil admission and the assessment of children with special needs, for example. Under the Race

Relations Act 1976 local authorities are obliged to provide interpreters to enable ethnic minority communities to have equal access to services. There are also legal obligations to provide interpreters for particular procedures – for example assessments under the Mental Health Act 1983. Although most local authorities have interpreting services, there is often a charge for their use. Or sometimes the range of languages that can be catered for does not correspond those needed by recently arrived refugee communities.

Local authorities should consider the following policy and practice issues

- Many local authorities outside Greater London state that finding able interpreters in key refugee languages is a huge challenge. The Refugee Council would dispute this, and believes that the way that local authorities treat interpreters is the cause of the problem. Most local authorities employ interpreters on a sessional basis. It is not worthwhile for an Albanian speaking interpreter to move from London to the North East, for example, if he/she is only going to be employed for a few hours a week.

- Local authorities should consider offering interpreters short term contracts and help them find accommodation, to make it easy for interpreters to move for work.

- Local authorities should carry out regular needs assessments to ensure that the range of languages provided meet the needs of the local community.

- Local authorities should consider sharing interpreting services with neighbouring local authorities.

- Interpreters should be supported and supervised. Managers of interpreting services need to organise support groups. Feedback from users of interpreting services should be encouraged.

- Interpreters should be encouraged to study for qualifications, for example the Diploma in Public Service Interpreting or a Certificate in Community Interpreting.

- LEA and school staff should be surveyed, to see if they have any language skills that could be utilised.

- Interpreters should be used for key interviews such as school admission and special needs assessment, even if a parent or child speaks some English, as misunderstandings can arise.

- LEAs should not rely on family members to interpret in sensitive situations, as it may be inappropriate to discuss some subjects in front of relatives.

Key staff should receive training on how to work with interpreters and examine the following points

- Staff need to know they should actively listen to both the interpreter and the parent or child.

- In any interview situation, it is important to check first that the parent and interpreter speak the same language and dialect and that the parent is happy with the interpreter provided.

- Any interview using an interpreter takes twice as long as without – sufficient time should be allowed.

- It is important to allow time for pre-interview discussion with the interpreter, to explain any technical words and the content of the interview.

- It is important that the interpreter is asked to explain any policy about confidentiality.

- During the interview it is important to check regularly that the parent and/or child has understood everything.

- It is important to have a short post-interview debriefing with the interpreter.

Asylum-seekers and refugees also rely on the services of other statutory service providers, including the Benefits Agency, FE colleges, the police and the National Health Service. Healthcare issues, in particular impact on families with children. Refugees' health needs fall into five areas: access to healthcare, interpreting and translation issues, health issues specific to refugees, mental health and cultural issues and sensitivities

Access to healthcare

Asylum-seekers and refugees have unequal access to healthcare and related social services. There are four reasons for this. Firstly, newly arrived refugees may not know how the healthcare system works. As healthcare is usually organised differently in a refugee's country of origin, a family may not know how to register with a GP, that they have to make appointments, or know about the range of services available in this country – for example the work of the health visitor.

Secondly, in order for asylum-seekers without access to benefits to secure free prescriptions, dental care and so on, they have to fill in a 14-page form called HC1. This is returned to a central NHS administration unit and a Certificate called HC2 is returned to the asylum-seeker. The certificate provides access to free treatment for a six month period, then the process has to be repeated. Although asylum-seekers supported by NASS are given some initial help in obtaining HC2, this cumbersome bureaucratic process has acted as a barrier to healthcare in the past.

Housing conditions, particularly in Greater London, have made refugees a highly mobile population. This prevents continuity of healthcare. Refugees are also more likely to be refused registration with a GP than other sectors of the population. In cost-conscious times someone who does not speak fluent English may be perceived as being more expensive to treat. All these factors mean that teachers and the school medical service should not assume that a refugee family is registered with a GP.

Many refugee children may miss the school entrance medical examination (usually carried out in a child's second term at school) and immunisations. The LEA, as a purchaser of healthcare, should be encouraged to look at its contract with the school medical service, and ensure that refugee children receive a school entrance medical examination soon after they arrive at a new school.

Health issues specific to refugees

Most refugees in the UK have come from poor countries which are experiencing conflict. The primary healthcare system in these countries may be overburdened or have broken down. People may not have been immunised. Some groups of refugees may also have travelled through refugee camps where there is inadequate sanitation and insufficient clean water. These past experiences mean that asylum-seekers may arrive in the UK suffering from communicable diseases, particularly tuberculosis, gastro-intestinal infections and parasites and malaria. The school medical service must be made aware that a child has arrived from a particular country. Refugee children may also have suffered from war injuries (this is true of about 20 per cent of Somalis fleeing northern towns during 1988). These may not have been treated. A small minority of young refugees may have been tortured in their home countries and bear the physical scars of torture.

Malnutrition is a condition experienced by some newly-arrived asylum-seekers, particularly those who have spent time in refugee camps. Refugees living in bed and breakfast hotels in the UK may also suffer from malnutrition, as they may not have proper cooking facilities and have to rely on take-away meals. And it is debatable whether asylum-seekers supported by NASS and surviving with so little cash can afford a balanced diet (Sellen, 2000). The school medical service must be made aware of these issues. Schools must ensure that school meals meet nutritional guidelines, and that refugee children do not miss out on health education. Some schools provide breakfast for children, or have homework clubs for homeless children where they also receive food. Food technology departments in schools must ensure that young refugees receive health education and information about a balanced diet, particularly if they are unaccompanied.

Refugees may also be at risk of certain diseases and conditions because of their ethnic origin. Most common are two blood disorders: sickle cell disease or trait and beta thalassaemia or trait. These are both haemoglobinopathies as they affect the haemoglobin in the red blood cells. People inherit genes that determine the form of their haemoglobin. Most people inherit the HbA gene from both parents, making them HbAA. Unfortunately there are some abnormal forms of haemoglobin such as sickle haemoglobin (HbS) and beta thalassaemia haemoglobin. The gene for sickle haemoglobin is common among people of African and African-Caribbean origin. The gene for beta thalassaemia is common in the eastern Mediterranean, Turkey, Kurdistan, Iran, parts of India, southern China, Vietnam and West Africa. In Cyprus one person in seven has beta thalassaemia trait, although the frequency of the gene differs from region to region. In the past people who have sickle cell trait or beta thalassaemia trait were more likely to survive malaria, which is why the gene has survived.

A person who inherits HbA from one parent and HbS from another will have sickle cell trait – HbAS – but will normally have few symptoms. But a person who inherits the sickle gene from each parent (HbSS) and so has sickle cell anaemia will often feel tired and be breathless after exercise and perhaps prone to infections, but will be able to lead a normal life for much of the time. But sickle cell anaemia can suddenly worsen and cause severe pain. Such crises are caused where the irregularly shaped red blood cells block blood vessels, precipitated by dehydration or strenuous exercise, so teachers need to know how to create a crisis-free life for young people with sickle cell anaemia. Affected children should avoid heavy exercise. They should always stay warm and must not be allowed to become dehydrated. They should not be forced outside at break-time in winter, and a sensitive school should provide a legitimate reason for them to stay indoors, such as being a library monitor.

Those who carry a single copy of the beta thalassaemia gene are healthy themselves. Children born to parents who both carry the beta thalassaemia gene have a 25 per cent chance of being suffering from thalassaemia major. Children with thalassaemia major are normal at birth but gradually become more anaemic. In the past most children with thalassaemia major died in their first decade. Today children are treated with regular blood transfusion and injections of a drug called Desferal which removes excess iron from the body.

Female genital mutilation

This is a major health concern facing some refugee communities in the UK. It is a controversial issue, generating strong feelings among refugees and healthcare professionals. If those at risk are to be supported it is essential that the relevant caring professions have good links with each other. Female genital mutilation is practised in many African countries, as well as in Yemen and Oman, and in their refugee and migrant diaspora. It is carried out by Muslims, Christians, Jews and animists. Many people believe it is justified by religious teaching, although it has no basis in any religious creed. It some countries female genital mutilation is part of a girl's rites of passage into adulthood. In some societies, too, an uncircumcised woman is viewed as shameful and unclean. Female genital mutilation is also used by families as a means of controlling girls' sexuality, and to deter them from marrying outside their ethnic group. It takes three forms: circumcision, excision and infibulation. Circumcision involves cutting the hood of the clitoris, whilst excision involves the removal of the clitoris and all or part of the labia minora. The most severe form of genital mutilation is infibulation, which involves the removal of the clitoris, labia minora and part or all of the labia majora. The two sides of the vulva are then stitched together and eventually scar tissue forms. A small opening is left for the passage of urine and blood.

Most women in Somalia, eastern Ethiopia and northern Sudan are infibulated, usually at between five and ten years old. Female genital mutilation has been banned in Eritrea, and is not an issue that now affects Eritrean refugees in the UK. Female circumcision is practised among certain ethnic groups in southern Sudan, eastern Uganda and northern Congo (Zaire) and many parts of west Africa. In certain countries female genital mutilation may affect some ethnic groups but be unheard of in other regions.

In the UK female genital mutilation is an issue which mostly affects the Somali, Sudanese and Yemeni communities. Although illegal, the operation still takes place in the UK, amid great secrecy. Other parents take their daughters to Africa or the Middle East during the summer vacation. There are immediate risks to a girl's health, as well as long term complications. An infibulated woman may suffer from chronic bladder and uterine infections. At marriage a husband will cut some of the scar tissue, to enable the marriage to be consummated. Sexual intercourse is likely to be painful for an infibulated woman. Complications during childbirth are unavoidable: in Somalia a pregnant woman has her scar cut open and is then re-infibulated at every delivery. Labour is longer, and there is an increased risk of infection, maternal and child death and perinatal brain damage.

There has been little research into the psychological consequences of female genital mutilation. But there is no doubt that such a practice is traumatic, and has overwhelming psychological effects on a girl. That a woman's body has been violated, her central organ of sexual pleasure removed, and sexual intercourse made painful is likely to have major psychological consequences. Teachers should be aware of the practice and its consequences. Girls who have been infibulated are extremely unwilling to take part in physical education. They may frequently be absent as menstruation can be very painful. It will also take an infibulated girl a very long time to pass urine: in schools where children have little privacy this can lead to questions, teasing and desperate embarrassment.

In both African and European countries there are promising initiatives among women's groups and by governments, aimed at ending the practice of female genital mutilation. In Eritrea it has been banned for some years. In Somalia the Somali Women's Democratic Organisation has called for legislation, to be backed up with an educational campaign. The Somali Government appointed an official commission on infibulation, banned the operation in hospitals and funded an educational campaign. But the achievements and organisational base of the campaign ended as Somalia plunged into chaos in 1991.

Legislation in the UK prohibiting female genital mutilation came into force in 1985, with the Prohibition of Female Circumcision Act. Female genital mutilation has been incorporated into child protection legislation by local authorities, and there have been nearly forty cases where there has been action to protect girls at risk. But intervention is often difficult, and many social workers face the dilemma of whether intervention will permanently divide a girl from her family.

FORWARD, the Sudanese Women's Group and the London Black Women's Health Action Group are among the organisations working to eradicate the practice. Among the Somali and Sudanese communities more and more individuals and organisations are willing to speak out against the practice, often in the face of hostility. They view female genital mutilation as a form of child abuse and an infringement of human rights. But educational campaigns among communities that practice female genital mutilation are underfunded, badly coordinated and do not reach all members of relevant communities (Minority Rights Group, 1992).

Many operations take place during the summer vacation, in the UK and sometimes in a Middle Eastern or African country. It is often the teacher who is the first person outside the family to know that a child is intending to travel abroad. If teachers believes that a girl is at risk they should inform the headteacher or someone with child protection or pastoral responsibility. Advice can be sought from agencies such as FORWARD. A meeting with the girl's family should be arranged in order the explain the school's concerns. It should be made clear to the family that the practice is illegal in the UK. It is inevitable that this meeting will be difficult. If the outcome of the meeting is unsatisfactory, a child protection officer in the local social services department should be informed.

Mental health

Refugee adults and children have specific mental health needs related to persecution and exile. These are examined in Chapter Nine. But it should be stressed that good links be forged with the schools psychological service and child and family consultation clinics.

Sex education and cultural issues

The Education Act 1993 makes sex education a compulsory subject is all secondary schools. Governors of secondary schools are responsible for developing school policy on sex education, involving parents in the process. Human reproduction has to be taught in the science curriculum but schools now have freedom to decide how they will teach the broader issues of sex education. Parents can also withdraw their children from sex education classes. Primary schools are now being encouraged to teach sex education, and school governors have the responsibility for deciding if and how it will appear on the curriculum. Attitudes towards sexuality differ between different ethnic and religious groups; religious and ethnic diversity raise many challenges for those developing positive sex education policies. The following issues should be addressed by those working in a multicultural environment.

Assumptions

Teachers and youth workers often make assumptions about the attitudes that people from different religious and ethnic backgrounds may have to issues such as sex and HIV/AIDS. But any group will have as wide a range of opinions as the majority group. Religious groups also approach issues of sexuality in many different ways: for example there is no Islamic consensus on homosexuality. Among many 'progressive' teachers there is the belief that religions offer only negative perspectives on matters of sexuality. This attitude can affect the self-esteem of young people brought up in a religious tradition. Teachers and youth workers must not perpetuate stereotypes, and must take into account the wide range of opinions within minority groups.

A student-centred approach

The best way of finding out the wide range of opinions within a particular community is to listen to young people, and identify issues that concern them. Sex education must address the concerns and needs of young people. In achieving this end it may be necessary to distinguish between the young person's needs and the concerns of those who may speak on their behalf: parents, community leaders and those with particular political agendas. It may be necessary to acknowledge inter-generational conflict.

Gender

Girls from all cultural backgrounds might well not speak openly in mixed groups about issues concerning sexuality. It is essential that young women are able to spend time in single sex groups. Sex education should also explore issues such as gender roles in a relationship. But again it is important that teachers do not make assumptions about the role of women and men in different cultures. In every refugee community there are many personal differences in the position of men and woman, and ideas about masculinity and femininity.

Case Study: The Health Support Team

Following Kensington, Chelsea and Westminster Health Authority approval of mainstream funding in January 1998, a nurse-led Health Support Team (HST) was set up by Parkside Health Trust. The HST's aim is to improve access to primary healthcare services for people in temporary accommodation in Bayswater and Paddington area of London, predominantly refugees and asylum-seekers. The project also aimed to ease the burden of having extra work from such patients in general practice.

This project has been implemented in close collaboration with GP practices, the Community Health Council and voluntary agencies. The registration protocol used is a comprehensive tool to assess health needs prior to registration with the practice. Additionally, it collects information which practices will require as part of the new patient registration process. The assessment record and subsequent care plan are bilingual and copies are held by the patient. They are encouraged to share these documents with the agencies with which they come into contact.

Initial feedback suggests that this is providing a comprehensive and detailed picture of individual health needs. This is particularly useful for easing the administrative burden for practice staff in local GPs' surgeries. A protocol for nurse prescribing is currently being developed. A secondment of a practice nurse from one surgery to the HST is done on a rota basis for one day per week with an aim of sharing skills, experience and increasing collaboration. This particular model could be useful in areas with large hostels for asylum-seekers.

Department of Health Section 36 Funding has been submitted on behalf of a group of local GPs, to set up a rolling monthly practice staff training programme. Workshop training sessions had been arranged to look at issues such as working with victims of torture, benefits entitlements for refugees/asylum seekers and working with interpreters.

Taken from *A Refugee Health Strategy*, (Acimovic, 2000)

HIV/AIDS

HIV and AIDS are issues affecting every young person in the UK. But refugee communities present special problems in terms of HIV prevention work and service delivery. Some refugees have fled from countries where the rate of heterosexual HIV infection is greater than in the UK. But HIV education in the UK has mainly been directed at the gay community and intravenous drug users. There is an assumption that HIV/AIDS are a 'gay disease'. Clearly this must be challenged – but without stigmatising refugees who come from Sub-Saharan Africa. As well as developing school-based sex education programmes, LEAs and health authorities should be meeting with and supporting community groups active in HIV prevention. There are several successful HIV/AIDS initiatives among the Zairean and Ugandan communities.

Non-governmental organisations

Asylum-seekers and refugees are reliant on the services of non-governmental organisations. These can range from large national refugee charities such as the Refugee Council, Refugee Action or the Scottish Refugee Council, non-refugee charities such as Barnados or the Children Society, both of which have specific projects working with refugees, small, locally based welfare organisations such as Welcare, or the Family Services Unit, or refugee community organisations. LEAs should collate information about local agencies that can support refugees and make these contacts available to schools. Perhaps most central to the lives of refugee families are refugee community organisations.

Making links with refugee community organisations

There are over 350 refugee community organisations in the UK. These self-help groups work with particular communities. Although many asylum-seekers also use the services of refugee agencies when they first arrive, refugee community organisations offer *long term support* and enable refugees to gain control over their own lives.

Refugee community organisations vary in size and in the activities they perform. Some have paid staff; others depend on the energy of volunteers. Some groups have been successful in attracting funds – others not. Some community organisations represent certain ethnic, political or religious groups from one particular country. Schools must be sensitive to these differences and be aware that many newly-arrived asylum-seekers and refugees may be wary of certain community groups and individuals from their home country.

Among the services that refugee community groups offer are

- advice on immigration law, welfare rights and housing
- café facilities, food parcels and second hand clothing
- English language classes, employment training and careers advice
- home language teaching and supplementary education for refugee children
- senior citizen's clubs
- women's groups
- cultural events and outings
- youth clubs
- the production of newsletters and information
- campaigning on issues affecting refugees from that community.

It is important that schools develop good links with refugee community organisations in their locality. If a school wishes to improve the participation of refugee parents in its activities, community groups can be approached and asked to encourage refugee parents. Refugee community groups can sometimes be asked to provide interpreters or to mediate where a serious problem has arisen. Refugee community groups can also be invited to speak to students or to be involved in activities such as cooking, storytelling and other cultural projects.

Bibliography

Acimovic, S. (2000) A Refugee Health Strategy, unpublished paper, from the Refugee Council

Audit Commission (2000) *Another country: interpreting dispersal under the Immigration and Asylum Act 1999*, London: Audit Commission

Carey-Wood, J. Duke, K., Karn, V. and Marshall, T. (1995) *The Settlement of Refugees in Britain, Home Office Study 141*, London: HMSO

Dorkenoo, E and Elworthy, S. (1992) *Female Genital Mutilation: proposals for change*, London: Minority Rights Group

London Borough of Haringey (1997) *Refugees in Haringey: a research report*, London: LB Haringey

Health of Londoners Project (1999) Refugee health in London, London: East London and City Health Authority

Home Office (2000) *Full and Equal Citizens: a strategy for the integration of refugees into the UK*, London: Home Office

Kaye, R (1992) 'British Refugee Policy and 1992: the Breakdown of a Policy Community'. *Journal of Refugee Studies*, Vol 5 No 1 pp 47-65

Refugee Council (1997) *The Development of a Refugee Settlement Policy in the UK*, London: Refugee Council

Sellen, D. *et al* (2000) *Young Refugee Children's Diets and family Coping Strategies in East London*, London: London School of Hygiene and Tropical Medicine

Shackman, J. (1997) *A right to be understood: a training pack for interpreters*, Cambridge: National Extension College

PART TWO
Refugees in Schools

5

Towards an Education Policy for Refugee Students

When we came to England we stayed with out friends, all our family stayed in one room. We didn't go out that much and the room was very small. We were there for about a month, I think. I knew my mum didn't have any money for the things I wanted, so I didn't ask for anything. But I wanted some toys and games and other things.

I wanted to go to school, but my first day at school, I cried, as I didn't want to be there. I didn't make any friends, nothing. I didn't understand anything and I didn't have any friends. I thought I would understand the teacher, but I didn't. My face was red, I think. After some time because I didn't understand any English, they took me to a special class.

Metin, a Kurdish boy who has just left primary school.

Everybody kept staring at me. I was embarrassed and shy. Even at dinnertime I was scared to have my dinner. They were talking about me. I know they were talking about me because they were calling my name. I was really upset then.

I told my Mum and Dad and they told me when I get to learn English they wouldn't say anything to you. I kept crying and said to my Dad, 'I don't want to go to school, I don't want to see them laughing at me and see them talking about me.'

I had two Turkish friends at school, but not that close. Sometimes they helped me, but most of the time they didn't. When they translated anything they were embarrassed. They were embarrassed that the other kids would say, "Don't talk to that girl, she doesn't speak English.

Teachers were always helping me with my work. There was a separate teacher who came to help me. I really like that teacher. I was happiest with her and not with the children in the class.

Serpil, an 11 year old girl from Turkish Kurdistan.

In December 2000 there were an estimated 69,000 refugee children in UK schools; about 70 per cent of them in Greater London. (Refugee Council, 2000). The largest communities were Somalis, Kosovars, Sri Lankan Tamils, Congolese and Turkish Kurds. This chapter aims to outline responses to refugees within the education system and concludes with a positive educational framework for supporting refugee pupils at an LEA, school and classroom level.

A legacy of policies

Today's refugee children are the latest in a long line of migrants and refugees who have entered British schools. Although separated by 200 years, the educational response to Huguenots and eastern European Jews was very similar. From 1680 until 1970 schools adopted *assimilationalist* policies towards refugees and migrants. Teachers aimed to make 'little Englishmen' out of them as quickly as possible. The Jewish Free School, first established in London's East End, had the stated aim of rapidly integrating Jewish students into British society. Students were discouraged from speaking Yiddish. Teachers concentrated on basic English literacy.

Such policies continued until the late 1960s. The educational response to children from eastern Europe, and indeed from the Indian Subcontinent, was to provide resources to teach English as a second language. The Local Government Act 1966 provided a special fund – Section 11 – targeted at groups whose language and culture was significantly different from the rest of the community. But racial prejudice began to make the assimilation of visible minorities an impossibility, even for new arrivals who considered rapid assimilation desirable. Moreover, migrants from the Indian Subcontinent and later Ugandan Asians fully intended to maintain their language and cultures in the UK. Research also began to show that bilingual children performed better in schools where there was bilingual teaching and/or bilingual resources. Students preferred schools and teachers who valued their home culture. Educationalists developed a different model: multiculturalism.

Multicultural education aimed to celebrate linguistic and cultural diversity. There were two distinct goals:

• to improve provision for children from ethnic minority groups

• to prepare children from the majority community for life in a multi-ethnic society.

Schools began to use bilingual resources and to celebrate Muslim, Jewish and Hindu festivals, as well as Christmas. Advisory teachers in multicultural education were appointed. The Swann Report (1985) marks a point when multicultural education policies had maximum impact, and describes many good practices in multicultural education.

From the mid-1970s multicultural education was criticised as being a liberal response to the deep-rooted problem of racism. Multicultural education did not overcome the underachievement of certain groups of school students, particularly African-Caribbean boys, nor address the many manifestations of racism in British society. Some schools and LEAs began to develop policies which aimed to confront racism and promote equality of opportunity. These explored the following issues

- the **curriculum** and whether it reflected the needs and experiences of minority groups
- whether **school resources** confirmed stereotyped views or had positive representations of all sectors of society
- how schools dealt with **racist incidents**, both inside and outside the school gates
- how students from ethnic minority communities were treated in **streaming and setting** practices
- **school discipline** – were some ethnic groups more likely to be excluded from school?
- the **assumptions** and **expectations** that teachers held about students from different groups
- the **recruitment**, retention and career progression of teachers from ethnic minority groups.

A large number of LEAs and schools played lip-service to antiracist education. But in reality only a relatively small number of schools had good policies which worked. Anti-racist education became politicised instead of being seen as good educational practice and many teachers were discomforted by being asked to examine their own attitudes and assumptions.

Policies for refugees in the 1990s

Just when the greatest numbers of refugee students were being admitted to English schools, the Government changed education policies in a way that seriously undermined their educational opportunities. The changes wrought by the Education Reform Act 1988 and continued throughout the 1990s with initiatives such as the Literacy Hour have made huge demands on teachers' time and energy. In such a climate many schools are unable to respond fully to the needs of refugee students and have no time to develop imaginative policies for their support.

Successive cuts in public expenditure and the greater delegation of LEA budgets to schools have reduced the power of local government to generate progressive policies or plan strategically for the arrival of refugees. Throughout the 1990s central government also challenged the multicultural consensus, prompted by lobbying from the New Right, which was adept at using the media to castigate antiracist education. Populist politicians have lobbied for the dismantling of teacher training institutions, seen as the power-base of progressive ideas. Emphasis is now on classroom-based training, and student teachers have far less time to read and reflect upon antiracist approaches or develop new ideas and resources.

An antiracist agenda for the 21st century

Good multicultural and antiracist education still survives in some schools. New ideas are emerging, *inter alia* Roger Hewitt's research into adolescent racism in the London Borough of Greenwich (Hewitt, 1996) and the Burnage Report – an investigation into the racist murder a 12 year old boy in a Manchester playground (Macdonald *et al*, 1989). Researchers such as Stuart Hall maintain ethnic and personal identity is shifting as a result of globalisation. The core of globalisation theory is that the world is increasingly interconnected, more and more a single economic, social and cultural entity in which the idea of a nation state is becoming increasingly defunct. Concepts of personal and national identity are shifting. Globalisation theory has also been used to explain growing refugee numbers. A nation state that has collapsed violently or seen a reduction in its powers has less control over social order and is less able to prevent conflict and to promote justice and equal opportunity.

Hall believes that globalisation has led to

- an erosion of national identity and its replacement with cultural homogeneity in some instances (the global McDonald culture)
- the strengthening of national and ethnic identity in other instances as a way of resisting globalisation. Thus newly unemployed workers may turn to narrow nationalism as a strong ideology in the face of economic stress
- the greater juxtaposition of different cultures in the same neighbourhood (or school)
- the development of new identities of hybridity to replace old national identities in other instances. For example, young refugees who may have spent their first five years in one country and the next ten years in the UK may well have their own hybrid identity.

The use of different strategies to create identity are examined by other refugee researchers. Asikainen (1996) looks at the construction of identity among Bosnian refugees in Finland. After the war in Bosnia there was greater awareness of ethnicity and religious affiliation among Bosnians. Asikainen suggests that a refugee narrative 'involving a heightened awareness of ethnic/religious or political affiliation' is constructed among refugees by mobilising collective memory. This refugee narrative serves many useful purposes by

- enabling people to share experiences
- helping refugees to create enemies and feel angry with them
- creating a sense of togetherness in exile
- helping some people to create a new identity as a refugee
- enabling a person to make sense of a war and of being a refugee.

Understanding identity is important for those working with refugee children. They need to know how refugee children construct new identities in exile, as a means of coping with their new life. Children may also construct new national narratives involving a heightened awareness of ethnic, religious or political affiliation. This sometimes leads to conflicts in schools between different groups of refugee children, such as ethnic Turks and Turkish Kurds.

The study of identity also throws light on the new forms of racism emerging in western Europe. 'Race' is becoming increasingly equated with nation. New English and British identities are being invented by the popular press and politicians and then compared with other identities, with the 'other' always being constructed as negative. Thus English identity becomes 'not a refugee, not a black'.

But new hybrid identities are also emerging and these may be a useful in creating a common agenda for opposing sides in a conflict. For example 'football fan' has been used to create a common agenda for Serbian and Bosniak men living in Leeds and they have formed a multi-ethnic football team. The creation of 'common agendas' and the 'commonality of experiences and aspirations' between refugees and non-refugees as a tool of combating racism has been recommended in advice given to the Refugee Council. For example, schools, perhaps via citizenship education, can engage in work that examines the commonality of experiences of refugee and non-refugee pupils.

Refugee children in our schools

The numerous legislative and policy changes targeted at asylum-seekers and refugees, along with the educational changes, have had a major effect on the lives of young refugees in schools. But other social and educational factors influence their schooling, some of them unconnected with the refugee experience. It is important to remember that within a given refugee community there is a great deal of heterogeneity and refugee children have no single neat set of educational needs.

Refugee students have come from many different countries. But within one national group refugee children will

- have different class origins
- come from different ethnic and linguistic groups

- come from families with different religious observances and different political affiliations
- have different educational backgrounds: some may not have attended school at all, while others may have attended English medium schools in their home countries
- have different experiences of persecution and flight.

LEAs and schools, therefore, need flexible policies to be able to meet the varied needs of refugee students. However, some issues, needs and problems do arise frequently with significant numbers of refugee children, including

- having an interrupted education in the countries of origin
- having horrific experiences in their home countries and flight to the UK, for a small number of whom this affects their ability to learn and rebuild their lives
- experiencing a drop in their standard of living and status in society
- changing care arangements: losing parents or usual carers
- having parents who are emotionally absent
- living with families who do not know their educational and social rights
- encountering problems securing a school place, free school meals or uniform grants
- speaking little or no English on arrival
- experiencing a lack of EAL support
- enduring bullying or isolation in school
- finding it difficult to study in the further or higher education sector because of their immigration status or lack of access to benefits.

A local authority framework

As well the factors that combine to disadvantage refugee children in schools, there are also positive examples of good educational provision at LEA, school and classroom level. The Refugee Council services a working group called the Steering Group on Refugee Education, made up of teachers, advisors, inspectors and education officers. The group has been meeting for ten years to exchange information about refugee issues and good educational practice, and to lobby for resources for refugee students in schools. The Refugee Council and the Steering Group encourage the following practices to be implemented by local government. The ideas raised below are developed in the case studies and in subsequent chapters.

- LEAS need to participate in **multi-agency planning** at a local authority level (see Chapter Four).
- Access to good quality **interpreting services** are central to the successful induction of refugee children in schools (see Chapter Four).

Duties to asylum-seeking and refugee children in English schools

- LEAs have a duty to provide full-time education for all children of compulsory school age resident in that LEA, as outlined in Section 14 of the Education Act 1996.

- LEAs and schools have a duty to provide free school meals for all refugee and asylum-seeking children on means tested benefits. If the asylum-seeking or refugee family are in receipt of Job Seekers' Allowance or Income Support, that obligation is outlined by the Education Act 1996. If the asylum-seeking family is being supported by a local authority or by the National Asylum Support Service, under Section 6 of the Immigration and Asylum Act 1996, that entitlement to free school meals is outlined in Section 117 of Schedule 14 of the Immigration and Asylum Act 1999.

- LEAs have a duty to provide certain educational support to children in public care, who are looked after under Section 20 of the Children Act 1989 (see Chapter 12).

- LEAs and schools, as both employers and education providers, have to comply with the Race Relations Act 1976 and the Race Relations (Amendment) Act 2000 – they must not racially discriminate. The new Race Relations (Amendment) Act also obliges public authorities *positively* to promote good race relations. The new Act also gives the Commission for Racial Equality the responsibility for preparing a statutory Code of Practice for LEAs and schools on how to fulfil their race equality duties. The new Education Code of Practice for LEAs and schools on how to fulfil their race equality duties. The new Education Code of Practice will come into force in early 2002.

- OFSTED can inspect schools for social inclusion and support for refugee children (see OFSTED, 2000).

- A written **educational policy** on support to asylum-seeking and refugee children is helpful, especially if it outlines issues of educational entitlement, as well as good practice. The London Borough of Camden and Gloucestershire County Council both have a comprehensive refugee educational policy document that can be used as a model for other local authorities.

- The LEA should consider conducting a **refugee survey** of its school children and users of early years and youth services. Further information about how to conduct a refugee survey is given on page 77.

- **Schools admissions** staff need to ensure they are aware of the entitlements to education of asylum-seeking and refugee children and that they are sensitive when interviewing refugee families who may speak little English.

- **Educational psychology teams** should have staff with designated responsibility for refugees.

- Where there are a significant number of refugee children in the LEA, **a refugee support teacher(s)** could be employed. At the time of writing, some 32 LEAs throughout the UK employed refugee support teachers. Their job involves

  - working with individual refugee children, often those whose needs extend beyond learning English
  - helping schools develop their own practices to support refugee children
  - delivering INSET
  - acting as a contact point on refugee issues within an education department.

A number of local authorities have multi-disciplinary refugee support teams where educational psychologists, teachers and educational social workers operate together. Some refugee support teams employ bilingual staff and classroom assistants. Where educational psychologists and education welfare officers do not work closely with refugee support or EAL teams, it is still important to have staff with responsibility for work with refugee children. The job of an educational welfare officer is to make sure that children attend school and most work with children already on a school roll. In some areas, the educational welfare officer's job has been widened to include work with homeless families and those in temporary accommodation. Officers may help children access a school place, as well as helping the family obtain free school meals and uniform grants – an essential job given the difficulties faced by many refugee families in securing school places.

All local authorities now have to have an officer with responsibility for the **education of looked after children** and this may include a large number of unaccompanied children. Such staff need to be aware of the specific needs of unaccompanied refugee children.

Traveller education services need to work closely with refugee support and EAL teams where local refugee communities include eastern European Roma.

Staff in **grants and awards teams** will be concerned with asylum-seekers and refugees who may wish to progress to further and higher education. They will need clear information about the different entitlements that different immigration status confers.

Libraries and leisure services have a significant and varied role to play and need to make sure that they are meeting the needs of refugee communities. Libraries should ensure that they hold books in relevant refugee languages. Library space can be used for exhibitions about new local communities and to promote awareness and positive images of refugees. The internet can also be used creatively with refugees: for example, Lewisham Refugee Network and

How to carry out a refugee survey

Ethnic monitoring of the uptake of services and job recruitment allows service providers or employers to ascertain whether certain ethnic groups are under-represented as users or employees. Ethnic monitoring may also be used to argue for funds for projects that target specific ethnic groups.

The DfEE is also moving towards a system where pupil achievement will be monitored by ethnic category in order to highlight areas of concern. Unfortunately, the ethnicity categories chosen will not benefit those specifically interested in the achievement of refugee pupils. The DfEE has elected to use broad categories such as Black African, Black Caribbean, Black Other. This means that unless LEAs supplement this classification, Somali pupils will be included in the same category as pupils of Nigerian origin and a Turkish Kurd might be classified as 'Middle Eastern' or European Other'.

This lack of precision has led some LEAs to conduct refugee surveys, to calculate the total number of refugee pupils. The information collected has often be used in funding bids, most usually for funds from the Ethnic Minority Achievement Grant.

Refugee surveys can be conducted in two different ways.

*   by asking children if they are asylum-seekers or have refugee status or ELR

*   using a range of different data such as LEA language surveys and National Asylum Support Service data.

A few local authorities require schools directly to ask pupils if they are asylum-seekers or refugees and use this information in refugee surveys. While this may be the most accurate way of approaching a refugee survey, asking such a direct question might arouse fear and suspicion among some refugee families. An alternative would be to look at information collected in annual language surveys and to supplement this with other information. Most urban local authorities carry out language surveys where a child's home language is recorded, sometimes with the country of birth. This can indicate if a child is likely to be an asylum-seeker or refugee – a child who speaks Krio or Somali, for example, is highly likely to be a refugee.

However, there are difficulties in calculating refugee numbers for some linguistic groups. For example, children who speak Arabic, French or Turkish may or may not be refugees. Here you will need to use supplementary evidence, such as finding out the country of birth, whether the family is supported by the National Asylum Support Service or seeing if the child speaks other languages also. For example, a Turkish speaking child who also speaks Kurdish is likely to be a refugee.

As from 3 April 2000, all LEAs will be informed of children being supported by the National Asylum Support Service. This may aid statistical accuracy in conducting LEA refugee surveys.

Lewisham libraries ran a project for young Kosovars based in a library where young refugees were able to use the internet to access Albanian language news and Red Cross family tracing information.

Swimming pools and other leisure outlets need to ensure that asylum-seekers supported by the National Asylum Support Service are able to use services at a concessionary rate. The use of leisure services as well as libraries should be subject to ethnic monitoring, to ensure that use is representative of the whole community.

About 40 per cent of all refugee children in the UK attend **refugee community schools**. LEAs should ensure that these schools, which may teach the home language, as well as supplementing the mainstream curriculum, are funded and supported. For example, the London Borough of Greenwich has a funding programme for its community schools including many refugee community schools. The receipt of funds is contingent on participating in teacher training programmes.

The **Youth Service** needs to be involved, to ensure that refugee children have full access to youth clubs, leisure, after-school and holiday projects. The Youth Service needs to monitor the uptake of its services to ensure that no ethnic group is excluded. Refugee community organisations should be supported in their development of youth services and the new ConneXions strategy in England must meet the needs of refugees.

Early years providers need to be actively involved, as refugee children are under-represented in early years provision. The new English Early Years Development Plans require that local authorities account for services for refugee children. Further information about early years provision is given in Chapter Fourteen.

Funding for refugee support work in education

Asylum-seeking children, as all children, have their mainstream education funded, through an annual allocation of monies from the DfEE (in England), the Welsh Assembly, the Scottish Executive or the Northern Ireland Office. Local authorities and schools receive an allocation of funds based on pupil numbers at an annual census day. This is called a Form Seven Census in England. For schools admitting large numbers of asylum-seeking pupils or other mobile groups, this annual census presents problems. A school may have no refugee pupils on roll on the day of the census and the school and the LEA will receive no funding for them until the following year. Within days refugee pupils may be admitted. LEAs and schools can also access funding for specific projects to support refugee children, in their learning of English, for example. The support of refugee children in schools can be funded

- directly by a local authority
- by EMAG funds in England
- by other sources of funding such as the Single Regeneration Budget, Education Action Zones, Sure Start and the Excellence in Cities programme.

Additionally, in July 2000, the DfEE announced that it would give an additional £500 grant per child to all schools outside Greater London who have received asylum-seeking children dispersed by the National Asylum Support Service.

Throughout the late 1990s the funding of specific refugee support work in education has become a political issue, with many teachers and education officers claiming that central government funding is not sufficient to meet the needs of newly arrived asylum-seekers and refugees. In England, funding for the educational support of refugee children mostly comes from local authorities and the DfEE administered EMAG – part of the Schools Standards Fund – replacing Section 11 grant in 1998.

In Wales, the Welsh Assembly makes grants available to local authorities for the support of children from ethnic minority communities. In Scotland there is no dedicated fund for such children's educational support, but funding is met directly by local authorities. Section 11 funding was never activated in Scotland and there is no EMAG-like grant, as local authorities and the Scottish Executive argue that the needs of ethnic minority communities in Scotland can best be met by the appropriate delivery of mainstream local authority services.

EMAG, and before it Section 11, have always been controversial sources of funding. From a refugee perspective, the main problems associated with EMAG are

- funding is insufficient to meet refugee children's needs to learn English. In reality teachers' time is solely targeted at beginners. Few children who have achieved some competence in English receive additional help.
- funding has decreased at a time when the numbers of children requiring EAL support have increased. A Section 11 fund of £130.8 million in 1993/94 was cut to an EMAG fund of £83 million in 1998/99.
- there is no contingency in the EMAG grant. Local authorities have to make an annual bid for EMAG funds. But the arrival of asylum-seeking children in a local authority is usually unpredictable, with many LEAs unable to claim monies for children who arrive mid-way through a financial year. As asylum-seekers began to be dispersed outside London, many coastal and northern local authorities complained that they were not receiving additional monies to meet the students' needs.
- Unlike Section 11, EMAG is reluctant to allocate grants for funding dedicated educational psychologists and educational social workers to sup-

port refugee children. But good practice indicates that the complex needs of refugee children are best met by multi-disciplinary teams.

- EMAG does not fund home language teaching, even though this has educational and psychosocial benefits for refugee children. The DfEE policy is that home language teaching is the responsibility of communities
- non-governmental organisations are unable to access grants from EMAG.

There are other sources of funding available to local authorities and schools working with refugee children (including the £500 grant of July 2000). Several LEAs have managed to access Single Regeneration Budget funding for refugee support projects. In England three Educational Action Zones are likely to have a major component of refugee support work within them. A small number of Sure Start and Excellence in Cities projects also have specific refugee components. However, research being carried out by the Refugee Council in 2000 indicates that refugee children have been neglected in many of the poverty and regeneration focussed special grants.

Funding models

The Refugee Council believes that the additional educational needs of newly arrived refugee children will involve costs of £110-£120 per child per week. There are three ways of organising support at an LEA level.

1. The **Integrated Refugee Support Team**, where all the additional educational needs of refugee children are met within the team. Team members may include refugee support teachers whose job it is to provide EAL support and organise any other support required. Refugee support teachers may also act as a contact point within the LEA, organise in-service training and help schools develop their own practices. Educational welfare officers who assist with school admissions, home-school liaison staff and educational psychologists may also work in an integrated refugee support team.

2. A specialist **Refugee Support Teacher**(s) whose job is to work with refugee children whose needs go beyond that of learning English: for example a child who is not coping as a result of an overwhelmingly traumatic past experience. The Refugee Support Teacher may also act as a contact point within the local authority, run in-service training and help schools develop practices. The London Borough of Brent organises its work in this way.

3. No dedicated specialism by LEA staff, but refugee children's needs met by EAL teachers, educational welfare officer and so on.

Whatever the method of working, a local authority should think about the following items when costing support for refugee children.

- *EAL support* – A minimum of five hours of in-class support and/or small group work per week should be given to a newly-arrived child.

- *Assistance with school admission* – It takes at least three hours of work per child by an educational welfare officer or similar to arrange school admission, free school dinners and uniform grants. Where interpreters are needed, their time will have to be costed.
- *Refugee support teachers* – At least 10 per cent of refugee children may have an educational need above that of learning English. Where refugee support teachers are not providing general EAL support, a level of at least one refugee support teacher per 400 children is needed.
- Dedicated time from an *educational psychologist*.
- *Books, tapes, dictionaries* and other teaching resources are needed.
- Budgets for organising *in-service training*.

School policy and classroom practice

The two testimonies given at the beginning of this chapter show how the educational experiences of refugee children in UK schools can vary. While there is much good practice to support refugee pupils, bullying, often of a racist nature, is an almost universal experience of newly-arrived refugee children, and leads to much misery. Arguably there also needs to be greater mainstream teacher competence in meeting children's EAL needs, as well as greater attention to what schools can practically do to support refugee children. These themes are outlined below and developed later in the book

The prime responsibility for ensuring that the educational needs of refugee children are met lies with the school. The role of refugee support teachers and other LEA services should be viewed as complementing the professional role of the classroom teacher. The starting point for changing school policy is to listen to what refugee children and their carers have to say about school and to observe critically what is happening to children in the classroom and playground. Refugee children are often clear about what they like about school and what support they need. For example, a group of Eritrean refugee children living in Sweden who were interviewed about they liked about school praised

- teachers who made some adjustment to their teaching methods, recognising that refugee children were often used to a more formal education system
- teachers with clear and high expectations
- teachers who asked them about themselves
- teachers who made an effort to include refugee children's experiences in the curriculum
- teachers who took racism seriously.
- schools which invited in members of refugee community organisations
- teachers who came to special cultural occasions held by refugee communities. (Taken from Melzak and Warner (1992) *Integrating Refugee Children in Schools*.)

Refugee children's particular educational and psycho-social needs may well be similar to other groups of pupils in a school. Schools should examine their existing practice: to meet the pastoral needs of children who have had stressful life experiences, to support bilingual children, to promote equal opportunities and to challenge racism. For changes in school policy and practice to succeed, they need to be given the backing of the headteacher and senior management team. School governors need to be kept informed of developments and involved as much as possible in changing policy and practice.

Some schools have used **in-service training** as a catalyst for change in a school, inviting in outside speakers. Refugee parents and past students can often relay moving testimony of their experiences. It is useful to involve support staff in in-service training, as school secretaries are often the first point of contact a refugee family has with a school. Lunch-time supervisors must be sensitive to issues of bullying and participate in the school's code of practice for dealing with such incidents.

OFSTED reports can also be used as a catalyst for change, as OFSTED **inspections** should examine the quality of support for refugee children, as well as EAL support, whether the school is meeting children's cultural needs, as well as the schools links with parents and communities. The 2000 *Framework for Inspection* has clear requirements for assessing issues of ethnicity and social inclusion. The process of drawing up a School Development Plans can also offer the opportunity to examine how a school supports refugee children. A few schools have targeted refugee children in their School Development Plans, committing the school to bring about change.

Working parties can be used to develop new policy and practice in schools: a number of schools have set up refugee working parties, or used existing bodies to carry out tasks to change policy. A few schools, mostly in London, have members of **staff with designated responsibility for refugee children**. Although they can act as a contact point within the school, the disadvantage is that other teachers may feel they need not take responsibility for dealing with the problems that refugee children may encounter. Whole school involvement in changing policy and practice to support refugee children is the key to success. Although a working group may draw up a school's refugee policy, the whole staff and governors should be able to comment on policy and feel that their comments are taken seriously. All staff must feel that they own school policy. This is of particular importance when dealing with emotive and controversial aspects of refugee policy, or in parts of the UK where refugees suffer public hostility and racial harassment.

Admissions and induction policy and practices needs to be examined so that a welcoming environment is provided for refugee children. Admission and induction policy is examined in greater detail in the next chapter.

Refugee children have specific **language** needs – most newly-arrived asylum-seeking children enter the school system speaking little or no English. Particular attention should be given to supporting language learning for children whose prior education has been interrupted. Schools should pay attention to children who are Stage Three and Stage Four language learners. As literacy is such a major feature of the work of schools throughout the UK, programmes such as the Literacy Hour in England should be accessible to children for whom English is an additional language. The English language needs of refugee children are discussed in Chapter Seven.

Refugee children also need to maintain and develop their **home language**. There is now clear evidence that children who continue to study in their first language perform better in school (in a second or third language) than those who are not able to develop their first or home language (see for example, Gravelle, 2000). The maintenance and development of the home language is also conducive to a positive sense of identity and essential for refugees who aspire to return home. Schools should encourage children to sit examinations in languages such as Arabic, Turkish, Tamil, Farsi and Chinese, of all which offer acccreditation in the UK. Schools with large numbers of refugee children from one particular linguistic group should look towards teaching that language as part of the mainstream school curriculum.

Schools, in collaboration with other professionals, need to examine the support they give to refugee children who have had traumatic experiences and may be manifesting disturbed behaviour. Many refugee children's **emotional and psychological needs** can be met within schools, bringing in outside agencies where appropriate. Art, drama and autobiography can be utilised to help children settle into school. Other children may need referral to specialist agencies such as the school psychological service, Child and Adolescent Mental Health Services and voluntary sector mental health projects. The psychological needs of refugee children are examined in Chapter Nine.

Bullying is commonly experienced by newly-arrived refugee children, particularly those who speak little or no English. The media coverage associated with the passage of recent asylum legislation, benefit cuts and the arrival of refugees in areas such as southern coastal towns have undoubtedly contributed to hostility towards refugees, perpetrated by both children and adults. Schools have a clear duty to counter bullying and racist behaviour. In England, the DfEE obliges schools to record and report racist incidents and now requires schools to have in place school behaviour strategies that include effective ways of combating bullying and racial harassment. Anti-bullying and **antiracist strategies** should determine clear sanctions for offenders, help build an atmosphere of respect in schools and use curricular opportunities, such the Citizenship programme of study in England, to make all students aware of why people become refugees. Chapter Ten looks at how schools can effectively challenge racism.

Case study – Salusbury Primary School and Salusbury World

Salusbury Primary School is a large primary school in the London Borough of Brent. Some 12-15 per cent of its 600 pupils are asylum-seekers or refugees. Although the school is located in a prosperous part of London, there are several bed and breakfast hotels nearby in which asylum-seekers and refugees are placed, often by local authorities other than Brent. The refugee children living in these hotels come from many different countries, although most are currently from Iraq, Somalia and Kosova. The children face social deprivation on many levels. Statutory sector support is minimal, especially for those for whom Brent is not responsible.

The refugee families living in the hotels are highly mobile. They may be housed there for a week or stay for as long as two years. With families moving frequently, the school has faced many additional administrative burdens, as the enrolment of pupils takes time.

A small number of refugee children have exhibited disturbed behaviour, often made worse by their inability to communicate in English or be understood. Salusbury Primary School has used an impressive range of strategies to help children settle into the school. A charitable trust has funded welcome packs for all newly-arrived refugee children who need them. Children are given pens, pencils and felt pens, to enable them to take part in lessons on their first day at school. Established pupils are expected to welcome new pupils into school and show them the cloakroom, toilets, canteen and so on. Children translate for each other. The school has also been able to tap into the strong informal support network of refugee parents in the area: some of them interpret or help in classrooms. The school staff noticed that some children felt very insecure in the playground and hated breaktime so the school playground was redesigned to provide quiet sitting areas.

There is a small LEA team working with refugee children in Brent. This project – the Travellers and Displaced Persons' Support Team has previously placed a teacher who speaks Somali and Arabic to work in the school. The school also has a long-standing commitment to human rights education and uses assemblies and lessons to examine issues such as migration and the reception of newcomers.

In 1997 the school set up an independent charity to extend its work with refugee families – Salusbury World. One of its first tasks was to raise money to refurbish a disused room to use as a drop-in centre for refugee children and their carers. In 1999 funding was secured from the National Lottery Charities Board which provided for a project co-ordinator and the conversion of a room. The project is now based in a room on the school site. A gallery has been built in the room, giving office space. Downstairs are activity tables, a refreshment area, a library of bilingual books and cupboards containing donated clothing and toys.

In term time, Salusbury World runs an after school and homework club three evenings a week. The club makes use of parent and community volunteers. In order to break down barriers between the school and Salusbury World, refugee children can bring their friends to the after school club. This has helped contain resentment that might be felt over 'special' provision for refugee children. Integration has also been promoted by getting all children at the school competing to design the logo of Salusbury World and involving them in the launch of the project.

During the school day, the project coordinator offers advice and advocacy services for refugee parents who may have problems with their asylum cases or with benefits or housing. She tries to ensure that families have good legal representation and visits hotels to make contact with families. Both Salusbury World and the school have noted that the casework undertaken by the project coordinator has freed a great deal of teacher time.

In term time, refugee parents are able to study English at a nearby centre run by Brent Adult and Community Education Scheme.

In the school holidays, Salusbury World organises a holiday club for refugee children. This is not restricted to children enrolled at Salusbury School and offers activites such as sport, reading, art and photography. The project coordinator has used photography in an imaginative and therapeutic way. Children used cameras to take pictures of their families, friends and surroundings. Photographs were then laid out and used to prompt discussion on topics such as people the children have lost. The photographs of hotel rooms were also used to initiate talk about the difficulties of living in crowded conditions. Another topic was built on the people missing from the photographs – the family and friends children may have lost or left behind.

Salusbury World represents value for money and is replicable in other schools. The project has mobilised a great deal of voluntary support within the community and has strengthened informal refugee support networks. The advocacy service offered by the coodinator have helped lessen some of the social stresses that impact on refugee families. The after-school club enables children to read or complete homework tasks. Although charitable funding has been granted to the project, other schools could look to statutory sources to fund similar work.

Case study – refugee support teachers in Newham schools

The London Borough of Newham is an inner city local authority with a large refugee population. The largest communities are Somalis, Somali Bravanese, Congolese (Zairean), Tamils, Angolans, Colombians and Kosovars. About ten per cent of the school population are refugees and all secondary schools in the LEA have significant numbers of refugee children. Many Newham schools face pressures in settling refugee children who arrive as unplanned admissions during the school term. Some are newly arrived in the UK, others have moved home many times, as they shift temporary accommodation. One of the focuses of the work of the refugee support teachers has been to help schools adapt their admission and induction practices for refugee children.

The LEA has run a refugee support team since 1994, initially two teachers, working in primary and secondary schools. The team is funded by the Single Regeneration Budget and has been increased to eight: three refugee support teachers work in primary schools and three in secondary schools, plus two family workers employed to help sort out welfare problems. Refugee support teachers are delegated to secondary schools and work in just one school for one term, or longer and aim to help schools develop good practice to support refugee children and to support individual children who are not coping.

The refugee support teachers based in Newham secondary schools have initiated much good practice in individual schools, such as

- identifying key staff in each secondary school who can take forward refugee support work after the refugee support teacher moves on

- initiating meetings with members of schools' senior management teams while working in a particular school, to examine ways of supporting refugee children in that school

- implementing in-service training to schools on issues such as mid-term admissions, supporting refugee children in mainstream classes and supporting refugee children under severe stress

- preparing translated welcome leaflets that give information about particular schools

- setting up a classroom friends scheme for newly-arrived refugee children and training the befrienders

- developing life story work in schools

- developing after-school clubs and a youth club activity centre for mid-term admssions

- participating in multi-agency meetings that attempt to coordinate services to refugees in Newham

- producing an information booklet about the Bravanese community.

Young refugees who arrive in the UK late in their educational careers, perhaps in the middle of GCSE courses, have particular educational needs. They need to spend their time at school meaningfully and directed towards clear career paths after school. All too often, however, **newly-arrived 14-19 year old asylum-seekers** are denied school places or given no targeted support and consequently perform badly at GCSE. Young refugees arriving late in their educational careers may also fail to secure a college place, or be directed to a course that does not meet their long term academic aspirations. But there are ways in which they can be supported. A school can enrol them with a younger age group, enabling them to study for examinations starting as near as possible to the beginning of the course. Alternatively, schools and colleges can organise one year 'access to GCSE courses' targeted at young people whose first language is not English. The needs of 14-19 year old refugees are examined in Chapter 13.

Research such as that conducted by the University of Warwick in 1998 indicates that many refugee **parents** have very little involvement in their children's education (Vincent and Warren, 1998). They may have come from countries where there is little tradition of parental involvement in schooling. Refugee parents may speak little English, or not be confident enough to make contact with the school. Schools themselves can be unwelcoming places. Chapter 11 examines ways of making positive links with refugee children's home and communities.

For refugee children living in temporary accommodation, after school and summer holiday clubs, as well as youth work provision, is particularly important.

Both Salusbury World and staff in the London Borough of Newham started from small beginnings, but over time they have developed classroom and whole school approaches that offer real support to refugee families. Both of these projects show that teachers and schools can make a significant difference to refugee chidren's lives.

Bibliography

Arshad, R., Closs, A. and Stead, J. (1999) *Doing our Best: Scottish School Education, Refugee Pupils and Parents – a strategy for social inclusion*, Edinburgh: Centre for Education in Racial Equality in Scotland.

Asikainen, E. (1996) 'The Construction of Identity among Bosnian Refugees in Finland' in *Journal of Refugee Studies*, Vol 9

Bourne, J. and Blair, M. (1998) *Making the Difference: teaching and learning stratgies in successful multi-ethnic schools*, London: DfEE

Camden Education and Camden and Islington Health Authority (1996) *Meeting the Needs of Refugee Children: a checklist for all staff who work with refugee children in schools*, London: Camden Education

London Borough of Camden (1997) *Refugee Education Policy* (Local Authority Report to Council)

Children of the Storm (1998) *Invisible Students: practical and peer-led approaches to enhancing the educational and emotional support for refugee children in schools*, London: Children of the Storm

Daycare Trust (1995) *Reaching First Base: guidelines of good practice on meeting the needs of refugee children from the Horn of Africa*, London: Daycare Trust

Department of Education and Science (1985) *Education for All: the Report of the Committee of Inquiry into the Education of Children from Ethnic Minority Groups (Swann Report)*, London: HMSO

Economic and Social Research Council (2000) 'Extraordinary childhoods: the social lives of refugee children' ESCR Research Briefing 5.

Gillborn, D. and Gipps. C. (1996) *Recent Research on the Achievement of Ethnic Minority Pupils*, London: Office for Standards in Education

Gilroy, P. (1990) 'The End of Anti-Racism' in *New Community*, Vol 17 (1): 71-83

Gloucestershire County Council (2000) *A Policy for the Education of Refugees and Asylum-Seekers* (unpublished policy report)

Gravelle, M. (ed) (2000) *Planning for Bilingual Learners,* Stoke on Trent: Trentham Books

Hall, S. (1992) 'The Question of Cultural Identity' in (eds) Hall, S.; Held, D. and McGrew, T. *Modernity and its Futures*, Cambridge, Polity Press

Hewitt, R. (1996) *Routes of Racism: the social basis of racist action*, Stoke on Trent: Trentham Books

Klein, G. (1993) *Education Towards Race Equality*, London: Cassell

Language and Curriculum Access Service Enfield (1999) *Refugee Education Handbook*, London: Language and Curriculum Access Service Publications

Macdonald. I. (1989) *Murder in the Playground: the Burnage Report,* London: Longsight Press

McDonald, J. (1995) *Entitled to learn? A report on young refugees' experiences of access and progression in the UK education system*, London: World University Service.

Melzak, S. and Warner, R. (1992) *Integrating Refugee Children in Schools*, London: Minority Rights Group

OFSTED (2000) *Evaluating Educational Inclusion: guidance for inspectors and schools*, London: OFSTED

OFSTED (2000) *Framework 2000: Inspecting Schools*, London: OFSTED

Power, S., Whitty, G. and Youdell. D. (1998) Refugees, Asylum-seekers and the Housing Crisis: no place to learn' in (eds) Rutter, J. and Jones, C. (1998) *Refugee Education: Mapping the Field*, Stoke on Trent: Trentham Books

Refugee Council (2000) *Helping Refugee Children in Schools*, London: Refugee Council

Refugee Council and Save the Children (2000) *In Safe Hands: a video training pack about supporting young refugee children*, London: Refugee Council and Save the Children

Rutter, J. and Jones, C. (1998) *Refugee Education: Mapping the Field*, Stoke on Trent: Trentham Books

Save the Children (1997) *Let's Spell It Out: Peer Research by the Horn of Africa Youth Scheme*. London: Save the Children

Shelter (1995) *No Place to Learn: Homelessness and Education*, London: Shelter

Troyna, B. (1992) 'Can You See The Join? An historical analysis of multicultural and anti-racist education policies' in (eds) Blair, M., Gill, D and Mayor, B. (1992) *Racism and Education: Structures and Strategies*, London: Sage

Vincent, C and Warren, S. (1998) Supporting Refugee Children; a focus on home-school links. Unpublished research report from the University of Warwick.

6

A Warm Welcome:
Admission and Induction

All I could say when I started school was 'hello' and 'goodbye'. I felt left out. I had to put my hand up all the time and point to what I didn't understand. A lot of the time I was just copying from others. I didn't like going to school because of the bullying. It would have been useful to have someone from my own country or someone who shared the same languages (Arabic and Tigrinya) at school with me then. Mohamed

All students who arrive after the start of the year need special induction procedures. Induction is designed to help students settle into a new school and become effective learners as quickly as possible. It aims to make the first crucial weeks in a new school a happy experience. A good induction policy is particularly important for refugee students. For one thing, almost all refugee students arrive in a school mid-term. Secondly, they often come from countries where the education system is different and schools may be differently organised. The style of teaching is usually more formal; laboratory practicals or group work might be unknown. The range of subjects taught in a child's home country might also be different. Drama and learning through play may be quite new and not perceived as educational. And lastly, refugee children may have had their school life interrupted because of war or unrest in their home countries.

Rapid enrolment and regular attendance at school is highly desirable for asylum-seeking and refugee children, for linguistic and psychological reasons. The Refugee Council considers that they should all be offered a school place within three weeks of arriving in a local authority. Their entitlement to a school place is clear. In England the DfEE Code of Practice on School Admissions *Annex B Guidance on Pupils from Overseas and DfEE Guidance on Support for Children of Asylum-Seeking and Refugee Families* (2000) outline the rights of asylum-seeking and refugee children to education. They have the same entitlement to schooling as other children. Parents are obliged to ensure that their children receive an education. Schools and LEAs must offer school places in accordance with their published admissions arrangements and must ensure that all children resident in that local authority receive full time education. The obligation of an

LEA to provide a school place is outlined in Section 14 of the Education Act 1996. In drawing up admissions arrangements, schools and LEAs must comply with the Race Relations Act 1976.

In Wales, the National Assembly's Education Department has issued a Code of Practice on Admissions which came into effect in April 1999. This outlines the right of all children to appropriate education. In Scotland, educational provision for asylum-seeking and refugee children is premised upon the requirements of the Education (Scotland) Act 1980. This legislation requires all education authorities to provide an adequate and efficient education for all pupils at school in Scotland. The Act also states that all children are entitled to the provision of primary and secondary school education regardless of immigration status or length of stay in an area. The Race Relations Act 1976 requirements also apply to Wales and Scotland.

In Northern Ireland, schools and Education Boards have greater freedom in determining school admission but the Race Relations (Northern Ireland) Order 1997 extends much of the same protection against discrimination afforded to ethnic minority groups in England, Scotland and Wales, and its requirements are monitored by the Commission for Racial Equality (Northern Ireland). This new legal instrument can also be used to ensure that asylum-seeking and refugee children gain access to mainstream education.

Nevertheless, it has been difficult to secure school places for some refugee children. At the time of writing, about 1,500 were without school places, mostly in England. The groups mostly affected were children who arrived in the UK late in their educational careers. Pressure to achieve league table targets and new performance related pay has meant that a minority of schools have illegally refused to admit refugee children. In recognition of this problem the DfEE changed policy on league tables. From July 2000 any child arriving new to the UK in Years 5, 6, 10 and 11 and speaking little or no English does not have to be included in school and LEA league tables for a two year period. However, this policy change does not address a fundamental problem: what is a meaningful education for a young person who arrives in school in Year 11? Evidence shows that despite this policy change many schools are still unwilling to take Year 11 arrivals.

Some LEAs have educational welfare officers or new arrivals teachers who help asylum-seeking and refugee children, as well as others, to enrol at school. Monies allocated to Asylum Consortia by the Asylum Support Directorate at the Home Office could be used to employ local authority new arrivals teachers/workers to enrol and settle asylum-seeking children in school.

Once children have a school place, the initial meeting and interview with parents/carers and their children is a time for relationships to be established.

Many schools wonder whether they can ask parents if they are asylum-seekers or refugees and how much they can ask them about prior experiences. It is the Refugee Council's view that the initial interview with parents/carers should make them feel they can trust the school with information and provide key *educational* information about their child. It is reasonable to ask parent/carers about languages spoken at home and past schooling and about their relationship to the child, as many refugee children have experienced changes of carer. Families can also be asked if they are in receipt of benefits or asylum support vouchers, as this will affect the administration of free school meals. Schools are required to see proof of date of birth, but the Refugee Council does not support demands to view passports or immigration documents. (At a future date, the National Asylum Support Service may inform LEAs that asylum-seeking children are being allocated housing in that LEA and this information may be passed on to schools.) However, once parents/carers trust a teacher, they may well volunteer other information about the child.

Investing time in developing good induction policy is almost certainly time well spent, anticipating and preventing problems later. Regarding their induction policy schools should question their practice as follows

- Does the school or local authority provide information on schooling? Is this information translated into relevant languages?

- Does the school use trained interpreters when interviewing new students and their parents? How easy is it to obtain interpreters if they are needed? Does your local authority have an interpreting and translation unit? If not, could you lobby for one to be set up?

- Who conducts the first interview with a child and parents/carers? Is that teacher aware of and sensitive to refugees' possible past experiences? Has the teacher received any in-service training about refugees? Is it always the same teacher who conducts the interview?

- What type of information does the school request from parents/carers? Are they assured that information they give the school will be treated as confidential? How does the school record and store confidential information and who has access to it?

- Is the school aware of the young person's dietary, religious or health care requirements?

- Is the refugee child registered with a GP? Do refugee children receive a school medical examination when they enter school? Are staff in the school medical service aware of the particular health care needs of refugee children?

- Is the new student interviewed to assess his or her past educational experiences and future needs? Is the new student interviewed by a teacher of

English as an additional language? Some local authorities, for example Barking and Dagenham, have developed assessment material for newly-arrived bilingual pupils. Could your LEA do this? Can a child be assessed in their first language? How are the child's past experiences and current needs recorded?

• Are parents/carers shown around the school when children are admitted? Does the school explain about the subjects their child will study and how children are helped to learn English? Does the school talk about possible differences in teaching methods between the UK and the child's home country?

• Does the school or local authority have material for refugee parents that explains the British education system? Is this translated into the appropriate languages? If not, could this be done?

• Are parents informed about their rights to free school meals, travel and uniform grants?

• Do parents receive information about the school's particular requirements, such as uniform and homework policy? Is this information translated? Does the school have the opportunity to talk to parents about school rules and requirements?

• Do students receive any welcome materials such as a map of the local area, plan of the school, name of their class teacher and timetable. Is this material accessible to students who speak little or no English?

• Is the tutor group informed that they will be receiving a new arrival?

• Is there a befriending system for newly-arrived students in their first days? Are befrienders briefed for the job, which should include ensuring that the new student knows where the toilets are, what to do about lunch, where to go for different lessons, and that they are introduced to the teachers.

• Are all relevant teachers given important information about new students via staff meetings or a notice board?

• Is a student's progress reassessed after a specified period, for example half a term? Are there procedures for monitoring progress?

• Can students who are not coping be withdrawn for small group tuition? Are there guidelines and resources for small group tuition?

The final point – withdrawal of students – is controversial. During the 1960s and 1970s many bilingual children were withdrawn for EAL support to language centres or, less usually, to special classes within their school. Children were taught EAL using a pedagogy based on the teaching of modern languages in schools or of English abroad. By being withdrawn from the mainstream, many bilingual children missed important parts of the curriculum, and also the opportunity to converse with their English-speaking peers. This policy of withdrawal began to be questioned by educationalists in the 1970s, when research into language acquisition recognised that children learn an additional language through many different routes, including working with an EAL teacher, interaction with peers and through the subject matter of lessons. Children learn the language of maths by studying maths and a big motivation for leaning English is wanting to join in lessons. (For an overview of the debate, see Jaine, 2000.)

For refugee children, inclusion within mainstream provision has special significance – attending school is in itself therapeutic and a normalising experience in a life that may have been far from normal. Withdrawing children for whom English is an additional language can also shift the responsibility for teaching them from mainstream to specialist provision. Withdrawal began to be discouraged on educational grounds in the 1970s and early 1980s as LEAs adopted a more inclusive policy. Then in 1985/6 the Commission for Racial Equality conducted a formal investigation into the English language support offered to children in Calderdale LEA. Here children who had newly arrived from the Indian sub-continent were required to take an English test. Those who did not pass were placed in a separate language class or language centre. Children who attended a language centre spent months or even years there and followed a much narrower curriculum. The Commission for Racial Equality referred its findings (the Calderdale Judgement) to the Secretary of State for Education, who agreed that Calderdale's separate provision was discriminatory and thus unlawful under the Race Relations Act 1976.

Following the Calderdale Judgement, language units were closed. Some LEAs actively discouraged all withdrawal, including small group teaching in schools. A more flexible approach is now emerging, as there may be some circumstances where withdrawal to a small tutor group on the school site may be beneficial for newly arrived refugee children. A minority of refugee children are so traumatised and disorientated by recent experiences that they might be unable to cope in class. The Refugee Council believes that for this small group withdrawal may be appropriate during the first few weeks in a new school, as part of an induction procedure.

Some refugee children may have had an extremely interrupted education and have little or no prior literacy. For them, some withdrawal may also be advantageous. Children who have acquired some oral and written English but are encountering specific problems with, for example, tense forms, may also be withdrawn. Small groups may well be therapeutic, enabling children to form supportive friendships and exchange experiences.

Fourteen to nineteen year olds arriving in the UK may encounter specific educational difficulties because they are expected to enrol immediately on an examination-based course. Some schools have organised one year access courses where small classes of students study a number of subjects including maths, English, science, computers and humanities while receiving EAL support. After a year students enrol for GCSEs, NVQs or A-Levels in school or a local college. Obviously, separate provision is justified for this group of students.

Although the present consensus is to integrate refugee children into mainstream schooling, the debate on separate provision is not dead. Separate classes and programmes of study for EAL students still exist in parts of the UK. Kosovan children who arrived on the Kosovan Programme in 1999 were educated in reception centres in many of the local authorities that received them (although their arrival at the end of the school years and their housing in reception centres may have militated against their immediate integration into schools). More worryingly, in 1998 and 1999 certain LEAs in London and the South East began to voice concern that educating asylum-seeking children was an expensive exercise and not worth undertaking, as many asylum-seekers would eventually be removed from the UK. This view was undoubtedly prompted by a growing hostility to asylum-seekers at local government level (see Chapter Two) and was also an issue concerning league tables. Two local authorities have drawn up proposals for separate educational provision for asylum-seeking children, and one of them systematically denied school places to over 450 of these children. Thankfully, the DfEE continues to support inclusive education, but those involved in the education of refugee children must remain vigilant.

Case study – South Camden Community School

Camden LEA has employed refugee support teachers since 1991 when Somali and Eritrean refugee children began arriving in the local authority in growing numbers. There were some 1,641 refugee children in Camden schools in 1997 of whom nearly one third were from Somalia. Other large groups included Kosovars, Congolese (Zaireans) and Eritreans. The local authority presently employs seven refugee support teachers, some working across the local authority and some in designated schools. Their posts are presently funded by the local authority and the Ethnic Minority Achievement Grant.

South Camden Community School is a large comprehensive based on one site. The largest ethnic minority group are Bangladeshis; the largest refugee group Somalis. The school has had an unhappy recent history. Both Bangladeshis and Somalis living in the area have been and still are the victims of racial harassment. In 1992, a white student at the school was murdered after escalating ethnic conflict in the area, whereupon the school, supported by the Refugee Coordinator in the LEA, embarked on raising staff awareness about the needs of refugee pupils. Whole school in-service training was organised and the school employed one member of staff as a part-time refugee pupil coordinator. The rest of her timetable is as an EAL teacher on induction courses for newly arrived bilingual students.

When new refugee pupils arrive in the school, the school nurse receives details of their medical history. She sees each child and evaluates their physical development milestones as well as looking for signs of psychological distress. All newly-arrived refugee students, as well as other newly-arrived bilingual students enter a full-time induction programme when they first enter the school and this is slowly reduced as appropriate. During this induction period, children are assessed by EAL specialists and by an EAL maths specialist to gage their entry level into the SMILE maths system. Mainstream teachers receive this assessment information. The new pupils are taught the school procedures and inducted into learning and teaching styles. If they need it, they are taught 'survival' English in modules on travel and journeys, school, food and study skills. Some refugee pupils are able to enter the mainstream curriculum after a few days; others may stay longer in the induction programme and be taught other curriculum units in subjects such as maths and science.

Newly-arrived bilingual pupils who arrive in Years 11 and 12 are offered a one year Council for Education in World Citizenship course in place of GCSE if their English does not equip them to follow GCSE provision. The one year course offers an introduction to living in the UK, as well as modules drawing on students' past experiences. Students taking this course are encouraged to sit Pitman's English examinations. After completing the course, students can enter courses in the sixth form or attend a local college.

South Camden Community School has developed the Prior Education Certificate. This lists the schooling that newly-arrived bilingual children have received in their home countries, including attendance at *maddrassah*, languages of instruction and the subjects they have studied. The Certificate also includes a short section that cites key educational achievements. For one boy who had two years attendance at a *madrassah* this read 'Mohammed knows by heart seven short chapters of the Holy Koran'. The Prior Education Certificate gives value to children's past educational and life experiences and boosts their self-esteem. The Certificate is also used as a tool for pupil assessment and helps develop teacher understanding of other education systems.

The school also hosts the Horn of Africa Club, an after-school club targeted at children from Somalia, Sudan, Eritrea and Ethiopia, although others attend too. Funded and supervised by staff from Camden's refugee team and volunteers, it enables children to complete homework with the assistance of volunteers and provides a supportive and welcoming environment. A Somali parents' group and a Somali community language school, sensitively accommodated, also meet in the school.

South Camden Community School has achieved much support for refugees due largely to the dedication of its own refugee coordinator and the LEA's. Both have tried to build stability in their work, as refugee support projects must not be seen to be reliant only on the efforts of particular members of staff.

Case study – new arrivals teams

Several LEAs employ teams of EAL teachers working with newly-arrived children who have EAL needs. In England, teams are mostly funded by the Ethnic Minority Achievement Grant. Lancashire, Birmingham, Wolverhampton, Lewisham and Glasgow LEAs all have new arrivals teams.

Lewisham local authority in south London had an estimated 2,618 refugee children in its schools in 1998, the largest being Somalis, Kosovars, Colombians and Tamils. Within the Ethnic Minority Achievement Project the LEA employs a member of staff responsible for supporting new arrivals, who also act as a source of expertise about refugee children in the LEA. Lewisham has published some bilingual phrase books in Albanian, Somali, Turkish and Vietnamese, providing survival phrases for children newly-arrived in school.

The LEA has also funded a New Arrivals Worker, based at Lewisham Refugee Network, a community organisation working with all refugee groups in Lewisham. The New Arrivals Worker's job includes finding school places for children, enrolling and settling them in the new school. The New Arrivals Worker has been able to challenge at LEA level some of the institutional factors that prevented refugee children from enrolling in school – the administration of uniform grants, for example.

Bibliography

Bolloten, B and Spafford, T (1998) 'Supporting Refugee Children in East London Primary Schools' in Rutter, J. and Jones, C. (eds) *Refugee Education: Mapping the Field*, Stoke on Trent: Trentham Books

Camden Education (1996) Refugee Education Policy, London: Camden Education, unpublished report

Camden Education and Camden and Islington Health Authority (1999) *Meeting the Needs of Refugee Children: a checklist for all staff who work with refugee children in schools*, London: Camden Education

Commission for Racial Equality (1986) *Teaching English as a Second Language: Report of a formal investigation in Calderdale LEA*, London: Commission for Racial Equality

Hall, D. (1995) *Assessing the Needs of Bilingual Pupils*, London: David Fulton

Hirson, J. (1999) New To Schooling: a survey of practice. Unpublished research report available from the Refugee Council

Jaine, S. (2000) 'Teaching English as an Additional Language: time for a productive synthesis' in Shaw, S. (ed) *Intercultural Education in European Classrooms*, Stoke on Trent: Trentham Books

Language and Curriculum Access Service Enfield (1999) *Refugee Education Handbook,* London: Language and Curriculum Access Service Publications

Lodge, C. (1998) 'Working with Refugee Children: One School's Experience' in Rutter, J. and Jones, C. *Refugee Education: Mapping the Field*, Stoke on Trent: Trentham Books

Refugee Council (2000) *Helping Refugee Children in Schools*, London: Refugee Council.

7

Supporting Children Whose First Language is not English

I could speak some English when I started school, but not very well because I had studied English in India. Classwork was OK, but homework was difficult. I was quite worried that students might pick on me. However, two students looked after me very well and one of them could speak Dari, my own language a bit.
Mukhtar, from Afghanistan.

This chapter aims to highlight key issues affecting refugee children in their learning of English. The teaching of English as an additional language (EAL) is well researched and some of the extensive literature is listed in the chapter's bibliography.

Refugee children arrive in the UK speaking – and sometimes reading and writing – a wide variety of languages. It is important for teachers to remember that refugee children are competent speakers of at least one language. Their skills in their first language should be valued and encouraged. Bilingualism should be viewed as an asset not a problem. Research has shown that bilingual children are more likely to make good progress in schools which value a child's home language and culture.

Some children, for example those from Sierra Leone or Nigeria, may have attended English medium schools in their home countries. Others will have learnt English as a foreign language. Some refugee children will have had little or no contact with the English language or the Roman alphabet and some will have received little or no prior education and not be literate in their home language. Children's linguistic needs will be very different but most newly-arrived children will require help in developing their speaking, reading and writing skills in English.

Funding for English as an additional language

In England, most EAL support in schools is currently funded by the DfEE's Ethnic Minority Achievement Grant (EMAG), part of the School Standards

Fund. This pays for specialist EAL teachers and bilingual classroom assistants. The DfEE provides about 57 per cent of EMAG funding, while the LEA is expected to match fund the rest.

In the past LEAs ran EAL teams centrally. Although there still is some provision for funding peripatetic EAL teams in rural local authorities, DfEE guidelines now dictate that at least 85 per cent of funding for EAL support has to be delegated to schools. This can works in two ways: either schools employ EAL specialist teachers and bilingual classroom assistants and have them on staff role, or the LEA continues to organise a central EAL support service and schools choose to purchase the service from the LEA. This requirement for delegating EMAG funding to schools was introduced in 1998. The advantage of this policy shift is that now EAL staff are on a school payroll and their specialism is less marginalised. The disadvantage is that some schools may opt not to provide EAL support or to cut it and then refuse to admit bilingual children.

EAL support in Wales and Scotland is administered differently. The Welsh Assembly funds the Ethnic Minority Achievement Grant, part of the Grant for Education Support and Training. Unlike its English counterpart, funding is provided to the LEA and not the school. The grant is paid at a rate of 70 per cent of project costs, with 30 per cent LEA match funding. The Scottish Executive provides grants for EAL support for school-aged children, with Scottish education authorities bidding for financial support as part of mainstream educational funding. As in Wales, EAL support is managed centrally by an LEA.

How students are given language support

Schools and LEAs organise their EAL language support for bilingual students, including refugees, in a variety of ways. EAL support can be given by

- withdrawing the child to special classes within the school for some lessons every week
- giving the bilingual child EAL support by an EAL specialist within the classroom, where they can listen to and converse with native English speakers
- giving EAL support within the classroom by a bilingual classroom assistant.

Developing the English of bilingual pupils should be seen as the responsibility of all teachers, but once bilingual students are withdrawn from the mainstream it is easy for teachers to view EAL as the sole responsibility of a specialist teacher. One of the many advantages of EAL teachers working in collaboration with classroom teachers is that the mainstream teacher will be encouraged to learn new skills in English language support.

There may be occasions, however, when it is appropriate for bilingual students, particularly in secondary schools, to be withdrawn for a few lessons a week for a limited period of time. It is hoped that in the current economic climate schools will retain sufficient flexibility in teacher allocation to allow for this. If students are to be withdrawn from certain lessons, this should always be discussed with the students, and with subject teachers concerned. Older bilingual students may be withdrawn if

- they have little or no previous schooling and lack literacy in their home language
- they are total beginners in English
- they request help with particular GCSE or other course assignments
- Stage Two and Three language learners are having specific problems with, for example, certain tense forms, may be withdrawn for a few lessons, to concentrate on particular problems
- they are having problems coping and are withdrawn or aggressive, so they can develop a trusting relationship with an adult or other peers, and possibly discuss and write about some of the events that led to their becoming refugees.

In-class EAL support

In an ideal situation the EAL teacher is seen as an equal partner with the class teacher, participating in planning lessons and developing materials with the class teacher, and introducing topics to the whole class. This is partnership teaching. It has been found to be effective, but can be costly in terms of staff time.

Alternatively, the EAL teacher or bilingual classroom assistant goes into lessons and works solely with bilingual students on particular tasks. This may be appropriate if, for example, students are working on GCSE assignments, but the EAL teacher may seem to be marginalised, particularly if they are not permanently based in that school. By association, the bilingual students might seem to be marginalised too. It can also fuel resentment if native English speakers feel that bilingual students are getting more help with work than they are. Mainstream teachers should always introduce EAL support teachers to the whole class and explain why they are present in the lesson.

Bilingual classroom assistants

Among some EMAG teams and in some schools the proportions of bilingual classroom assistants to EAL teachers is growing. The reason is simple: a bilingual classroom assistant can be employed on a sessional or full time basis at £6 per hour while an EAL teacher has to be salaried. Bilingual classroom assistants come from a wide range of backgrounds. Some may have been qualified and experienced teachers in their home countries. Others may have little or no experience of working with children. But few bilingual classroom assistants have prior experience of teaching English through the mainstream curriculum.

The advantages of employing bilingual classroom assistants are that they can act as interpreters when parents visit school and become a bridge between the school, home and community, providing useful information about particular groups. Local authorities who keep a sessional pool of bilingual classroom assistants providing support in a wide range of languages have the capacity to react quickly to the unplanned arrival of new groups refugee children.

But there can be problems in employing large numbers of bilingual classroom assistants. If skilled only to provide bilingual support, for example through the medium of Somali, the assistant will not be able to meet the needs of children who speak other languages. The retention of good assistants is another issue. When an interpreter can earn £16 per hour and a bilingual classroom assistant only £6 per hour during term time, it is not surprising that many of the best bilingual classroom assistants leave education. Accordingly, bilingual classroom assistants should be given sufficient training to be able to provide quality language support. There should be a clear career structure to enable them to become qualified teachers. Some LEAs do this: organising training courses for bilingual classroom assistants in partnership with universities.

Lack of resourcing: a key discrimination

Although bilingual children learn best in mainstream education, they will need an EAL specialist working alongside them in class. In a large urban secondary school with beginner bilingual children in many classes and perhaps forty classes running at any one time, many EAL specialists are going to be needed to ensure in-class support in most lessons. Yet this does not happen in practice. Few schools employ more than five teachers of English as an additional language – most employ one or none. Newly-arrived bilingual children are unlikely to receive more than five hours EAL support per week; those who have achieved Stage Two or Stage Three levels of English even less.

The Refugee Council considers this to be discriminatory, particularly since many other children with additional educational needs do receive full-time support. Perhaps some national standards of entitlement to EAL support could be promoted by the DfEE/Scottish Executive and the Welsh Assembly. Such standards could be incorporated into a National Language Strategy, something this country presently lacks.

Mainstream teacher competence

Children for whom English as an additional language make up some 7.5 per cent of the school population of England, according to DfEE statistics – a significant number. Yet most teacher training colleges place little emphasis on developing trainee teachers' skills in teaching children for whom English is an additional language. Throughout the UK, many young teachers enter the profession with little or no training for this. All good teachers of EAL in schools are actively engaged in improving the language awareness of mainstream teachers. But they face an uphill struggle now that far more schools have bilingual pupils because of the dispersal of asylum-seekers throughout the UK. Asylum-seekers are being settled in seaside towns and other predominantly white areas where schools have little experience of teaching bilingual pupils.

The Literacy Hour and literacy initiatives

The Literacy Hour in England and literacy initiatives in Scotland and Wales are not always accessible to newly arrived bilingual pupils. The Literacy Hour demands a set amount of whole-class teaching, as well as increased emphasis on phonics, both of which may present problems for newly-arrived bilingual children.

Accordingly, the DfEE has published National Literacy Strategy guidance and teacher training materials on English an additional language. The National Association for Language Development in the Curriculum, as well as some local authority EAL support teams, have produced their own good practice guidance. A number of EAL teams, such as Manchester City Council and Lancashire County Council, also have dedicated Literacy Hour specialists working within their teams.

To help make the Literacy Hour accessible to newly-arrived bilingual pupils teachers can

- involve EAL staff in the planning of Literacy Hours, ideally planning the lessons together
- choose texts with clear print and clear illustrations
- choose texts that are representative of all children's backgrounds and experiences
- use the home language when introducing new words and texts. Dictionaries and glossaries can be obtained in many different languages
- use bilingual classroom assistants/teachers to introduce a new text to target pupils, for example by having bilingual staff tell the story or explain the text in the home language, or introduce new texts in a short 'warm-up' session
- support the introduction of new texts with visual aids and artefacts
- provide lots of guided support by getting children to produce story boards for a particular text, or use writing frames
- encourage parents to listen to their children read new books
- revisit texts in paired reading sessions, pairing bilingual learners with fluent speakers of English

- spend more time discussing the meanings of words, especially examples of idiomatic language
- use sentence level work to develop children's understanding of grammar such as tense and the use of prepositions
- utilise guided reading sessions to allow teachers to work with small groups of children. Different texts can be used and matched to the abilities of reading groups, so teachers can select books that are accessible to children with English as an additional language.

Support for children with little or no prior education

In some schools and LEAs significant groups of refugee children may have had interrupted schooling or none at all. This is true for some children from Somalia, Angola, the Democratic Republic of Congo, Sierra Leone, Kosova, Turkish Kurdistan, Afghanistan and for Roma from Romania, the Czech Republic and Slovakia. As well as being a refugee in a strange country, children with interrupted prior education may feel frustrated or inadequate because of their inability to read, write or complete other tasks, their lack of opportunity to handle, choose and read books, and be unfamiliar with classroom equipment and furniture.

Children whose schooling was interrupted at secondary level pose serious challenges to schools. A few local authorities and schools have developed specific projects to address the needs of this group. For example the Multicultural and English Language Support Service of the London Borough of Barnet used to include the 'New to Schooling Project' for students, mostly from Somalia. In 1998 the project published an advice leaflet for teachers containing useful background information and ideas to help children develop their reading and writing skills.

At North Westminster Community School in central London, a member of the EAL department conducted research into the support of refugee children new to schooling (Hirson, 1998). In response to her findings, children with little or no prior education are now placed on Stage One of the school's Special Needs Register and are being taught a pilot course by the EAL and Special Educational Needs Department.

Good practice to support students with little or no previous education may include

- having a dedicated teaching room for small group teaching (not every school has an EAL room)
- ensuring that EAL assessments on entry to school pick up children with interrupted education, by asking children and their carers about prior education and getting children to complete tasks or write in their home languages

- for young people arriving aged 14 plus with limited prior education, there should be a clear progression pathway on to further education. This might include provision of 'access to GCSE courses'
- teaching material must reflect the real experiences of secondary aged children. Books aimed at young children do nothing for older children's self-esteem, but there is more appropriate teaching material targeted at older children with reading difficulties. Alternatively, desk-top publishing equipment can be used to scan and adapt teaching material for younger children as appropriate.

Helping bilingual students in the classroom

As part of the induction interview, an EAL teacher should find out what languages newly-arrived bilingual students speak, if they are literate in their home language, and what level of education they reached before coming to Britain. The EAL teacher should assess the language acquisition stage of new students and the information made available to all subject teachers.

Helping a beginner learn English

The following suggestions may help beginners feel welcome in a class, and start learning English.

- Make sure you pronounce their names properly, and try to greet them every lesson.
- Make sure students know your name: introduce yourself and write down your name for them.
- Sit the students next to sympathetic members of the class, preferably those who speak the same language and can translate.
- Try to encourage students to contribute to the lesson by using the home language.
- Do not worry if beginners say very little at first, as plenty of listening time is important when starting to learn a new language. It helps the student to 'tune in' to the sounds and intonation of the new language. But obviously just listening all the time is frustrating for students.
- Try to teach beginners some useful basic phrases such as yes, no, miss/sir, thank you, please can I have ....., I don't understand.
- Encourage them to help give out equipment, and collect books, so they have to make contact with other students. But don't treat them as the class dogsbody!
- Encourage the students to learn the names of equipment, symbols or terms essential for your subject. Use pictures and labels. Students can make their own 'dictionaries' for key words for your subject. There are also some commercially published dual-language lists of key words for different subject

English Language Acquisition Stages

Most EAL projects require that schools assess the English language needs of bilingual pupils but there are no nationally agreed criteria for assessment. Many LEAs and schools still use a four stage assessment model, as below.

Stage One: Beginner Bilingual – Students may remain silent in the classroom, or use a little English if encouraged to do so. They have minimal or no literacy in English. If involved in learning activities in groups they need considerable support or to be able to use their home language.

Stage Two: Developing Bilingual – Students can participate in all learning activities, but it will be evident from their speaking and writing that their first language is not English. Students will be able to express themselves orally in English quite successfully, but they need considerable support in writing and reading English.

Stage Three: Developing Bilingual – Students have sufficient English language skills to enable them to be successfully involved in all activities. Their oral and written English is developing well, but their written English will tend to lack complexity and show evidence of structural errors associated with this stage of language acquisition.

Stage Four: Fluently Bilingual – Students are totally fluent in English. They write like native speakers.

Recently, some LEAs in England began moving towards a new system, promoted by the Qualifications and Curriculum Authority, by which EAL levels are subsumed within National Curriculum levels. A child who arrives in an English school is assessed in *listening, speaking, reading and writing* according to a series of steps and levels. For example, when assessing a child's listening skills:

Step One 'Pupils listen attentively for short bursts of time...'

Step Two 'Pupils understand simple conversational English...' They listen and respond to the gist of general explanations by teachers where language is supported by non-verbal cues.'

Level One (threshold level) 'With support, pupils respond appropriately to straightforward comments or instructions addressed to them. They listen attentively to a range of speakers, including teacher presentation to the whole class.'

Level Two (secure level) 'In familiar contexts, pupils follow what others say about what they are doing and thinking.'

There have been serious disagreements among EAL professionals about this approach. Many consider that additional language acquisition cannot be slotted into a system geared to assessing the learning of concepts, skills and knowledge in subjects such as mathematics.

areas (see Further Resources). Short vocabulary lists can be provided for each lesson.

- Ask students for the home language equivalents of English words.

- If students are literate in their first language, try to obtain bilingual dictionaries, and encourage students to use them. Students may have their own dictionaries at home.

- If students are literate in their home language, teachers can use books in it for initial reading lessons. It may be possible to obtain books in the home language for particular subject areas. Using such materials will not impede learning English. Students are far more likely to feel confident about using English and not worrying about making mistakes if they feel their mother tongue is valued.

- Collaborative learning activities are very helpful for learning English. But working in groups with other students will be a new experience for many refugee children, as most have come from countries where the educational system is more formal than the UK. Other students in a group need to be supportive too.

- Visual cues are extremely helpful, for example videos, slides, pictures, diagrams, flash cards and illustrated glossaries.

- Reading material can be made easier by oral discussion, relating it to a student's own experiences. If reading material is recorded on cassette, a student can listen and read simultaneously.

It is important to maintain students' confidence in learning a new language, and help them feel they can complete written work, however simple. Beginners will initially need to copy, and may need practice with handwriting. They can also copy labels on to pictures or diagrams, copy simple sentences under pictures, match pictures to names and fill in missing words in text from a list supplied (cloze procedures). Beginners should always be given homework if other pupils receive it, even though it needs to be very simple.

Helping second stage learners

Second stage learners can engage in all the learning activities in a classroom, and their understanding of conversation and oral instruction is generally quite good but they will need considerable support with written work and reading. Their understanding of text will be helped by visual clues, for example watching the video of a novel before studying it as a class reader. Class or group discussions of texts also help, as do role play and audio cassettes to listen to before the lesson. Teachers can prepare simple summaries of the main points of books, texts or lessons.

Written tasks for second stage learners need to be structured. Appropriate tasks include

- Sequencing – putting statements in the right order before writing them out, as a pair or group activity and using writing frames
- Filling in charts and tables which can then be used as a basis for writing sentences
- Deciding on true/false statements
- Providing structured questions, designed so that the answers will generate a piece of continuous writing when put together. This helps students who find continuous writing difficult.

Teachers should provide models of the type of writing they want to see, for example the correct layout of a letter, or the results of a scientific experiment. Certain maths schemes, such as SMILE, require a a good understanding of English and require adaption if they are to be used successfully with beginners and second stage learners.

Helping third stage learners

These students can cope with the demands of the curriculum and will be able to produce extended pieces of writing, albeit with errors. Unfortunately the language needs of third stage learners are neglected in many schools, and as a consequence their skills are not developed to full fluency. Many children who reach this stage never go on to write fluent academic English

Teachers must remember that the English language skills of a third stage learner are still developing. They will still need help with reading and writing and in extending their vocabulary. Written work will benefit from the provision of models and plans. When written work is marked it would be helpful to explain their grammatical mistakes. It is also important to look at words that students are not using: a piece of writing may be competent but use only a limited range of tenses and vocabulary. Can students be shown alternative expressions and extra tenses? Do they still need to learn how to use reported speech and the passive voice?

English language qualifications

Bilingual students face many formal and informal assessments of their communication skills, particularly when applying for jobs or progressing on to further and higher education. For those wishing to enter higher education, a qualification in English is usually a requirement. Most institutes expect students to have obtained GCSE English or an equivalent qualification. But this examination is designed to assess the native English speaker and assumes familiarity with cultural references.

The Cambridge Examination Syndicate administers three different English as a foreign language qualifications geared towards the needs of non-residents. One of these examinations – the Cambridge Certificate of Proficiency – is accepted by many educational institutions as the equivalent of GCSE grade C. (The Cambridge First Certificate in English and the Cambridge Lower certificate are not acceptable entry qualifications for higher education). Pitmans examinations in English provide alternative qualifications.

Bibliography

Barnet, London Borough of (1998) *New to Schooling: guidelines for schools*, London, London Borough of Barnet Multicultural and English Language Support Service

Bourne, J. and Blair, M. (1998) *Making the Difference: teaching and learning strategies in Successful Multi-Ethnic Schools*, London: DfEE

Committee of Inquiry into the Education of Children from Ethnic Minority Groups (1985) *Education for All: The Report of the Committee of Inquiry into the Education of Children from Ethnic Minority Groups (Swann Report)*, London: HMSO

Cummins, J. (1996) *Negotiating Identities: Education for Improvement in a Diverse Society*, Ontario, USA: California Association for Bilingual Education

Edwards, V. (1998) *The Power of Babel: teaching and learning in multilingual classrooms*, Stoke on Trent: Trentham Books

DfE (1991) *Partnership Teaching,* London, HMSO

DfEE (2000) *National Literacy Strategy: Supporting Pupils Learning English as an Additional Language*, London: DfEE

Gibbons, P. (1991) *Learning to Learn in a Second Language*, Newtown, Australia: Primary English Teaching Association

Gravelle, M (1996) *Supporting Bilingual Learners in Schools,* Stoke on Trent: Trentham Books

Gravelle, M. (2000) *Planning for Bilingual Learners,* Stoke on Trent: Trentham Books

Hall, D. (1995) *Assessing the Needs of Bilingual Pupils,* London: David Fulton

Hirson, J. (1999) *New to Schooling: a survey of practice*, Unpublished research report available from the Refugee Council

Lancashire County Council (1999) *National Literacy Strategy Guidelines for Primary Schools*, Preston: Lancashire County Council

McWilliam, N. (1998) *What's in a Word? Vocabulary Development in Multilingual Classrooms*, Stoke on Trent: Trentham Books

National Association for Language Development in the Curriculum (1998) *Provision in Literacy Hours for Pupils Learning English as an Additional Language*, London: NALDIC

Qualifications and Curriculum Authority (2000) *A Language in Common*, London: QCA

Richardson, R. for Brent Language Service (1999) *Enriching Literacy: Text, Talk and Tales in Today's Classroom*, Stoke on Trent: Tretham Books

Skutnabb-Kangas, T. and Cummins, J. (eds) (1998) *Minority Education*, Clevedon, UK: Multilingual Matters.

8
Home Language Maintenance and Development

The UK has a rich linguistic heritage, and refugees' languages are part of it. Surveys in Greater London – the most ethnically diverse part of the UK – indicate that almost 200 languages are spoken by school students.

Since the late 19th century and the entry of Jewish refugees from eastern Europe, there has been an educational debate about the use of the home language. At first education policy aimed to integrate refugee children as quickly as possible into 'British' society. Children were taught to speak, read and write the English language, but little attention was given to their home language or culture or to their experiences within the school system. Some educationalists believed that bilingualism actually hindered a child's progress in learning English. (Sadly, this belief still has currency today, perhaps because it is a 'common sense' belief. Some refugee parents are reluctant to send their children to community schools to study the home language lest it hinders their acquisition of English. Teachers will need to invest time in explaining the importance of home language development.)

In the late 1960s opinion began to change. Assimilist policies were seen as unworkable and unpopular because they ignored cultural and linguistic diversity. Schools and LEAs began to move towards linguistic diversity, among other goals. In the 1970s and 1980s some LEAs encouraged schools to have policies to enable bilingual children to value and maintain their home languages. They supported bilingual teaching and home language teaching. They gave mainstream teachers in-service training on language issues and bilingualism, and funded some community schools. The Swann Report articulated many of these positive policies, but did not see home language teaching as part of statutory provision. It recommended instead 'the establishment of comprehensive programmes of support by LEAs for existing programmes of language maintenance by the 'language communities' concerned.' The Report highlighted the lack of funding and poor premises of supplementary schools, suggesting that school premises be made available to community schools *free of charge*. It also recommended that LEA advisers be used to train volunteer teachers and that there should be more home language teaching in mainstream schools – after the school day.

None of this advice was ever implemented. By the late 1980s the tide had shifted against bilingual education. The New Right made multicultural and anti-racist education one of its targets for attack. Community schools and bilingual education became an unfashionable cause. A further blow to the community school movement was dealt with the implementation of the Education Reform Act 1988. This brought in new arrangements for the financial management of schools, introducing the principle of Local Management of Schools (LMS; DMS in Scotland). What LMS means in practice is schools control their own expenditure, including paying caretakers for opening school buildings at weekends. Suddenly community schools faced large bills for premises, and some were forced to close. While LEAs have the power to make 'directed lettings' (free use of premises) under the Education Reform Act 1988, few refugee community schools are aware of this and consequently few received the free used of premises.

Central government policy makers have never supported bilingual education – where children are taught in their home language in mainstream education – or community language teaching. While some LEAs and schools may have attributed value to linguistic diversity, the attitude of central government to home language teaching has been hostile. The Section 11 grant of the Local Government Act 1966, used to fund EAL teaching until 1999, has never been available for home language teaching. The DfEE's stated policy on funding home language teaching is that the responsibility for it lies with ethnic minority communities. In England, EMAG funding is not available for home language teaching.

The benefits of bilingualism

The advantages of bilingualism are now recognised by educationalists. Refugee children undoubtedly need to learn English as quickly as possible and children with a high level of skill in their home language have a great advantage in the learning of English.

Imagine you are back at school, but in France. Now imagine that your new teacher is trying to teach you about fractions. Because you learned maths in an English-speaking school, you will have already developed a range of concepts about numbers. While you are learning in your new language, you will be making connections with what you already know in French. It would be much more difficult to learn about fractions in a new language had you not already learned about them in English. If you have made sense of things in one language it becomes easier to do so again in a second.

Children who arrive in a school with a strong command of their home language are in a favourable position to learn English. They are known as additive bilinguals, as they are adding a second language to the one they already know. Younger children whose language skills are less well developed are in a less favourable position to learn English. One of the most unfavourable times to start learning English is at the age of five, when the fragility of the first language does not support the learning of a second. However, very young children can easily develop two languages at the same time. The key factor is the extent to which the home language is continuing to develop. But once they start school, English gradually replaces their home language. If their English is not well developed they risk falling behind in their learning, as neither the home language nor English may be adequate for classroom learning (Gibbons, 1991).

Equally linguistically vulnerable are the refugee children who have had an interrupted or non-existent prior education. With less linguistic and conceptual development, they have fewer pegs on which to hang their new learning so it is essential to continue to learn in their home language. Unfortunately, few bilingual children are given this opportunity in the British state education system. It is underfunded and marginalised refugee community schools which are meeting this need. This is an educational scandal.

Research also shows that children who continue to learn in their home language have superior linguistic skills to monolingual children (Lambert and Peal,1962, Vygotsky, 1978). Additive bilingual children have two words or phrases to describe the same idea or object. Fluency in the home language will enable them to communicate with parents and other members of the community. A person's sense of identity is also closely linked to language; home language teaching and positive language policies help children promote their own identity through language.

So refugee community schools play a key role in meeting the children's psychological needs. Positive links with culture and community have been identified by researchers such as Baker, Elbedour, ten Bensel and Bastien as mediating factors that prevent children manifesting distress. Refugee children who have positive links with their community, language and culture are much less psychologically vulnerable than children who have few links with peers from their own community.

Refugee children negotiate questions of personal identity on a daily basis. They have to be able to resolve questions of identity and have positive feelings towards the culture of home as well as the school. Many refugee children meet friends from their own community and debate such questions. And one important place where such discourse happens is the refugee community school. There children can meet compatriots of their own age, negotiate complex questions of identity and forge a positive relationship with the language and culture of the home. And since many refugee families aspire to return home if political conditions change, knowing the language of their home country will enable children to re-integrate more easily.

Bilingual education and home language teaching

In an ideal world bilingual students should have the opportunity – if they want it – of developing their home language in mainstream education. Nursery and infants schools can employ teachers and classroom assistants who speak the child's home language, on a permanent or peripatetic basis. In primary and secondary schools the first language can be used as a medium of instruction alongside English, so that the child may be taught for a set part of the school day in, for example, Somali, and for the rest of the time in English. Bilingual education has been adopted in some US cities with large Hispanic communities of this kind but in only a few isolated cases in the UK, partly because the provision of bilingual education has huge resource implications for schools and LEAs.

Instead, community languages such as Urdu, Bengali, Turkish, modern Greek, Farsi, Chinese or Spanish are taught as a modern language, in both primary and secondary schools. This is usually referred to as mainstream home language teaching. Several refugee communities helped develop GCSE examinations in their respective community languages. But such initiatives have been dealt a double blow, by cuts to LEAs budgets and introduction of the National Curriculum, which defined 'modern foreign languages' as only the European Community official languages plus Japanese, Chinese (Mandarin) and Chinese (Cantonese), Russian and Arabic. The languages of the Indian sub-continent and Vietnamese are excluded and may be squeezed out of the timetable in inner-city schools. Vietnamese was lost as a GCSE subject and attempts to develop a new GCSE in Somali have failed.

There are also practical constraints to providing mainstream home language teaching in school time. Refugee communities are often small and widely dispersed; if only a few speak a particular language in a school, it is much more difficult to make provision for their language learning. The Refugee Council believes that LEAs could examine ways of sharing resources across their boundaries. Two local authorities could employ a teacher of Vietnamese or Somali, for example. Some groups of schools have organised and paid for home language teaching outside school hours, enabling students from several schools to attend. And certain further education colleges are offering classes in refugee community languages aimed at children and families. In London, for example, language classes are being offered in Kurdish, Turkish, Arabic, Chinese (Cantonese) and Tigrinya.

In both Denmark and Sweden children with refugee status (but not asylum-seekers) have the right to home language teaching. In Denmark bilingual children have the right to this if there are twelve or more children from a particular language group in a given municipality. In Sweden five or more children from a particular linguistic group are required before a municipality will fund afternoon or after-school classes. But in both countries the work of teachers of minority languages is unrecognised by mainstream education and some teachers receive little supervision, although the Swedish government has recently introduced a programme to strengthen their competence. The UK should learn from these European models.

Supporting the home language in primary and secondary schools

Even when refugee children's home languages cannot be taught in schools there is still a great deal that teachers can do to support and value them. This support may not always extend students' skills in their language, but the psychological implications are considerable. The following practice recommendations have been found helpful in schools.

*   Ask students about their first language(s) and praise bilingualism! Students should feel that their teachers are genuinely interested in their languages.
*   Assess newly-arrived children's past educational experiences, including home language skills. Bilingual students can be asked about home languages and whether they are literate in them. If students are literate in their home languages, they can be asked to produce a piece of writing. Even without being able to read what students write, a teacher can learn much from the way students approach the task, the speed and confidence with which they write, and their handwriting. Obviously if the writing is translated, more will be learned.
*   As well as samples of work in English, put students' writing in their first language in their profile folders.
*   EAL and English teachers can ask students to write about themselves in English and in their mother tongues, as part of autobiographical work (see Chapter Nine). These testimonies can be typed on a word processor: many school ICT departments now have programmes in a range of scripts.
*   Teachers should try to increase their knowledge of the language skills of their students so they can show sensitivity: for example not asking students to write if they are not literate in their home language.
*   Schools should include home language and dual language books in class and school libraries, and encourage bilingual students to read them. Refugee community organisations and EAL teams should be able to tell teachers where they can obtain such books. Schools should purchase bilingual dictionaries for students.

- Schools should pay the examination fees of students who wish to sit GCSE, A-Level and other examinations in community languages and make all administrative arrangements for them to sit the examination at school.

- Schools can run language awareness courses for all students, and bilingual students can contribute. Younger children can do surveys about the languages spoken in their class or school, and present the results in the form of bar graphs and charts. Schools can put up signs and posters in different community languages and displays by students in different scripts. Bilingual parents can be invited in to tell stories or read poetry in various languages.

- Schools should also try to find out as much as possible about local refugee community schools. They or the LEA could compile a list of them and encourage students to attend.

- Most community schools welcome visitors. Mainstream teachers can arrange to visit community schools attended by their pupils.

- Mainstream schools should look favourably on approaches made by volunteers or community schools to use premises to teach children's home languages, while maintaining close contact with them. LEAs should be encouraged to make 'directed lettings' to such refugee community schools.

The Minority Rights Group's Voices project

The Minority Rights Group has collected and published a series of dual language testimonies written by refugee children in London schools – *Voices from Angola*, and *Eritrea, Somalia, Sudan, Uganda, Zaire* and *Kurdistan*.

The Minority Rights Group worked with refugee students and EAL teachers to collect the testimonies. After the accounts were typed all the students had the chance to change their testimonies before the books were published. For the refugee students who wrote and produced these accounts it has been a hugely affirming project. The *Voices* series is now being used with newly-arrived refugee children who can read the accounts in their home language and English. Many of the refugee children who have used the books have been heartened by reading about other children in a similar position; there is no doubt that *Voices* has been a great psychological boost to refugee children in many schools and a valuable teaching aid. The testimonies in the *Voices* series also raise awareness among teachers and all students about refugees from these countries and can be used as a resource when teaching about such issues as migration.

EAL teachers in schools can undertake their own Voices projects, helping refugee students to prepare their testimonies, and producing them on desk-top publishing software. There is software available in many different scripts, and schools and community groups often have access to it.

from *Voices from Somalia*
Mohammed Warsame, 13 years old
Hackney Downs School, London

Waxaan ku koray oo aan degganaa ilaa intaan imanayey Ingland Jeniwary 1990. Waxaan degannaa miyiga Burco oo aanu guri weyn ku lahayn. Dugsi maan gelin – waxaan rarci jiray xoolahayaga. Shaqaadayduna taasay ahayd. Waxaan kici jiray subixii sideeda. Waxaan qabto waxaa ugu horreyn jiray inaan xoolaha si aanay u baxsan. Waxaan kale oo lisi jiray riyaha iyo geela. Hooyaday iyo walaakay ayaa iyana i caawin jiray. Caanaha ayaanu cabi jiray oo subag, burcad iyo ciirba ka sameysan jiray. Waxaabahan waxaan ka helaa imminka dukaamada waaweyn sida Seynsburi iyo Tesko. Hooyaday waxay u iib geyn jirtay subagga iyo caanaha Ceerigabo. Markaa ayey noo keeni jirtay khudrad iyo wixii kale ee aanaan haysan ama sameysan karin. Maalin walba shaqo joogto ah ayey ahayd xoolo raac, guri sameyn oodis. Aad bay u hawl badnayd laakin waqtigu markiiba wuu ku dhaafayey.

I grew up in Bur'o in Somalia, and lived there until I came to England in January 1990. I lived in the country in a big house. I didn't go to school – I looked after the animals we kept. I looked after camels and sheep and goats all day – that was my job. I would get up at about eight o'clock in the morning. My first task was to water and feed the animals. All day I would sit out in the hills watching the animals, making sure they did not wander off. I would also milk the goats, camels and sheep. My mother and brother also helped with the milking. Our family used the milk for drinking and we made butter and cheese and yoghurt too. I can get some of these things here in Hackney from Sainsbury's and Tesco's. My mum would sell the milk and cheese in the market in Erigavo. Then she would buy fruit and vegetables and anything else we could not grow or make ourselves. It was the same every day – everyone was very busy working in the house or with the animals or fixing fences or repairing the buildings. The work was hard but time passed quickly.

Refugee community schools

For most refugee children, the community school (supplementary or Saturday school) is the only place they can develop their home language skills. Every Saturday morning over 15,000 refugee children can be found leaning their home languages in classrooms and living rooms throughout the UK. They are pupils in schools run by refugee communities. Despite the enthusiasm of the students, the importance attached to them by communities and the clear educational benefits, the refugee schools are scarcely recognised for their work by mainstream education and are consequently starved of resources.

The supplementary school movement has a long history in Britain and long precedes the academic debate about the value of maintaining the home language(s). The earliest voluntary classes were started in the late 19th century by Jewish refugees from eastern Europe. Children gathered at weekends to learn Hebrew and to study religious texts. After the Second World War, Polish, Ukrainian and Hungarian refugee communities organised their own schools. Today, nearly 70 Polish schools still remain in the UK, accommodating about 4,500 pupils and 450 volunteer teachers. Many of these schools are organised by priests and meet in church premises.

In the 1960s immigrants from New Commonwealth countries began to set up their own community schools. Some taught South Asian languages and organised cultural activities. Others gave religious instruction, as well as language teaching. At the same time Britain's African-Caribbean community began to organise a different type of school. Concerned at the underachievement of their children in mainstream education, African-Caribbean parents organised their own supplementary classes with the emphasis on the three Rs. Today African-Caribbean supplementary schools are as popular as ever, with at least 300 schools in the UK.

In the 1970s the countries of origin of immigrant communities changed, with asylum-seekers arriving from areas of conflict in Africa, Asia and South America. New refugee communities groups were formed and new schools were started by Afghan, Armenian, Assyrian, Chilean, Iranian, Kurdish, Tamil and Vietnamese refugees. The period 1975-1985 saw many refugee community schools given local authority funding. (Before its abolition in 1990, the Inner London Education Authority gave financial support to 104 organisations running supplementary schools.)

Refugee community schools today

The Mother Tongue and Supplementary Schools Resource Unit, a charity and pressure group working to support community schools, estimates that approximately 100 refugee community schools in Greater London have access to funding and premises. There are probably a further 100 refugee community schools meeting outside the capital, as well as other classes of children who meet in living rooms and whose teachers do not enjoy access to funding and regular premises. Among them are tiny *Madrassah* (Koranic schools) run by Somali refugees, teaching the Koran, Arabic and Somali.

Refugee community schools are performing different functions. Most teach the languages of the country of origin and many, particularly those working with Muslim children, give religious instruction. Many schools teach their students the history, geography and culture of the country of origin and some supplement the mainstream curriculum, running classes in English, maths and other school subjects. Some schools organise youth clubs and leisure facilities and may offer youth advice sessions, for example on drugs and smoking, and organise summer holiday activities.

The Refugee Council periodically publishes a *Directory of Refugee Community Schools* (see Further Resources). Since its first directory appeared in 1990, a large number of schools have ceased to function, particularly those organised by some of the newer and less established refugee communities. Promoting stability is a key issue facing those working to strengthen the community school movement, and access to funding and premises is the main obstacle. Another issue, as asylum-seeking families have lost their access to cash, is that some children cannot afford bus fares to travel to community schools.

At present the major **funders** of refugee community schools are parental contributions, local authorities, the Trust for London and BBC Children in Need. The most generous local authorities were the London Boroughs of Islington, Southwark, Lewisham, Greenwich, the latter linking funding to training and development targets. Funding is available but many of those in newly established schools need help in fundraising.

Premises are also essential as schools must be accessible to children without private transport. They need to have storage space so that books and other equipment need not be moved every weekend, Some local authorities have provided free premises and this should be encouraged. The Education Reform Act 1988 gives LEAs the power to direct school governors over access to school premises and charging policy.

Many refugee community schools identify **teacher training** as a major need. The Resource Unit for Supplementary and Mother Tongue Schools is setting up an accredited course for volunteer teachers. Other agencies have adopted different approaches. The London Borough of Greenwich funds a number of community schools, but links funding to a programme of professional development of teachers. In Kensington and Chelsea, eleven community schools have formed a consortium to resource and develop their schools. The consortium has secured funding from the National Lottery Charities Board for a teacher advisor who will help organise teacher training, and help the schools secure funding and advise on their curricula and extra-curricular activities. Albanian language, Polish, Somali and Tamil supplementary schools have joined together into their own organisations. The Kosova School, the federation of Albanian language classes, is presently planning volunteer teacher training.

Training is needed in the production of **teaching resources**. Many schools have to make their own resources as it is impossible to purchase teaching materials from countries such as Somalia and Afghanistan. Community schools could make greater use of desk-top publishing programmes in different scripts if they had the expertise and funding to purchase computers and programmes. Local education authorities and mainstream teachers could easily become involved in training teachers and this would help create a stronger partnership between mainstream and supplementary schools.

Despite all the hurdles facing community schools, they survive. Their importance to refugee communities is illustrated by the energy and determination with which they have been set up and maintained. But statutory support remains disappointing, and leaves many community schools in a precarious position. The following practice recommendations would promote stability and quality provision in refugee community schools.

Practice Recommendations

- LEAs should accept responsibility for supporting supplementary schools and have a local strategy to ensure that their needs for training, premises and funding are met. Premises should be made available on favourable terms and schools granted sufficient funding.

- LEAs should compile up-to-date lists of community schools in their areas, and make these lists available to mainstream schools.

- LEA advisors should be encouraged to be involved with community schools by offering training.

- Schools should consider forming themselves into Consortia or federations. This would enable them to lobby more effectively for funding, implement training and maintain a central library of teaching resources.

- Community schools should be encouraged to run open days and invite mainstream teachers, councillors and officials in education departments, community education and race units.

- Supplementary schools should examine ways of broadening their activities by providing summer holiday projects and youth advice sessions.

Case study: The Iranian Community Centre's supplementary school

The Iranian Community Centre (ICC) set up its first Farsi class in 1984 attended by a small number of children living in Ealing. As the numbers increased funding was secured from the former Inner London Education Authority. Today the ICC runs its classes in a school in Islington. Over 70 children now attend the school. There are three levels of Farsi on offer. The supplementary school also offers EAL for children, EAL for adults, dance, music and drama.

The Farsi teachers use a range of teaching aids; through play and games children widen their vocabulary. ICC has no problem recruiting volunteer teachers from within the Iranian community. But they do have problems maintaining a regular commitment from some teachers, particularly in the latter part of the school year. Parents work in close partnership with the supplementary school teachers. They help in class and in the library. While their children learn Farsi, parents can take part in EAL classes. There is an active parent's association. The ICC used to order teaching material from Iran, but this has now become impossible. New Farsi books are being published in other countries, but there is no money to buy them. A shortage of funds means that ICC cannot afford to print its own materials.

After the abolition of the Inner London Education Authority in 1990 three London LEAs gave funding to the ICC to run the school. But these grants were not renewed and the operation of the school was threatened. Today the ICC receives funding from the BBC Children in Need. This does not meet all the school's costs and parents are also asked to make a contribution.

Case study – the Kosova School

The Kosova School is a federation of five Albanian language schools meeting across London. The schools have been running for varying periods of time, although most were founded after 1998. At first, the schools were independent of each other. They were largely unfunded and were run by volunteer teachers who received no payment for their time and effort. Neither did the teachers receive any expenses – an issue, as most of them were un-employed. Although the children attending the classes were enthusiastic, some of the schools were in danger of closure. The schools then formed a federation – 'Kosova School'. Its running was taken over by Albanian Youth Action, a voluntary sector youth group. Albanian Youth Action has both offices and funds and provided the stability needed to develop the school. Funding proposals have been put together for the development of the five schools. Extensive teacher training and further classes are planned, as well as a play-group for younger children.

There is good access to teaching resources, as staff from Albanian Youth Action visited Albania in 1999 and purchased over 1,200 school books. These are available on loan to any Albanian language school in the UK. The work of Kosova School has been supported by a recognised supplementary curriculum of four hours of teaching per week, targeted at 6-16 year olds in mother tongue schools. The curriculum includes Albanian language lessons, culture and history. It is recognised by the Kosovan administration and the Albanian government, and is being used in Germany, Sweden and Switzerland. It forms the basis for teaching in mother tongue schools in the UK.

Bibliography

Abdelrazak, M. (2000) *Towards More Effective Supplementary and Mother Tongue Schools*, London: Resource Unit for Supplementary and Mother Tongue Schools

Baker, P and Eversley, J (Eds) (2000) *Multilingual Capital: the languages of London's Schoolchildren and their relevance to economic, social and education policies,* London: Battlebridge Press

Baker, R. (1983) 'Refugees: an overview of an international problem' in Baker, R. (Ed) *The Psychological problems of Refugees*, London: British Refugee Council

Committee of Inquiry into the Education of Children from Ethnic Minority Groups (1985) *Education for All: The Report of the Committee of Inquiry into the Education of Children from Ethnic Minority Groups (Swann Report)*, London: HMSO

Cummins, J. (1981) 'The role of primary language development in promoting educational success for lan-guage minority students' in California State Department of Education (Ed) *Schooling and language minority students: a theoretical framework,* Los Angeles: California State University

Cummins, J. (1996) *Negotiating Identities: Education for Improvement in a Diverse Society*, Ontario, USA: California Association for Bilingual Education

Elbedour, S., ten Bensel, R. and Bastien, D. (1993) 'Ecological integrated model of chidlren of war: individual and social psychology' in *Child Abuse and Neglect*, 17.

Gibbons, P. (1991) *Learning to Learn in a Second Language*, Newtown, Australia: Primary English Teaching Association

Gravelle, M. (ed) (2000) *Planning for Bilingual Learners,* Stoke on Trent: Trentham Books

Lambert, W. and Peal E. (1962) 'The relation of bilingualism to intelligence' in *Psychological Monographs*, 76

Linguistic Minorities Project (1983) *The Other Languages of England*, London Routledge and Kegan Paul

Refugee Council (1998) *Refugee Community Schools Directory*, London: Refugee Council

Resource Unit for Supplementary and Mother Tongue Schools (2000) *Directory of Supplementary and Mother Tongue Classes 1999-2000*, London:Resource Unit for Supplementary and Mother Tongue Schools

Skutnabb-Kangas (1984) *Bilingualism or not: the education of minorities*, Clevedon: England: Multilingual Matters

Skutnabb-Kangas, T. and Philipsson, R. (1994) *Linguistic human rights,* Berlin: Mouton de Gruyter

Vygotsky, L. (1992) *The Mind in Society: the development of higher psychological processes*, Cambridge, USA: Harvard University Press.

9

The Psychological and Emotional Needs of Refugee Children

How many Goodbyes Do You Know?
There's the 'I hope to see you again' goodbye
the 'I don't care if I never see your ugly face again' goodbye
the 'can't see my grandma again' goodbye
the 'praying to the person who's going to Heaven' goodbye.
There's the 'waiting to say goodbye' goodbye
the 'butterfly on a cup' goodbye
the 'goodbye mama, goodbye, I'll never see you again' goodbye.
There's the 'nalingiyo mingi' goodbye
The 'je t'aime vrais beaucoup, mais il faut que je parte' goodbye.[1]
How many goodbyes do you know?
Written by a group of refugee children and reproduced with thanks to the Medical Foundation and Leah Thorne.

Refugee children will have experienced a multiplicity of different stressful events and may overcome and cope with some or all of them. Like adults, most children cope with the multiple stresses of being a refugee; some remain psychologically vulnerable, however, and a few manifest disturbed behaviour. This chapter examines the factors that influence a refugee child's psychological well-being and then suggest ways in which schools can give emotional support.

Refugee children's experiences

Refugee children undergo many different events in their journey to Britain and in rebuilding their lives in this country. These events add up to LOSS, TRAUMA and CHANGE.

Loss

Refugee children may have lost their parents, other key carers, brothers and sisters, extended family and friends. They may have lost their home, their

---

1. *nalingiyo mingi* (Lingala) I love you very much
   je t'aime vrais beaucoup, mais il faut que je parte (French) I love you very much but I have to go.

material belongings and toys. They have certainly lost their familiar surround-ings and familiar ways of doing things. And they may find they have lost their parent's attention and support in a new country.

Trauma

Refugee children may have experienced or witnessed

- high intensity war, bombing or shelling
- the destruction of their homes
- the violent death or family friends
- the injury of family of friends
- getting separated from family
- being injured
- the arrest of members of their family or friends
- being arrested, detained or tortured
- being forced to join armies or militias
- rape
- grave shortages of food, water or other necessities
- the fear of discovery or arrest
- hostility in their new homeland
- material deprivation in their new homes
- being with people who do not understand or know about the violent events they have experienced.

Change

Refugee children may experience major cultural changes such as learning a new language and a different set of cultural norms. They may find themselves in a totally different type of school and face changes in their standard of living and status in society. Relationships with their parents are likely to change as they appear more vulnerable or become more protective or authoritarian towards them.

When working with refugee children it is important not to make assumptions about their experiences or label them automatically as 'different' or 'traumatised'. Every child's experiences of loss, trauma and change is different and each child reacts differently.

Adverse and protective factors

After a traumatic experience such as bereavement it is normal to manifest strong emotional reactions, but with time these usually lessen. Children's reactions to such events vary vastly in both the short and long term. Many factors influence psychological well-being. The duration and intensity of trauma, the child's age, the child's personality and character, the quality of childcare and the experiences in a new country all affect how the child will come to terms with being a refugee. Certain *adverse* or *risk factors* make it more likely that problems will arise. Other *protective* factors help guard a child against long term psychological distress.

Adverse factors which make it more likely that a child will suffer long-term psychological stress include

- traumatic events which are overwhelmingly intense or last for a long time. Repeated exposure to stresses, both acute and chronic, greatly decrease a child's ability to cope
- experiencing inconsistent childcare; a child may have lost parents and have a difficult relationship with new carers. Others may have lost their parents' attention
- seeing exile as inexplicable, and being unable to understand the changes in their lives. Younger children are more vulnerable because they find events such as death more difficult to understand
- economic insecurity and circumstances such as poor housing
- suffering bullying and/or isolation at school.
- having academic problems at school
- being isolated from other people from their home country
- having low self-esteem and little to look forward to
- being unable to talk about traumatic events for fear of disclosing secrets
- being a child who withdraws or gets angry when things go wrong
- having problems unrelated to the refugee experience that make coping more difficult, for example a learning disability.

Protective or *mediating* factors make it less likely that a child will suffer long term psychological stress. They include

- having parents who can give their children full attention and good quality childcare
- having an extended family network
- having access to other people, particularly from their own community, who give friendship and support
- having some understanding about the reasons for exile. Obviously younger children may have an incomplete understanding of such stressful experiences and be more vulnerable. Children who are able to integrate their experience into their belief system are less likely to suffer long-term distress

- having access to permanent housing, a permanent immigration status, and enjoying a reasonable standard of living in a new country
- being able to maintain some links with their homeland
- remembering good things about life in the home country
- being happy in a new school, making friends and being able to achieve at school
- feeling optimistic about the future and about making progress are important protective factors
- children who have good self-esteem are more likely to overcome traumatic events
- being able to talk about stressful events and thus gain mastery over them
- being able to ask for help when things go wrong
- having a hobby or interest to pursue.

Some psychologists/psychotherapists have further developed the concept of adverse and protective factors. Ron Baker, a social worker and himself a child refugee, formulated a 'relationship web' (Baker, 1983 see Figure 2).

A well-adjusted person is centred by a series of relationships. What exile does is to strip refugees of their anchors. Those who provide education and social care for refugees should be helping them reconstruct the links on the web. Thus schools can help children establish new friendships and re-establish language, role and status.

It is useful for teachers to think about adverse and protective factors when working with refugee children. Schools and teachers who wish to promote well-being should try to maximise the protective factors in a child's life and and minimise the adverse factors, as much as they have control over them. (For a further discussion on adverse and protective factors see Rutter, 1985, Elbadour *et al*, 1993 and Bolloten and Spafford, 1998).

Schools, too, have to prepare children for their future. As future citizens, refugee children, (as well as all others!) must learn to solve conflicts. When considering the support they can offer, teachers and others who work directly with refugee children should ask themselves

- What qualities in the internal and external world of refugee children will afford them psychological protection?
- What do refugee children need from adults in order to enhance their development?
- What psychological interventions are needed to ensure that refugee children (and future generations) can develop into mature, creative adults who will build a society based on co-operation rather than violence?

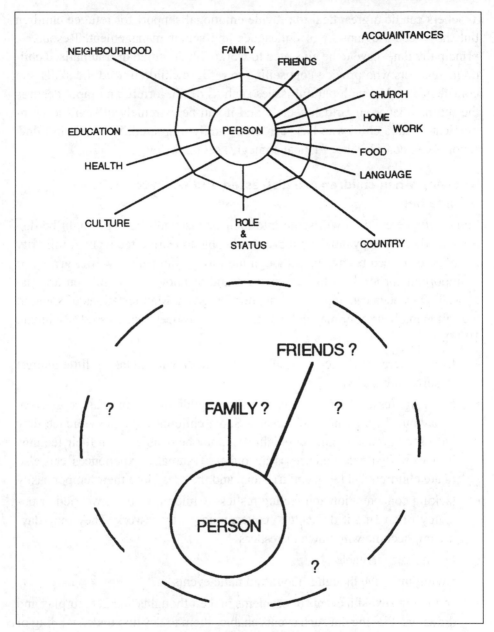

Figure 2

Providing emotional support for refugee children is an integral part of a school's refugee policy and cannot be considered in isolation from matters such as providing a welcoming environment, good home/school liaison and EAL support. A school which meets a child's academic and social needs is one where that child will feel happy. Conversely no amount of counselling will enable a child to feel happy if he or she is encountering racism at school or not making educational progress.

Teachers can do a great deal to provide emotional support for refugee children but they need the support of colleagues and senior management. Resources, principally time, have to be allocated to work with unsettled or traumatised children. Teachers who provide counselling to refugee children need the skills and confidence to deal with painful issues such as death, torture and rape: death is the ultimate taboo in British society and it can be extremely difficult to communicate with a child who has seen their family murdered. With this in mind, schools can consider the practical strategies set out below.

Knowing when children are distressed and when to seek outside help

Some refugee children will settle into their new schools. Others might be disorientated or unhappy at first but eventually able to learn effectively. A minority manifest disturbed behaviour, although not always immediately after arrival. It is important for teachers to be observant and to know when children are distressed. Only then can appropriate support be given. Manifestations of some of the following behaviour may indicate that a child is deeply distressed (Richman, 1993).

- losing interest and energy or being very withdrawn and taking little interest in surroundings
- being aggressive or feeling very angry. Children can manifest aggressive behaviour for a number of reasons. Some children copy the violence they have seen around them. Young children may be unable to put their feelings into words so use violence as an outlet. Traumatic experiences can also make children feel tense and irritable, and they may lose their temper easily
- lacking concentration and feeling restless. Children who are worried or unhappy often find it difficult to concentrate on their work. They may daydream, become withdrawn or restless
- feeling very irritable
- having intrusive thoughts about traumatic events
- acting out stressful events or problems in their thoughts and in their play and drawings. Playing out such events enables them to develop understanding of these events and gain control over difficult emotions. When children play out violent or traumatic events time and time again it indicates that they are not getting over the experience
- physical symptoms such as poor appetite, eating too much, breathing difficulties, pains and dizziness
- losing recently acquired skills and faculties, for example keeping dry at night
- nightmares and disturbed sleep
- crying and feeling overwhelming sadness

- being nervous or fearful of certain things such as loud noises
- being unable to form relationships with other children, perhaps being too sad and withdrawn to want to play, or unable to trust other children. A newly arrived child might also not understand what other children are doing. Refugee children may be isolated because they are rejected by other children, who see them as different or because of their disturbed behaviour
- having difficulty relating to adults because they mistrust them. Sometimes refugee children keep away from adults because they fear loss: they are reluctant to show affection to a significant adult lest that person disappear.

If some or many such patterns are manifest, schools should consider referring the child to another agency that has expertise in working with distressed children. Schools need to find out about relevant agencies – is there anyone in the school psychological service or the local child and family service who has expertise in working with refugee children? (The quality and type of service offered by child mental health services and schools' psychological services are highly variable, and not all professionals have experience of working with children from different cultural and linguistic backgrounds.) Other specialist services in the locality may be of use.

Working with parents

If a child experiences difficulties at school it is essential to develop good communications with parents and other key carers at once, using an interpreter if needed. Sometimes parents' and children's problems may be closely interlinked. Exile often disrupts family relationships: children may lose parents or key carers. More frequently, children lose the attention of their parents, who may be so preoccupied by basic survival and their own problems that they cannot give young children the attention they need. Where parents are emotionally absent, it is important to ensure that they receive social support.

Refugee parents can lose status in the country of exile, particularly if they are dependent on children for interpreting or face long periods without work. Intergenerational conflict, too, can be an issue among some refugees, where the values and aspirations of parents differ from those of their children.

Ensuring that children and families have access to social and community support

For many refugees isolation and lack of support are significant risk factors. If refugee children are experiencing difficulties at school, it is important to check that they and their families have the support of community groups, after-school clubs, access to playgroups and nurseries, befriending schemes and English classes. Successful psychological interventions for young refugee children are often those which enhance parental competence.

Strategies for individual children

Any child who gives cause for concern should be observed over a period of time. Teachers should avoid jumping to hasty conclusions or labelling children and should try and find out about their background and the reasons for their behaviour. Children can be asked why they are feeling sad or angry. After this the teacher can think about a strategy for support.

Training

In-service training should aim to increase teachers' knowledge about refugee children's background, and to develop their listening and communication skills. Naomi Richman has written an excellent training manual *Communicating with Children* (Richman 1993). Aimed at working with children enduring difficult circumstances, the book offers useful information and training exercises. It looks at issues such as being a good listener, creating trust and starting a conversation, and can be used for school-based in-service training. Specialist organisations such as the Medical Foundation for the Care of Victims of Torture offer in-service training. Some teachers may also want to consider validated counselling courses.

Talking to children

Many schools have well-planned pastoral care and one of the most important things a teacher can do is to talk to distressed children, listen to what they say and take their communication seriously. To do so, the teacher has to make a regular time to be free. A room or an office which affords privacy should be set aside at breaktime or after school. Teachers also need to consider their own listening and communicating skills: to be sympathetic and non-judgmental, to use prompts when a conversation dries but not to say 'I know exactly how you feel'. A useful activity in staff development is to work in pairs and or small groups and discuss what makes a good listener. Teachers/child care workers can then use this exercise to improve their own listening skills.

Counselling

A small number of refugee children will need more intervention. Some schools offer individual or group counselling to children who have suffered abuse or stressful experiences, usually facilitated by teachers who have obtained counselling qualifications or by other professionals. But with not all societies having the same attitude towards counselling services, some refugee families may view counselling as inappropriate.

Play

Those who work with younger refugee children can use play with individuals and small groups of children to make sense of their experiences, explore issues such as fear and trust and help newly-arrived children settle in. Play therapy is a well-established discipline and many projects working with children who have experienced abuse will employ a play therapist. But there has been comparatively little work done to bring the philosophy and skills of the play therapist into schools in order to help refugee children reflect on their lives and begin to settle.

Play therapists approach their work from different psychological paradigms, some of which are outlined in *The Handbook of Play Therapy* (McMahon, 1992) or *Play Therapy* (Cattanach, 1995). What appears to be the most useful theoretical basis for work with refugee children is social construction theory, which holds that all people construct a narrative about themselves. Play therapy should aim to give young children an understanding of the distortions in that narrative. For example, a refugee child whose mother is always crying might interpret that parental upset as being his fault and construct a narrative around this. Play therapy could help this child reconstruct this story.

Play is a universal and all children play in different ways. As young children develop and start to find out about the world, they will engage in sensory and exploratory play. This type of play is useful in helping new arrivals settle down. As children grow older, they begin to develop projective play – using toys and objects to replicate the real world. Refugee children can use projective play to represent events in their lives. For this to be useful, children will need lots of small objects, human figures, puppets and so on, although care must be taken to ensure that they are representative of the child's culture. Children can use puppets, props and dressing-up clothes to act out emotions or events.

In order to use play in a therapeutic way, a school or other organisation will need to provide items and conditions that enable them to play, such as

- time – to let play evolve and develop
- space – living in refugee camps, in hiding or in temporary accommodation in the UK does not allow children to play and fully express themselves
- privacy – in certain play situations
- favourable attitudes from adults
- suitable play materials. These need not be expensive and could include materials for encouraging sensory and exploratory play such as sand, water play, cornflour, noise putty and slime. A treasure basket containing materials of different textures or objects that make different noises can be used to encourage such play. Also useful are small toys, figures and other objects that facilitate the telling of stories, and puppets, props and clothes for role-play.

A key issue to consider is the extent of adult intervention in play. Adults will need to establish some ground rules – violent play and destruction of toys should be prevented, so it is advisable to observe the children's play for a while. But adults can intervene, acting out roles during role-play and providing guidance and verbal prompts, perhaps to explore particular avenues.

Autobiography and creative writing

Children can be encouraged to write about themselves, their home country and present circumstances, keep a diary or make a scrapbook or picture book about themselves (The Life Story Book). Such autobiographical techniques are frequently used with refugee children and help develop understanding of complex events and feelings. Younger children can use paints and crayons to draw about themselves, and work with an adult to write down captions to their drawings. Autobiographical techniques that can be used with refugee children include

- making a map about their home country and then using it to prompt discussion about home

- making 'feelings cards' – a child (or an adult if a child cannot write much English) writes about things they are feeling on postcards and then talks about them with a teacher or helper. This activity is best used in one-to-one settings. It is important to begin with positive feelings then progress on to more difficult feelings

- My World activities. This can be done with groups of children. Each draws himself/herself at the centre of a piece of paper (or sticks a photograph at the centre) and then draws pictures of things and people who are important, radiating from 'me' at the centre. The drawing can be used to prompt discussion and reflection

- the same activity can be adapted to 'My World Back Home', where the child draws things and people left behind

- children can write about their journeys to the UK or make artistic representations of them

- good memories and bad memories – children can be encouraged to write about, talk or draw their memories, starting with good memories. If this is done in a small group where they trust and respect each other, children can share their writings and find commonality of experiences and feelings. The poem at the start of this chapter was produced by a group of refugee children examining their memories

- teachers can initiate group discussion, writing and art about how children would put the wrong in the world right, or work towards a more hopeful future

- refugee children can compose letters to friends and relatives about life in the new country. The letter need not be sent (and often cannot as post offices seldom function where there is war). The letter can be used as a prompt for discussion

- opposing forces – refugee children can be encouraged to produce creative writing or art on particular themes, for example, safety versus danger; security versus fear; power versus helplessness; assertiveness versus anger; justice versus injustice.

Art

Art can be utilised in the same ways as creative writing and play: to enable children to express themselves and develop understanding of complex events and feelings. Art therapy is extensively used in the health service and a growing number of art therapists are also facilitating work with refugee children (see for example, Kalmanowitz and Lloyd, 1997).

There are times and places where a Registered Art Therapist should be used – for work with very disturbed refugee children, for example. But primary school teachers, art teachers and care workers can be trained to use art with refugee children in ways that help them settle. It is best to give children time to use new art materials such as crayons, oil pastels, paints, plastercine, clay and collage materials before any directed activity is planned.

The aim of using art with refugee children is twofold – to boost self-esteem by creating something and to help them reflect on events and feelings. Art can be used to explore autobiographical themes, such as those described above. Other useful techniques include

- self portraits
- mask production and discussion of facial feature and feelings
- the Desert Island – here children work in groups of four or five around a large sheet of paper, painting the items they would wish to bring to their desert island. There is space for painting personal items as well as communal space for children to paint together. The activity is a good prompt for talk.

Art Therapy for Groups (Liebman, 1986) is an excellent resource for such activities.

Drama and puppetry

Drama and puppetry can be used similarly, to express feelings and reflect on events. Drama allows children to communicate ideas and feelings that would be too difficult to say directly. Children can create a piece of drama or a puppet show that allows them to express their own experiences, while distancing themselves from the characters in the drama. Children can also use drama and puppetry to experiment with different types of endings to stories.

Providing safe places

Starting a new school can be terrifying for refugee children. British schools are large and noisy and they may feel lost, especially with few friends and little or no English. Although able to cope during lesson time, they may find breaktime overwhelming. It is important that schools have safe areas such as a room or a quiet space where children can sit if they do not feel like participating in playground activities.

The pastoral curriculum

Bereavement will affect everyone at some time in their lives and learning about loss, death and bereavement is important. Some schools have excellent resources about bereavement for use in religious education or personal and social education. Schools need to use the pastoral curriculum to examine bereavement and loss. In this way refugee children will not feel different and will realise that other children also have bad experiences.

Learning from others

Imaginative mental health initiatives are being tried with refugee children all over the world and much can be learned from them. Here are two examples of interesting initiatives, one from the UK and the other from Zambia. Other replicable refugee mental health projects are described in *Restoring Playfulness* (Tolfree, 1996).

Case Study – Enfield 1993-98

From 1993-98 this London local authority funded a multi-disciplinary refugee education team and a separate multi-disciplinary early years team. The education team comprised six refugee support teachers, a part-time educational social worker and a part-time educational psychologist. The teachers provided in-class support for children, worked with refugee children who had particularly severe difficulties, provided in-service training and helped schools develop their own support practices. The educational social worker assisted families to solve housing and welfare problems. The educational psychologist's role involved the assessment of individual children, therapeutic work with refugee children, in-service training of teachers and helping schools develop their own pastoral care and support groups. She also ran a drop-in group for teachers, parents and others who had concerns about a particular child, helping those who came to the group develop support strategies for children. Sadly, funding for the educational psychologists' posts ended in 1998 when the DfEE did not approve this element of the Ethnic Minority Achievement Grant.

Case Study – Ukwimi Refugee Settlement

By 1991 Ukwimi Refugee Settlement, eastern Zambia, was home to 22,000 Mozambican refugees. Most were subsistence farmers, but among them were some professionals. They had been caught in the civil war between the Mozambican Government and Renamo guerrillas. Research carried out by the International Catholic Child Bureau indicated that many of the refugees had lost immediate family, witnessed violence, or had been used as forced labour by Renamo.

The International Catholic Child Bureau was asked to implement a programme to support war-traumatised refugee children. Mothers of pre-school children were given training to help them understand the importance of play. The schoolteachers in the settlement were brought together for a series of training sessions. In the first session teachers were asked to identify children about whom they felt concern. They were taught to understand the concept of stress, and to recognise when children are showing stress-related behaviour.

Next, the teachers attended a two-day introduction to counselling. This course identified the differences between a teacher and counsellor, but also offered some experience of counselling. The teachers were subsequently visited by the trainers and given further support in their schools. There was no evaluation of the course, but after six months the teachers were asked to report back on the work they had done in their schools. Although implemented in a poor country, this could be a model for training in the UK.

Bibliography

Ajdukovic, M. and Ajdukovic, D. (1992) 'Psychological well-being of refugee children', *Child Abuse and Neglect*, Vol. 17, p 843 – 854

Baker, R. (1983) 'Refugees: an overview of an international problem' in Baker, R. (ed) *The Psychosocial Problems of Refugees*, London: British Refugee Council

Blackwell, D. and Melzak, S. (2000) *Far from the battle but still at war: troubled refugee children in school*, London: The Child Psychotherapy Trust

Bolloten, B. and Spafford, T. (1998) 'Supporting Refugee Children in East London Primary Schools', in Rutter, J. and Jones, C. (eds.) *Refugee Education: Mapping the Field*, Stoke on Trent: Trentham Books

Case C. and Dalley, T. (1992) *The Handbook of Art Therapy*, London: Routledge

Cattanach, A. (1995) *Play Therapy: Where the Sky Meets the Underworld*, London: Jessica Kingsley

Doktor, D. (1998) *Arts Therapists, Refugees and Migrants: reaching across borders*, London: Jessica Kingsley

Elbedour, S., ten Bensel, R. and Bastien D. (1993) 'Ecological integrated model of children of war' in *Child Abuse and Neglect*, Vol 17, p 805-819.

Eth, S. and Pynoos, R. (eds) *Post Traumatic Stress Disorder in Children*, Washington: American Psychiatric Press

Harris, A. and Hewitt, M. (1990) *Talking Time*, London: Learning by Design

Kalmanowitz, D. and Lloyd, B. (1997) *The portable studio: art therapy and political conflict*, London: Health Education Authority

Liebman, M. (1986) *Art Therapy for Groups: a handbook of themes, games and exercises*, London: Routledge

Machiodi, C. (1990) *Breaking the Silence: art therapy with children from violent homes*, New York: Brunner/ Mazel Publishers

McCallin, M. (ed) (1993) *The Psychological Well-Being of Refugee Children*, Geneva: International Catholic Child Bureau

McMahon, L. (1992) *The Handbook of Play Therapy*, London: Routledge

Melzak, S. (1994) What do you do when your parents are crying? Unpublished paper, The Medical Foundation

Nylund, B., J.-C.Legrand and Holtsberg, P. (1999) 'The role of art in psychosocial care and protection for displaced children' in *Forced Migraiton Review*, Vol 6 December 1999

Richman, N. (1993) *Communicating with children – Helping children in distress*, London: Save the Children

Richman, N. (1998) *In the Midst of the Whirlwind: a manual for helping refugee children*, Stoke on Trent: Trentham Books

Rutter, J. and Hyder, T. (1998) *Refugee Children in the Early Years: issues for policy makers and providers*, London: Refugee Council and Save the Children

Rutter, M. (1985) 'Resilience in the Face of Adversity – Protective factors and Resistance to Psychiatric Disorder' in *British Journal of Psychiatry*, 147

Tolfree, D. (1996) *Restoring Playfulness: different approaches to assisting children who are psychologically affected by war or displacement*, Stockholm: Radda Barnen

Young Minds (1994) *War and Refugee Children: the effects of war on child mental health*, London: The National Association for Child and Family Mental Health

Yule, W. (1998) 'The Psychological Adaption of Refugee Children' in Rutter, J. and Jones, C. (eds.) *Refugee Education: Mapping the Field*, Stoke on Trent: Trentham Books.

10
Challenging Racism and Xenophobia in Schools

In June 1992, Ruhollah Aramesh, a 24 year old Afghan refugee, was murdered by a gang of racists in south London, while defending his sister from racial abuse. Ruhollah Aramesh was a much-liked volunteer interpreter at the South London Refugee Project and at the Refugee Council. He had intended to study medicine at university. On that summer day a life full of promise was extinguished.

Ruhollah Aramesh is one of twenty-eight people murdered by racists during the last fifteen years. As well as British citizens, their numbers include refugees from Somalia, Sri Lanka, and Sudan: people who had come to the UK seeking refuge from persecution. Another victim was Ahmed Abokar from Somalia, murdered in 1989 by ten white youths who repeatedly punched and stabbed him in the head. Ahmed had been working with the Scottish Refugee Council in Edinburgh. Although his attackers made racist remarks in court, only one of the ten was prosecuted. He was jailed for 21 months.

For every murder there are hundreds of thousands of incidents of racist abuse, racial attacks, spitting and other abuse, most of which goes unreported. And the majority of perpetrators of racial harassment are young.

What do we mean by racism?
A great many refugees who are in contact with refugee agencies report experiences of racism – ranging from physical attack to verbal abuse and spitting. They also report discrimination by employers and other institutions. Racism can take many forms and it is important to understand this, and to understand how opinions of different ethnic groups are formed.

The word 'race' is misused. Sociologists tend to use the words 'ethnic group' or 'ethnic minority'. An ethnic group is any group who shares a distinctive culture; where it forms a minority of the population it is an ethnic minority group.

Racial prejudice means negative and unfavourable feelings about a particular ethnic group, that are not based on knowledge or fact. Treating people differently because they belong to a particular ethnic group is racism and it can take may forms. People can be victims of violent attacks, as well as being treated differently by employers and other institutions in society. Institutional racism describes an institutional culture in a school, public service or business, in which there is discrimination on grounds of race, whether intentional or not. The Stephen Lawrence Inquiry (Macpherson *et al*, 1999) focused on institutional racism within the police force and made good practice recommendations for the police and other public institutions. These have growing relevance today with the dispersal of asylum-seekers.

Increasing hostility

The numbers of attacks on refugees appears to be mounting, although at present there is no research on this. The negative media coverage of asylum has undoubtedly fuelled public hostility, as has the badly planned dispersal of asylum-seekers. The experiences of one local authority illustrates what can go wrong and how interested parties can work to put matters to right (see opposite).

Racial violence is perpetrated by a small number of individuals, but for this to happen, there is almost always tolerance of racism within the larger community, as well as widespread negative feelings towards ethnic minority groups. The case study opposite indicates how such negative perceptions can develop, which may ultimately lead to violent attacks. Factors contributing towards the racial harassment of refugees may include

*   existing local tensions
*   high unemployment and bad housing, leading the to the easy scapegoating of refugees
*   negative portrayals for refugees in the local media
*   inflammatory statements by local politicians
*   ill-planned dispersal of asylum-seekers
*   no local consultation over plans to house asylum-seekers
*   little previous settlement by ethnic minority communities
*   failure by the police to pick up on growing tensions and to protect victims effectively
*   failure of schools to challenge hostility to refugees from non-refugee pupils and their families.

The everyday experiences of refugee pupils in schools

Refugee pupils' experiences of racism in schools mirror what is happening in the wider community. All studies on the experiences of refugee pupils reveal that many experience racial harassment in their schools and neighbourhood. In one study in the London Borough of Hackney in 1995 thirty-two refugee children were

Case Study

R is a small industrial local authority in Yorkshire. Asylum-seekers have been housed there since 1999, when London local authorities began placing families and single people there. In the summer of 1999 the local authority also received Kosovan evacuees who arrived as part of the Kosovan Humanitarian Evacuation Program. R is set to receive further asylum-seekers dispersed there by the National Asylum Support Service (NASS).

The local authority planned to commission accommodation for some 180 NASS-supported asylum-seekers in a hostel in a former pit village. A private company planned to build a large prefabricated hostel in one village. There was no consultation about the hostel and news of it leaked to local people, who were very angry. As a result there have been considerable local objections to this hostel. Police were called to one meeting about the hostel, because a council official who was there to hear concerns about the hostel feared for the safety of himself and his colleagues.

The site of the hostel is close to sheltered housing for the elderly. Some of the residents of this housing then organised a sleep-out protest on the site of the planned asylum hostel. The protests have attracted a great deal of coverage in the local media, with the refugees being described in very negative terms. Some press articles described refugees as beggars and members of armed gangs.

The protests were then followed by racial attacks on refugees already living in the area. At least three refugee school children have been attacked on their way to school. At the time of writing some 16 asylum-seeking children, mostly of secondary school age, have failed to secure a school place. Head teachers have been refusing to take these students, as a result of pressure from white parents and fears for league table performance.

In the Summer of 2000 Refugee Council staff local to the area held a community based meeting to talk to organisations working in the area as well as any local residents. Over a day, they explained why refugees were being moved to the local authority and sought to dispel myths. The meeting was successful in that many local residents and members of tenants' associations were brought on the side of refugees. The climate in the authority has improved since this initiative.*

* The application to house refugees in R was rejected in early 2001.

interviewed. They were from a range of national groups, including Bosnians, Turkish Kurds, Somalis and Vietnamese. All the children were judged by their parents and teachers to be 'coping' in school but nineteen of them reported that they had suffered racial harassment and nine had moved school as a result.

Let's Spell It Out – Save the Children's peer-led research – reported that over half the refugee children reported **bullying** in their schools and over 25 per cent reported the existence of racism, although fewer freely admitted to experiencing bullying themselves (15 per cent) or racism (30 per cent). Most common were comments against refugees and Africans. The children in the research were targets of racism from both white and black UK-born students. Less than half the refugee children surveyed knew if their schools had anti-bullying or anti-racist policies and these were rarely seen as effective (*Save the Children*, 1997).

Isolation is another common experience among refugee children. The Refugee Council's Education Adviser interviewed thirty two refugee children studying in London schools. Only one child reported that he had ever visited the home of a fellow pupil judged to be 'British'. Lack of language contributes towards isolation, but arguably so does negative media coverage with its portrayal of refugees as the 'alien other'.

Moreover, refugee children and their families have unequal **access to support** and redress after racial harassment. Many crimes are not reported to the police, an issue facing all ethnic minority communities. But under-reporting is made more likely by lack of English and a real fear some refugees have of the police, based on experiences in their home country. In such circumstances, the police must meet with refugees to allay their fears, and local authorities should fund racial harassment prevention projects that employ people who speak the refugees' languages. The third-party reporting of racial harassment is also something that can be considered – where community groups, schools, colleges and other groups can telephone the police to report racial harassment on behalf of refugees. Some local authority asylum teams have police officers seconded to them, another positive practice.

Racial harassment in schools

Roger Hewitt offers an important and unique study of the perpetrators of racist action and the impact on them of anti-racist policies. He claims that fifteen years of antiracist and multicultural education policies have changed the attitudes and behaviour of many school pupils but that there remains a core of racist youth in the predominately white areas he studied in the London Borough of Greenwich (Hewitt, 1996). Hewitt distinguishes between the 'passive' racism of private jokes, graffiti and racist opinions and the 'active' racism of assaults and verbal abuse. Active racism, he observes, is almost always carried out by groups of young people, suggesting that peer pressure may encourage assaults or abuse, and that active racism requires the perpetrators to feel safe. Hewitt's research in Greenwich leads him to conclude that

- Greenwich was ethnically divided with areas where ethnic minority communities did not live or even visit. The ethnic divide was perpetuated by the sons and daughters housing policy which allowed local authority homes to be passed on to the next generation
- the main agents of reproduction of racist attitudes were the peer group
- the policing of racist attitudes came more from the peer group than from parents, although parents might exert pressures on girls not to have boyfriends from ethnic minority groups
- white males seemed more vulnerable to peer pressure. Indeed it was girls that articulated the clearest arguments against racism. Hewitt believes that

anti-racist policies have to give more direct and indirect support to these exceptional girls

- most children in the predominantly white areas had little social contact with children from ethnic minority backgrounds until they entered secondary school, by which time they were becoming aware of themselves as part of a specific peer group

- the majority community played down the racist element of violence and abuse

- local authority antiracist policies were widely interpreted by the majority community as being 'unfair to whites', stoked by coverage of antiracist initiatives in the right-wing tabloid press. The clumsy management of some local authority antiracist initiatives may also have caused resentment among the majority community

- two domains of school activity were considered 'unfair to whites': discipline and the way cultural differences were dealt with.

- some schools dealt with disciplinary incidents in a way that stressed the school's antiracist policy rather than asserting the fundamental wrong of the offence

- schools often portrayed minority cultures as unitary, in events such as 'Africa Week'. Students from the majority community cannot identify with this simplified 'culture' so feel they have no culture. Hewitt stresses the need for schools to portray minority cultures in a true to life complex form. School celebrations of diversity must not exclude whites

- antiracist initiatives must run side by side with practices that address other oppressions such as poverty and sexism.

The themes he identified are developed by other writers. The Burnage Report, sitting after the racist murder of a Bangladeshi boy at a Manchester school in 1986 is one such (Macdonald *et al.*, 1989). (Burnage School now has a large number of Somali pupils.) The Stephen Lawrence Inquiry also took evidence from educationalists, and since it reported local authorities have produced reports and action plans to challenge racial harassment and promote good community relations (Macpherson *et al.*, 1999). In England, the DfEE has requested that all schools monitor racial incidents and report them annually to the LEA, parents and governors.

Also telling is the research *Refugees – from a small issue to an important cause*, carried out for the Refugee Council by Rainey, Kelly, Campbell, Roafe, an advertising agency. The researchers interviewed two groups of young adults, none of whom had strong views on immigration or refugees, in an attempt to identify strategies that could be adopted by refugee agencies to generate sympathy towards refugees. The interviews highlighted that refugees in the UK were not part of everyday life, as they were 'hidden away' in hostels. None of the interviewees had had any social contact with refugees so it was easy for media stereotypes to take hold. Although many interviewees expressed superficial sympathy towards refugees, this was not coupled with identification. Refugees' backgrounds and plights were considered to be 'other-worldy'. The use of statistics and hard facts had limited use in challenging popular stereotypes of refugees. Rather, refugee agencies should stress that refugees are ordinary people in extraordinary circumstances, by drawing on personal testimony and asking '*how would you feel if ..*'. questions. As one interviewee said: '*Instead of making it a charitable thing – oh look at the poor refugees – it makes you think about refugees as people like you.*'

An approach that stresses common humanity, challenges the negative stereotypes and the construction of refugees as 'alien other' should be used in the planning of projects that aim to raise awareness about refugees and challenge hostility to them. Often the arts – creative writing, poetry, testimony and the visual arts – can be employed to do this in a way that reaches into the psyche of all children.

So what can schools do?

Schools need to consider five different areas in work to challenge racism.

- **an evaluation of previous antiracist work** – what initiatives have been implemented before and did they work?

- **school ethos** – does the school promote human rights and respect for all? Or do pupils have low self-esteem or attend a school with an atmosphere of barely contained violence?

- **multi-agency work** – how does the school work with other agencies in society that should be involved in challenging racism? These may include parents, the police, youth groups, tenants' organisations, Race Equality Councils, football clubs, local authority housing departments and others. As Hewitt stressed, multi-agency work to challenge racism is usually the most effective and many areas have multi-agency working groups on racial harassment. In schools it is essential to involve all parents in projects and work on issues of race and justice, by inviting parents to attend assemblies and look at displays of work, for example, and informing them about what is going on.

- **effective monitoring and sanctions** – monitoring should be consistent and schools need guidelines to all staff (including lunchtime supervisors) on what constitues racial harassment and what does not. Sanctions against pupils who perpetrate racial harassment are needed and these should be seen by all to be fair. These sanctions should be understood by all pupils and staff and carried out consistently. Northamptonshire County Council has published an excellent resource for use among pupils and staff, to help them develop effective ways of dealing with racial harassment in schools. *Learning for All* (Commission for Racial Equality, 2000) also offers useful guidance.

• **using the curriculum to promote diversity and equality** – schools can use the curriculum to raise awareness about refugees in a way that stresses their humanity – the arts in particular offer many opportunities. Suggestions for curricular projects are described below.

Primary English can involve Literacy Hour work on refugee stories and testimonies; writing stories and accounts of refugee migrations; interviewing refugees; making presentations about relevant issues.

In the *secondary English* curriculum students can, for example, develop their speaking and listening skills by role-play and debate about refugee issues, presenting information, negotiation. Students can be given non-fictional texts to read such as newspapers articles about refugees, autobiography, diaries, letters and leaflets. Students can develop writing skills by setting out to inform others about refugees, or presenting written arguments, stories and narrative about refugees.

Primary history can deal with the growth of multi-ethnic UK; the era of the Second World War; local history projects about migration and oral history of refugees.

Secondary history can consider the Huguenots; Jewish migration in Victorian Britain; the growth of multi-ethnic Britain 1880-1970; the era of the Second World War and the Holocaust; the development of the United Nations and International Humanitarian Law; the Colonisation of Africa and post-colonial Africa; the Arab-Israeli conflict; the Viet Nam War and relevant Oral History work.

Primary geography can research refugees' countries of origin; prepare projects on migration and journeys; and examine links with other countries in an interdependent world.

The secondary geography curriculum can examine similar issues and also explore the impact of refugee migration on the host society.

Religious education can concern itself with religious festivals of many faiths; or with some of the many cases of persecution because of religious beliefs. Stories in religious texts can be used as a basis for looking at the way that society treats the outsider (Jesus' flight to Egypt or the *Hegira* – Mohammed's journey from Mecca to Media – for example). Religious education also involves the study of contemporary moral issues, for example poverty, war, the arms trade, social justice, race and immigration issues and responsibility to others.

Art can include looking at art forms from other countries and using art to represent feelings.

Cross-curricular themes in primary schools might include danger and being scared; loss; children's rights; safety; how we treat others; justice and issues of identity.

Sociology/social studies

The social studies curriculum examines race and immigration issues and pressure groups within a democratic society.

In *integrated humanities*, refugee issues can be examined in work that considers equality and inequality, conflict and cooperation, freedom and constraint, justice and injustice, pressure groups and political movements, nationalism and internationalism, poverty, wealth and welfare.

In September 2002, all English secondary schools are required to have a citizenship programme of study in place and this will embrace many of the issues suggested above. Citizenship education, according the DfEE's Advisory Group, involves three strands, namely political literacy, social and moral responsibility and community involvement – the active citizen.

Citizenship education can be cross-curricular, or it can be implemented as a subject in its own right. Teachers can adopt a concepts approach, examining concepts such as equality and diversity, for example. Or they can adopt a skills-based approach, involving problem-solving and the development of conflict resolution skills. Or teachers can adopt an enquiry-based approach and raise such questions as *Can you believe everything you read in the papers?* All three approaches offer opportunities to examine refugee migration in a way that challenges racism and promotes equality and diversity.

Curricular projects in schools

More and more UK schools have refugee students and teachers need to be sensitive to their needs, particularly when initiating class projects on refugees. Refugee children may have experienced traumatic events in their home countries or during their escape. They may have seen members of their family injured, arrested or killed. Such horrific events cannot easily be discussed in classrooms.

Refugee children may not want to talk about their home country or family circumstances because they are worried about family left at home, or because they feel that it might jeopardise their chances of staying in the UK or eventually returning home. They may not want to be made to feel different from other children. And they may feel embarrassed about the popular images of their home country. For example, some Somali children in London schools have felt unable to admit their origin because the only image their teachers and fellow pupils have of Somalia is of famine and war.

But there are many ways of making refugee students feel secure, while at the same time increasing all the students' knowledge, such as producing displays about life in students' countries of origin. Schools can invite parents and members of refugee communities to talk to students. Importantly, all school work on refugees must seek to humanise those who flee, and encourage non-refugee students to feel empathy towards their refugee classmates.

Teaching about controversial issues

Sometimes teachers are afraid to tackle issues like the movement and reception of refugees because they see them as controversial and requiring much knowledge to be properly understood. Teachers may assume that they must solve or at least confront the problems in advance of presenting them to children and that this will not be easy when issues are contestable. They may decide to ignore controversial issues completely.

The curriculum resources produced by the Refugee Council take the approach that children should be helped to understand how different opinions are formed. Many of the activities give children the opportunity to explore different opinions and the complex feelings generated by examining how we receive newcomers in our society. And more and more projects in schools throughout the UK are looking at refugee issues in schools. During Refugee Week 1999 some 800 schools held assemblies, engaged in fundraising and collections, or organised projects of work about refugees. Many schools produced dramas or made videos, others

Case study – The Welcome Leaflet: A whole class project at Fir Farm School.

This project was carried out with a Year Four group in a primary school in Enfield, London, and facilitated by a Refugee Support Teacher employed by the local authority.

The project aimed to encourage the class to think about the situation for refugee pupils when they arrive in a new school and produce a welcome leaflet for new pupils arriving in a school mid-term. The school had recently admitted refugee and non-refugee pupils mid-term and the Refugee Support Teacher wanted to involve both groups of students. She discussed the project with the new pupils before introducing it to the rest of the class. The project started by a discussion about what the first days in school felt like. The children were then asked to write about what made them feel better at this stressful time. A class list was made from this which included 'play with them at play time' and 'don't leave them out of a game'.

The Refugee Support Teacher then suggested making a booklet to help new pupils settle in and the children did this collaboratively, some designing covers and others making lists of the teachers. After the booklets were produced, there was following-up work including writing poems about being new. All the work was a way of looking at some of the issues faced by refugee children that involved the whole class.

worked with arts organisations to produce displays. Older pupils have participated in debates. The examples of good and inspiring citizenship education projects are too numerous to mention. The case study on page 143 is just one example.

Bibliography

Student material for use in citizenship education is listed in Further Resources at the end of the book.

Association of Chief Police Officers (2000) The Policing of Asylum Seeker and Refugee Communities, unpublished report

Audit Commission (2000) *Another Country: implementing dispersal under the Immigration and Asylum Act 1999*, London: Audit Commission

Commission for Racial Equality (1988) *Learning in Terror: survey of racial harassment in schools and colleges*, London: Commission for Racial Equality

Commission for Racial Equality (2000) *Learning for All: standards for racial equality in schools*, London: Commission for Racial Equality

Commission for Racial Equality (2001) *Strengthening the Race Relations Act*, London: CRE

Fekete, L. (2000) *The Dispersal of Xenophobia*, London: Institute of Race Relations

Hewitt, R. (1996) *Routes of Racism: the social basis of racist action*, Stoke on Trent: Trentham Books

Klein, G. (1993) *Education Towards Race Equality*, London: Cassell

Macdonald. I. (1989) *Murder in the Playground: the Burnage Report*, London: Longsight Press

Macpherson, W. et al (1999) *The Stephen Lawrence Inquiry: the report of the Inquiry by Sir William Macpherson of Cluny*, London: HMSO

Northamptonshire County Council (1990) *Dealing with Harassment and Racist Incidents in Schools*, Northampton: Northamptonshire County Council Education and Libraries

Rainey, Kelly, Campbell, Roafe (1997) Refugees – from a small issue to an important cause, unpublished report to the Refugee Council

Richman (1995) They Don't Recognise our Dignity: a study of young refugees in the London Borough of Hackney, unpublished report from City and Hackney Community NHS Trust

Refugee Council (1996) *Refugees: We Left Because We Had To,* London: Refugee Council

Refugee Council (1998) *Refugees: a primary school resource*, London: Refugee Council

Save the Children (1997) *Let's Spell It Out: Peer Research by the Horn of Africa Youth Scheme,* London: Save the Children

Searchlight (1995) *When Hate Comes to Town: community responses to racism and fascism*, London: Searchlight Educational Trust

Supple, C. (1999 2nd ed.) *From Prejudice to Genocide; learning about the Holocaust*, Stoke on Trent: Trentham Books

11

Home and Community Links

I didn't know what is going on in the school. The teacher just says that my child is doing well, he is fine. I didn't know how he fitted in. It was a big surprise to me when he failed all his GCSEs. Somali mother.

Schools make contact daily with other organisations and individuals. Some of the most successful schools are those which have strong links with parents, the caring professions and other groups. This chapter looks at some of the links a school must make with parents and community groups if it is to offer real support to refugee children.

Home/school liaison

In recent years there has been a great deal of rhetoric stressing the importance of parental choice and parental involvement in education. Since September 1999 all parents of children in English schools have had to sign 'Home-School Agreements'. But still many refugee parents have little contact with their child's school and that may be only when problems arise, for example when a child is in trouble. Why is this so?

Refugee parents who are newly-arrived may be unfamiliar with the workings of the education system, having come from countries where there is little parental participation in education and events such as parents' evenings are unfamiliar. Past experiences may make refugee parents suspicious of authority and wary of contact with schools. Their uncertain position may also make them nervous of challenging institutions. Language is another factor preventing parental participation; over 70 per cent of adult refugees arrive in the UK speaking little or no English. Refugee families may feel that their stay in the UK is temporary and not want to invest their emotions in their children's schooling. Finally, many newly-arrived asylum-seeking and refugee parents are under such stress that becoming involved in their children's school or even sorting out problems that arise seem low priority for parents struggling to cope. Positive home/school liaison policies must take these issues into account.

Siraj-Blatchford (1993) describes the type of ethos that schools should aim for to encourage good links with parents from ethnic minority groups and offers a basis for good practice:

- make all parents feel that they are wanted and have a positive role to play
- show parents that they can always make their feelings and opinions known to staff, and that these will be dealt with respectfully and seriously
- demonstrate that parents' linguistic, cultural and religious backgrounds are valued
- show that the school is part of the community it serves.

Carol Vincent and Simon Warren developed some of the ideas above in their research report *Supporting Refugee Children: a focus on home school links* (1998). They suggest that schools that focus solely on issues of achievement may erect impenetrable boundaries between school and home and suggest that the following should be considered:

- Every school should have a teacher responsible for home/school liaison and that teacher should be aware of refugee issues.
- Not all refugee children are cared for by both parents: many experience changes in their care arrangements, so schools need to check with whom a child lives and ensure that sensitivity is shown when invitations to 'parents' evenings' are sent out.
- Essential information should be translated and schools should book trained interpreters for school admission interviews and any assessments of the child's background.
- Schools and LEAs should work together to prepare welcome booklets which explain about the education system and the school. Model school letters can be prepared and translated, for such things such as invitations to parents/carers' evenings. Such information can be shared across LEAs to economise on costs.
- Parents should be made to feel welcome when they first come to the school and be shown around and introduced to staff and other parents. School staff should talk about the possible differences in learning methods between the UK and the child's home country.
- Schools can organise social events such as a coffee morning for parents who are new to the locality.
- Parents should be invited to help in the school's activities – many refugee parents have skills that can usefully be employed in schools.
- Advice material for refugees can be stocked in parents' rooms.
- Schools should investigate sources of funds for projects to support refugee parents and carers, including statutory funds for parental literacy or EAL, Education Action Zone monies, or non-statutory funding.
- More effort is needed to recruit educational welfare officers and teachers with a home/school liaison brief from refugee communities. Such bilingual staff could be shared between two or three LEAs which have only a few refugees.

Examples of successful projects

The Refugee Council runs an out-of-school Family Learning Workshop funded by the Further Education Funding Council's Adult and Community Learning Fund. Parents and children learn together on Saturdays and during the school holidays. Children receive support in maths, English, IT and study skills, often using games to make the learning process fun. Parents are given an introduction to IT and help with English and also information about the education system and how they can help their children at school.

The London Borough of Lewisham has organised thirteen English language classes for parents, based in the schools their children attend, also funded by the Adult and Community Learning Fund.

A primary school in Hounslow which has fifteen computers linked to the internet, has set up an after-school computer club for parents. Albanian-speaking parents have been encouraged to come on a designated evening. The club runs from 3pm-6pm and children and parents are welcome. There are refreshments and parents can access the Albanian language press on the internet. At the same time, teachers can drop in and talk to parents about their children's education.

A school in Newham has set up a project entitled 'Somali Families Learning Together', after Somali parents told teachers that they did not know how to help their children with homework. The school had some free time when the computer room was not used and this was set aside each week for Somali parents to work with their children. A crèche for under fives was set up in a neighbouring classroom and staffed by a classroom assistant who was also a qualified nursery worker. Parents were able to develop computer skills, find out about schooling and homework help, and meet other parents. Is the sessions, parents chose books and read with their children. The Refugee Education Team in the LEA helped the school put together a mini-library of dual language books and tapes. The school is now looking for other sources of funding to extend the project.

Making links with refugee community groups

There are over 400 refugee community organisations in the UK. Although most are in Greater London, more groups are forming outside the capital. These self-help groups work with specific communities. They may offer long-term support and help refugees to gain control over their own lives. Refugee community organisations vary in size and in the activities they perform. Some have paid staff; others depend volunteers. Some refugee communities, for example, the Iranians, are supported by several successful and well-organised community groups. Other communities, for example, eastern European Roma, are less well represented by community groups.

Some refugee community organisations represent specific ethnic, political or religious groups from particular countries. Schools must be sensitive to these differences and be aware that many newly-arrived refugees may be wary of community groups and individuals from their home country.

Among the services that refugee community groups offer are

- advice on immigration law, welfare rights and housing
- English language classes, employment training and careers advice
- supplementary schools for refugee children
- senior citizens' clubs
- women's groups
- cultural events and outings
- the production of newsletters and information
- campaigning on issues affecting refugees from that community.

It is important that schools develop good links with refugee community organisations in their locality. If a school wishes to improve the involvement of refugee parents in its activities, it can ask the relevant community groups to encourage refugee parents to respond to the school's overtures. Refugee community groups can sometimes provide interpreters to mediate in an emergency. They can also be invited to speak to students or be involved in activities such as cooking, storytelling and other cultural or awareness-raising projects. Schools can research and list local community organisations and individual refugees who could be invited in to help.

Bibliography

Bastiani, J. (ed) (1997) *Home-School Work in Multicultural Settings*, London: David Fulton

Kahin, M. (1997) *Educating Somali Children in Britain,* Stoke on Trent: Trentham Books

Siraj-Blatchford (1993) *The Early Years: laying the foundation for race equality*, Stoke on Trent: Trentham Books

Vincent, C. and Warren, S. (1998) Supporting Refugee Children: a focus on home-school liaison. Unpublished report of a research project conducted by the University of Warwick.

12
Unaccompanied Refugee Children

When I was in Kosova I didn't know the significance of my room. I thought living alone in a hotel would be like living in my own house. When I came to London I was 14 years old and I decided to ask for asylum. The Immigration in Croydon told me that I would have to find someone who was over 18 to look after me because I too young to live alone. I found a friend and he undertook to look after me. In the social services office where I was registered they found me a hotel together with my friend.

The hotel they found us was a catastrophe. It wasn't painted, the two beds in our room were broken and very old and small and the springs dug into my back. They didn't change the sheets once in two weeks. The entire hotel was the same, children were crying all night, some of the residents were coming in drunk at 2am and at midnight there was singing and shouting. I was all alone without my family.

My mind was always in Kosova with my family who I left in danger of the Serb police. Also I was afraid of the drunken residents because I didn't know how to cope with such people. On the first morning when I wanted to cook breakfast, I was made to go five flours down to the kitchen, which was dirty, like the toilet on the floor below my room.

We had to wait in a queue for the toilet, as well as for the kitchen. After one month I told the hotel boss that I wanted to change my room, and he said 'Yes, why not.' I went with him to look at another room: it was so small that I had to jump from the door on to the bed because there wasn't space for more than a bed.

I lived in the hotel for more than six months and during that six months I was registered in school with the help of the friend I had lived with. After I was registered in school, they changed my hotel and sent me to a better one. But it was too far from my school and it took me one hour to get there. I told my teacher it was very difficult for me to come to school. The next day she called the social services and asked them to bring me near my school.

After three months they changed my hotel and sent me to a flat. There I had my own room and my friend had his own room. The flat was good and we were happy there. We only got this because of my school and the other agencies who were helpful and kind in getting us a flat after a whole year of staying in hotels. At the beginning I didn't want to get the flat together with my friend because he was someone I never knew before. But the Council told me that if I didn't share with him I would have to stay in the hotel for ever and he would stay on the street.

I continue in my school and I am happy with what I have. But I have missed my family in Kosova and they will never be forgotten. I still remember how I left my family, at my house's old scratched door, crying with tears in their eyes.

K aged 15, who attends Albanian Youth Action, a youth group.

U naccompanied children are the most vulnerable of refugee children, because they lack the support of a family. Family separation or loss, however, never occur in isolation – an unaccompanied refugee child will have experienced other traumatic events such as war.

Who are unaccompanied refugee children?

In 1999 some 3,339 asylum-seeking children arrived by themselves in the UK and were identified as unaccompanied asylum-seeking children by the Immigration and Nationality Directorate of the Home Office. This figure is misleading and underestimates the numbers of unaccompanied refugee children in the UK. The UNHCR defines unaccompanied children as 'those who are separated from both parents and are not being cared for by an adult who, by law or custom has responsibility to do so' (UNHCR (1994) *Refugee Children: Guidelines on Protection and Care* Geneva: UNHCR). The UN Convention on the Rights of the Child and the Children Act 1989 define a child as anyone under the age of 18 years. Using UNCHR's definition, unaccompanied refugee children include

- children who have become separated from their parents and have arrived in the UK by themselves
- children who are being cared for by older siblings, distant relatives and family friends – people who would not by custom be their usual carers
- children who arrived in the UK with family but whose care arrangements break down after arrival.

Flight

Children flee on their own for a variety of reasons. Their parents may have been killed or imprisoned. They may have become separated from their parents during war. Many parents arrange for their children to travel to another country because they fear for their safety. Risk factors can include war, or being associated with a persecuted political or minority group. In at least 25 countries children under 18 make up significant percentages of national armies, guerrilla groups or both. Parents may send children away to prevent forced recruitment; for this reason more male unaccompanied children reach Europe than do girls.

Most unaccompanied children arriving in the UK have been sent by their parents, although contact with parents is often negligible. Some come to the UK with family friends, other are brought by an agent. Some are handed over without warning to a community organisation, or simply abandoned. A significant number of unaccompanied refugee children arrive in the care of older siblings – usually just a few years their senior.

In the last four years unaccompanied children have arrived in the UK from over 50 different countries of origin. Since 1997 the largest group have been from Kosova. About 1,500 unaccompanied Kosovan children arrived in the UK in 1999, mostly boys and young men. Other significant groups of unaccompanied asylum-seeking children arriving in 1999 included Afghans, Albanian nationals, Chinese nationals, Eritreans, Ethiopians, Iraqis (including Iraqi Kurds), Somalis, Sri Lankan Tamils and Turkish nationals.

National policy

British asylum law currently makes little distinction between adult and child asylum-seekers although there are some concessions. When applying for asylum (see Chapter Three), unaccompanied children are given a Statement of Evidence Form in which to describe evidence of persecution. They are usually not required to attend oral interviews with immigration officers. Immigration Rules also acknowledge an unaccompanied child's vulnerability. Unaccompanied children whose asylum application has been refused and who face removal or deportation are obliged to have a country of origin report prepared. This is meant to assess the conditions faced by the child if returned, in particular if there is an appropriate person to care for that child.

Despite these concessions, the process of applying for asylum is complicated and stressful. Not all unaccompanied asylum-seeking children have skilled immigration lawyers who can develop a good rapport with a child or adolescent. In acknowledgement of this, the Home Office funds a panel of advocates whose job is to guide unaccompanied children through the asylum process *inter alia*. The Panel of Advisers for Unaccompanied Children is coordinated by the Refugee Council (see Further Resources).

The Immigration and Asylum Act 1999 makes it clear that the responsibility for unaccompanied asylum-seeking children under 18 years lies with local authority social services departments under the provisions of the Children Act 1989. No unaccompanied asylum-seeker under 18 is meant to be supported by the National Asylum Support Service. Instead there is the Special Grant for Un-accompanied Asylum Seeking Children, administered by the Department of Health, which is payable for support offered under Section 17 and Section 20 of the Children Act 1989, although not all local authorities who support such children receive it.

Central government has also encouraged some good practice initiatives. In 1995 the Department of Health published practice guidelines and a training pack on unaccompanied refugee children. The DfEE and the Department of Health have a published circular: *Guidance on The Education of Children Being Looked After by Local Authorities* (2000). It recommends that all local authorities have a teacher or education officer who has clear responsibility for looked-after children. It also recommends that looked-after children do not spend more than 20 days out of education.

At a local government level, all social services departments are required to produce Children's Services Plans which are submitted to the Department of Health. These offer the opportunity to examine services to unaccompanied refugee children. In 1999, the Department of Health also published *Quality Protects Management Action Plans* at national and local level, which aim to improve the life chances of children in need. These programmes of work may also present opportunities for examining services to unaccompanied refugee children.

Care options

In England and Wales, the Children Act 1989 provides the legislative framework that is meant to guide how unaccompanied asylum-seeking and refugee children have their care needs met. The Children Act 1989 brings together all legislation pertaining to the welfare of children. Areas covered in the Children Act include

– definitions of parental responsibility
– definitions of 'children in need'
– legal procedures for protecting children
– amendments to adoption and fostering law
– the obligations of local authorities to provide care for children in need or on remand
– secure accommodation for children
– the regulation of residential care services.

There are also regulations and guidelines to support the Children Act. These are not primary legislation but can be used for judicial review. Local authorities also have their own guidelines and procedure. Under the Children Act, local authorities have a duty to ensure the welfare of 'children in need' up to the age of 18. Additionally, local authorities have to provide services for some children leaving care. According to the Children Act, a child is defined to be in need if

> he is unlikely to achieve or maintain, or have the opportunity of achieving or maintaining, a reasonable standard of health or development without the provision for him of services by the local authority; his health or development is likely to be significantly impaired, or further impaired, without the provision of such services; or he is disabled.

A local authority is obliged to provide services to support children in need which are appropriate to a child's race, culture, religious background and linguistic group, and this applies to unaccompanied refugee children. The Children Act also stresses the need for children to be kept informed about decisions affecting them and for effective partnership between statutory and voluntary organisations.

The Children Act 1989 makes a local authority social services department responsible for providing support to all children 'in need' living within its boundaries. For unaccompanied refugee children this is taken to be the local authority to which the child first presents. The social services departments have two care options available

1. After assessment the child may be formally 'looked after' or 'accommodated' under the provisions of Section 20 of the Children Act 1989. A 'looked after' child will have a named social worker and has clear legal entitlements to things such as a care plan, independent visitor and support after he or she leaves care.
2. A child/young person may be supported under the provisions of Section 17 of the Children Act 1989. Here a social services department assesses the child and concludes that he or she requires support services such as accommodation.

Department of Health guidance recommends that all unaccompanied asylum-seeking children under the age of 16 years are 'looked after'. The Department of Health leaves the decision for assessing and supporting 16 and 17 year olds to the discretion of local authority social services departments. In practice most 16 and 17 year olds are supported by Section 17 of the Children Act, where quality of services varies considerably. Given these legal guidelines, the usual care arrangements for unaccompanied asylum-seeking and refugee children are

Placement with close relatives – the children are cared for by close relatives such as aunts and uncles after they arrive in the UK. While many children are happy being cared for by close relatives, some are not and there is no statutory requirement under the Children Act for the on-going monitoring of unaccompanied children where they are being cared for by close family.

Informal care – many asylum-seeking and refugee children who arrive in the UK without their parents are cared for by siblings, distant relatives or family friends. Sometimes social services departments will know of informal care arrangements; in other cases they will not. Strictly speaking this informal care should be regarded as a private foster placement by a social services department and thus subject to monitoring, but in practice this is rare.

Often informal care is successful, sometimes it is not. Unaccompanied refugee children may be rejected by their carers when life gets tough in the UK. Children being cared for by siblings who are only a few years older are of particular concern. There may be the usual sibling conflicts and sometimes the younger child may not accept the authority of an older sibling.The older sibling may not know of services offered by social services that can lessen the stresses such young carers' experience.

Fostering – some unaccompanied refugee children who are 'looked after' under Section 20 of the Children Act are fostered, particularly if they are very young. Usually they are placed in a children's home where they are assessed and at a later date they are moved into a foster home. Ideally, a foster family should be of a similar ethnic and linguistic background, and receive proper support from the local authority. Although a few local authorities have invested considerable resources in recruiting foster carers from refugee communities, there is a national shortage of refugee foster families. Many refugee families simply do not feel settled enough to put themselves forward as foster families. As a result refugee children may be placed with a foster family from the same region – for example an Eritrean family caring for a Somali child – or matched in a cruder way, according to skin colour or religion. While some cross-cultural fostering works well, research shows that among refugee children there is a high level of breakdown of cross-cultural foster care.

Unaccompanied refugee children may be placed with foster families many miles away from the local authority that is responsible for them. A growing number of unaccompanied asylum-seeking and refugee children have recently been placed in private foster care outside Greater London, where they may be isolated and deprived of contact with members of their own community.

Residential care – about 40 per cent of unaccompanied refugee children cared for under Section 20 of the Children Act stay in residential homes, run by a local authority, voluntary agencies or privately. Some local authorities and organisations such as the Refugee Council have homes specifically for refugee children. In such homes children have a great deal of contact with members of their own community and the support of trained staff. In other cases, unaccompanied refugee children are housed in a non-specialised children's home, where they may have little contact with members of their own community. They may be housed with other children who have severe emotional and behavioural problems. As with fostered children, unaccompanied refugee children in residential care may be placed in a home many miles away from the local authority responsible for them.

Supported local authority accommodation – some older unaccompanied refugee children are provided with their own housing but supported by a social worker. In Australia and Canada unaccompanied refugee children often share housing and support workers, but this option is rarely used in the UK.

Section 17 support – the majority of 16 and 17 year old unaccompanied asylum-seeking and refugee children are supported under Section 17 of the Children Act, where services for them range from adequate to very poor. Some are placed in hostels with supportive staff and access to named social workers. They may receive a cash allowance for their maintenance. Other young asylum-seekers are placed in bed and breakfast hotels, supported by vouchers and may not have a named social worker.

Concerns

Services to unaccompanied asylum-seeking and refugee children vary considerably. In some local authorities they are looked after and given Section 20 support but in others very few are supported in this way. The poor quality of services offered to 16 and 17 year olds is a growing concern and appears to have worsened since 1996. This has undoubtedly been caused by the passing of responsibility for supporting asylum-seekers without benefits to social services. Asylum-seekers became unpopular with local government and this included unaccompanied children, for whom local authorities were unwilling to invest financial resources.

While the Home Office makes very clear that unaccompanied children will not be supported by the National Asylum Support Service, there remain many questions about what happens to these young people when they turn 18. They may become the responsibility of NASS, be supported by vouchers and be moved out of London under the dispersal programme, even if they have made friends and settled. The NASS has undertaken not to move 18 year olds 'in the year of an examination course'; nevertheless significant numbers of 18 year old asylum-seekers may be uprooted and moved.

Cases of disputed age have been given undue prominence by some social services departments: a young person may claim to be 17, while a social worker claims they are 19. It is worth reflecting on why these disputes arise. An asylum-seeker may arrive in the UK without any documentation or with forged documentation that gives an incorrect date of birth. Since 1996 there has also been a financial incentive to claim to be under 18, in order to try and qualify for Children Act support rather than vouchers.

About 25 per cent of unaccompanied refugee children have no contact with people from their own community. This problem has grown as more children are cared for in homes and foster placements outside London.

Little extra support is generally given to refugee children being cared for by older siblings.

Most unaccompanied refugee children receive little support and guidance when leaving care, particularly those who arrived aged 16 or 17 and were supported under Section 17 of the Children Act, as they have no entitlement to a leaving package of support.

Access to good lawyers is another key concern: young unaccompanied asylum-seekers need a lawyer who can communicate with them as well as being a skilled asylum lawyer.

The quality of education for this group is often unsatisfactory. Access is an issue: many 15 year olds arriving in the UK fail to secure a school place. Research undertaken in the London Borough of Camden in 1998 indicated that at least 50 per cent of 16-19 year old refugees were not in school or college, including the majority of young Kosovars. Because so few UK-born young people in local authority care progress to further or higher education, some residential social workers have low educational expectations of refugee children living in children's homes. Unaccompanied refugee children, however bright, are rarely encouraged to progress to university and may be channelled into un-suitable vocational courses.

Young Kosovars seem a particularly vulnerable group (see page 223). The proximity of Kosova to western Europe and its comparative wealth means that the Kosovan exodus is a mass migration rather than an elite migration. Young Kosovars, therefore, come from all socio-economic classes and significant numbers are from working class families with little tradition of education. The poor quality of support provided to 16 and 17 year olds and the severely inter-rupted prior education of almost all of them has made them additionally vul-nerable. Enrolment in post 16 education is low and research carried out in 1999 shows disproportionate numbers of young Kosovars to be entering the criminal justice system.

The teacher's role

Many unaccompanied refugee children are eager to learn, and often develop trusting relationships with their teachers. This can mean that teachers and lecturers are often the first outsiders to know when care arrangements are going wrong. Such problems may include the breakdown of informal and formal foster placements or unsuitable hostel accommodation. **Practical strategies** that schools can adopt to support unaccompanied children include

Making links – it is essential that teachers working with unaccompanied refugee children understand their experiences and needs and be informed about referral agencies. Schools and LEAs must ensure that they develop good links with social service departments and refugee organisations. Since younger unaccompanied refugee children will be 'looked after', good contact should be made with the LEA officer/teacher who has responsibility for the education of looked after children.

• Schools should ensure that sibling or relative carers are aware of support available from the social services department.

• The schools should be clear about the local authority's policy for looked-after children and refugee children.

• Schools should ensure that unaccompanied refugee children know about the Red Cross Tracing and Message Services. They should also make them aware of befriending schemes and other support initiatives such as summer holiday schemes.

School admissions – when admitting new pupils, school staff should be aware of the wide range of care arrangements for unaccompanied refugee children and use an admission interview to gather information on care arrangements. Where children are living with unrelated adults, the school should ensure that the social services department is informed – with the knowledge of the family – so they can assess whether private fostering regulations apply.

Advice and support of a significant adult – unaccompanied refugee children do not have access to the advice and support that parents can give. They may find it more difficult to get up in the morning, complete homework, and organise their time. Parents give advice – on suitable careers for example. It is important that schools give unaccompanied children extra support, guidance and encouragement. For children who have few contacts with others from their culture, schools can play a positive role by encouraging such contacts.

Teachers may find themselves in the role of a significant adult in the life of an unaccompanied refugee child, in terms of advice and authority, praise for achievement, understanding their experience before and after flight, help in conflict resolution, further education and careers advice. Where such a child is encountering major problems, schools have a duty to investigate, and work with other agencies to ensure that the child receives appropriate care. This will require time and patience and may require teachers to step outside their role.

Specified teachers should be encouraged to participate in care planning and statutory reviews of looked-after children. Teachers should be prepared to challenge poor practice and to complain on behalf of children who are not getting a good service or being listened to by social services.

In its guidance on the education of 'looked-after' children, the DfEE recommends that headteachers in primary schools and heads of year in secondary schools 'hold a watching brief for all children being looked after by social services'. This indicates good practice that should be encouraged.

Sensitivity – schools need to avoid exclusive language and thinking, such as letters to 'parents and guardians' and 'parents' evenings'. Sensitivity needs to be extended into curricular areas where children might be asked to do projects on their family.

The asylum process – teachers can offer support to unaccompanied children in the asylum determination procedure. They need to be aware that an unaccompanied refugee children might have had no appropriate legal advice about making an asylum claim, even if looked after by a social services department. Teachers might keep a watchful eye on such children's asylum applications, in liaison with a social worker, to ensure that they are being represented by a good lawyer, but should not contact the Home Office directly on their behalf or help them make their asylum claim – instead contact a legal adviser.

Schools should ensure that children know about the Refugee Council's Panel of Advisers for Unaccompanied Refugee Children and help them make contact if they wish. The school staff need to understand about the process of making an asylum claim, so they can support children at particularly difficult times, such as following a refusal, or through the appeals process.

The school might consider making a report to support the child's claim, or helping collect evidence to support an asylum claim or appeal. A few teachers have worked with children to make audiotapes of children describing their experiences of persecution, for later use by the child's lawyer.

School curriculum – schools should ensure that the experience of evacuees and unaccompanied refugee children are included in any treatment of refugee issues or certain periods of history such as the Spanish Civil War or Second World War.

Some curricular flexibility may be needed to enable children who arrive in Years 10 and 11 to engage in schooling (see Chapter Fourteen).

LEA responsibilities – The DfEE requires there to be a named person at senior management level in every LEA who has overall responsibility for the education of looked-after children. That person needs to be aware of refugee children's needs and to work closely with those responsible for refugee education in the LEA.

The LEA should lobby to ensure that unaccompanied children's education is not interrupted by unplanned or badly thought through moves of housing, which necessitate their changing school or college.

Refugee support teachers and those responsible for the education of looked-after children should have access to Department of Health/Social Services Inspectorate practice guidance on asylum-seeking children.

The Panel of Advisers for Unaccompanied Refugee Children

The Home Office funds an advocacy service for unaccompanied refugee children called the Panel of Advisers for Unaccompanied Refugee Children. The Refugee Council has administered it since 1994. Some 40 advisers have been recruited and trained. They come from a wide range of ethnic groups. Children are paired with advisers according to factors such as ethnic background and gender. The children's advisers will befriend a young person; guide them through the asylum process; give advice; help that young person stake a claim to statutory rights; and offer some kind of cultural link.

Unfortunately the Panel of Advisers has no statutory power to ensure that children have their care needs met. Pressure of work means that some unaccompanied children are supported for only a short time, but the Refugee Council runs a drop in service to supplement the one-to-one work of the Panel. Other organisations such as the Medical Foundation for the Care of Victims of Torture are running long term befriending schemes for unaccompanied refugee children.

Children ask for support from the Panel of Advisers. They may also be referred by immigration officers, social workers, lawyers, community groups, teachers and other professionals. If a child is referred to the Panel of Advisers, consent should first be obtained. The relevant social services department should also be informed. The Panel aims for better treatment of unaccompanied refugee children, and tries to address some of the concerns raised by childcare professionals.

Bibliography

Amnesty International (UK) (1999) *Most Vulnerable of All: the treatment of unaccompanied children in the UK*, London: Amnesty International (UK)

Ayotte, W. (1998) *Supporting Unaccompanied Children in the Asylum Process*, London: Save the Children

Bell, A. (1996) *Only for Three Months: The Basque Children in Exile*, Norwich: Mousehole Press

Department for Education and Employment (1994) *The Education of Children Being Looked After by Local Authorities*, London: Department for Education and Employment

Department of Health (2000) *Guidance on The Education of Children Being Looked After by Local Authorities, Circular LAC (2000)* 13, London: Department of Health and Department for Education and Employment

Department of Health/OFSTED (1995) *The Education of Children who are Looked After by Local Authorities*, London: HMSO

Department of Health Social Services Inspectorate (1995) *Unaccompanied Asylum-seeking Children: a practice guide*, London: HMSO

Department of Health Social Services Inspectorate (1995) *Unaccompanied Asylum-seeking Children: a training pack*, London: HMSO

Gershon, K. (Ed) (1989) *We Came as Children*, London & Basingstoke: Papermac/Macmillan

Jackson, S. (1988) *The Education of Children in Care*, Bristol Papers No 1: University of Bristol (School of Applied Social Services)

Munoz, N. (1999) *Other People's Children: an exploration of the needs of and the provision for 16 and 17 year old unaccompanied asylum-seekers*, London: Children of the Storm and London Guildhall University

Ressler, E., Boothby, N. and Steinbock, D. (1988) *Unaccompanied Children*, New York and Oxford: OUP

Rutter, M. (1985) 'Resilience in the Face of Adversity – Protective Factors and Resistance to Psychiatric Disorder', in *British Journal of Psychiatry*, 147, pp 598-611

Save the Children (1999) *Seeking Asylum in the UK: a leaflet for adults supporting unaccompanied children with legal representation and the asylum process*, London: Save the Children

United Nations High Commissioner for Refugees (1994) *Refugee Children: Guidelines on Protection and Care,* Geneva: UNHCR, p 121

United Nations (1989) *Convention on the Rights of the Child*, New York and Geneva: United Nations

Utting, W. (1991) *Children in the Public Care*, London: HMSO

Wicks, B. (1989) *The Day They Took the Children*, London: Bloomsbury

Williamson, L. (1998) 'Unaccompanied – but not unsupported' in Rutter, J. and Jones, C. (eds.) *Refugee Education: Mapping the Field*, Stoke on Trent: Trentham Books

Williamson, L. (2000) 'Unaccompanied refugee children: legal framework and local application in Britain' in Bloch, A. and Levy, C. (eds.) *Refugees, Citizenship and Social Policy in Europe*, London: Macmillan.

13
Meeting the Needs of 14-19
Year Old Students

I arrived when I was 15 and missed school for a whole year because no school would take me. The next September I started at college, on a access course. There were lots of refugees on the course, from Kosova, Somalia and lots of places. My best friend was Ayse, she was Kurdish. We stayed on the course, but lots of my friends left after a while, because they moved hotel, because they moved house. It sounds silly but one Kosovan boy left because he couldn't face the others, his friends, because he hadn't got the money to buy new clothes or a telephone. I don't even think he had the money to buy lunch.

In Ethiopia we just listened to the teacher, took notes and prepared for the exam. We never did homework assignments, or practicals in science or presentations... Here we do group work and practicals and we have to research and use books in the library to find the answers. There, there was only the teacher and one textbook for the course and that's it.

(Testimonies collected by Jeremy McDonald and Jill Rutter).

Adolescence is a difficult time for all young people. They are undergoing physical and emotional changes and having to make decisions that will affect the rest of their lives. Having to cope with life in a new and unfamiliar country can add serious extra strain at an already trying time. While most young refugees do arrive with parents or other adult carers, more 14-18 year olds than younger children are unaccompanied. Refugees who *arrive* in the UK aged 14-19 may face particular educational and social problems, namely

- an interrupted education
- faulure of many 14 and 15 year olds to gain access to secondary schooling, despite their rights
- high geographic mobility in the UK. Children may move school, further disrupting their education, or may drop out of a college course because they cannot afford to travel back to it (asylum-seekers are not allowed to receive access funds in FE colleges)

- financial hardship with attendant educational implications, as the testimony opening this chapter illustrates
- lack of social support for unaccompanied young asylum-seekers aged 16 to 18
- failure of 16-19 year old refugees to secure access to appropriate courses in colleges of further education, with many of the academically able being channelled towards vocational courses
- lack of careers advice tailored to the particular needs of refugees
- lack of access to youth work
- rules that prevent asylum-seekers receiving access funds to meet cases of hardship

A research project published in 1998 indicated that about half of 15-19 year old refugees in one central London local authority had no contact with any education provider. Some 39 per cent of the case-load of a neighbouring Young Offenders' Team was taken up with refugee clients, mostly young Somali and Kosovan men. Of all refugee groups, those who arrive in the UK between the ages of 14 and 19 years are at risk of becoming a 'lost' generation.

Students' experiences in schools

In June 2000, the Refugee Council estimated that about 1,500 asylum-seeking and refugee children had failed to secure a school place in the UK, of whom at least 60 per cent were newly arrived 14 to 16 year olds. Because of the pressure to meet league table targets, some schools were unwilling to enrol refugees who had little or no English, midway through a GCSE course.

In July 2000 the DfEE made an important policy change: children and young people who arrive in England with little or no English in Years 5, 6, 10 or 11 of their schooling no longer have their examination results included in school and LEA league tables. This may ease the problem of schools refusing to enrol such students, but it does not answer the fundamental question – what is a meaningful educational experience for a young person who arrives in the UK aged 14-16? This is a question that the DfEE and equivalent bodies in Wales, Scotland and Northern Ireland have not addressed. For these young people, full-time school attendance is essential, as well as being a legal requirement. Part-time courses offered in separate units (the practice of some local authorities) do not meet their educational needs and are in all probability illegal. Once in a school, these adolescent students have certain educational options:

1. Some may be integrated into GCSE courses straight away, most likely those who have attended English-medium schools in their home country, or are from English speaking families or are notably academically able. The latter will need English language support. For these students the main educational obstacle may be catching up with GCSE course work.

2. Students start as near as possible to the start of Year 10. The league table opt out may make this easier.

3. Starting GCSE courses after a short induction course to include basic English, study skills, an introduction to new subjects, as well as IT. The study skills aspects of induction should not be neglected, as many young refugees have little experience of research, writing essays or preparing assignments.

4. A one year 'Access to GCSE' course. One London school runs such a course for about fifteen students aged between 15 and 18. Students mix with their peers during class periods, assembly and games. On the course they study maths, English, IT, science and humanities, as well as a modular creative arts course. Students are also encouraged to study for qualifications in their languages, for example Arabic, French, Farsi or Turkish. After one year, many students sit GCSEs and progression to further GCSEs, vocational qualifications and A-Levels is high.

5. A similar one year course for 15 year olds in a local college. Several London colleges run such courses and offer high quality provision. But there may be some young refugees for whom a school place, with greater supervision and pastoral support, may be more appropriate.

6. The new 'key skills' (Higher Skills in Scotland) qualifications may offer opportunities to provide accreditation for courses aimed at refugee children and young people with little or no prior education. From Autumn 2000 students will be able to study for qualifications in numeracy, communication, problem solving, working with others and information technology. Alternatively the Welsh Joint Examination Committee offers a Certificate of Educational Achievement in a range of subjects.

The Refugee Council is concerned about the lack of English language support available to children studying in the top sets. Setting takes place in most secondary schools and is almost universal in GCSE maths. (It is applied in other subjects to a lesser degree.) Regrettably, children with English as an additional language still end up in the bottom sets in some schools. Even in more enlightened schools, simple economic choices may prevent children for whom English is an additional language from studying in a top set. English language support teachers are in short supply in all schools, so many schools group their English language learners in one or two classes, in an attempt to achieve maximum access to classroom-based support. But seldom are those 'top set' classes.

In line with setting, many GCSE boards offer 'tiered' GCSE courses, with students sitting the same subject at different ability levels. A teacher has to decide the level at which a student should be entered, effectively capping the grade that can be achieved. In mathematics, students may sit papers at higher, intermediate or foundation tier and the foundation tier cannot yield more than a grade D at GCSE. A number of London teachers have expressed their concern about refugee students who have superior mathematical skills to their UK-educated peers being entered in 'foundation' tiers because of the setting system or because of prejudice towards bilingual learners.

Another difficulty is that few LEAs or schools provide any English language support for those aged 16-18 who choose to remain in the school system. This effectively means that students who are English language learners have to attend sixth form colleges or FE colleges if they wish to continue their education.

Colleges of Further Education

Young refugees arriving after the age of 16 usually attend colleges of Further Education or tertiary colleges – if they choose to continue with their education. In order to meet their needs colleges must examine their policies on issues such as initial assessment, the range of courses, pastoral support and careers advice.

Processes of enrolment and assessment of students vary widely. Staff who administer college admission need training on the entitlements of asylum-seeking students. The Refugee Council is concerned that many academically able young refugees are channelled towards vocational courses in FE colleges – courses that do not fulfil their long-terms needs and aspirations – as well as wasting talent. This appears to stem from poor quality initial assessment.

The range of courses on offer varies across the UK, and so does the quality of some English language support in the FE sector. For example, in an east London local authority with one of the highest populations of refugees there is no sixth form provision in schools. The Sixth Form centre has a very limited number of courses providing English language support. There is only one local FE college and although this offers a wide range of courses with English language support, the demand for them is high. At the time of writing some 800 young refugees were on this college's waiting list for English language or English language supported courses. In many parts of the UK to which asylum-seekers are being dispersed there are few English language courses on offer.

The courses need to take into account the likelihood of an interrupted education. Colleges can, for example, offer access courses for those hoping to go on to further study. English language support should be available on mainstream courses where needed, and all tutors should receive training in working with bilingual students.

Pastoral support is another issue. Many young refugees have experienced violence or other stressful events. Once in the UK, they may be lonely and isolated. Colleges of Further Education can be impersonal places, particularly for those studying part-time. Student counsellors should be aware of the particular needs of young refugees. The college should ensure that it is a welcoming place, perhaps organising social events for those who may be isolated. A number of FE colleges have attached youth projects working with specific groups of students, for example, Tower Hamlets College in London employs a Somali youth worker.

Careers advice for young refugees

At age 16, the end of compulsory education, five different options face young refugees. They can remain at school, enrol at a sixth form or tertiary college, enrol at a college of further education, enter a training scheme or obtain a job. At 18, similar decisions have to be made; for any young person the many possible choices can be confusing. A career adviser's role is to help young people make informed decisions about their future employment and education paths, and help them progress into further and higher education, training or into employment. Careers advisers have to assess needs, advise and teach any young person skills such as interview techniques, but for young refugees additional factors may arise such as whether their immigration status affects access to further and higher education. Refugees will often have especially poor information about the UK job market and the further and higher educational system, and their confidence and future aspirations may have been negatively affected by the experience of becoming a refugee and living in exile.

Asylum-seekers are classified as overseas students until a decision is made about their case. This means that they are liable to pay an overseas student's fee for a full-time course in higher education – far more expensive than a home student's fee. Overseas students are not entitled to student grants and loans. Young asylum-seekers may have their future opportunities restricted because of this ruling. Careers advisers need to be aware of this situation, and advise students accordingly. Young people granted 'exceptional leave to remain' in Britain are home students as regards fees. But they need three years ordinary residence before they can qualify for a maintenance grant and this limits their career options too.

Cultural factors influence young people's choice of career. In refugees' countries of origin people may rely on word of mouth or government notice-boards to search work, rather than newspaper advertisements. Recruitment and selection procedures may be quite different, so young refugees will probably need particular support from careers advisers to improve their job search skills.

The status of certain jobs varies from country to country – for example, teaching is a high status job in Sri Lanka but not in Poland – and these perceptions affect the career aspirations of young refugees. Young people also need knowledge about the types of job available, but research shows that many refugees are misinformed about the British job-market (Marshall 1991). Many believe that mining and heavy industry employ large numbers of people in the UK, when in fact more people are employed in tertiary industries such as banking, finance, retailing, education and the health service. Careers advisers must not assume that young refugees have accurate knowledge about the British job market, and must be prepared try and correct their misconceptions.

Many young refugees aspire to return home at the earliest opportunity. This too will influence their career choices as many will choose jobs or courses that are relevant to their return. Others may be unwilling to commit themselves to long courses of study in the UK.

Finance for educating 16 to 19 year olds

Rules on fees and awards are complex. Those advising young refugees should consult the *Refugee Council's Information Service Handbook* or the *Refugee Education Handbook* (World University Service, 2000). Schooling from 5 to 16 is free for all asylum-seekers. Refugees and people with ELR may continue to attend schools or colleges of further education free of charge up to the age of 19. At colleges of further education asylum-seekers aged 16-19 may be obliged to pay a tuition fee for a full-time course, although this depends on the policy of the college. Many colleges allow all 16-19 year olds to study free. In England, there is also a Further Education Funding Council (soon to be Learning and Skills Council) concession that allows all unaccompanied asylum-seekers free full-time study.

If a college does charge asylum-seekers overseas students rates, young asylum-seekers might be able to study on courses funded by the European Social Fund. Alternatively, asylum-seekers not in work can study on part-time Scheduled Courses (up to fifteen hours per week direct teaching time and only be charged a 'concessionary' fee). In England the Learning and Skills Council will reimburse colleges who provide such part-time Scheduled Courses for asylum-seekers. A Scheduled Course's legal basis is outlined in the Further and Higher Education Act 1994. Scheduled Courses are listed every two years by the Further Education Funding Council and presently include

- all basic English language, literacy and numeracy
- access courses
- GCSEs and the new A-Levels
- vocational qualifications.

Some unaccompanied children can study full time and claim income support, although the DSS is restrictive about which 16 to 18 year-olds can claim while in relevant education. Relevant education is defined by the DSS as non-advanced further education courses (up to and including A-level) of more than 12 hours per week (*IS (Gen) Regs 13*).

Some 16 to 18 year-olds can obtain income support while in relevant education and will not be required to sign on (*IS (Gen) Regs 13*) and this applies to all unaccompanied refugees – a person who 'has no parents nor any person acting in the place of parents'.

Those who have refugee status and have, within twelve months of arriving in the UK, started an English language course of more than fifteen hours per week are allowed to claim income support. This concession lasts for a maximum of nine months.

In England, the Careers Service is undergoing a period of change, as part of large-scale changes in 16-19 education. Connexions, new support scheme for 13-18 year olds, will bring together the Youth Service and the Careers Service. Vulnerable young people may be provided with salaried 'personal advisors' by Connexions, offering scope for supporting some young refugees.

Access to youth work

Many newly arrived young asylum-seekers spend their first months or years in the UK in temporary housing, often a bed and breakfast hotel or hostel. Conditions are invariably overcrowded and young people may find it difficult to study. Leisure opportunities are also restricted so there is a particular need for youth clubs and summer holiday projects for those living in hotel or hostel accommodation.

Young refugees can find themselves in adult roles in the family, for example, frequently having to act as interpreters and this can cause tensions within the family. Many young refugees also have anxieties about their sexual or cultural identity. Their opinions may be in conflict with their parents'. The process of acceptance into British society may require them to break away from their own cultural roots. Some young refugees are able to live happily in a bicultural environment – behaving like a British person when with local friends and adopting the cultural norms of their homeland when with compatriots. Others find themselves on the fringes of two cultures and not fully accepted by either, and this can affect their self-esteem and sense of identity. Questions about identity can be resolved by meeting with other young people who have similar experiences. The youth club is a place where young people can meet with others in a similar situation.

Positive youth work with refugees requires special skills. A refugee population is geographically mobile and may not be familiar with youth work as a concept. Extra effort is needed to publicise youth clubs, requiring good links with refugee community groups, schools, colleges and houing providers. Youth workers must be sensitive to the needs of refugees, and familiar with working in a multicultural environment. Ideally, youth services should employ some refugees.

In Greater London, it is community groups who are the principal providers of youth work for asylum-seekers and refugees. A research project conducted in 2000 mapped 26 community youth projects, offering a variety of different activities including advocacy and advice, holiday schemes, music and arts, sport, supplementary education and health advice (Norton and Cohen, 2000). A number of young refugees have set up their own projects; these include the Horn of African Youth Scheme and Ethio-Youth England.

Within LEAs and colleges there is little youth work provision targeted at young refugees, although one London LEA has a large and well-funded refugee youth project and a few tertiary colleges in London have targeted programmes. There is one new Connexions partnership in London working with asylum-seekers and refugees. But funding for youth work has become increasingly difficult to obtain and youth work carried out by LEAs has suffered large budgetary cuts in recent years. It is a trend that must be reversed if the social needs of young refugees are to be met.

Bibliography

Gillborn, D. and Youdell, D. (2000) *Rationing Education: policy, practice, reform and equity*, Buckingham: Open University Press

Marshall, T. (1991) *Cultural Aspects of Job-Seeking*, London: Refugee Council

Marshall, T. (1992) *Careers Guidance with Refugees*, London: Refugee Council

McDonald, J. (1995) *Entitled to Learn: a report on young refugees' experiences of access and progression in the UK education system,* London: World University Service

McDonald, J. (1998) 'Refugee Students' Experiences of the UK Educational System' in Rutter, J. and Jones, C. (eds) *Refugee Education: Mapping the Field,* Stoke on Trent: Trentham Books

Norton, R. and Cohen, B. (2000) *Out of Exile: Developing Youth Work with Young Refugees*, London: National Youth Agency

Refugee Council (2000) *Information Service Handbook*, London: Refugee Council

World University Service (2000) *The Refugee Education Handbook*, London: World University Service.

14

Early Years Provision

When I first went to the nursery I didn't like it and I used to try and run out of the door with my Dad. I didn't know what the food was. I didn't know what I was eating. There was a nice teacher there and she helped me. I liked the toys there. Vlora, an Albanian girl now aged 6, remembering her nursery school.

Certain social factors mean that the refugee population in the UK has an exceptionally great need for early years provision. Yet research conducted by the Refugee Council and by the London Borough of Islington's Women's Equality Unit indicates that refugee children are under-represented in most forms of early years provision. This chapter highlights ways that early years providers can address this inequality, in the light of recent Government initiatives such as Early Years Partnerships and Development Plans, and describes positive practice to support young refugee children in early years provision.

The new English early years framework: opportunities for refugees

Wide variations in the amount and nature of early years provision between different local authorities, poor strategic planning at local authority level, inadequate information about what is available, has made access to early years services a lottery. Many parents and carers have effectively been excluded from the job market. As successive Governments have tried to cut unemployment (most recently through the New Deal for the Unemployed), early years provision has been pushed higher up the political agenda. New initiatives such as the National Childcare Strategy and Early Years Development Plans have been introduced, and with them the opportunity to ensure that the specific needs of young refugee children and their carers are met.

The National Childcare Strategy pulls together all recent Government initiatives on childcare, strengthening links between childcare and adult training opportunities. Childcare Partnerships will be created locally to provide childcare and after-school care for working parents. Such provision will be funded by adult training providers, the New Opportunities Lottery Fund, further education colleges and local authorities. Childcare Partnerships will work alongside the new Early Years Development Partnerships convened by local authorities. These Partnerships are obliged to include representatives from early years providers from all sectors, local employers, parents and relevant interest groups. Early Years Development Partnerships will deliver, *inter alia*, the planned expansion of nursery education. All four year olds whose parents want it are now entitled to free nursery education and this entitlement will be extended to three year olds in future.

Early Years Development Partnerships have to draw up Early Years Development Plans. The first were submitted in 1997 and ran from April 1998 until March 2001. Early Years Development Plans will provide for the further expansion of nursery education and the integration of child care and nursery education. Early Years Development Partnerships are required to assess local need, consult widely on the Plans, as well as promoting equality of opportunity for all children. Thus Early Years Partnerships and Plans offer the opportunity to consult with refugee parents and community organisations, assess the needs of refugee children, and develop comprehensive and innovatory services to meet their needs. In 1999, new Early Years Development Plans were required to account for services provided for refugee children: an addition welcomed by refugee charities.

Local authority social service departments are also required by the Department Of Health to draw up Children's Services Plans – a product of collaboration between local authorities, health authorities, the voluntary sector and other appropriate groups. This creates another opportunity for planning for the needs of refugee children.

OFSTED is required to inspect all nurseries and other child care, including child minders and these inspections require an assessment of whether children's particular ethnic or linguistic needs are being met.

Two other DfEE-led initiatives offer opportunities for developing quality early years provision for refugee children. The Sure Start project is targeted at England's poorest 125,000 under threes. Monies will be allocated to innovatory parent education, childcare and healthcare projects. A network of twenty five Early Excellence Centres is being set up, offering quality integrated nursery provision. Integrated nursery provision has been built on the pioneering work of the Dorothy Gardner Centre in Westminster and others. Such centres combine childcare and nursery education with a range of other services for young children and their families, such as toy libraries, parent and toddler groups, holiday play schemes, family literacy classes, English classes for adults, counselling, health visitor clinics, surgeries offering welfare rights and other advice, and support for children with special educational needs. Integrated nurseries may also offer childcare training courses such as the NVQ Level Two and Three courses in

Childcare and Education. As refugee families may have a wide range of social needs and have difficulties accessing statutory services, a range of provision of this kind on one site is a real attempt meet their needs.

Refugee children's needs

Refugee children have a particular need for quality early years provision. The age profile of refugee communities in Britain is younger than the non-refugee population: in 1996 some 77 per cent of asylum applicants were under 35. There are proportionally more refugee children under five than that of the population as a whole. Additionally, a greater proportion of refugees with young children are in further or higher education. Many newly-arrived refugees are attending English classes or obtaining new qualifications. Unpublished research conducted by the Refugee Council in 1989 indicates that some groups of refugee parents are more likely to work unsociable hours than the general population. But while need for childcare is greater, the ability to pay for it is less.

Refugee children also need social contact with other children and adults who speak English. At least 70 per cent of refugee children come from homes where little or no English is spoken. As many refugee families have little social contact with families in the majority community, the nursery or school is often the only place children can use English.

The changes in asylum legislation and policy, described in Chapter Two, have added to refugee families' stress and reduced some parents' ability to cope with young children. The parent who cries in front of their child or is emotionally absent is often a refugee parent. Quality early years provision will give stressed refugee parents a break and can enable them to rebuild their own lives.

The uptake of early years provision

Across the UK, refugee children are under-represented in most forms of early years provision. Despite an expansion of early years provision, this inequality persists. In one London local authority, where refugee children comprise 6.5 per cent of all children, there were only nine refugee children in all its nursery provision in 1997. Reasons for under-representation include

Housing mobility – changes to housing legislation introduced in 1993, 1996 and 1999 mean that asylum-seekers are usually housed in temporary accommodation. Even after an asylum-seeking family receives a positive decision about their case and is granted refugee status or Exceptional Leave to Remain, the family may have to wait months or years until they receive permanent social housing. Many LEA nurseries have waiting lists for places, so families move before a nursery place is available. A place in a social services nursery usually requires a formal assessment of a vulnerable family's needs and high housing mobility may prevent this.

Lack of knowledge of local services – many refugee producing countries in Africa and Asia have little or no early years provision. Asylum-seeking families arriving in the UK seldom know about the range of early years provision available. And since over 70 per cent of asylum-seekers speak little or no English, it is difficult for them to find out about provision. In particular, parents may not know about projects such as parent and toddler groups, one o'clock clubs, play buses and toy libraries.

Poverty – the support arrangements for asylum-seekers introduced in April 2000 mean that adult asylum-seekers are given a cash allowance of £10 per person per week plus vouchers amounting in total to 70 per cent of the level of income support. All children under 18 get a cash allowance of £10 per week and vouchers amounting to 100 per cent of income support. Additionally, the unemployment rate for some refugee groups is very high, for example 75-90 per cent for adult Somali households (LB Tower Hamlet, 1993, LB Barnet, 1995). Many nursery places are beyond refugees' financial means. Even parent and toddler groups that make a small charge might be unaffordable for an asylum-seeking family forced to live on NASS support.

Cultural factors – in some refugee communities infants are always cared for by the mother and her extended family, so putting them in the care of strangers could attract disapproval. Other mothers, particularly those who speak little English, feel uneasy about young children being cared for by people who do not know their language, dietary arrangements, religion or customs.

Inaccessibility – some early years provision may not be accessible for large families without private transport. A part-time nursery place may not be a priority if it requires a one hour journey on public transport.

Unwelcoming services – some types of early years provision, such as playgroups, one o'clock clubs and mother and toddler clubs may be used by a regular group of children and carers who may make 'outsiders' feel unwelcome.

Addressing under-representation

Quality strategic planning by the new Early Years Partnerships, monitoring use provision and outreach and consultation with refugee groups are clearly important in addressing the under-representation of refugee children in early years settings. Below are some policy and practice recommendations for those involved in planning and consultation.

Policy recommendations: planning services.

• All local authorities and Early Years Partnerships in areas where refugees have settled should ensure that there is a person with designated responsibility for refugees.

- The new asylum support consortia and local authority housing departments should make links with health visitors and early years services to ensure that the latter know where to find asylum-seeking and refugee children, to facilitate access to services.

- Where nursery waiting lists operate, local authorities should consider prioritising the most socially excluded refugee children.

- Ethnic monitoring of uptake of early years services is essential and evidence shows poor ethnic monitoring of voluntary sector early years services. But for ethnic monitoring to highlight issues about refugees' use of services, it must use detailed categories (see Chapter Five).

- Child minding offers employment opportunities to refugee women. Local authorities can organise training courses targeted at refugee women, perhaps with English language support. Training should be coupled with a small grants scheme to enable the women to purchase toys and safety equipment.

Policy recommendations – consulting with refugees

It is important to be aware of the shortfalls of consultation. Meetings will be most readily attended by those who have transport and babysitters, while those who most need early years services are most likely to be excluded. Question-naires and written responses to consultations are more likely to come from better educated, English speaking or more confident parents. Those who are consulting refugees need to keep full ethnic data for the local population and the uptake of local services.

Early Years Partnerships and managers of early years services in local authorities should arrange to meet key refugee groups. A start could be made by contacting existing refugee community organisations. Their addresses are usually held by the local authority, race equality councils or by national organisations such as the Refugee Council. However, not all refugees are in contact with community groups. They might not live close to community organisations that could support them. Some refugees may not wish to be in contact with compatriots they do not know or trust. Some refugee women have also indicated in surveys that com-munity organisations can be very male-dominated and unlikely to be concerned about 'women's issues' such as childcare. Alternative methods of consultation include contacting refugee parents via health visitors or schools.

Consultation meetings should be held in venues that feel safe and welcoming. Care should be taken to avoid all religious holidays and festivals. Transport and crèche facilities should be considered when consulting refugee parents of small children. Publicity material about consultation meetings should be translated if needed and interpreters might be needed at meetings. Information about early years provision should be available in key community languages.

Policy recommendations – the voluntary sector

Voluntary sector organisations are an integral part of early years provision in the UK, offering a wide range of services. Some also lobby for better early years services or provide training. About five refugee community or small refugee organisations presently run playgroups or sessional nurseries – a very small proportion – although there are many parent and toddler groups run by refugee community organisations. Interest is growing among them in developing services for young children, prompted by employment training programmes aimed at refugees and the New Deal for the Unemployed, but they will need considerable support from early years teams in order to achieve these aims.

Policy recommendations – voluntary sector playgroups and toy libraries

There is much evidence to suggest that these are under-utilised by refugee children (for example LB Islington, 1997), possibly because refugee parents are unaware of them, or because playgroups can feel unwelcoming to newcomers. Voluntary sector playgroups and toy libraries should be encouraged to keep ethnic data on the use of their services. Local authority early years teams and local Pre-School Learning Alliances should be helping voluntary sector groups to publicise their services. Local Early Years Partnerships should be ensuring that the training needs of play workers are met. The play resources and books used by such projects should reflect the cultural background of local children. As all voluntary sector early years provision has to be registered and inspected, inspections can be used to push for changes in practice that ensure that the needs of refugee children are met.

Policy recommendations – training

Voluntary sector and private training providers may be involved in training early years staff. A few, such as Praxis, are offering child-care courses targeted at refugee women. Arguably more training providers should be doing this. Training providers may also run crèches for those attending their courses. Again, all too few do so. Child-minding itself offers work opportunities for refugee women. Refugee community organisations and local authority early years teams should be working together to recruit, train and register child-minders from refugee communities. As attitudes to issues such as discipline and toilet training differ between (and within) ethnic groups, training and support for refugee child minders should be sensitive to the different backgrounds of refugee women. Child minders may need access to funds to enable them to buy pushchairs, toys and safety equipment. A refugee woman living in accommodation that is below the standard for child minding registration could possibly pair up with another woman in more suitable housing.

Improving practice for refugee children in nurseries

Central to Early Years Development Plans should be the development of expertise in meeting the needs of refugee children in local authority and community nursery provision. Currently the awareness of refugee children's backgrounds and specific needs varies from nursery to nursery. Many of the principles of good early years practice naturally apply to refugee children too, including a commitment to equal opportunities, parental involvement and play as a child's right.

Specifically, refugee children need nurseries that

- can meet their psychological needs, by, for example using play to help a child settle
- respond to their language needs
- can challenge racism and promote cultural diversity
- involve parents who may not be confident in speaking English
- can support families who may be experiencing stress and economic deprivation.

Practice issues: psychological needs

Refugee children's psychosocial needs are discussed in Chapter Nine. The youngest are a psychologically vulnerable group. They are more dependent on the care of their parents or other adults and any event that disrupts the quality of childcare is likely to affect them severely. In her work with children evacuated in the Second World War or who lived through the Blitz, Anna Freud observed that it was not so much the actual experience of war or its material privations which adversely affected young children but rather the degree of emotional stress shown by parents and other significant carers. Torture, armed conflict and the stresses of being an asylum-seeker in the UK can make parents emotionally unresponsive to their children, with major consequences for those children. Very young refugee children may also have an incomplete understanding of death, persecution and exile and come to believe that exile is 'their fault'.

As discussed in Chapter Nine, refugee children manifest their distress in many different ways. For very young children the effects of a traumatic experience may be manifest in their play. Although there are cultural differences in the way that children play, certain aspects transcend cultural variations. Refugee children who have survived persecution and are experiencing distress may display some of the following factors in their play:

- a preoccupation with war and violence
- an identification with the oppressor: a child may re-enact war, taking the role of the oppressor, perhaps being violent to other children

- aggressiveness in play
- rigid and/or emotionless play, with a lack of elaboration of their experiences, or simply being unable to play
- characteristic drawings, showing violence or featuring very small children.

Play can indicate how the young child is coping with the refugee experience. It can also be a means of healing. Play offers children the chance to explore reality and make sense of the world and their reactions to it. It also offers children the chance to gain confidence through interacting with peers and exploring their environment. As many refugee children have lost self-esteem and trust in peers and adults, play can help them regain lost confidence and make new trusting relationships with adults or other children.

To facilitate play as a healing process, a key worker system should be put in place. The key worker system enables a child to develop a close and trusting relationship with one adult, crucial for children who may have been let down by adults or have lost parents or other carers. Consequently, early years workers need to think about how they can promote play, to facilitate children's healing. A starting point is to look at what a child needs to play, such as:

- *space* – children who have spent time in refugee camps or hiding in a cellar may not have had the space to play in the past. In the UK, refugee children who are living in bed and breakfast hotels or hostels may still be very confined
- *materials* – items such as water or plastic containers, as well as manufactured toys
- *time* – play evolves and develops over time
- *favourable attitudes* to play from adults around them.

Asylum-seeking children living in a bed and breakfast hotel with stressed or emotionally absent parents are likely to be missing most or all of what they need for play. A meaningful way to support such children would be to organise a parent and toddler group, crèche or visits to local play facilities.

Early years workers can then establish healing play. For example, in one Save the Children project in Bosnia-Hercegovina, a worker noticed that during free play a group of children sat in the home corner looking subdued. Then they would pick up toy telephones, make a call, become very agitated and throw the telephone on the ground. The early years worker made no attempt to stop this drama, as she felt that the children were playing out scenes they had witnessed and needed to interpret. Over time, the children gave her a role in their play, whereupon she introduced new props, so that children could develop their play.

The following types of play may be useful for refugee children

- sensory and exploratory play
- drama, including mime, puppetry, the use of miniature figures and mask-making which allows children to play out feelings and problems
- painting and drawing
- opportunities for free play, particularly in home corners, allows children to use play to interpret stressful events that have taken place in their lives
- using stories, followed by discussion, acting and play. For example, *A Bear Called Paddington* could be used to help children act out a story-line about the theme of being new.

Practice issues: language

Over 70 per cent of refugee children come from homes where little or no English is spoken so the nursery could be their first contact with the English language. Developing a language policy in a nursery is crucial to meeting the needs of refugee children. Language is also a key component in the building of personal identity. If children's home language is not present or valued in the community in which they live, it is hard for them to develop positive self-esteem. Good practice includes

- ensuring that staff receive training on meeting the language needs of children
- informing parents about the nursery language policy and stressing to parents the importance of speaking and reading to children in their home language
- finding out from families which languages are spoken at home
- trying to employ bilingual early years workers who speak relevant languages
- learning a few words in relevant languages, particularly greetings. Find out from parents how children will tell you when they need to go to the toilet or when they are thirsty
- purchasing resources such as bilingual tapes and books
- making labels and signs in relevant languages
- encouraging parents to come in and read stories or teach songs
- letting children teach staff and other children some words in their home languages
- remembering that children can understand what is said before they can express themselves fluently. It is important to keep communicating with children and ensuring that their environment is language-rich
- being a good language model by speaking slowly to children, but in a natural voice.
- encouraging productive language such as hellos and good-byes.

Practice issues: challenging racism

Research indicates that children as young as two or three distinguish between different skin colours and attach different social values to them (see Derman Sparks, 1989). Children may reject a black doll, for example. Many of the ideas young children develop about ethnicity are in line with the views of their adult carers. Sometimes children may use racist terms of abuse, perhaps not knowing their full meaning or potential impact. So if children are to develop positive views about ethnic diversity, anti-racist and multicultural education has to start in the early years.

Nurseries should examine their recruitment practices to ensure that staff are representative of the community. Early years workers also need to be confident in dealing with racist name calling and fights among young children. Verbal abuse should not be ignored. A useful way of dealing with abuse is to ask the children how they would feel if they were spoken to that way. Nurseries should not ignore physical differences in clothing or skin colour but be open and positive about people's differences. One of the best ways of promoting diversity is to ensure that stories and dolls reflect different ethnic groups.

The early years are an important time for learning the social skills and values needed in adult life. The curriculum should enable children to explore values such as sharing and respect. It can be used to examine issues such as moving, fear, justice, being new and ethnic diversity, for example

- telling children folk-tales from refugees' countries of origin and inviting in parents or others from the community to tell stories

- using resources that depict refugees (and other minority groups) doing every-day things like shopping and cooking. Teachers should acquire resources and examples from a wide range of cultures: dual language books should be pur-chased and black dolls used alongside white dolls. But it is important to look at resources critically. The Working Group Against Racism in Children's Resources (1990) has published a useful guide for the selection of resources for young children. Teachers may want to develop their own checklist to ensure that resources do not perpetuate bias or stereotypes

- celebrating Muslim, Jewish and Hindu festivals as well as Christmas and Easter

- children should be encouraged to use their home language. There should be labels and signs in relevant languages. Teaching all the children songs in the various languages of the children in the group helps to celebrate bi-lingualism.

Practice issues: parental involvement

Parental involvement is essential in early years education but research conducted by bodies such as the Refugee Council and the University of Warwick has shown that refugee parents are less likely have meaningful involvement in their child's education than most other groups. Parental involvement is examined in Chapter Eleven and in the case study below.

Some local authorities such as Camden and Tower Hamlets have produced written information, translated into relevant languages, explaining how parents or carers can work with the nursery to help young children learn at home (see Further Resources). But these leaflets are no substitute for talking to parents about how they think they can help their child learn and should be used to back up advice.

Case Study: Enfield Under Fives Home School Liaison Service

The project is run by the Education Department of the London Borough of Enfield, and works with ethnic minority communities within its boundaries. The project was initially funded in 1995 by Section 11 and by the London Borough of Enfield. In 1998, responsibility for funding fell solely on the local authority as the funding criteria of the new Ethnic Minority Achievement Grant were too restrictive. It has now been granted Sure Start funds to work in one part of Enfield and is bidding to be included in a new Early Excellence Centre.

The project employs three teachers, seventeen bilingual support workers and a part-time educational psychologist. It works in nursery and reception classes in 26 schools in Enfield. Bilingual Support Workers help children in these classes learn English. The teachers and bilingual support workers speak twelve languages between them, including Amharic, Swahili, Tamil and Turkish.

The project provides pre-school programmes for children and families in the year before they start school, making regular home visits, taking books, toys and games. Play sessions and toy libraries are also provided for these children in their pre-school year. The Under Fives Home School Liaison Service runs a multicultural library and toy library loan service. It liaises with schools, health visitors, social services nurseries, playgroups and community groups. Project staff also visit children's homes and community organisations to explain about the range of early years provision available in Enfield.

The educational psychologist runs a drop-in surgery for teachers, bilingual support workers, community groups parents and anyone working with children who are causing concern, where they can discuss strategies for supporting the children. She also carries out individual assessments.

Case Study: Praxis

Praxis is a voluntary organisation working with refugee and migrant communities in London. It offers educational advice and has received funding from the National Lottery to run a childcare course for refugee and migrant women.

Praxis has organised a course leading to the City and Guilds Certificate in Sessional Crèche work, moderated by a further education college in Newcastle, qualifying students to be sessional crèche workers. Unlike many access courses, the City and Guilds Certificate in Sessional Crèche Work follows an NVQ format and students can go on to study for an NVQ in Child Care and Education. This part-time course runs for six months and includes a work placement. Students also have to prepare a portfolio of work for assessment. The women on the course come from a wide range of backgrounds; while all speak good English, some do need help in reading and writing. The course offers the scope for giving some individual English language support.

Praxis also runs other training courses for refugee women. It is hoping to open a nursery for its trainees at a later date, to enable more refugee women to attend training.

Bibliography

Brown, B. (1998) *Unlearning Discrimination in the Early Years*, Stoke on Trent: Trentham Books

Cattanach, A. (1995) *Play Therapy: Where the Sky Meets the Underworld,* London: Jessica Kingsley

City of Westminster (1998) Consultation Document of Integrated Nursery Settings in Westminster. Unpublished local authority document

Commission for Racial Equality (1996) *From Cradle to School: a practical guide to racial equality in the early years*, London: Commission for Racial Equality

Daycare Trust (1995) *Reaching First Base: guidelines of good practice on meeting the needs of refugee children from the Horn of Africa*, London: Daycare Trust

Derman Sparks, L. (1989) *The Anti-Bias Curriculum: tools for empowering young children*, Washington DC: National Association for the Education of Young Children

Early Years Trainers Anti Racist Network (1994) *Children without Prejudice: a video pack*, Liverpool: EYTARN

Hyder, T. (1998) 'Supporting Refugee Children in the Early Years' in Rutter, J and Jones, C. (eds) *Refugee Education: Mapping the Field*, Stoke on Trent: Trentham Books

Lane, J. (1998) *Planning for Excellence; Implementing the DfEE Guidance for the Equal Opportunity Strategy in Early Years Development Plans, and introducing a Framework for Equality*, Liverpool: Early Years Trainers Anti-Racist Network

Lynch, E. and Hanson, M. (1992) *Developing Cross-cultural Competence: a guide for working with young children*, London: Jessica Kingsley

Praxis (1998) Unpublished research on childcare provision in refugee community organsiations, London: Praxis

Refugee Council and Save the Children (2001) In *Safe Hands: a video training pack for those working with young refugee children,* London: Refugee Council and Save the Children

Rutter, J and Hyder, T. (1998) *Refugee Children in the early years: issues for policy makers and providers*, London: Refugee Council and Save the Children

Siraj-Blatchford, I. (1994) *The Early Years: laying the foundation for racial equality*, Stoke on Trent: Trentham Books.

PART THREE
Refugee Groups in the UK

■ Refugees from Afghanistan

Over 18,000 Afghan refugees have fled to the UK since 1979. In 1998 Afghanistan's population was 23 million. The capital is Kabul.

Ethnic groups: Afghanistan is a multi-ethnic society and there is an ethnic dimension to the conflict. The largest group are the Pushtuns (Pathans), comprising about 38 per cent of the population. They live in eastern and southern Afghanistan (and also in Pakistan). Also living in eastern Afghanistan are the Baluch. Three major ethnic groups live in northern Afghanistan: the Turkmen, Uzbeks and Tajiks. Central Afghanistan is peopled by Hazara, Aimaq and Nuristani people. Central control of power has always been weak in Afghanistan. Afghans owe their first loyalty to their family, and then to the clan and ethnic group to which they belong.

Languages: Pushto and Persian (Dari) are the two official languages. Pushto is spoken by about 60 per cent of the population, mostly in southern and eastern Afghanistan and is the first language of the Pushtuns. Pushto is also spoken in the North West Frontier Province of Pakistan, although with dialectal variations in pronunciation, vocabulary, spelling and grammar. Pushto is an Indo-European language, mostly closely related to Persian. It is written from right to left in the Perso-Arabic script, with a number of additional letters to accommodate sounds not found in Persian or Arabic.

Persian is spoken by about 30 per cent of the population, mostly in western Afghanistan and this dialect of the Persian language is usually called Dari. There are major differences between the spoken Dari dialects of Afghanistan and many of the Farsi dialects of Iran although some Farsi dialects are similar to some Dari dialects. Generally, a speaker of Dari would not be able to communicate easily with a Farsi speaker. A standard written form of Persian is used in Iran and Afghanistan, although there are differences in the written form used in Iran and Afghanistan. Persian is written from right to left in the Perso-Arabic script. It uses 32 letters, all primarily used as consonants although four have secondary uses as vowel sounds. As in Arabic, other vowel sounds are indicated as marks, known as points, placed above or below the letters. Modern Persian books for adults omit the points, but schoolbooks use point marks.

Tadzhik is spoken in north west Afghanistan, on the border with Tajikistan. Most linguists consider Tadzhik to be a dialect of Persian. In the Republic of Tajikistan this language is written in the Cyrillic script, but in Afghanistan it is still written using the Perso-Arabic script. Hazara and Aimaq, spoken in central Afghanistan, are also considered dialects of Persian. Uzbek is spoken by over one million people in Afghanistan and is also the national language of Uzbekistan. It belongs to the Altaic language family. Originally written in Perso-Arabic, this is still the case in Afghanistan, but the Soviet Union Uzbek was later written in the Cyrillic script. Turkmen is spoken by about 500,000 people in north west Afghanistan and is also the national language of Turkmeniya. It is an Altaic language, closely related to Turkish. In Turkmeniya it is written using the Cyrillic script, but in Afghanistan it uses Perso-Arabic letters. Uzbek, Persian and Pushto have an extensive literature, in the form of poetry and some modern novels. Afghan Sikhs speak Punjabi as their home language.

Names: The naming system differs between ethnic groups. But most Afghans have two or three names: a first name, followed by the father's first name, and then sometimes a family or descriptive name. The first names used are usually Islamic. The descriptive name can relate to a person's characteristics or their place of origin. In western Europe this descriptive name is often used as a family name. Thus a woman will take her husband's descriptive name when she marries. Otherwise a woman will keep her two names after marriage.

Religion: Almost all Afghans are Muslims. The majority are Sunni Muslims, although about 15 per cent are Shi'a Muslims and another two per cent are Ismaeli Muslims. There are also small populations of Sikhs, Hindus and Jews, although many of them have fled abroad in recent years. The exodus of Afghan refugees to the UK has included a number of Afghan Sikhs, mostly from Kabul and Jalalabad.

The Sunni Muslim Taliban emerged in 1995, as an organisation of fundamentalist Muslim students who drew most support from the Pushto population. Many of the Taliban had been refugees in Pakistan, where they attended *madrassah* run by fundamentalist clerics. The Taliban's Islam has also been influenced by the Wahabi Movement of Saudi Arabia. Its founder, Mohamed Ibn Abd-al-Wahab interpreted the Koran in its fundamentalist form. In Afghanistan, the Taliban have followed this literal interpretation of Islam, leading to extensive human rights violations. The Taliban's religious police, supported by the *shari'a* (the code of Islamic law) are empowered to search houses and carry out physical punishment such as amputations and beatings. The treatment of women by the Taliban has been brutal. They have been largely excluded from employment, although some women are now allowed to work in hospitals under strict control. Women are obliged to wear the *burqa*, a garment that covers the entire body. They are prohibited from leaving the home without a male relative. In 1998, the Taliban prohibited women receiving medical treatment in the absence of her husband, brother or father. As many Afghan women have lost all family members, restrictions on female employment and healthcare are particularly harsh.

The Taliban have also banned certain recreational activities such as videos, music, kite-flying and chess. Dolls and soft toys such as teddy bears are also banned, due the Taliban's injunctions against the representation of living beings.

Shi'a Muslims faced persecution in Afghanistan. Most Shi'a are Hazara, from central Afghanistan. One of the elements in the recent conflict is that the Hazara wished to claim a larger share of power in Afghanistan.

Shi'a Muslims are those who believe that Ali and his descendants are the leaders and successors to Mohammed. Ali was the Prophet Mohammed's cousin and husband of his daughter Fatima. (Sunni Muslims believe that the Prophet Mohammed had no successors.) Ali was killed at Kerbala (now in Iraq), and this is a major place of pilgrimage for Shi'a. About 12 per cent of the world's Muslims are Shi'a, the rest being Sunni, or belonging to other smaller sects. Sunni and Shi'a Muslims worship at different mosques. The day of Ashura, marking the death of Husain, the prophet's grandson and another Shi'a leader, is an important Shi'a festival, marked by processions.

Ismaeli Muslims believe that Karim Aga Khan is a direct descendent of the Prophet Mohammed. They face persecution in Afghanistan because radical Muslim clerics consider them heretics or non-Muslims.

Education system: State education in Afghanistan has been severely disrupted because of fighting and is in a state of near collapse. In addition the Taliban have severely restricted the education of girls and prohibited the employment of most female teachers

Primary education is meant to start starts at six or seven, and last for six years. The medium of instruction is either Pushto or Dari, depending on the part of the country. English was taught as a second language in the latter part of primary education but this has been largely discontinued by the Taliban. Koranic Arabic is taught in all schools.

There is an entrance examination for admission to secondary education, which is not compulsory. Secondary education can last for six years and is divided into two three-year cycles. From

13-16, pupils study at a middle school (*Maktabeh Motevaseteh*) and then spend another three years at a high school (*Doreyeh Aali*). At 19, students sit for the Baccaluria examination, considered equivalent to GCSE. Some secondary school students are able to study technical subjects such as teaching or agriculture.

Boys and girls study different subjects. In 1990, gender segregation was introduced in all schools. As Taliban took control of Afghanistan, they shut girl's schools and decreed that girls should receive no education after the age of eight. Some parent sent girls to Iran for their education, others organised informal home schools. These were tolerated by the Taliban in various parts of the country until the Taliban shut more than 100 of them in June 1998.

A few girls' primary schools remain open, teaching girls for one or two years. There are also some Taliban-approved Koranic schools for girls. In parts of Afghanistan not controlled by the Taliban, there are more opportunities for girls. Nevertheless, over 90 per cent of girls and 65 per cent of boys are not enrolled at any school. Most children in rural areas drop out of school, if they attend at all. The literacy rate is 12 per cent for men and three per cent for women.

Economy: Afghanistan is a mountainous country. Its economy is agricultural, and the main crops are wheat, fruit, vegetable and livestock. Little has changed in the countryside during the last 500 years. The rural and urban economy has been disrupted by war and Afghanistan is one of the world's poorest countries.

A chronology of events: The country which is now Afghanistan has been colonised by many different empires in the last 2,000 years. From 1767 to 1973, Afghanistan was ruled by a succession of tribal leaders and kings. Governments ruled from Kabul, although central control has never been strong. In 1883 Afghanistan's present borders were drawn. At this time Afghanistan was a neutral country between two powerful empires: the British and Russian Empires.

1919 – A new government comes to power in Afghanistan and attempts a programme of modernisation. It tries to abolish the veil for women. This so angers many traditional leaders, that no government dares try further reforms until the 1950s.

1933 – King Zaher Shah comes to the throne. He introduces a new constitution and land reforms. Political parties are legalised.

1973 – King Zaher Shah is deposed. Mohammed Daoud, the King's cousin and former Prime Minister installs himself as president. His new government initially includes members of all political parties but as time passes opposition is suppressed. Some opposition politicians flee the country.

1978 – Mohammed Daoud is killed in a coup. The People's Democratic Party of Afghanistan (PDPA) comes to power. This party follows a communist ideology, and draws most support from urban areas. The new government starts an ambitious programme of reforms, targeted at the poor. There are major land reforms, and a literacy campaign in launched. Although the reforms sound good, they are hastily and insensitively carried out. Many people oppose the reforms and some use violence to stop them being implemented. At the same time the PDPA becomes divided by bitter arguments. Those who oppose the PDPA are arrested, killed or have to leave the country. Between 1977 and 1980 over 200,000 people flee.

1979 – Afghanistan's President is killed by members of a PDPA faction. Hafizullah Amin becomes the new president, and human rights violations worsen. Armed resistance to the PDPA grows stronger; these fighters are known as *mujahideen*. By the end of 1979 the PDPA appears to be losing control. On 27 December 1979 Soviet troops enter Afghanistan.

1980-82 – After the Soviet invasion the *mujahideen* grow more organised. They are supplied with arms by the USA, Saudi Arabia, France and the UK. Fighting worsens, and by 1982 3,300,000 refugees have fled to Pakistan and 2,850,000 to Iran. Nearly 5,000,000 Afghans are internally displaced. Life for refugees is very hard with many basics being in short supply. By **1986**, the *mujahideen* control much of the countryside, while the Afghan Government controls urban areas. Fighting is worst in rural areas, and nearly 30 per cent of Afghan villages are destroyed.

1989 – Soviet troops withdraw from Afghanistan. The Afghan Government, led by President Najibullah, is expected to fall within weeks. But it survives, partly because the *mujahideen* are not united in their opposition. Fighting continues, especially around Kabul, Kandahar and Jalalabad.

1992-94 – The Government of Najibullah falls in April 1992 and the President takes shelter in the UN compound in Kabul. But the *mujahideen* are not united, and cannot form a replacement government that enjoys the support of the majority. Rabbani eventually becomes president, but has no power. Fighting breaks out between different factions. It is concentrated in Kabul and other parts of eastern Afghanistan. By 1993 there is intense fighting between four factions in Kabul. The population drops from 2,000,000 to about 500,000. There are no public services, and the city is on the brink of famine. The *mujahideen* are divided along ethnic, religious, ideological and personal lines. Refugees continue to return from Iran. But the return of refugees from Pakistan is halted by fighting.

1994-1996 – A new political group emerges called the Taliban. They are mostly young Pushto speaking men, many of them educated in fundamentalist *madrassah* while in exile in Pakistan. They soon take control of much of Afghanistan. They capture Jalalabad, and Kabul in September 1996. One of their first acts is to enter the UN compound in Kabul and hang ex-President Najibullah. After the fall of Kabul, Afghanistan is effectively partitioned. The Taliban control all the predominantly Pushtun areas of the country, plus the major cities of Kabul and Herat. Opposition forces control most of the non-Pushtun areas and are led by General Dostam and Commander Masoud. General Dostam has his stronghold in the northern town of Mazar-I-Sharif and draws his support from the Uzbeks and other peoples who live in northern Afghanistan. Commander Masoud draws his support from Tadzhiks, some ex-communists and people who believe in democracy. Throughout late 1996 and 1997 there is fierce fighting between the Taliban and anti-Taliban forces. The latter form the United Islamic Front for the Salvation of Afghanistan and base their headquarters in Mazar-I-Sharif.

1998 – The main battlegrounds move north of Kabul. The city enjoys a break in fighting. While not supporting the Taliban, many ordinary people welcome this relief. The severe interpretation of *shari'a* causes severe hardships for some groups, particularly girls and women. Although the Taliban control nearly 90 per cent of the country, there is no functioning central government. Instead, local Taliban commanders have considerable discretion and the harshness of interpretation of *shari'a* can vary from area to area. Peace talks between representatives of the Taliban and opposition forces collapse. There is fighting in Mazar-I-Sharif between ethnic Uzbeks and the shi'a-dominated forces of the Hib-I-Wahdat. Then in August 1998 the Taliban capture Mazar-I-Sharif. They massacre an estimated 8,000 men, women and children in revenge for the killings of 2,000 Taliban in 1997. Most of those who are murdered are ethnic Hazara.

1999 – Fighting between the Taliban and opposition forces continues. Amnesty International issues a report on the detention and killing of political personalities, thus drawing attention to a new wave of assassinations of moderate Afghans. At the end of 1999 some 2,600,000 Afghans are refugees and about 600,000 internally displaced.

2000 – An Ariana Afghan Airlines plan is hijacked to London Stanstead. A number of those on board claim political asylum in the UK, amid much negative media coverage.

2001 – Over 500,000 displaced Afghans are at risk of famine.

Afghan Refugees in the UK – Statistics

Year	Applications for Asylum	Refugee status as percentages	ELR	Refusal
1993	315	1	76	23
1994	325	25	5	70
1995	580	2	93	5
1996	675	5	85	10
1997	1,085	3	87	10
1998	1,295	2	94	4
1999	3,975	1	92	7

For many years Germany, the USA and Canada were the major western destinations of Afghan refugees. Small numbers of asylum-seekers have been arriving since the 1970s but in 1997 figures increased greatly and the community here now numbers about 18,000 people. Most Afghan refugees live in Greater London with the biggest communities in the London Boroughs of Brent, Ealing, Hounslow, Richmond and Westminster. Since the local government and Home Office dispersal programme, smaller Afghan communities have been growing up elsewhere in the UK.

The community is very diverse and its numbers include

- refugees who arrived in 1973 after the coup d'etat
- opponents of the PDPA government
- people associated with the PDPA government who fled after 1992
- opponents of the various factions of *mujahideen*
- Sikhs and Ismaeli Muslims
- Shi'a Muslims, mostly ethnic Hazara, who had made their homes in cities like Kabul
- refugees who have come into conflict with the Taliban including people associated with international aid organisations.

Almost all the refugees who have arrived since 1992 have experienced high intensity warfare, the economic deprivations of armed conflict and intolerable violations of human rights. The refugees express diverse political and religious opinions and some are observant Muslims, others are not. Almost all Afghan refugees are from urban areas. Most worked as professionals or merchants in Afghanistan. Many are highly qualified. Until recently almost all Afghan asylum-seekers were afforded refugee status or Exceptional Leave to Remain in the UK. But since March 2000 the proportion of positive asylum decisions has fallen dramatically. This is undoubtedly a political decision, made after the hijack of an Afghan plan to London Stanstead.

A number of Afghan refugee children in UK schools have had their education interrupted. Others may have attended private English medium schools in Pakistan before coming to the UK, so children's previous educational experience can be very varied.

There are several active community organisations in London and elsewhere.

Bibliography

Amnesty International (1997) *Women in Afghanistan*, London: Amnesty International

Marsden, P. (1998) *The Taliban: War Religion and the New Order in Afghanistan*, London: Zed Books

Minority Rights Group (1992) *Afghanistan: a nation of minorities*, London: Minority Rights Group

Refugee Council (1998) *Persian and English School Words*, London: Refugee Council

Ruthven, M. (1984) *Islam in the World,* London: Penguin

School of Oriental and African Studies (1989) *Courtesy and Survival in Pushto and Dari*, London: SOAS.

■ Refugees from Albania

Growing numbers of asylum applicants from Albania have been lodged with the Home Office, some 1,310 in 1999 alone. Albania is the poorest country in Europe. Its north east corner is poorest of all and it is in this region that traditional social attitudes to women's freedom still apply.

After 400 years of Ottoman rule, Albania gained its independence in 1912. In 1928 President Zogu retitled himself King Zog. The Italians invaded Albania in 1939 and incorporated it and much of Kosova into 'Greater Albania'. In 1943, following Italy's truce with the Allied Powers, Nazi Germany invaded Albania. The Germans were resisted by communist-led partisans and, following German withdrawal in 1944, the National Liberation Front took control of the country. From 1945 until 1985 Albania was led by Enver Hoxha, who pursued rigid communist policies and isolated Albania from much of the outside world. Religious activity was banned and all political opposition brutally repressed. Ramiz Alia succeeded Enver Hoxha. The Albanian Government slowly began to distance itself from Hoxha's legacy. Following the collapse of other communist regimes in eastern Europe, the pace of reform quickened. In December 1990 independent political parties were legalised. At this time thousands of Albanians commandeered ships and sailed to the Italian port of Brindisi where most were interned and returned to Albania. The first multi-party elections took place in 1991. The communists won 60 per cent of the vote in an election that was criticised for being unfair. Continuing unrest, however, forced the resignation of the communist government and in June 1991 a new 'Government of National Stability' was formed. In 1992, elections to the new Assembly were won by the Democratic Party of Albania (DPA). Sali Berisha of the DPA was elected President.

In spring 1997 much of Albania experienced a breakdown in law and order, following the collapse of pyramid selling schemes. Some 1,600 people died in the violence (*Amnesty International*, 1998). A former communist (the Communist Party had been renamed the Socialist Party of Albania) was appointed head of government. In elections held later in 1997, Rexhep Mejdani, a SPA member, was elected as president with Fatos Nano as head of government. But the DPA boycotted parliament from October 1997 to March 1998, citing unfair practices by the ruling SPA.

Much of the countryside in northern Albania still lies outside the control of government. Local warlords and criminals exert control of these areas. Albanian gangs have become involved in the trafficking of drugs and people. Political opposition has been subject to harassment by both police and the national intelligence service. DPA activists remain at risk. Some journalists and human rights activist have also faced harassment. Another group at risk are those who expose corruption or the activities of criminal gangs.

As a consequence of the breakdown of law and order in northern Albania and the resultant worsening of the economic situation, there has been a population movement to the south. Many of the displaced are living in shanty towns around southern cities such as Tirana. Albanians have also moved abroad.

Asylum-seekers and migrants leave by sea, to Italy or make illegal journeys by land. In the UK a small number of Albanian asylum-seekers have masqueraded as Kosova Albanians in the hope of gaining refugee status, although dialectal differences between Albania and Kosova make this deception difficult. This practice has contributed to tension between those who have left Kosova and Albania in some UK schools, colleges and hostels. About 3,000 Albanian nationals live in the UK, in contrast to some 29,000 Kosovan Albanians. Many fled during or after the Second World War and were opposed to the rule of Enver Hoxha. More recently, Albanian asylum-seekers have swelled the community; their numbers including Albanian Roma.

Bibliography
Vickers, M. (1999) *The Albanians: a modern history*, London: IB Tauris.

■ Refugees from Algeria

Since 1992 over 7,000 Algerian refugees have fled to the UK.

In 1998 Algeria's population was 30 million, of whom 50 per cent live in urban areas. The capital is Algiers.

Ethnic groups: About 74 per cent of the population identify themselves as Arabs. The main minority ethnic group are the Berbers, who comprise about 25 per cent of the population. The Berber population is concentrated in the east and south of Algeria in the mountains of Kabylia, Chaouia, the Mzab and the Sahara. Their migration into Algeria predates that of the movement of Arabic speaking peoples. Their home language and culture is distinct from that of the Arabic-speaking majority. The Tuaregs are nomadic Berbers living in southern Algeria.

Languages: Arabic is the official language of Algeria. About 15 per cent of the population speak one of the Berber languages. French is also widely spoken by the educated urban elite.

Arabic belongs to the Semitic sub-group of the Hamito-Semitic language family and is mostly closely related to Maltese and modern Hebrew. The Arabic language was confined to the Arabian peninsula until the 7th century AD. Later the expansion of Islam carried the language across the Middle East and to North Africa. The Arabic language uses 28 letters, mostly consonants. Vowel sounds are indicated using marks, known as points, above or below the letters. Most modern Arabic books for adults omit the points but schoolbooks and religious texts use them. Arabic-speaking children who are learning English will have to learn to use the vowels as an integral part of words. Arabic is written from right to left in Arabic script. Arabic nouns and adjectives are either masculine or feminine. Like all Semitic languages, Arabic is characterised by triconsonantal roots. For example *kitab* (book) is based on the root consonants 'k', 't' and 'b'. From these root letters other words can be made, for example *anna aktob* – I write, *maktub* – letter, *maktaba* – bookshop and *katib* – clerk.

Classical Arabic – the language of the Koran – is taught in *madrassah* and in schools in Algeria. A modern, simplified form of classical Arabic, known as Modern Standard Arabic is used as a written language throughout the Arab world. Modern Standard Arabic is the language of government and the medium of education in Algeria. When two Arabic speakers from different countries meet, they will generally converse in Modern Standard Arabic. Young children and adults who have not been to school will be unable to speak or write Modern Standard Arabic. In UK schools, a young child from Algeria will find it hard to understand one from Iraq speaking colloquial Arabic.

Spoken Arabic varies from country to country. The different spoken dialects can be divided into two families: western Arabic and eastern Arabic. Western Arabic dialects are spoken in Algeria (also in Morocco, Tunisia and western Libya) and are most closely related to the spoken Arabic of Tunisia. Major cities such as Algiers, Constantine and Oran are identified as centres of their own urban dialects that in turn differ from dialects spoken in rural Algeria. There are sometimes mutual difficulties in comprehension between different Algerian dialects.

Not all Algerian refugees in the UK speak Arabic as their home language. There are small numbers of Berber refugees, mostly living in London, who use one of the Berber languages/dialects at home. About 14 per cent of the population of Algeria use Berber as their main language. There is a linguistic debate as to whether the Berber languages, sometimes known collectively as Tamazight, constitutes a single language plus a number of dialects, or are separate languages. Berber languages belong to the Hamito-Semitic language family, but are not closely related to Arabic. The most widely spoken Berber language in Algeria is Kabyle. Other important dialects are Chaouia and Tamazight. The latter has been used to develop a standardised Berber language. Berber languages are primarily spoken languages, although an ancient Berber script survives among some Tuareg. Standardised Tamarzight is taught in a few schools; there are also Berber radio and television programmes. In 1998, after pressure from Islamic parties, a law was implemented in Algeria to impose the use of Arabic in all government departments and in business. This caused widespread protest among the Berber population. Many Algerian refugee families speak French.

Names: Algerians may use an Islamic naming system of a first personal name, followed by the father's name and sometimes the grandfather's name. Alternatively, a person may have a first personal name, followed by a family name, or a name that denotes their place of origin.

Religion: Some 99 per cent of the population are Sunni Muslim. Some Algerians may be secular in their outlook while others are observant Muslims. Throughout the 1980s, high unemployment, inflation and political discontent led to the growth of Islamic fundamentalism as an ideological alternative. The *Front Islamique de Salut* (FIS) was established in 1989. Originally organised through mosques and Islamic organisations, the FIS promised social justice and better welfare services and gained its support from the urban poor. Between 1992 and 1998, the FIS organised armed opposition and claimed responsibility for attacks on Algerian police, armed forces and civilians. The *Group Islamique Armée* (GIA), an extreme Islamic militia, has not called a ceasefire.

Algerian refugees living in the UK reflect these religious and political differences. Many are secular and middle class whose lifestyle may make them targets of the Islamic militia. Some Algerian refugees have fled to the UK because they are associated with the Islamic groups and fear persecution by the Algerian security forces and they are likely to be observant Muslims.

Education system: Education is compulsory from six to 15 years in Algeria. School starts at six years and primary education lasts nine years with children attending an *École Fondamentale*. During the first seven years of primary education, all children study the same courses. At the end of primary education, pupils sit the *Brevet d'Ensiegnement Fondamentale*. Secondary education starts at 15 and lasts for three years. Students attend a Lycée and choose specialist courses after which they sit the Baccalaureat examination. A *Baccalaureat* pass is considered to lie between GCSE and A-Level standard. The literacy rate is 73 per cent for males and 49 per cent for females.

Economy: Algeria is a middle income country. Some 95 per cent of its export earnings come from the sale of oil and petroleum products. Other important products include steel, wheat, grapes, citrus fruit, olives, tobacco and dates. The economy is heavily state-influenced – a legacy of the post-independence policies of the Front de Liberation Nationale (FLN). Over 400 key enterprises are still state-owned, although there have been recent moves towards a free market economy. These economic changes have led to growing unemployment, as inefficient state-owned industries close. Youth unemployment is particularly high, fuelling discontent in urban areas.

A chronology of events: The first evidence of settlement in the area that is now Algeria dates to about 8000 BC. By about 1000 BC, north African people speaking Berber languages inhabited today's Algeria and had formed their own states. The Berber population was subdued by invading Phoenicians who established power bases at Carthage and Annaba. But by 250 BC Phoenician power was waning, caused by the revolt of many of its Berber subjects. By the end of the second century BC, several large Berber Kingdoms had emerged in the region. Berber rule lasted until 24 AD, when much of the North African coast was annexed to the Roman Empire. North Africa emerged as a cosmopolitan and prosperous part of the Roman Empire, producing cereals and olive oil. The coastal towns supported large Christian and Jewish populations. There were continued uprisings against Roman rule. As the Roman control of North Africa weakened, the Berbers returned. The Algerian coast also suffered invasions of Germanic Vandals and the Byzantine forces of the Emperor Justinian.

642-800 – The first Arab military invasions land in North Africa, converting the Berber population to Islam. Paradoxically, the spread of Islam among the Berbers did not guarantee their support for Arab rule. Rather, high taxes and discriminatory treatment at the hands of the Arab population alienated many Berbers. There were revolts against Arab rule.

800-1100 – Much of modern Algeria is ruled by a succession of Arab dynasties. Urban culture becomes increasingly Arabised. This period of history is marked by constant conflict and economic decline. Contributing to political instability was a major migration of Arab Bedouin from Egypt in the first half of the 11th century. The Bedouin sacked Arab towns, leaving them in ruins, and sent farmers fleeing from the fertile coast. As a result of the Bedouin incursion into the countryside, rural inhabitants adopt the Arabic language.

1100-1516 – The area that is modern Algeria continues to be ruled by Arab dynasties, but experiences greater stability. The coastal towns grow in prosperity. In 1516 Islamic mercenaries invade coastal Algeria. They are later given the support of the Ottoman Sultan who loans them additional 2,000 soldiers. With the aid of this force, much of coastal Algeria is brought under the control of the Ottoman Empire. Although nominally under Ottoman rule, most rural people still owed allegiance to Arab and Berber chieftains. Ottoman rule lasts until 1830.

1830-1842 – French forces conquer Algeria. Northern Algeria is formally annexed in 1842. French rule is consolidated by European settlers. The French authorities take possession of Ottoman lands and sell them to settlers. Other property is bought from native Algerians at rock-bottom prices. Called *colons* or *pieds noirs* (black feet), the European settlers were peasant farmers or the urban poor from southern Italy, France and Spain. Some were criminal deportees. Many of the settlers became permanent residents. This migratory movement causes massive disruption to traditional society. By 1845 Algeria was under the control of three types of civil administration: European communes, 'mixed' communes and indigenous communes. In the aftermath of the Revolution of 1848, Algeria loses its status as a colony and becomes and integral part of France. With the advent of the Second Empire in 1842, Napoleon III returns Algeria to French military control. In **1866**, drought and the sale of seed grain cause widespread starvation among Algerian farmers.

1871 – The Franco-Prussian War: France loses Alsace-Lorraine to Germany. Refugees from Alsace Lorraine put pressure on the French Government to make new land available to them in Algeria. Over 5,000 settlers arrived in Algeria and an equal number of Algerians are uprooted from their land to make way for them. The drought, hunger and loss of farmland lead to a revolt in the Berber areas.

1908-1930s – Algerian nationalism grows, partly as a result of proposals to conscript young men into the French army. Some nationalist groups called for full integration and citizenship rights in France. Others campaign for Algerian independence. Islamic groups are active in the campaign for equal rights. At the same time, the settlers mobilise their allies in France to resist changes. In **1936**, growing unrest in Algeria prompts a newly-elected French Government to accede to some of the demands of Algerian nationalist groups. Under the Viollette Plan full political equality would be extended to certain members of the Algerian elite but because of opposition by the settlers it is never implemented.

1939-45 – Nazi Germany defeats France and establishes the quisling Vichy Government. Most French settlers support the Vichy Government, but it threatens the human rights of the Muslim and Jewish population of Algeria. Algeria falls to the Allied powers in 1942. By 1943, the main nationalist groups in Algeria have abandoned their campaign for full integration with France and call for self-determination. The French administration responds by promoting reforms based on the Viollette plan. By the end of the war there was unprecedented support for independence. Tensions explode on 8 May 1945 with the banning of an independence march. Some 103 Europeans are killed, followed by reprisal attacks on Muslims in which at least 6,000 people die.

1952-1954 – By 1952 Algerian political leaders have fled the country in increasing numbers. Among them is Ahmad Ben Bella. In exile in Cairo, he and eight others found the Comite Revolutionnaire d'Unite et d'Action, renamed the Front de Liberation Nationale (FLN) in 1954. In the same year the FLN organises military opposition in Algeria. On 1 November 1954 the FLN begins a war of national independence.

1960s – Over one million Muslim Algerians are killed in the war of independence. Despite opposition from European settlers, the French Government agrees to a ceasefire in March 1962. Algeria becomes an independent country in 1962 and a new government is formed with Ben Bella as President and the FLN holding all political power. The majority of European settlers leave immediately. In addition to war damage, the exodus of the settlers leaves Algeria deprived of most of its skilled workforce. In 1965, Ben Bella is deposed in a bloodless coup led by Colonel Houari Boumedienne. In the next ten years, rising oil revenues and the policies of a state-controlled economy transform Algeria from a poor agrarian society into an urbanised industrial society. The army grows in power in post-independence Algeria.

1975-1978 – Boumedienne drafts a new constitution, enhancing his political power. In December 1976 he is re-elected unopposed. In 1978 he dies. One-party rule continues with the FLN choosing Colonel Benjedid Chadli as presidential candidate.

1986-1989 – A decline in income from oil exports, increasing unemployment, price rises and cuts in public expenditure spark a wave of strikes and violent demonstrations. By 1989, the Fronte Islamique de Salut (FIS) had emerged as the main opposition group.

1990s – President Chadli agrees to FIS demands for an early election. At the same time, there are demonstrations against religious intolerance and new laws against the use of French and Berber languages in education. In 1991, opposition to Government economic policy leads to national strikes. In a general election, the FIS emerges as the clear leader. In 1992, the Government is dissolved and Chadli is forced to resign under pressure from military leaders. The second round of elections is cancelled. A five member High Council of State, chaired by Muhammad Boudiaf replaces the FLN Government. A state of emergency is declared and the FIS is outlawed. Violent clashes erupt throughout the country. In June 1992 Boudiaf is assassinated. By the end of 1992, the Islamic opposition has become more fragmented and increasingly radicalised. The GIA emerges, as a more extreme Islamic organisation that operates in cells. Armed opposition grows, led by the FIS and the GIA. Islamic extremists target policemen, soldiers, civil servants, politicians, journalists, teachers and other member of the educated urban elite. At the same time the security forces intensify their campaign against the armed Islamic groups and people suspected of supporting them. The 'Ninja', the hooded security forces, brutally murder innocent people as a means of spreading fear among potential supporters of Islamic parties. The police and security forces are also accused of using widespread torture in an attempt to break the power of the terrorists.

In January 1994 Liamine Zeroual is appointed Head of State. A transitional government, culminating in presidential elections is announced. In 1995 President Zeroual wins presidential elections boycotted by many political parties. By the end of 1995 up to 40,000 people have been murdered. In 1997 elections to the legislative assembly are held. The National Democratic Rally, the party seen as the main supporter of President Zeroual, wins most seats. Following the temporary release of the Abassi Madani, leader of FIS, its armed wing declares a ceasefire and enters negotiations with the Government despite much internal opposition. The killings, however, continue: since the start of the violence over 80,000 people have lost their lives.

In 1998, Matoub Lounes, a popular Berber singer, is murdered by Islamic extremists, prompting demonstrations. President Zeroual announces that he plans to leave office after presidential elections to be held in April 1999. The presidential elections are held, in an atmosphere of violence. Six of the seven candidates withdraw beforehand, leaving Abdelaziz Bouteflika, perceived as the army's choice, as the winner.

Algerian Refugees in the UK – Statistics

Year	Asylum applications	Refugee status as percentage	ELR	Refusal
1992	150	6	31	63
1993	275	7	7	86
1994	995	1	1	99
1995	1,865	2	1	97
1996	715	2	1	97
1997	715	14	1	86
1998	1,260	61	3	35
1999	1,385	71	5	24

The Algerian community numbers about 7,000, mostly living in central London. Because France has close political relations with the Algerian Government, many Algerians, particularly those associated with Islamic groups, fear deportation from France so prefer to seek asylum in the UK.

Algerians have fled to the UK for different reasons so the community is socially diverse. It includes journalists and human rights activists whose work has put them at risk from the Islamic militias. Also at risk from Islamic militia are those with a secular lifestyle, members of the communal guards and people associated with the security forces. Others have fled because they are associated with Islamic groups, including many young men, whose lack of English has contributed to difficulties accessing services and finding work. Another issue of concern has been high refusal rates prior to 1997. The liberal media has highlighted cases of torture victims being refused asylum in the UK.

There is a small community organisation based in London. Other Algerian refugees have been supported by mosques. No one community organisation can, therefore, hope to represent Algerian refugees.

Bibliography

Home Office (2000) *Country Assessment: Algeria*, London: Home Office Immigration and Nationality Directorate

Stone, M. (1997) *The Agony of Algeria*, New York: Colombia University Press.

There is much information about Algeria on the internet. The US Library of Congress has a detailed historical background on www.loc.gov.

■ Refugees from Angola

Over 16,000 Angolan asylum-seekers have arrived in the UK since 1989, although not all have remained. In 1998 Angola had a population of 12 million. The urban population has been doubled by large numbers of internally displaced people. The capital city is Luanda.

Ethnic groups: There are seven main ethno-linguistic groups in Angola and many smaller minorities. The conflict in Angola has an ethnic dimension. The largest ethnic group are the Ovimbundu, comprising about 37 per cent of the population. They speak Umbundu as their first language. Ovimbundu live in all parts of Angola but are concentrated in the central highlands. Jonas Savimbi, the UNITA leader, belongs to this group.

The Kimbundu (sometimes known as the Mbundu) comprise 26 per cent of the population, split into 20 sub-groups. Their traditional homeland is around Luanda, and in the northern and central regions. They speak Kimbundu as their first language and have traditionally supported the MPLA. The Bakongo make up about 15 per cent of the population, living mostly in northern Angola and in Cabinda (as well as Congo-Brazzaville and the Democratic Republic of Congo). They speak Kikongo as their first language and traditionally gave their support to the FNLA. The *Lunda*-Chocwe are another significant ethnic group living in north east Angola, as well as Zambia and the Democratic Republic of Congo. They speak dialects of Lunda-Chokwe. The Ambo live in southern Angola and Namibia. They speak dialects of Oshivambo. Other ethnic groups living in Angola include the Nhandeca-humbe and the Ganguela. Angolans of Portuguese origin and mixed race live in Angola. Many occupy senior positions in Government and give strong backing to the MPLA.

Languages: The official language of Angola is Portuguese. The most important African languages are Umbundu and Kimbundu which some linguists argue are a single language with dialectal differences. Kikongo is spoken by about one million people living in northern Angola. Chokwe is spoken by about one million people in north east Angola. All Angolan languages are closely related Bantu languages, belonging to the Niger-Congo language family.

Names: Angolans usually use the European naming system: a first name followed by a family name. Many Angolans have Portuguese first names and some Angolans also have Portuguese family names.

Religion: Between 80 and 90 per cent of the population hold traditional beliefs but most in the urban areas are Roman Catholic. There are also small numbers of Methodists, Baptists and people belonging to African churches. Many Bakongo belong to the Kimbanguist Church, also found in the Democratic Republic of Congo. Members of the Tocoist church, another African church, have faced persecution.

Education system: Schooling starts at six or seven and is compulsory for eight years – although many poorer Angolan children never attend school. *Ensino de Base* (primary education) lasts eight years and is divided into three cycles or levels lasting four years, two years then two years. At the end of the third level students must pass a national examination to go on to *Ensino Medio* (secondary education). *Ensino Medio* lasts four years and finishes with the Secondary School Leaving Certificate, comparable to GCSEs. Students who complete secondary education may go on to university but only after working for the state for two to five years. Some two or three year pre-university courses offer an alternative route to higher education. The medium of instruction in all schools is Portuguese. The literacy rate for men is 49 per cent, and for women 33 per cent. Literacy rates are much lower in rural areas. The state education system has been severely disrupted by war.

Economy: Angola is basically an agrarian economy, and about 71 per cent of the labour force work as farmers. The main crops are maize, sugar cane, palms, coffee, cotton, sisal and vegetables. Angola is a fertile country and was once a major food exporter but the civil war has disrupted farming. Fighting has been concentrated in the main food producing area. Angola has had to import food since the mid- 980s, and suffered famine in 1989-90, 1993-94 and in 1999.

Angola has many natural resources and is potentially one of the richest countries in Africa. There are extensive oil reserves in Cabinda, and 90 per cent of the country's export earnings come from crude oil and petroleum products. There are also many mineral reserves such as iron ore, copper, gold, diamonds, uranium, phosphate, lead and zinc. The war has totally disrupted the economy. Domestic commerce is at a standstill, and in many areas the only functioning economy is the barter system. There is virtually no industry and a very poor infrastructure. Malnutrition is widespread.

A chronology of events: In the 13th century Angola waves of peoples speaking Bantu languages moved south into Angola, displacing the Khoi San. The first Europeans arrived in 1482 when Diego Cao, a Portuguese explorer, reached the mouth of the River Congo. Colonisation was first carried out by trade missions and then by military expeditions. For over 300 years Portuguese colonisers made a great deal of money out of the slave trade, offering certain ethnic groups money for the capture of slaves, which precipitated much internal conflict. War and slavery reduced the population from 18 million in 1450 to about eight million in 1850. The slaves were transported to North America, Brazil, Sao Tome and Portugal, nearly half perishing during the journey.

By 1850, the Portuguese controlled the coast of Angola, and Angolan traders and local lords the interior. Slavery was still legal. In 1884, the Berlin Conference grants Angola to the Portuguese. The boundaries are set in 1891. Military campaigns between 1895-1921 give Portugal control of the interior. Portuguese are encouraged to settle in Angola to strengthen their presence. Some Angolans are given a missionary education, then jobs in commerce and government. They are known as the *assimilados* – assimilated Angolans.

1945-1960 – Portuguese migration to Angola triples and the number of settlers reaches 350,000. Many of the Portuguese migrants cannot read or write and face direct competition with Angolans for jobs. It is the latter who lose out, and begin to agitate for independence and an end to discrimination against Angolan people. In 1956 the Popular Movement for the Liberation of Angola (MPLA) is founded, supported mainly by the Kimbundu living around Luanda. It seeks an end to Portuguese rule. Soon other resistance movements are formed, including the Union for the Total Independence of Angola (UNITA) and the National Front for the Liberation of Angola (FNLA). UNITA draws most of its support from the Ovimbundu, and the FNLA from the Kikongo.

1960s – The war of independence begins in 1961. MPLA militants storm Luanda's prisons while Portuguese targets are also attacked in north west Angola. The Portuguese army responds by bombing villages and using napalm. Over 60,000 refugees flee to Zaire. By 1965, the war has forced 400,000 Angolan refugees into Zaire. Most settle in the border area. In 1968 the war spreads south and refugees flee to Zambia.

1970s – The MPLA, FNLA and UNITA fail to resolve disagreements. More Angolans are killed in fighting between the three liberation movements than are killed fighting the Portuguese. The super-powers worsen the conflict by arming different groups. The West backs UNITA, the Chinese the FNLA and the Soviet Union the MPLA. In 1974 Dr Salazar's dictatorship is overthrown in Portugal. Within days the new Government announces it will leave its colonies. The three independence movements sign a ceasefire. The MPLA, FNLA and UNITA meet in Portugal in 1975 and sign the Alvor Agreement. This outlines the structure of an interim Government and plans for free elections. But by March violent clashes erupt again between the three liberation movements. The MPLA then establishes a government in Luanda. The FNLA and UNITA then establish an alternative government in Huambo. The South African Government sees Angola as a potentially wealthy rival and its troops invade Angola. (Angola is a socialist and multi-racial country, and the MPLA allows the African National Congress and the South West Africa People's Organisation to have bases in Angola for their guerrilla war against South Africa.) Cuban troops arrive to support the MPLA and together manage to drive back the South Africans.

From 1976-1980 there is a lull in the fighting and some economic recovery. The US Congress stops much military aid to UNITA, rendering it less active. The Angolan Government is able to make big improvements in healthcare and education.

1980s – President Reagan promises more US military aid to UNITA. South Africa also increases aid to UNITA and resumes bombing southern Angola, destroying economic targets such as railways and factories. Refugees continue to flee to Zambia and Zaire. By 1984 over 600,000 people are internally displaced in Angola. Drought and the spread of civil war lead to severe food shortages in 1984. The South African and Angolan Governments sign a peace agreement but UNITA continues to receive South African military aid. In 1987 the MPLA shifts away from strict Marxist policies and moves towards a mixed economy. The US and African states put pressure on UNITA and the MPLA to negotiate a peace settlement. A ceasefire is signed but due to different interpretations, hostilities are soon resumed. Both sides of the conflict are accused of human rights violations.

1990s – By 1990 over 400,000 Angolans are refugees in Zaire and Zambia. There is famine in rural areas. In 1991 a peace agreement is signed by UNITA and the MPLA, to be monitored by the UN. But it excludes representatives of parties from the small oil-rich enclave of Cabinda, who seek independence for Cabinda.

Elections are held in September 1992 with the MPLA securing 57 per cent of the vote and UNITA 32 per cent. UN monitors declare the elections to be generally free and fair but Jonas Savimbi, President of UNITA, refuses to recognise the result. UNITA soon reorganises its army and begins to seize towns and villages. The civil war escalates and attempts to negotiate a ceasefire fail. The MPLA is reduced to maintaining control in western Angola, and some towns in the central provinces. Over two million people are internally displaced and over 500,000 are refugees in neighbouring countries. A ceasefire is declared in November 1994 after peace talks are held in Zambia. The UN continues to monitor the peace, with 7,000 staff. The UN's mandate includes monitoring the demobilisation of Government and UNITA troops, collecting UNITA weapons and selecting 26,500 UNITA troops for integration into the Government army. Violations of the ceasefire agreement continue.

In 1997 the UN force is replaced by a smaller UN Civilian Observer Mission. The UN imposes sanctions on UNITA because it fails to meet its obligations or demobilise its soldiers. There is fighting in Cabinda between Government forces and separatist guerrillas. By 1998 half of Angola is still under UNITA control although the peace agreement is meant to provide for the integration of the country. Ceasefire violations continue and previously de-mined areas are re-mined. UNITA keeps at least 30,000 experienced fighters. The unrest in the Democratic Republic of Congo further destabilises Angola. Full scale war resumes. In 1999 the UN withdraws all its peacekeepers, stating that there is no peace to keep.

Over 2,300,000 people have been internally displaced by fighting and 350,000 have fled as refugees, mostly to Zambia and the Democratic Republic of Congo. Angola is on the brink of famine as fighting has disrupted almost all food production. About 70 per cent of the population now lives in Government controlled urban areas and all towns and cities host thousands of internally displaced Angolans. The remaining 30 per cent of the population live in areas that have become inaccessible to aid agencies.

Angolan Refugees in the UK – Statistics

Year	Applications for Asylum	Refugee Status as percentages	ELR	Refusal
1989	235	58	25	17
1990	1685	11	22	67
1991	5780	1	2	97
1992	245	1	1	99
1993	320	1	1	99
1994	605	1	1	98
1995	555	1	1	98
1996	385	1	4	95
1997	195	3	38	59
1998	150	2	17	81
1999	545	24	41	35

Source Home Office. Numbers exclude dependants.

The numbers of Angolans fleeing to the UK peaked in 1991. Today Angolan refugees who have the financial means to escape to Europe are finding it difficult to apply for asylum. The security situation in Angola makes it difficult to travel and flee the country.

Angolan refugees in the UK have often fled human rights violations. Both UNITA and the MPLA Government have killed, imprisoned or executed people suspected of supporting opposition groups. The Angolan refugee community is ethnically and politically diverse. Some refugees support the MPLA and have fled UNITA, others are UNITA supporters and have fled from Government persecution. There are a small number of Bakongo refugees living in the UK, as well as Angolans of mixed race. In the 1990s almost all Angolan asylum-seekers were refused asylum in the UK, giving major cause for concern to refugee and human rights organisations. Reports and representations were made to the Home Office about the quality of asylum decisions for Angolans.

In 1998, as the security situation deteriorated in Angola, deportations of Angolan asylum-seekers were suspended. A number were granted Exceptional Leave to Remain, as part of a Home Office 'backlog clearance' exercise aiming to clear cases that went back before 1993.

The Angolan community in the UK numbers about 16,000. Most live in Greater London, particularly in central London, Lambeth and Newham. They face many of the problems of other groups of refugees, such as difficulty in finding settled accommodation, employment and EAL classes. There are several community organisations working with Angolan refugees, some of which reflect the political and ethnic differences in the Angolan community. There are funded community organisations in the London boroughs of Kensington and Chelsea, Lambeth and Waltham Forest, a Bakongo organisation in Newham and a community school in Westminster that teaches Portuguese to children.

Bibliography

Brittain, V. (1998) *The Death of Dignity: Angola's Civil War*, London: Africa World Press

Jamba, S. (1995) *Patriots*, London: Penguin

Tvedten, I., Wright, S. and Bowman, L. (eds) (1997) *Angola: the Struggle for Peace and Reconstruction*, Boulder, Colorado: Westview Press

Warner, R. (1995) *Voices from Angola*, London: Minority Rights Group.

■ The Armenians

The UK's Armenian community numbers about 16,000. Most have arrived in the last 20 years. The Armenian homeland is located in the mountains of eastern Turkey and the Caucasus. The Armenians were converted to Christianity around 300 AD, and have their own church and patriarch, following an early schism from the church of the Roman Empire.

Most Armenians speak Armenian as a first or second language. It constitutes a separate branch of the Indo-European language family, although it has borrowed many Persian words. It uses a distinct script, written from left to right.

Eastern Turkey never experienced long periods of peace, and over the centuries the Armenians have been ruled by many different empires. In the 15th century much of Armenia became part of the Ottoman Empire. By 1827, and the Russian conquest of the Caucasus, large numbers of Armenians found themselves living in the Russian Empire. But the most tragic event in Armenian history was the genocide of 1915. In 1908 there was a revolution in Turkey; the Sultan was removed and replaced by more democratic government. The revolution was led by the Young Turks who were extremely nationalistic. There was increased repression of Turkey's minority groups, and the Armenians were suspected of sympathies with enemy powers. Violent attacks on the Armenians started after the military setbacks in the First World War. Nationalists used them as a scapegoat. Starting in 1915, 1,500,000 Armenians were shot, or died of starvation and disease. Thousands were deported from their homelands, and died on death marches. One third of all Armenians died in this holocaust. The perpetrators of this crime were never brought to justice and even today the Turkish Government denies that it ever occurred.

Some 500,000 Armenians fled into exile to Russia, other Middle Eastern countries, France and the USA. Many of those who fled to Russia and the Middle East have had to face another exile. Since 1965 some 410,000 Armenians have fled from their homes in Cyprus, Iran, Lebanon and Syria and another 200,000 from Azerbaijan in 1990-91 after inter-ethnic conflict and war between the two new republics of Armenia and Azerbaijan. Of all the Armenians alive today about four million live in Armenia. There are small minorities elsewhere in the former Soviet Union; 500,000 in Lebanon, Turkey, Syria and Iran; 500,000 in the USA and about 250,000 in France.

About 13,000 Armenians live in London, mostly in the west London boroughs of Ealing, Kensington and Chelsea and Hammersmith. Recent refugees have settled around an old established community, probably the oldest refugee community in the UK. In the 13th century after a Mongol invasion of parts of Armenia, some refugees settled in England. Later Armenian textile merchants settled in Plymouth, Liverpool and Manchester. At the beginning of the 20th century came refugees escaping massacres in Turkey. But most have arrived in the last 20 years, fleeing civil war and human rights abuse in Cyprus, Lebanon and Iran.

The Armenian community is very diverse. Some members have achieved great success in commercial life. Other more recent arrivals are struggling to make new lives and face most of the problems of other groups of refugees. There are a large number of elderly Armenian refugees in the UK.

The Centre for Armenian Information and Advice (CAIA) is an active community group, working to support refugees. It offers an advice service, giving information on immigration law, welfare rights and housing. There are several ESL classes and a playgroup for children. The CAIA also runs Armenian classes for young people born in the UK, or those married to Armenians. It runs training and careers advice for Armenian women, and also produces a newsletter, which goes to almost every Armenian living in the UK. An Armenian radio programme is broadcast once a week, and there is a unique library of information about Armenia. The CAIA also collects funds for refugees displaced by fighting in the Caucasus.

Bibliography
Marshall Lang, D and Walker, C. (1991) *The Armenians*, London, Minority Rights Group.

■ Refugees from Bolivia and Ecuador

A small number of asylum-seekers from Bolivia and Ecuador have arrived in the UK, amounting to about 2,000 people.

Those caught up in the anti-narcotics drive in Bolivia are at risk of human rights abuse, as are those who are critical of the Government. In Ecuador there are documented instances of arbitrary arrest, extra-judicial execution and torture and those critical of the Government are also at risk. Most refugees settle in east and south east London. Spanish speaking, they use many of the same Latin American support groups as Colombians.

■ Refugees from Bulgaria

Between 1989 and 1999 some 2,630 asylum applications from Bulgaria were lodged with the Home Office. Human rights abuses, particularly police brutality is well documented in Bulgaria, with ethnic Turks and Roma, the two largest minority groups most at risk. Throughout the 1980s and early 1990s the Bulgarian Government organised a campaign to eradicate the national identity of the Turkish minority (some 8.5 per cent of the population). Turks were forced to take Bulgarian names, the speaking of Turkish was banned and mosques were shut. Peaceful protest was met with police repression, followed by the mass expulsion of 250,000 Bulgarian Turks to Turkey in 1989. There were no records of ethnic Turks fleeing to the UK at this time.

Bulgarian Roma comprise an estimated 2.6 per cent of the population (US Library of Congress, 2000) or 750,000 people according to Kenrick (1998). As in many eastern European countries they face ill-treatment by the police and have little recourse to justice. In August 2000 Amnesty International reported the burning in police detention of one 16 year old Roma boy and the shooting by police of a 14 year old Roma boy. But despite this, there has been little or no migration of Bulgarian Roma to the UK according to key informants who work with Roma refugees.

Language surveys in Greater London listed 248 children in Greater London schools who speak Bulgarian, mainly in central London local authorities (Baker and Mohieldeen, 2000, p25). There are no community groups representing the Bulgarians, nor are there any home language schools at present.

Bibliography
Baker, P. and Mohieldeen, Y. (2000) 'Using School Language data to estimate the total number of speakers of London's top 40 languages' in Baker, P and Eversley, J. *Multilingual Capital*, London: Corporation of London.

■ Refugees from Burundi

Burundi has an estimated population of 5.8 million. Its capital is Bujumbura. The official languages are Rundi and French. Swahili is also widely understood. Many linguists consider Rundi (often known as KiRundi) and Rwanda (kinyaRwanda) to be the same language. Rundi is a Bantu language belonging to the Niger-Congo language family and is scripted in the Roman alphabet.

Some 84 per cent of Burundi's population are Hutu, 15 per cent Tutsi and about one per cent are Twa ('Pygmies' – many still living as hunter-gatherers). As in neighbouring Rwanda, Burundi has experienced decades of ethnic conflict. As in Rwanda, there are also major economic, social and political facets of the conflict.

Chronology: Pre-independence – Burundi's fist inhabitants were Twa. Between 1000 and 1500AD the ancestors of the Hutu migrated to central Africa. They practised settled agriculture and cleared much of the forest to plant crops. Between 1600 and 1800 a new group of cattle herding nomads migrated to central Africa from Sudan and Ethiopia. They were the Tutsi, distinguished by their height and finer features. They adopted Rundi, the language of the Hutus, and soon emerged as rulers. Today's Burundi (but not Rwanda) was ruled by Tutsi kings (called the *mwami*) and a princely class. Ordinary Tutsi and Hutu, however, were in much the same economic position and intermarriage was common.

In **1894** Burundi and Rwanda became part of German East Africa. During the First World War, Burundi was occupied by the Belgians who invaded from neighbouring Belgian Congo. In **1918**, after Germany's defeat, Belgium assumed administrative control of Burundi and was granted a League of Nations mandate to do this. The country was known as Ruanda-Urundi. In **1945**, after the creation of the United Nations, Ruanda-Urundi became a UN Trustee Territory, with the UN putting pressure on the Belgian colonial administrators to move the country towards democracy and independence. During colonisation, the Belgians favoured a small Tutsi elite. They also introduce identity cards, stating a person's supposed ethnicity. These policies accentuated differences between Hutu and Tutsi.

In 1961 the Belgians announced that they intended to leave Ruanda-Urundi and there was movement towards becoming the separate states of Burundi and Rwanda. In Burundi the two main political parties were the UPRONA, headed by Prince Louis Rwagasore and the Democratic Christian Party (PDC). (In the years immediately after independence the UPRONA tried to unite Tutsi and Hutu). UPRONA won the elections for the first government, but two weeks later Prince Louis Rwagasore was assassinated. His death led to divisions within the UPRONA and the start of the current conflict.

Post-independence: Burundi achieves full independence in 1962 with the *mwami* as head of state. He tries to grant equal political power to Hutu and Tutsi. In 1965 the newly-elected Prime Minister, a Hutu, is murdered. Hutu parties emerge victorious in the new elections but the *mwami* appoints a Tutsi prime minister. In response, the Hutu-dominated police-force rebels in a failed *coup d'etat*. Over 3,000 Hutu are murdered in Tutsi reprisal tacks and thousands flee as refugees to neighbouring countries. Two successful *coups d'etat* in Burundi in 1966 culminate in the overthrow of the *mwami* and the establishment of a republic headed by a Tutsi President. Most Hutu politicians and army officers are removed from their jobs.

In **1972** extremists in the Tutsi-dominated army murder at least 150,000 Hutus after an un-successful Hutu-led rebellion. Some 300,000 Hutus flee as refugees to Rwanda, Zaire and Tanzania. No-one is tried for the 1972 genocide.

1980s – human rights abuses worsen again. Members of Hutu opposition groups are detained and tortured. In 1987, in another *coup d'etat* Pierre Boyoya, a Tutsi, becomes president. The Tutsi-dominated army kills at least 20,000 unarmed Hutu. International pressure forces Burundi's President to appoint an Hutu prime minister. In the next three years, human rights conditions improve and more Hutu are appointed to senior civil service positions. But the Tutsi-led army resists change.

1990s – elections are held in 1993 and Melchior Ndadaye becomes Burundi's first Hutu President, but the campaign heightens inter-ethnic tensions. FRODEBU, the winners, fight as a Hutu party, while UPRONA is seen as a party that defends Tutsi interests. In October 1993, army officers surround the Presidential palace and Melchior Ndadaye is killed. The military coup is followed by violence. Tutsi and any supporters of UPRONA are killed in revenge for the *coup d'etat*. In other areas FRODEBU activists and Hutu are killed by the army. Over 50,000 people die and 700,000, mostly Hutu, refugees flee to Rwanda.

A new government is formed in early **1994.** Within two months its Tutsi President is dead, killed in an air crash with President Habyarimana of Rwanda. Burundi drifts towards civil war. Tutsi soldiers and militia kill civilians. Hutu militia also kill Tutsi civilians. Over the next six years some 20,000 people are murdered.

In response to continued attacks by Hutu militia, the Government announced a policy of 'regroup-ment', ostensibly to provide protection, but in reality to deny potential support or cover for armed opposition groups. Civilians are moved into secure camp areas, where conditions are appalling, food cannot be cultivated and there is little water or sanitation. Most international aid agencies are denied access to the camps, and thousands in them die of malnutrition and disease. In 2000 a peace agreement, brokered by Nelson Mandela, is signed in Tanzania. The Government is ambivalent about its intentions and extremist Tutsi parties boycott the peace negotiations.

There are about 1,000 Burundi refugees in the UK, most of whom have arrived since 1998. They come from all sides of the conflict. There is no community group working with Burundis, although some use other organisations providing services to francophone Africans.

Bibliography
Malkki, L. (1995) *Purity and Exile*, Chicago: University of Chicago Press
Minority Rights Group (1998) *Burundi*, London: Minority Rights Group.

■ Refugees from Cameroon

About 1000 refugees from Cameroon have arrived in the UK since 1998. Cameroon had a population of 16 million in 1999. The capital is Yaounde.

Cameroon is a multi-ethnic society, made up of over 200 different ethnic and linguistic groups. The official languages of education are French and English. The north-west and south-west of the country tend to be Anglophone, while French is the *lingua franca* elsewhere. Over 100 African languages are spoken, led by Fang, Bulu, Yaounde, Duala, Mbum and Fulani.

Cameroon became a German Protectorate in the 19th century. After the First World War, the country was divided into British and French zones of interest. In 1922, a League of Nations Mandate ensured that 80 per cent of the country became a French Protectorate and the rest the British-administered Northern and Southern Cameroons, administered as part of Nigeria. French Cameroun gained its independence in 1960, and in 1961 the former British and French colonies formed one united republic. Cameroon is now a member of the Commonwealth.

The same political party has remained in power since 1961. There is little toleration of political dissent, with government critics being subject to harassment, arrest, torture or imprisonment. Almost all refugees who flee to the UK have been active in opposition politics, or are independent journalists or human rights activists. Nevertheless, over 98 per cent of Cameroon asylum-seekers were refused refugee status or ELR in 1998 and 1999. There are also severe human rights violations in parts of northern Cameroon. Local militia have been accused of looting and rape and there is generally much less observance of the rule of law. But the Cameroon police and armed forces have responded by executing those suspected of belonging to these militia. There are also ethnic tensions between Fulani and other ethnic groups in Northern Cameroon.

Cameroon has achieved a high level of school enrolment, for a poor country. Most Cameroon refugees in the UK, both French and English speaking, are well educated, with the majority of adults having completed university education. There is one refugee community group, based in Croydon, south London.

Bibliography
Amnesty International (2000) 'Cameroon' in *Annual Report*, London: Amnesty International.

■ Refugees from Chad

Over 400 asylum-seekers from Chad have arrived in 1999 and 2000 – the first to come to the UK, although many refugees have fled armed conflict in Chad in the last 21 years.

Chad had a population of 7.5 million in 1999, belonging to over 200 different ethnic groups. The capital is N'Djamena. About 14 per cent of the population identify themselves as Arabs. The Sara are another large ethnic group, mostly living in southern Chad. There are ethnic elements in today's conflict. Some 55 per cent of the population are Muslim, the rest are Christian, mostly Roman Catholic, or follow traditional African beliefs.

Chad gained independence from France in 1960. From the start there was conflict between northern and southern peoples, made worse by the intervention of France and Libya. The French supported central government, dominated by southerners, while the Libyans abetted rebellion in the northern and eastern regions. Armed rebellion turned into civil war in 1979. Today armed conflict continues in the north.

Most Chadian asylum-seekers in the UK have been involved in opposition politics or are human rights activists, environmental activists opposing the Chad/Cameroon pipeline or independent journalists.

Bibliography
Whiteman, K. (1988) *Chad*, London: Minority Rights Group.

■ Refugees from China

Some 9,095 asylum applications from China were lodged in the UK between 1992 and 1999. A number were political opponents, some involved in the Tiannemen Square uprising. Others have suffered religious persecution including practitioners of Falun Gong, a form of meditation. But many Chinese asylum-seekers are young single men from the impoverished coastal Fujian province. The discovery of 58 bodies of young people from Fujian at Dover in June 2000 highlighted this migratory movement. Would-be migrants may pay traffickers up to £30,000 to secure passage to the UK. Once here, some claim asylum and seek work. Others might not draw attention to authorities and work, illegally, to pay off their debts, sometimes living in conditions akin to slavery.

■ Refugees from Colombia

Colombians are the largest group of Latin American refugees in the UK. About 8,000 have sought asylum in the UK, although the Colombian community is larger. Colombia had a population of 39 million in 1999. The capital is Bogota.

Ethnic groups: Colombia is a multi-ethnic society. Almost all Colombians are the descendants of Amerindians, Africans and Europeans, a large proportion of whom have inter-married during the last 500 years. About two per cent of the population belong to the many Amerindian indigenous groups living in remote rural areas, including the Amazonian jungle and the southern highlands. Another four per cent are of African descent and live mostly along the Pacific coast. Amerindians and African-Colombians are the most economically deprived ethnic groups and Amerindians have suffered disproportionately in the recent violence.

Some 58 per cent of Colombians identify themselves as mixed Amerindian and European ethnicity, sometimes described as *mestizos*. A further 14 per cent consider themselves to be of mixed European and African descent, with three per cent of the population being of African-Amerindian descent. Colombians of European descent continue to occupy most of the positions of power within government, the professions and business. Much social status is attached to having light skin and an old, respected Spanish family name. By the mid-1980s Colombians of mixed Amerindian-European ancestry had achieved some upward social mobility, although *mestizos* are still poor city dwellers or peasant farmers.

Language: The official language of Colombia is Spanish, spoken by almost everyone. Colombian Spanish differs from Castillian Spanish in its accent and pronunciation of some letters.

Names: Colombians use a Spanish naming system of personal name, followed by father's family name and then the mother's family name. For example

Maria	Moreno	Gonzales
	Father's family name	Mother's family name

Maria Moreno Gonzales would be commonly known as Maria Moreno. On marriage women usually adopt their husband's family name in place of their father's name, and replace their mother's family name with that of their fathers. In the UK, many Spaniards and Latin Americans use a hyphenated family name, to avoid names being wrongly recorded. Maria Moreno would become Maria Moreno-Gonzales.

Religion: Over 95 per cent of Colombians are Roman Catholic, but there are also Protestant and Jewish minorities living in Colombia.

Education system: Compulsory schooling starts at six and lasts until a child is 12. Secondary school follows, with a 'basic cycle' lasting four years. At 16 there are opportunities for specialisation. A young person can move to a vocational or technical school or follow more specialised courses at a comprehensive school, which may offer a wide range of courses. At 18, the *Bachillerato* examination is taken. A large proportion of children from wealthier families attend private secondary schools. There has been increased investment in education in the 1980s and 1990s, and more children from rural areas enrolled in state schools. But only 30 per cent of rural children attend school and only 18 per cent of them complete primary school. Many primary teachers lack graduate qualifications.

Economy: Economic inequality is one of the main causes of the current conflict. There are major inequalities of wealth with 70 per cent of arable land controlled by just three per cent of the population. Colombia is a middle income country. Its main exports are oil and petroleum products, textiles, processed food and drink, coffee, bananas, cut flowers, sugar cane, cotton and vegetables. A major illegal export is cocaine – often sent for processing in laboratories in other Latin American countries.

A chronology of events: Before the Spanish conquistadors arrived in the 16th century, Colombia was inhabited by Amerindian groups, including the sophisticated Chibca with their numerous, well-organised towns. The first Spanish to arrive were Alonso de Ojeda (1499) and Rodrigo de Bastida (1500), soon followed by Roman Catholic clergy and colonial administrators. During the 17th and 18th centuries, Spanish control was gradually extended into the interior of Colombia. There was much inter-marriage between Amerindians and those of Spanish descent, creating the majority *mestizo* population. African slaves were also transported to work

19th century – After growing opposition to Spanish rule with its high taxation, Colombians were granted some degree of self-government in 1810. But the ruling class were split between those who wanted to transform Colombia into a modern nation and those who wished to preserve links with the Roman Catholic church and Spanish colonial legacies. In 1819 Colombia (then called New Granada) gained independence, as part of Gran Colombia, comprising modern Panama, Venezuela, Colombia and Ecuador. Political tensions cause Gran Colombia to split in 1831. New Granada becomes an independent state, made up of modern-day Colombia and Panama.

In **1850** the Liberal Party and Conservative Party are formally established. Conflict between them continues to dominate politics to the present. In the 19th century the Liberals draw most of their support from urban traders, artisans and industrialists. They are anti-colonial and wish to transform New Granada into a modern nation so they seek to separate church and state, promote a more democratic form of government and invest in education. The Conservatives wish to preserve colonial structures and institutions and maintain strong links between church and state, as well as more authoritarian government. They are supported by large landlords and the Roman Catholic hierarchy. Landless labour and peasant farmers often gave their support to the party of the local landowner. Conflict between supporters of the two parties leads to political instability and periods of armed rebellion.

A new constitution is adopted in **1886**, conferring power on the President and national council. The country is renamed the Republic of Colombia. In 1899 supporters of the Liberal Party attempt a revolution, known as the War of a Thousand Days. It takes more than 100,000 lives and leaves the country devastated. Colombia is also too weak to resist Panamanian separatists, who in 1903, declare Panama an independent country. The war discredits the party factions that had supported it. Moderate members of each party assume power and in 1904 Rafael Reyes, a Conservative, is elected president. He pursues a policy of national reconciliation, forcing Liberal representation into government. Reyes also makes closer political links with the United States.

20th century – From **1934-38** President Alfonso Lopez Pumarejo embarks on considerable economic reforms. Known as the 'Revolution on the March', the reforms includes economic planning, changes to the taxation system and constitutional reforms such as the right to strike. Industrialisation is accelerated. The Liberals, recognising social changes, identify themselves with the growing demands of waged labour. In contrast, the Conservatives favour continued control by a small upper class.

1940s and 50s – Pumarejo is re-elected in 1942 but this time faces greater opposition to his reforms and a less stable economy caused by the Second World War. Army officers stage an abortive *coup d'etat* in 1944 and in 1945, Pumarejo resigns. Liberal leadership ends in 1946 with the election of President Mariano Ospina Perez, a Conservative. This ignites local tensions between the parties, resulting in violent political conflict, particularly in rural areas. The violence worsens in 1958 with the assassination of Jorge-Eliecer Gaitan, a popular and radical Liberal politician. In a riot that follows some 2,000 people are killed and much of Bogota is destroyed. Although order is restored to Bogota, civil war engulfs much of the countryside. The conflict is complex and is characterised by political rivalry, personal rivalry, class conflict and rural banditry. Conservative and Liberal leaders organise their own guerrilla armies but some guerrilla groups begin to operate independently of political leaders. Communists, too, begin to organise their own guerrilla units. Successive governments refuse to accede to the people's demand for economic change. In the period 1948-1958 – *La Violencia* – some 250,000 are killed and over two million displaced.

In 1958, after nearly five years of military dictatorship, constitutional changes are agreed in a pact between the Conservative and Liberal Parties. The Presidency is to be alternated between the two parties and posts in the cabinet, judiciary and civil service divided between them. Although the pact overcame some of the traditional political rivalries, it meant that no third party could challenge the Liberals or Conservatives. It also caused a great deal of voter apathy.

1960s and1970s – Rising poverty and a sense of political powerlessness lead some rural people to support left-wing guerrilla organisations, chiefly the Revolutionary Armed Forces of Colombia (FARC) and the National Liberation Army (ELN). In 1970, disenchanted members of another political party form another guerrilla army – M-19. Throughout the 1960s, the Colombian armed forces pursue a low intensity campaign against the left-wing guerrillas. Colombia's narcotics industry grows and certain drug barons begin to exert considerable political power.

1980s and 1990s – In 1982 Belisario Betancur Cuartas is elected President and in 1984, to facilitate peace talks with M-19, he signs a ceasefire agreement that prohibites any counter-insurgency activity by the Colombian army. With its hands officially tied, and supported by the large landowners, the army builds up right-wing guerrilla groups and death squads, to deny left-wing guerrillas any advantage after the ceasefire. This trend began the current conflict and since the mid-1980s an average of 25,000 Colombians have been murdered every year in the violence. In 1985 nearly 300,000 people were internally displaced. In some areas a triple alliance of drugs barons, the army, right- wing paramilitary groups and death squads target those suspected of sympathising with left-wing groups. All political opposition, human rights activities, trade unionists and community workers are also at risk. The counter-insurgency tactics of the Colombian army force thousands to flee, as does the fear of being murdered by the army and death squads and forced recruitment into paramilitary groups. About a third of internally displaced Colombians have fled left-wing guerrilla action, killings and kidnappings.

In 1998 Andres Pastrana is elected President on promises of peace. To create space for peace talks, he establishes a 'demilitarised zone' in southern Colombia, in part of the country largely controlled by FARC. Peace talks are initiated in 1999 between FARC and the Government but there are few signs that those who hold real power in Colombia – large landowners, the army and drugs barons – are ready to give up their hold.

Colombian refugees in the UK – Statistics

Asylum	Applications	Refugee status as percentages	ELR	Refusal
1992	280	4	30	64
1993	380	6	11	83
1994	405	1	4	95
1995	525	0.5	2.5	97
1996	1,005	3	1	97
1997	1,330	4	5	90
1998	425	15	6	79
1999	1,000	2	2	96

Source: Home Office. All Colombians granted ELR in 1999 were given it as part of a backlog clearing exercise by the Home Office. This group had lodged claims prior to 1996.

According to the Colombian Embassy about 25,000 Colombians live in the UK. These include asylum-seekers and refugees, as well as those who have entered on tourist or student visas. Many live in south east and central London and work in the hotel and catering industry. The Migrant Resource Centre estimates that about 80 per cent are visa overstayers – people whose legal permission to stay in the UK has expired and who might therefore be fearful of authority.

The numbers of Colombian asylum-seekers grew in 1996, as civil war and internal displacement worsened. Many came to join friends and family. In 1997, the Home Office introduced a visa requirement for Colombian nationals – a deliberate policy to deter asylum-seekers. Human rights and refugee organisations regard the Home Office treatment of Colombian asylum cases as a major cause for concern. Many are refused because the Home Office asserts that they have 'internal flight alternatives' – they could flee to other parts of Colombia.

Two community organisations provide support for Colombian refugees in London, one of which runs Spanish classes for children. Other Colombians use some of the many well-organised Latin American support groups. Colombian children are well represented in Spanish home language schools.

Bibliography

Refugee Council (1997) *Caught in the Crossfire: Colombian asylum seekers in the UK*, London: Refugee Council

Save the Children (2000) *War Brought Us Here*, London: Save the Children

Useful information about Colombia is available on the World Wide Web including

www.idpproject.org
Information about internal displacement in Colombia

www.loc.gov
Country study of Colombia, US Library of Congress.

■ Refugees from the Democratic Republic of Congo (formerly Zaire)

Over 23,000 refugees from the DR Congo have arrived in the UK since 1988. The DR Congo had a population of 48 million in 1998 of whom 29 per cent live in urban areas. The capital is Kinshasa.

Ethnic groups: There are over 200 ethnic groups in the DR Congo. About 80 per cent speak Bantu languages. Other groups include the Mangbetu and Azande (who speak languages from the Adamawa-Eastern language family, the Alur (who speak a Nilotic language, related to languages spoken in Uganda and southern Sudan and the Lugbara (who speak a central Sudanic language). There are also over one million Bwaka (pygmies) living in the forests of central Congo.

The main ethnic groups are: The Kikongo – about six million people who mostly live in western Congo, and speak the Kikongo language. Other Kikongo live in Angola and Congo-Brazzaville.

The Luba – about seven million people who live in south-east Congo and speak Tshiluba. At present there is conflict between Luba from Kasai province and Luba from Shaba province. During colonial times, Luba from Kasai were taken as indentured labour to work in the Shaba mines. Some of the Kasai Luba became successful in commerce, arousing resentment among the Shaba Luba. At least 40,000 Kasai Luba fled from Shaba Province in Autumn 1992, some of them to western Europe. Communal conflict between the Kasai Luba and the Shaba Luba was exploited by President Mobutu in order to undermine opposition.

The Mongo – about five million people living in central Congo. The Banyamulenge (also known as Banyarwanda or Goma) – about one million people of Rwandan origin (Hutu, Tutsi and Twa) – live on the border with Rwanda, a long-established settlement. The Banyamulenge are resented because of their ownership of land. Media sympathetic to the Congolese Government has also scapegoated the more prosperous Banyamulenge community, blaming them for the deteriorating economic situation. The whole region was destabilised in 1994 when over two million Rwandan refugees crossed the border. The killing of minority Rwandans were reported in 1998.

Languages: French is the official language and the language of government. All teaching is through the medium of French, although in school classrooms teachers will frequently use the local language. Fluency in French will obviously depend on how long a person has spent at school in the DR Congo. Four other languages have official status in the DR Congo: Kiswahili, Tshiluba, Kikongo and Lingala. Each is the language of trade and commerce in a particular region. All are Bantu languages.

There are at least another 200 other languages and dialects, mostly Bantu. A Congolese who has completed secondary education will probably be able to speak at least three languages: French, one or more major African languages and perhaps another home language. Lingala is the most prominent Congolese language, spoken in northern and north western Congo and around Kinshasa. It is also spoken in Congo-Brazzaville. Its prominence is due to its use in the capital and in popular music. It uses the Roman alphabet. Living mostly in the east along the border with Tanzania and Uganda are about three million people who speak a dialect of Kiswahili known as Kingwana. Like other Bantu languages, grammatical inflections occur at the beginning of the word, for example *kitabu* means 'a book' and *vitabu* means 'books'. Tshiluba is spoken by over four million people in southern Congo, Kikongo by about two million people in the far west and also in the Republic of Congo and in Angola. Lingala, Kiswahili, Tshiluba and Kikongo use the Roman alphabet, with some letter variations.

Names: Congolese refugees usually have French first names and African family names although some have African first and family names.

Religion: About 30 per cent of the population follow traditional beliefs. Some 40 per cent, mostly town dwellers, are Roman Catholic. Another 20 per cent are Protestant. About 10 per cent of people adhere to the Kimbanguist church, an African-led church founded in the 19th century by Simon Kimbangu. There is a small Muslim minority in northern Congo. Congolese Muslims are also known as Kindu Manyema. Jehovah's Witnesses were persecuted in the early 1990s and forbidden to practice their religion. The churches play an important role in the provision of services such as healthcare and education, and in implementing socio-economic development programmes.

Education system: During the colonial period the Roman Catholic Church ran most schools and played a major role in formulating educational policy. Education was basic; it reinforced gender roles, and deliberately sought to avoid creating an educated Congolese middle class. Today the church still runs many primary and secondary schools.

Primary education starts at six, although not all children enrol at this age. As in many African countries, students may remain in a class for more than one year, or miss parts of their education, so age is not always a realistic indication of how long a pupil might have spent in school. Primary education is theoretically compulsory, but only 60 per cent of boys and 40 per cent of girls enrol. Parents have to pay for state, church and private schools. The medium of instruction throughout is French. The primary school curriculum includes French, maths, moral and religious education, physical and natural sciences, PE, art and African languages. A *Certificat d'Études Primaires* is awarded to pupils who do well in the *Examen de Fin de Cycle*.

Secondary education is not compulsory and students have to sit an entrance examination to enrol. There are two parts to secondary education: a two year *Cycle d'Orientation*, and a three or four year *Cycle Superieur*. During the *Cycle d'Orientation* students study the same subjects as in primary schools, plus technology and sociology and finally take an examination: *Brevet du Cycle d'Orientation*. After the second part of secondary education students take the *Diplome d'État d'Études Secondaires*. Some pupils may study at a technical or vocational school. To go on to higher education students must take a university entrance examination. About half of all boys progress to secondary education, but only one third of girls. In rural areas and among the poor, girls are kept at home to look after siblings or work in the fields. The overall literacy rate is 53 per cent. Teaching is much more formal than in the UK and Congolese children will have had little experience of using a laboratory or other practical aspects of education. The schools are poorly equipped; wealthy Congolese send their children to private schools.

Economy: Main exports are copper, palm oil and coffee. It is the world's largest producer of copper and has considerable resources of other minerals such as zinc and tin, mostly located in Shaba Province. The DR Congo could become a rich country, but the wealth gives little benefit to the majority of its people; at least 80 per cent live below the poverty line in one of the poorest countries in the world.

Corruption is rife. In order to obtain basic services, almost everyone has to pay bribes to government officials. There has been scant investment in infrastructure and basic services. Transport is appalling and the war has further disrupted the economy. There is little investment in primary healthcare and malaria is widespread. The end of the Mobutu regime has produced no beneficial economic changes. There is hyperinflation and the purchasing power of ordinary people is being constantly and dramatically eroded, so many regions have reverted to a barter system.

A chronology of events: Before colonisation, the DR Congo was a collection of small states along the River Congo. Information about the country reached Europe between 1840 and 1870, through the journalistic coverage of David Livingstone and Henry Stanley's expeditions, financed by a Belgian trading company who signed trading agreements with local leaders. In **1884** the

Berlin Conference drew up the borders of the Free State of Congo, and declared it the personal property of the King of Belgium. It became a Belgian colony in 1908. The Belgians extract the country's timber and mineral resources, but do little to develop the infrastructure of the Congo. The native population is subject to harsh working conditions in the mines and forests, and all anti-colonial opposition is brutally suppressed.

1950s and 1960s – African political parties are allowed to operate for the first time but many draw support on a narrow ethnic basis. Only Patrice Lumumba's *Mouvement Nationale Congolaise* achieves a national outlook. In 1959 violent unrest follows the police repression of a peaceful political demonstration. To avert further bloodshed King Badouin of Belgium promises independence. In 1960 Patrice Lumumba becomes Prime Minister. Within days the army mutinies and Colonel Joseph-Desire Mobutu seizes power. A secession crisis starts in the Shaba region, due to local resentment of the extraction of the region's mineral resources. Belgium gives support to the secessionist movement. UN troops are sent to the Congo to maintain order. In 1961 Mobutu returns power to Joseph Kasavubu, who arrestes Lumumba and delivers him to Belgian mercenaries in Shaba, who kill him. A new Government is formed in 1962. The secessionist movement in Shaba ends, but unrest flares up in Kwilu. In 1965 Mobutu seizes power in a *coup d'etat*, and declares himself head of state. In 1967 a new constitution is adopted and Mobutu forms *Le Mouvement Populaire de la Revolution*.

1970s – By 1972 there is the sole legal political party and all citizens are automatically members of it. Mobutu is 'elected' President in 1970. Thousands of opponents are arrested, tortured or killed. He institutes 'Zairisation', renaming the country the Republic of Zaire. Place names are changed and people are encouraged to change their personal names and wear traditional dress. The copper mines are nationalised, but their wealth benefits only the elite. Nationalisation causes unease among western leaders and Mobutu later announces he has uncovered a US-funded conspiracy to overthrow his leadership. But Mobutu continues to receive support from the US, who see Zaire as an ally in the region.

The *Fronte Nationale de Liberation de Congo* invade Shaba province in 1977 and 1978 with support from the Angolan MLPA, a pro-Soviet liberation movement in Angola. Both invasions are repulsed by the Zairean army, with western support. Large numbers of refugees flee to Zambia. President Mobutu is re-elected in 1977 for another seven year term. Mobutu and Augustina Neto of the MPLA sign a peace treaty in 1978 in which Angola agrees not to support secessionist forces in Zaire.

1980s and 1990s – In 1982 a new party, *Le Union pour la Democratie et la Progres Social* (UDPS) is formed by thirteen former members of the National Legislative Council. The founders are imprisoned then sent into internal exile. The formation of the UDPS is followed by the founding of the FCD, a coalition of opposition groups with Nguza Karl-I-Bond its main spokesman. In 1983 Amnesty International publishes a report condemning human rights abuse in Zaire and criticises the Government for extra-judicial executions, the arbitrary arrest and torture of opponents and the torture, rape and ill-treatment of prisoners. Further unrest in Shaba is brutally put down by the army. Mobutu is re-elected in 1984 for a further seven years.

A further report from Amnesty International in 1986 highlights continued human rights violations. Opposition parties continue to be banned, and members are constantly under the threat of detention. Newspapers which criticise the Government are promptly closed. Forcibly re-patriated refugees are targets for detention and mistreatment. The incidence of extra-judicial executions and secret detention rises during the late 1980s. Local church organisations and Amnesty International find it increasingly difficult to trace detainees. Amnesty International is concerned about the violent suppression of demonstrations, often resulting in injuries and death. In 1987 a number of Jehovah's Witnesses are detained without trial. In 1988, Etienne Tshisekedi of the UDPS holds a political meeting at which three people are shot and 50 disappear. Tshisekedi is then detained and banished. Relations with the Belgian Government break down after the Belgian press publishes reports on corruption in Zaire. Mobutu orders Zaireans living in Belgium to return. Diplomatic relations are not resumed until 1990, when Belgium signs a treaty of cooperation with Zaire.

In **1989** student demonstrations are held in Kinshasa and Lubumbashi against increases in the cost of living and 50 students are killed. Kinshasa University and four other institutes are closed. UDPS members are arrested and beaten at a meeting to commemorate the assassination of Patrice Lumumba. Arrests of UDPS members escalate. There is increasing unrest in the Kivu region, bordering Rwanda, and numerous arrests. Mobutu announces reforms, including the right to form political parties and trade unions. But these are hollow promises. In May 1990 students at Lubumbashi University stage an anti-Government demonstration. Between 50 and 150 students are killed, and many others flee to Zaire. Student demonstrations and UDPS meetings are violently disrupted by security forces in 1991. Mobutu tries to appoint Tshisekedi as Prime Minister but he refuses. The National Conference, a forum to draft a new constitution, is opened and then closed again.

In **1991** the devaluation of the currency leads to massive price increases. The army riots and there is extensive damage to shops and businesses. The US and IMF suspend aid. French and Belgian armed forces intervene to protect expatriate communities. The reopened National Conference appoints Tshisekedi, leader of the UDPS, Prime Minister, but Mobutu sacks him and installs his own candidate causing further riots and bloodshed. Tshisekedi establishes a parallel government. Kasai Luba living in Shaba are attacked by Shaba Luba. At least 60 people are killed and 40,000 flee Shaba. Some politicians call for the expulsion of all Kasai Luba from Shaba Province. The riots are suspected of being an attempt to destabilise Tshisekedi's parallel government. In December the National Conference is dissolved and replaced by a 'Council of Wise Men', but most people regard it as too conciliatory.

In **1993** Mobutu issues a 5,000,000 Zaire note as payment to the army, despite opposition from Tshisekedi, who declares the note illegal tender. Retailers reject it. The army riots and shops and businesses in Kinshasa are looted. Mobutu sends in security forces and 1,000 people are killed, including the French Ambassador. It is alleged that Mobutu ordered the riots to conceal house-to-house searches for opposition members. Next, Rwandan minorities in Goma become the target of attack. More Kasai Luba flee Shaba after their houses are burned or property confiscated. Nearly 500,000 people flee Kasai Province, too, many suffering from malnutrition. Refugees also flee to Angola, Zambia, France, UK and Belgium. President Mobutu's position is maintained by security forces which report to him. The most powerful of these services are the *Division Special Presidentielle*, and *'les Hiboux'*, who work at night and are responsible for night-time arrests. In 1994 over two million Rwandan refugees cross the border into Zaire. Both the refugees and local Rwandan become the targets of harassment from the Zairean military and non-Rwandan groups. The security situation deteriorates in eastern Zaire.

Mobutu leaves Zaire for cancer treatment in Switzerland in **1996** and dies in 1997. Rebels soldiers organise themselves in north east Zaire and form the *Alliance des Forces Democratiques pour la Liberation du Congo-Zaire* (AFDL), dominated by local Tutsi and probably supported by the Rwandan and Ugandan Governements. It is led by Laurent Kabila, a veteran opposition leader. Both Rwandan soldiers and AFDL forces attack Hutu refugees in Rwandan refugee camps. An estimated 600,000-700,000 refugees return to Rwanda. Another 200,000 people flee deeper into the Congolese rain forest, and thousands die or are murdered.

The rebels sweep though Zaire and in **1997** they enter the capital and seize power. Kabila declares himself president and Zaire is renamed the Democratic Republic of Congo. The new Government announces that elections will be held in April 1999. It faces a momentous task: to rebuild the economy and rid the country of corruption. However, a ban is soon imposed on all political activity and key opposition leaders are not integrated into the new Government. Another 200,000 Rwanda refugees return home.

1998-2001 – In **1998** a rebellion starts in eastern Congo, with the *Rassamblement Congolaise pour la Democratie* seeking to oust Kabila. The rebels appear to be ex-Kabila supporters and are aided by the Rwanda regular army and the Rwandan and Ugandan Governments because Rwanda believes that Kabila is secretly supporting Rwandan Hutu extremists. The rebels soon capture a large part of the country but this initial success is stalled when Angola, Zimbabwe, Namibia, Chad and Sudan provide support for Kabila. The fighting destabilises a large part of the African continent. There are violent attacks on people of Rwanda descent, particularly Tutsis, in eastern Rwanda, Kinshasa and urban areas. Government propaganda has whipped up racism. In 2001 Kabila is assassinated and replaced by his son. Peace talks are resumed, but the civil war continues although there are political splits among the rebels. Insecurity and violence is endemic. Human rights violations are as serious as in Mobutu's time. Nearly 250,000 refugees fled the DR Congo to neighbouring countries and others have sought asylum in Europe. An estimated 1,300,000 people are internally displaced. The DR Congo also hosts thousands of refugees from Angola, Congo-Brazzaville, Sudan and Burundi.

Congolese refugees in the UK – Statistics

Year	Asylum Applications	Refugee Status as percentages	ELR	Refusal
1988	157	13	45	52
1989	525	81	3	16
1990	2,590	9	4	87
1991	7,010	1	1	99
1992	880	1	1	99
1993	635	1	1	99
1994	775	1	1	99
1995	935	1	1	98
1996	680	1	3	96
1997	690	7	13	80
1998	660	2	77	21
1999	1,240	15	40	45

Congolese refugees in the UK

The Congolese were the largest group of refugees entering the UK in 1991 and today the Congolese refugee community numbers about 23,000 people.

Until 1989 the numbers of Congolese claiming asylum in the UK was low and those who fled to Europe tended to claim asylum in France or Belgium where they would have historical and linguistic ties. Despite the high cost of getting there, many Congolese saw Europe as the only safe destination. During the time of Mobutu there were documented instances of the SIE, his external intelligence service, seeking out Congolese refugees in Rwanda and Angola and murdering or kidnapping them. Additionally, those fleeing ethnic conflict or human rights abuse in Shaba travelled via Zambia, from where there are more flights to London than there are to Brussels or Paris. There is also a belief that racial harassment is worse in France and Belgium than in England. Treatment of Congolese refugees by the Home Office is of great concern to the Refugee Council and other human rights organisations. Large numbers were detained on arrival during the 1990s and almost all asylum applications were rejected. Very few Congolese speak English, making applications difficult. Asylum applications are conducted sometimes in English and sometimes in French, on the assumption that all Congolese speak French. In fact by no means all do: fluency in French depends on how long they spent in school.

Despite a grave deterioration in the security situation in the DR Congo, the Home Office is continuing to refuse requests for political asylum, and in August 1998 stopped making decisions on all Congolese asylum applications. At the same time it suspended removals and deportations, effectively leaving over 3,500 people in limbo. In the past many Congolese have been refused asylum for failure to attend for interview, or failure to provide additional information to corroborate claims of persecution (non-compliance). In Zaire detention usually takes place without trial, and often in secret detention centres, not prisons, so additional evidence of detention can be hard to obtain.

Congolese refugees are a diverse community. They include the opponents of Mobutu and, since 1997, those associated with the Mobutu regime. Most Congolese asylum-seekers live in Greater

London with the largest communities in Haringey, Redbridge, Lambeth, Merton and Newham. The refugees tend to be young, many under 30 and are well-educated, often holding first and higher degrees. Immigration, housing and employment present major difficulties. There are Congolese community organisations in Camden, Haringey, Islington, Kensington and Chelsea, Lambeth and Newham, some reflecting particular political affiliations. At least two community schools teach French and Lingala to children.

Bibliography
Biddlecombe, P. (1994) *French Lessons in Africa*, London: Abacus

Healthy Islington 2000 (1994) The Islington Zairean Refugee Survey Report, London:Healthy Islington 2000 (unpublished report)

Kushner, T. and Knox, K (1999) *Refugees in an Age of Genocide*, London: Frank Cass

Warner, R. (1995) *Voices from Zaire*, London, Minority Rights Group

Useful, up-to-date information about internally displaced people in the DR Congo may be obtained from the website of the Internal Displacement Project on www.idpproject.org.

■ Refugees from the Republic of Congo (Congo-Brazzaville)

Over 1,000 asylum-seekers have arrived from the Republic of Congo during the last three years, fleeing a civil war that has created 800,000 internally displaced people and over 50,000 refugees.

The Republic of Congo had a population of 2.8 million in 1999. The capital is Brazzaville. It is a multi-ethnic country: the main ethnic group are the Kikongo (some 48 per cent of the population), mostly living in the south of the country. Other major ethnic groups are Sangha (20 per cent), M'Bochi (12 per cent and Teke (17 per cent). The latter mostly live in northern Congo. French is the official language and medium of education. Kikongo, Lingala and Teke are the mostly widely spoken African languages.

The Republic of Congo gained its independence from France in 1960. In October 1997, Denis Sassou-Nguesso toppled Pascal Lissouba, Congo's elected president. Civil war soon engulfed the country with supporters of Lissouba fighting Government forces and allied militia. Fighting flared up again in late 1998 and is now intense. All sides in the conflict are engaged in killing and looting. There are many arbitrary arrests. Journalists and human rights activists are threatened. Brazzaville lies in ruins and refugees have fled over the River Congo to neighbouring Kinshasa. Nearly a third of Congo's population are internally displaced.

Most refugees from the Republic of Congo are living in Greater London, where they use the services of refugee organisations working with other groups from francophone Africa, particularly the Democratic Republic of Congo, who speak the same languages – Kikongo and/or Lingala.

Almost all have had their asylum applications refused by the Home Office. This is a major concern to organisations such as the Refugee Council. However, in 1998, as civil war worsened, the Home Office suspended the deportation and removal of persons to the Republic of Congo, possibly unsafe. This caught some asylum-seekers in immigration limbo – their cases and appeals refused, but unable to be sent home. A humane response would be to grant asylum-seekers from the Republic of Congo permission to stay in the UK.

■ Refugees from Eritrea

Over 11,000 Eritrean refugees have fled to the UK since the mid-1960s. The peak years of arrival were 1989 and 1990.

Eritrea had a population of 3.8 million in 1999, plus an exile population of about 350,000. The capital is Asmara.

Ethnic groups: Most of the people identify themselves as Eritrean, although there are nine different ethno-linguistic groups.

Languages: About half of the population speak Tigrinya, and another 30 per cent Tigre. Tigrinya is spoken in the Central Highlands, while Tigre is spoken in north-west and northern Eritrea. Most

Tigre speakers are Muslim. Tigrinya and Tigre, like Amharic, are descended from Ge'ez, the ancient religious and literary language of Ethiopia. Both are written in the Ethiopic script, from left to right. There are 35 letters in the alphabet, plus seven vowel sounds that are added to consonants. Two dots placed after each word separate it from the next.

Arabic is spoken as a first language by the Rashaida people who live in the coastal region. Also spoken are Saho, Beja, Afar (sometimes known as Danakil), Baza, Barya and Bilen. These were not scripted until independence, when the Department of Education scripted them in the Roman script. All Eritrean languages belong to the Hamito-Semitic language family. Tigrinya and Tigre are Semitic languages. The other six are Cushitic languages and more closely related to Somali. Most Eritrean refugees in the UK speak Tigrinya, although a few speak Tigre or Saho. Many can understand Arabic, particularly Muslims or those who have travelled to the UK via the Sudan. Eritrean refugees who have been educated in Ethiopian or Italian schools will have been taught Amharic, English or Italian.

Names: Eritrean Christians use a first personal name followed by a religious name and their father's first name. The naming system is the same as that used by Ethiopian Christians. On official documents Eritreans may list their first personal name, followed by their father's and grandfather's name. Some Eritrean women take their husband's father's name on marriage; others keep their own father's name. Eritrean Muslims use a traditional Islamic naming system: a personal name, followed by their father's name and then their grandfather's name.

Religion: About half of the population are Christian, living mostly in the central highlands. The rest, living mostly in the coastal region and western lowlands, are Sunni Muslim. Most Christians belong to the Eritrean Orthodox Church, which split from the Ethiopian Orthodox Church in 1993. It uses a Coptic Rite, similar to the Egyptian Coptic Church, but has its own archbishop. Eritrean Christians celebrate Christmas, Epiphany and Easter, but on different days to those celebrated in the UK, because the Ethiopian religious calendar is divided into 13 months: 12 months of 30 days, plus another month of five days. During the reign of Haile Selassie, the Ethiopian Orthodox Church was used as a means of cultural and political domination. The new Government of Eritrea has tried to diminish the power of religious groups. Some Eritrean Christians are Roman Catholic, particularly the families of people who went to Italian schools. Eritrean Muslims may celebrate the main Muslim festivals, and have the same dietary requirements as other Muslims. A few Eritreans face religious persecution today. These include Jehovah's Witnesses and anyone suspected of supporting Islamic fundamentalist groups.

Education system: Eritrean refugees in the UK could have attended different types of school: Ethiopian schools in occupied Eritrea or in Ethiopia, Eritrean schools (post 1991), private Italian schools, schools in the liberated areas (pre-1991) or schools in refugee camps in Sudan.

In the Ethiopian system children started school at six, and spend six years there before moving on to junior high school for two years. Senior high school lasts four years. During the Ethiopian occupation the medium of instruction was Amharic in primary schools and English in secondary schools. About half of the teaching profession was Ethiopian. There was little investment in state education. Schools were starved of resources, and the University of Asmara was closed down. These factors caused many middle class Eritreans to send their children to private schools, mostly run by Italians.

The Eritrean People's Liberation Front (EPLF) ran its own schools in the liberated areas. Education was mostly in the local language and for older students through English. The EPLF developed its own curriculum and teaching resources, now modified for use throughout Eritrea.

Eritrean primary schooling now starts at age six or seven and lasts five years and is taught first in the local language, and later in English. Pupils move to middle school for two years and secondary school for four years, where they study for the Eritrean General Certificate Examination. The literacy rate in Eritrea is only 12 per cent. Children living in rural areas have little access to education, although there have been improvements in recent years. Most children are forced to leave school to work the land, or live too far away from a school.

Economy: Eritrea can be divided into the central highlands, the western lowlands and the eastern coastal lowlands. The central highlands rise to 2,500 metres and are bisected by fertile valleys. Most people in this region are settled farmers. The western lowlands extend to the Sudanese border. Most inhabitants are nomadic, although some parts are fertile enough to support settled agriculture. Soil erosion is a major problem. The eastern lowlands consist of a narrow coastal plain stretching along the Red Sea. It is a desert and the few people who live there are nomadic.

Under Italian rule Eritrea developed light industries, mostly in Asmara, or in the ports of Massawa and Assab. The first car factory in Africa was in Asmara, built by Fiat. After 1952 these industries were dismantled by the Ethiopian Government. Factories were taken apart and transported to Ethiopia. The railway from Massawa to Asmara was ripped up. There was virtually no investment in Eritrea's infrastructure. At independence in 1991 there was 150 kilometres of all-weather road in the country. The lack of agricultural investment contributed to the disastrous famines of 1974, and 1982-85.

Eritrea's economy also suffered war damage, particularly in the late 1980s. The border conflict with Ethiopia diverted precious economic resources to the war effort. Most Eritreans rely on agriculture for their livelihood. The main exports are hides and other animal products. The country also relies on the repatriated earnings of refugees and migrant workers. Nearly 70 per cent of Eritrea's food is in the form of food aid. Agricultural self-sufficiency is a major economic target of the Eritrean Government.

A chronology of events: Until the late 19th century Eritrea was a collection of small kingdoms ruled by local nobles and influenced by many of the great powers in the region, including the Turks, Greeks, Arabs, Egyptians and Persians. In 1871, Yohannes IV, an Ethiopian, united Ethiopia and Eritrea into a modern nation state. At the same time colonial powers were beginning to take an interest in the Horn of Africa. The Italians attempted to colonise the country, but in 1889 they were routed in battle and Menelik became Emperor of Ethiopia. He signed a peace agreement with the Italians, but was unable to drive them from Eritrea. It becomes an Italian colony. In the next 30 years over 60,000 Italian settlers arrive. They build roads, factories and a railway. Eritrea was also an important military base. Eritrean national identity begins to grow under Italian occupation.

In Ethiopia Emperor Menelik's daughter is succeeded in 1930 by Ras Tafari, a nobleman. He takes the name Haile Selassie. Using Eritrea as a base, the Italians, under Mussolini, invade Abyssinia (Ethiopia) in 1934.

1940s and 1950s – The UK declares war on Italy. Using Somali, Ethiopian and Eritrean soldiers, the British army drives the Italians out of the Horn of Africa and Eritrea becomes a British military administration and then as a British Protectorate until 1950. The Allied powers call on the UN to decide Eritrea's future. There are three options: incorporation within Ethiopia, federation with Ethiopia or independence. The UN decides that Eritrea should be federated with Ethiopia with its own regional government and other safeguards to preserve its autonomy. Emperor Haile Selassie's pro-western stance influenced the UN, as the USA and the UK, key members of the Security Council, wanted the important Red Sea ports of Massawa and Assab to remain in the hands of a friendly government. In 1952 the UN agreement comes into operation and almost at once Ethiopia begins to ignore large parts of the UN plan intended to safeguard autonomy. Eritrean factories are closed and moved to Ethiopia. There is no investment in the economy. Tigrinya and Arabic are no longer taught in Eritrean schools. Eritrean political parties and trade unions are banned. The Ethiopian Government begins to imprison its Eritrean opponents. By 1960 there are about 3,000 Eritrean political prisoners in Ethiopian jails.

In 1961 the Eritrean Liberation Front is founded to fight for independence but in 1962 the Ethiopian Government manages to get a majority of its supporters elected to the Eritrean assembly, then votes for complete unity with Ethiopia.

1970s – The Eritrean Liberation Front and the Eritrean People's Liberation Front (EPLF) fight among themselvesin a conflict that claims many lives. In 1974 famine hits large parts of Ethiopia and Eritrea. Haile Selassie's Government collapses, and a new military government takes power under Colonel Mengistu. The Eritrean people hope that the new Government will restore autonomy but it draws its support from the same people who backed Haile Selassie. The civil war continues, although the EPLF/ELF conflict ends. Colonel's Mengistu's Government – called the Derg – increases military spending, and receives military aid from its ally the Soviet Union. The policy of neglect in Eritrea, Tigray and other provinces continues. The war worsens in Eritrea. Over 30 per cent of the population flee from their homes. Some 250,000 refugees flee to the Sudan. The EPLF now the main group fighting for independence, makes many military gains, controlling much of Eritrea, where it sets up democratic local government and builds schools and clinics. The EPLF also enacts land reform. Faced with escalating warfare the EPLF makes a strategic withdrawal in 1978 from the cities it controls. The Ethiopian Government continues to launch attacks in Eritrea.

1980s – In **1983** and **1985** two disastrous famines strike Eritrea and Ethiopia. Soil erosion and the continued lack of agricultural investment reduce farmers to subsistence level. They have no savings, so when drought strikes they cannot buy food. Up to 300,000 people die, and millions of Eritreans and Ethiopians walk to refugee camps. Further famine hits Eritrea in 1987. The EPLF makes military gains in western and northern Eritrea but food shortages continue.

1990s – The EPLF captures the Red Sea port of Massawa. The Ethiopian Government bombs the city, destroying it. The EPLF offers to open the port for food aid shipments, but the Ethiopian Government does not allow this. Over 750,000 refugees are in the Sudan, some living in appalling conditions in refugee camps. Asmara and other towns held by the Derg are under nightly curfew. Human rights violations continue. The Derg collapses in **1991** as the EPLF and opposition forces in Ethiopia make military gains. The EPLF forms a provisional Government to rule the country until a referendum in April **1993**. A transitional Government is also established in Ethiopia, and relations between Eritrea and Ethiopia are good. The provisional Government offers the Ethiopians access to Assab, on the Red Sea. Most of Eritrea's population vote for independence in the referendum. Eritrea becomes Africa's newest country. It is, however, a one party state, tolerating no political opposition. In 1994-1995 the Eritrean Government consults extensively about reform of the constitution – but not with any political opponents. In 1996 a number of Eritrean political activists are assassinated. Relations with Ethiopia deteriorate following Eritrea's introduction of the Nafka, a new unit of currency. Relations with the Sudan are also tense, as each country accuses the other of harbouring opposition groups. In **1998** Eritrean and Ethiopian air forces bomb each other's towns, over disputed border areas. Fighting on land follows. Some 1,000 Ethiopians, many long resident in Eritrea, are expelled and Eritreans are also expelled from Ethiopia. The fighting worsens in early 1999. It continues on and off throughout the year.

In **2000**, after OAU and Algerian diplomacy brings the warring parties together, Ethiopia and Eritrea agree to a ceasefire. Some 30,000 combatants have died in the fighting and 750,000 Eritreans are internally displaced, including over 67,000 expelled from Ethiopia. At the same time, famine threatens much of western and central Eritrea.

Eritrean refugees in the UK

Eritrean refugees have been fleeing to the UK since the mid-1960s. As repression and war worsened in 1989-1990, numbers increased. They have recently increased again. In 1999, some 565 asylum applications were lodged with the Home Office. Recent arrivals include Eritreans who lived in Ethiopia before the 1998-2000 war and faced expulsion, and also Government opponents.

The Eritrean community in the UK now numbers about 11,000, mostly located in central London. where schools may well have Ethiopian and Eritrean students studying together. During the 1998-2000 border war, conflict in the home country was also played out in the UK with rival demonstrations and there were reports of fights between Ethiopian and Eritrean students. Most Eritrean refugees in the UK come from the central Highlands, particularly Asmara. Those who can afford to flee to Europe are generally from the commercial or professional middle classes. They may suffer a considerable drop in their living standards in the UK but suffer less unemployment than many other refugee groups. Eritreans are usually highly motivated students, from families who value education. In 1990 over 250 unaccompanied Eritrean children arrived in the UK having fled Addis Ababa and other parts of Ethiopia and Eritrea. Most were boys, fleeing the threat of conscription into the Ethiopian army.

There are nine Eritrean community organisations working in London. While some work with Eritreans of all political persuasions, a few are aligned with particular political groups. There is an Eritrean Saho community, working with Saho-speaking refugees. At least nine groups run community schools in London, teaching children a range of Eritrean languages including Tigrinya, Tigre, Arabic and Saho.

Bibliography

Keneally, T. (1989) *Towards Asmara*, London: Paladin

Pool, D. (1997) *Eritrea: Towards Unity in Diversity*, London: Minority Rights Group

Warner, R. (1993) *Voices from Eritrea*, London: Minority Rights Group.

■ Refugees from Ethiopia

There are about 12,000 Ethiopian refugees in the UK. They have been arriving since the 1970s, with the peak years of asylum application being the early 1990s.

Ethiopia had an estimated population of 59 million in 1999 of whom 12 per cent live in urban areas. The capital is Addis Ababa.

Ethnic groups: Ethiopia has over 80 ethnic groups and conflict between them has precipitated refugee movements. The largest is the Oromo, comprising about 40 per cent of the total population. The Amhara make up 26 per cent and live in central Ethiopia, around Addis Ababa, dominating Government until 1991. Tigrayans make up nine per cent and live mostly in the province of Tigray. The Sidama (nine per cent) mostly live in south west Ethiopia. Some six per cent are ethnic Somalis, mostly inhabiting the disputed Ogaden region. Smaller ethnic groups include the Afars and the Gurage.

Languages: Amharic is the official language, spoken by about one third of the population. About five million people in the province of Tigray speak Tigrinya. These languages belong to the Hamito-Semitic language family, and are derived from Ge'ez, the ancient literary and religious language of Ethiopia. Amharic and Tigrinya are written in the Ethiopic alphabet, and from left to right. Each consonant can be modified by additions that symbolise vowel sounds. Both languages have an extensive literature.

Other major languages include Oromo spoken by about 25 million people in southern Ethiopia and also spoken in Kenya. Sidamo is spoken by five million people in south west Ethiopia and Somali by another two million in the south east. Oromo, Sidamo and Somali are related languages. Oromo has recently been scripted using an Ethiopic script and today there are a few Oromo newspapers and journals. It also has a rich oral tradition of poems and folk tales. There have been attempts to transcribe Oromo into Roman script. Somali uses the Roman script and Sidamo is not scripted. There many other languages and dialects in Ethiopia. Most Ethiopian refugees in the UK speak Amharic, Tigrinya or Oromo as their first language and may also speak a second language.

Names: Most Ethiopian Christians have three names: a first personal name, followed by a religious name and then the person's father's first personal name. The religious name is determined by the day that the child is born or baptised. A few Ethiopians use just one personal name. On official documents the religious name may not be used. Ethiopian Christians may list their first personal name, their father's name followed by their grandfather's name. Women usually keep their name when they marry. Ethiopian Muslims use Islamic names, having a first personal name, followed by their father's and their grandfather's name.

Religion: Some 59 per cent of Ethiopians are Christian, 30 per cent are Sunni Muslim and about 11 per cent practice traditional religions. Afars and ethnic Somalis are mostly Muslim, Oromo are usually Muslims or animists. Ethiopian Muslim refugees will celebrate *Eid ul Fitr, Eid ul Adha* and the *Hijra*. They may observe the Ramadan fast, and have the dietary restrictions of other Muslims.

The majority of Christians belong to the Ethiopian Orthodox Church which uses a Coptic Rite, similar to the Egyptian Coptic Church, but has its own archbishop. Ethiopian Christians celebrate Christmas, Epiphany and Easter, but on different days to those celebrated in the UK. Church services are held in Ge'ez. Some Ethiopian refugees are devout and may abstain from eating meat during Lent, demand that meat is slaughtered in special manner, and may not eat pork. A child's birth is a time of great celebration: baby boys are usually circumcised at eight days, and children are baptised on the 40th day after birth. Ethiopian Orthodox refugees in the UK may worship at the Ethiopian Orthodox Church in Ladbroke Grove, in London. Others may attend Russian Orthodox or Greek Orthodox churches. A few Ethiopians are Roman Catholic, or belong to Protestant or independent churches. Jehovah's Witnesses and Pentecostalists have reported persecution.

Education system: Since the 1974 revolution there has been large scale educational reform. Primary, secondary and tertiary education is free. Education is compulsory until the completion of the eighth year at the end of Junior Secondary School. There is some nursery provision, but most children start school at six. Primary education lasts six years culminating in the Primary School Certificate. Students then spend two years at Junior Secondary School, and four years at senior secondary school. They take an examination at the end of Junior Secondary School and sit for the Ethiopian School Leaving Certificate at the end of senior high school. This examination is considered the equivalent of a GCSE pass at grades A, B or C on a subject-for-subject basis. The medium of instruction in primary schools is Amharic, Tigrinya or Oromo. In secondary schools it is English but local languages are extensively used in the classroom. The literacy rate is 47 per cent for men and 25 per cent for women. Many more people are literate in urban areas. In 1971 only nine per cent of men and one per cent of women were literate. On gaining power in 1974 the Derg declared education to be a priority and instituted a major literacy campaign.

Economy: Much of Ethiopia is mountainous, reaching heights of over 4,000 metres. The Ogaden, in eastern part of the country – bordering Somalia – is desert. The central highlands, around Addis Ababa, are the most densely populated part of the country. Most people rely on agriculture. Ethiopia is one of the poorest countries in the world, with a GNP per head of about £90 per year. Under the Governments of Haile Selassie and Colonel Mengistu there was very little investment in agriculture and in the infrastructure of many parts of Ethiopia. Tigray, Gondar and the Ogaden (and also Eritrea) were treated rather like a colony. Amharic landlords extracted money from tenant farmers while investing little in the regions. As a consequence most farmers existed (and still do) at subsistence level. Farmers have few savings to see out natural disasters such as drought. The main exports are coffee, animal hides and vegetables products such as beans and lentils.

A chronology of events: Ethiopia has been the seat of ancient civilisations, including the Kingdom of Axum dating from about 500 BC. But although an Ethiopian kingdom existed in various forms at different points in history, power lay in the hands of local nobles. It was not until 1871 that the country was effectively united under Yohannes IV, a northern noble. In 1889 the Italians attempt to colonise Ethiopia, but lose in a battle that kills Emperor Yohannes. The Italians withdraw to Eritrea, which becomes an Italian colony. Menelik becomes the new Emperor and signs a peace treaty with the Italians.

1930-1980 – In 1930 Ras Tafari, a nobleman, becomes Emperor, taking the name of Haile Selassie. During his rule there is continued neglect of regions of Ethiopia such as Tigray and Gondar. Much land is owned by wealthy landlords who reap the profits of tenant farmers but do not put money back. As a result peasant farmers exist at a subsistence level. Ethiopia (then called Abyssinia) attracts the attention of Italy's fascist Government. Using Eritrea as a military base, Italy prepares for war, and, by late 1935 invades the country. Haile Selassie flees to the UK. In 1941 the Italians are forced out of Ethiopia by British and African troops. Ethiopia and Eritrea are placed under British administration until 1952.

In 1952 Ethiopia gains independence and is federated with Eritrea. Haile Selassie is restored as Emperor. He gains most support from the Amhara, and his Government continues to neglect the needs of the non-Amharic majority. In Tigray, a province of six million people, there was only one road and five secondary schools in 1973. Haile Selassie is criticised for his policies during the famine of 1974, and is overthrown by army officers. There are hopes that the new Government, led by Colonel Mengistu, will improve the lot of Ethiopians and Eritreans, but it draws its support from the Amharic minority, the same people who backed Haile Selassie. The policy of neglect of Ethiopia's regions continues, while the new Government – the Derg – increases military spending. Human rights violations increase, and many opponents of the regime are imprisoned. In 1975 the Tigrayan People's Liberation Front is formed to fight for regional autonomy for Tigray. Somalis and Oromo also form armed organisations, and fighting erupts in Tigray and in Southern Ethopia.

1980s – In 1983 and 1985 most of Ethiopia suffers serious food shortages after the rains fail, especially Eritrea and Tigray. Fighting means that food cannot reach starving people. Over six million people are forced to leave their villages and walk to refugee camps in Sudan and Ethiopia. In 1987 famine strikes again.

1990s – Parts of Eritrea and Tigray are also threatened by swarms of locusts as fighting prevents aerial spraying. The Ethiopian Government resettles thousands of people on to collective farms in southern Ethiopia. Parts of Ethiopia are again threatened by famine in 1990, made worse by civil war. Opposition groups in Ethiopia unite to form the Ethiopian People's Revolutionary Democratic Front (EPRDF) which is dominated by the Tigrayan People's Liberation Front, and operates in cooperation with the Eritrea People's Liberation Front.

The military successes of the EPRDF puts the Derg under increasing strain. In May 1991 the Ethiopian Government collapses, and the EPRDF marches into Addis Ababa. It forms a transitional government announcing its commitment to democracy. During 1992-94 human rights violations decrease, but some opposition journalists are still imprisoned. The EPRDF attracts opposition from Addis Ababa's urban and Amharic-speaking middle class, who fear that the Government is dominated by Tigrayans, and does not take their needs into account. The Oromo Liberation Front continues in its armed opposition to the Ethiopian Government. Elections are postponed. Opposition to the Ethiopian Government by ethnic Somalis grows. Three main political parties represent this group: the moderate Somali Democratic League, the Ogaden National Liberation Front and al-Ittihad al-Islamia, an armed Islamic fundamentalist group. In July 1995, the Ethiopian armed forces attack al-Ittihad al-Islamia's guerrilla bases in Somalia. Tension also grows on the border with Djibouti, where there are armed attacks by the Afar Revolutionary Democratic Unity Front.

In 1996 a number of ethnic Somalis are arrested, after the attempted assassination of an ethnic Somali political activist by al-Ittihad al-Islamia. From 1998 to 2000 Ethiopia and Eritrea fight over disputed border territory. After lulls and periods of intense fighting, a ceasefire is signed in 2000. During the fighting some 67,000 Eritreans resident in Ethiopia are expelled and 270,000 Ethiopians are internally displaced. Parliamentary elections are held in 2000. The Oromo Liberation Front is not allowed to participate because it will not renounce violence.

Ethiopian refugees in the UK
There are about 12,000 Ethiopian refugees in the UK. They have been arriving in small numbers since the mid 1970s. Until May 1993 the Home Office did not keep separate statistics for Ethiopians and Eritreans. Asylum statistics from 1993 are listed below.

Ethiopian refugees in the UK – Statistics

Year	Asylum applications	Refugee status as percentages	ELR	Refusal
1993	615	1	98	1
1994	730	1	12	87
1995	585	1	7	92
1996	205	3	17	80
1997	145	9	15	76
1998	345	34	10	56
1999	455	31	12	57

Most Ethiopian refugees in the UK are Amhara from Addis Ababa and its environs. They include opponents of the Derg, and most recently opponents of the new Government.

The UK has also received smaller numbers of Tigrayan and Oromo refugees. The latter are still fleeing due to fighting in south east Ethiopia, as well as repression of Oromo political activists. The Oromo community numbers about 1,500 and there are about 1,000 Tigrayan refugees. Each have their own community associations. In London there are five community schools that teach Amharic and others that teach Oromo and Tigrinya. In some schools and colleges there has been tension between groups of Ethiopian and Eritrean students as a result of the recent border conflict.

Throughout the 1990s a steady number of unaccompanied refugee children from Ethiopia arrived in this country. They included ethnic Eritreans, children fleeing conscription, and the children of opponents of the Government. Most are brought out of Ethiopia by an agent and taken to Ethiopian community organisations in central London. Most Ethiopian refugees live in Greater London with the largest numbers in central and north east London.

Bibliography
Pankhurst, R. and Pankhurst B. (1998) *The Ethiopians,* Oxford: Blackwells

Marcus, H. (1995) *A History of Ethiopia*, Berkeley, CA: University of California Press

Tronvoll, K. (2000) *Ethiopia: A New Start*, London: Minority Rights Group.

■ Refugees from India

Between 1989 and 1999 some 18,145 asylum applications from India were lodged with the Home Office, peaking in 1994-1996. Indians were one of the largest groups to arrive during this period and accounted for 5.5 per cent of asylum applications. Indian asylum seekers are unlikely to be given asylum. In 1997, more than 99 per cent of asylum decisions were refusals. Although some applications may be unfounded, there are significant numbers of asylum-seekers from the Punjab and Kashmir who have fled armed conflict and/or human rights abuse. These cases are well documented. In particular, Sikhs associated with secessionism may be arrested, harassed and tortured in the Punjab and elsewhere in India. In Jammu and Kashmir an estimated 17,000 people were killed between 1989 and 1995 by guerrillas and Indian police and armed forces.

The Refugee Council sees very few Indian clients. Sikhs from the Punjab do, however, use the services of the Medical Foundation for the Care of Victims of Torture (some 341 Sikh clients between 1991 and 1998). All cited an experience of torture and almost were initially refused refugee status or ELR by the Home Office. Asylum-seekers from India seek the support of established organisations that deal with the welfare needs of UK-born Indians as well as refugees.

Within schools, asylum-seeking and refugee children from India may not be identified as 'refugees' by teachers but seen rather as part of a larger group of ethnic minority pupils. The researcher believes that this may not matter save in situations where a child has had an overwhelmingly traumatic experience and may need specialist psychotherapy.

■ Refugees from Indonesia

About 1,000 asylum-seekers from Indonesia have entered the UK, mostly in 1998 and 1999. Almost all are ethnic Chinese from Java who fled the targeting of their community during the political violence of 1998 and 1999. Very few refugees from Indonesia's other conflicts have reached western Europe as they lack the means to escape.

Within Indonesia over 500,000 people were internally displaced in mid-2000. They include

*   West Papuans on the island of Irian Jaya

*   Ethnic Madurese transmigrants in West Kalimantan (Borneo), where indigenous Dayaks and local Malays have attacked the mostly Christian Madurese settlers

*   Acehnese (Aceh is on the northern tip of Sumatra)

*   Victims of Christian-Muslim violence on islands such as Ambon and Halmahera (both part of the Moluccas islands in the province of Maluku)

*   Victims of violence on Lombok island.

Bibliography
Chin Ung Ho (2000) *The Chinese of South-East Asia*, London: Minority Rights Group

Good sources of information on Indonesia include the US Committee for Refugees (www.refugees.org) or Tapol (wwwww.gn.apc.org/tapol).

■ Refugees from Iran

Since 1980 over 28,000 Iranian refugees have arrived in the UK. The Islamic Republic of Iran has a population of 67.5 million (1997 estimate) of whom 69 per cent live in urban areas. The capital is Tehran.

Ethnic groups: Over the last 3,000 years different invaders and migrants have settled in Iran. Although 60 per cent identify themselves as Persians, the culture and people of Iran reflect these many waves of migration. Forty per cent of the population belong to minority groups, the largest of which are the Azeris, comprising 27 per cent of the total population. Others include the Kurds (15 per cent of the population), Turkmen (3 per cent), Baluchis (2.5 per cent), Arabs (2.5 per cent), Armenians (2 per cent), Assyrians and Jews. Refugees from all of these minority communities have fled Iran, in particular Kurds, Armenians and Jews.

Languages: Persian is the official language, spoken by most people in Iran, and also in western Afghanistan. In Iran it is generally referred to as Farsi; in Afghanistan it is called Dari. Persian is one of the world's oldest languages and belongs to the Indo-European language family. Since the 7th century it has been written in the Arabic script with a number of additional letters to accommodate extra sounds. Written from right to left, it uses 32 letters, all primarily used as consonants. Four of the 32 letters have a secondary use as vowel sounds. Like Arabic, other vowel sounds are indicated by marks, known as points, placed above or below the letters. Most modern Persian books for adults omit the points, but they are used in school books. Modern Persian has a standard written form that is taught in schools. Spoken Persian shows regional variations. Dari, Hazara and Aimaq, all spoken in Afghanistan, are considered to be distinct dialects of Persian.

Azeri is spoken by about five million people in the Province of Azerbaijan and is linguistically related to Turkish. Gilaki and Mazanderani are both related to Persian and are spoken in northern Iran along the shores of the Caspian Sea. Kurdish is spoken by many of Iran's five million Kurds, although the use of the language has been heavily discouraged. Between 1946 and 1979 it was forbidden to speak or write Kurdish, so most Iranian Kurds are not literate in their language.

Baluchi is spoken by about 500,000 people in South East Iran. Other languages include Arabic (500,000 speakers), Turkmen (500,000), Armenian (250,000) and Assyrian (100,000).

Names: Iranian men and women have a first personal name. This can be followed by their father's name and a family or descriptive name. Women usually retain their family names on marriage but children adopt their father's family name. In the UK a few Iranian women are now changing their family names when they marry.

Religion: Some 80 per cent of Iranians are Shi'a Muslims. The Kurdish minority are mostly Sunni Muslims. Other religious groups include Armenian Christians, Assyrian Christians, the Baha'i, Zoroastrians, Jews and a small number of Catholics and Protestants.

In the late 1970s soaring inflation and discontent with the Shah's autocratic regime provoked active opposition. The exiled Ayatollah Ruhollah Khomenei, supported by Islamic clergy, inspired millions of ordinary Iranians who were disappointed with the failures of Western capitalism and saw Islamic fundamentalism as a radical alternative. In 1979 the Shah was forced to flee, and his Government was replaced by a 15-member Islamic Revolutionary Council. Supreme power was vested in a religious leader – initially the Ayatollah Khomenei. After a brief power struggle, the Islamic clergy emerged as the only force capable of taking control of Iran. A new constitution and legislative changes were introduced, both based on *sharia* – Islamic law and religious teaching. As part of the new ideology women were rapidly removed from public life. An Islamic dress code was adopted. The age of marriage was reduced to nine years. Divorce laws were changed, preventing women from obtaining a divorce save under the most extreme circumstances. Married women convicted of adultery were punished by stoning to death. Sexual segregation in education has drastically reduced the opportunities available to women and certain professions are barred to them.

Many secular Iranians actively supported the overthrow of the Shah, but soon became disillusioned with the new regime. As the Government adopted more repressive measures, secular Iranians began to flee. Most Iranian refugees living in the UK are not religiously observant.

A small number of *Mujahideen Khalq* have fled to the UK. The *Mujahideen Khalq* are a Shi'a political group whose ideology is a mixture of socialism and Islam. Most of the *Mujahideen Khalq* are exiled in Iraq.

Iran's Islamic constitution recognises the rights of other religions, and Sunni Muslims, Christians, Jews and Zoroastrians are all represented in the *Majlis* – the Parliament. But Iranian Jews and Armenians have, nevertheless, been forced to flee. In 1979 Iran had a Jewish community of about 70,000 people. After the revolution Iran immediately aligned itself against Israel and made Zionist activity a crime punishable by death. Some prominent Jews were executed. At the same time the Ayatollah Khomenei publicly reassured Jews of their safety in Iran. But in the face of blatant anti-Zionist ideology many Jews felt unsafe. Between 1980 and 1992 over 55,000 Jews fled Iran, to Israel or to European countries. Many Armenian Christians have also fled Iran. Extremist elements in the Islamic clergy have harassed teachers in Tehran's Armenian schools, and some Armenian businesses have found it difficult to function. More information about the Armenian community is given on page 194.

The Baha'i faith has about five million adherents worldwide, including about 300,000 followers in Iran. This religion was founded in the 19th century in southern Iran and rooted in Shi'a Islam, although it is a separate religion. Followers believe that God's will has been revealed throughout the ages by a series of prophets, including the Lord Buddha, Zarathrustra, Adam, Moses, Jesus Christ and Mohammed. The Baha'i do not have the recognition afforded to other religious minorities and have suffered extensive persecution since 1979. Many holy places have been destroyed and the Baha'i have been ordered to recant their faith in public. In some parts of Iran local government officials have treated the Baha'i with great harshness and over 200 have been murdered. Hundreds more have been detained, imprisoned or tortured in an attempt to force them to renounce their faith. They also suffer systematic economic discrimination and are denied welfare benefits and pensions. In some parts of Iran the Baha'i have lost their land or been denied business licences.

Iranians of all religions celebrate the Yalda and Nourouz festivals. The Yalda festivals marks the longest night of the year, and has its roots in the Zoroastrian religion and in the ancient traditions of Persia. Nourouz is the Iranian New Year and is celebrated in the Spring.

Education system: Education is compulsory for five years between the ages of six and ten years, but this entitlement has not been fully implemented in rural areas. Children may attend nursery classes, but most children start school at six. Primary education lasts five years and culminates in a final examination, success in which entitles students to enter secondary education. Secondary education can last for seven years and is divided into a three year guidance cycle and a two or four year intermediate cycle. At the end of the guidance cycle students take a national examination called the Certificate of General Education. Those who pass are entitled to enter the intermediate cycle where students can specialise in either an academic, industrial, service industry related or rural and agricultural course. There are also specialist vocational schools. Students on academic courses take a general curriculum for three years and a final year of specialisation in arts, natural science, physics and mathematics or social sciences. The final *Diplom Metevaseth* or National High School Diploma is deemed to be the equivalent of a GCSE pass at grades A to C on a subject-by-subject basis. Students choosing vocational courses may study in programmes lasting for two or four years (British Council, 1998). The medium of instruction in all schools is Farsi.

The Islamic Revolution made extensive educational changes. All schools were immediately segregated, including nursery schools. In the early 1980s the curriculum was rewritten to reflect Islamic ideology. Many teachers and educational administrators left at this time. Religious teaching now plays a major role in the curriculum and in school life. The Armenian and Jewish communities have their own schools, as do other recognised religious minorities. These are obliged to follow the national curriculum and use Farsi as the medium of instruction. Private schools and coeducational schools are banned. The literacy rate is 71 per cent for men, compared with 50 per cent for women. Figures from 1994 indicate that 89 per cent of boys and 78 per cent of girls were enrolled in primary and secondary education. Levels of literacy are higher in urban areas and lowest in rural Baluchistan and Iranian Kurdistan.

Economy: About 30 per cent of the population are employed in agriculture, particularly the production of wheat, fresh and dried fruits. Carpet manufacture also employs many people. Iran has substantial oil reserves, which account for most of its export earnings. Central Iran and the areas around the Caspian Sea are the most fertile regions. Baluchistan is dry and infertile and one of the most impoverished regions.

A chronology of events: Iran has been inhabited since the 18th century BC by peoples speaking Indo-European languages. From the 10th century BC a recognisable Persian culture developed, and by 500 BC the Persians controlled a large empire, stretching as far as the Mediterranean and India. The Persian Empire later fell into the hands of Alexander the Great and subsequently parts of the Empire were conquered by the Seleucid Turks and the Romans. The area which is now Iran was brought under the control of the Arab Caliphate of Baghdad in the 7th century AD and Islamic thought and practice were introduced. After the collapse of the Caliphate of Baghdad, Persia attained autonomy under the rule of Seleucid and Persian dynasties. This was a time of great scientific and cultural achievement. In 1258 Persia was invaded by the Mongols. For three centuries political life was dominated by conflicts between the Mongols and the Ottoman Turks. Eventually a Persian monarch united the country, expelling the Turks. Persia was then ruled by a succession of dynasties. In 1906 it became a constitutional monarchy ruled by a Shah.

1909-1925: A treaty divides Persia into two areas – one under the economic influence of the UK and the other under Russia. The UK exploits the oil fields. During the First World War Persia is occupied by the British and Russians. Foreign occupation and widespread government corruption lead to popular unrest. In 1921 the Government is overthrown by Reza Khan, commander of the National Guard who installs himself as the Minister of War and later Prime Minister. In 1925, with the support of the *Majlis* (Parliament) Reza Khan ousts the Shah, and takes the throne. He tries to turn Persia into a modern and neutral state, abolishing the obligatory wearing of the veil, and modernising the health and education systems. He cancels British oil concessions. In 1935 Persia is renamed Iran.

1940s and 1950s: In 1941 Reza Shah refuses to allow a consignment of Allied arms to pass through Iran. After issuing an ultimatum, the British and Soviet armies invade Iran. Reza Shah is forced to abdicate in favour of his son, Mohammed Reza Pahlavi. Educated in Europe, the new

Shah is perceived to be more amenable to British interests. The 1949 constitution restricts the power of the Shah. Prime Minister Mossadegh attempts to reduce economic dependence on the UK and tries to nationalise the oil fields. In 1953 he is overthrown in a CIA-backed coup, and much political power returns to the Shah. Mossadegh is imprisoned, and thousands of socialist and nationalist politicians are killed or detained.

1960s: Iran experiences a period of increasing westernisation, greater penetration by trans-national companies, rapid economic growth, but increasing urban poverty. These changes are known as the 'White Revolution'. The Islamic clergy oppose the Shah's modernisation policies. Peaceful demonstrations, inspired by the Ayatollah Khomeini, are crushed by the armed forces and many demonstrators are killed. Khomeini is forced into exile.

1970s: A huge rise in oil prices increases Iran's oil revenue. The Shah launches an ambitious spending programme which fuels inflation and exacerbates tensions within Iranian society. The spending boom is followed by harsh austerity measures to control inflation. The poor suffer most from government spending cuts. Antagonism towards the Shah's regime increases. In 1975 all political parties except the Resurgence Party are banned. The Shah declares that all those who oppose the new order 'can take their passports and leave the country'. In 1977 Amnesty International criticises the Iranian Government's record on human rights. Protests mount in Iran, with numerous strikes and demonstrations. The best organised opposition to the Shah's regime comes from the exiled Ayatollah Khomeini. Many protests are violently suppressed and martial law is declared in 1978. In 1979 Shahpur Bakhtiar forms a new Government in a last-ditch attempt to avert a revolution. The Shah flees the country soon after; the Ayatollah Khomeini arrives in Tehran and Iran is declared an Islamic Republic. Governing powers are initially vested to a 15-member Islamic Revolutionary Council. The new regime launches an attack on Iranian Kurdistan. Other breaches of human rights soon become apparent.

1980s: An intense power struggle within the Government continues for two years. Abol-Hasan Bani-Sadr becomes President, and more elections are held for the *Majlis* (Parliament). The Islamic Revolutionary Council is then dissolved. Women are expelled from government offices. The universities are closed. There are numerous border conflicts with Iraq, tension is heightened when Khomeini calls for the Shi'a of Iraq to rebel against the 'atheistic Ba'athist regime'. In September 1980 Iraqi troops cross the Shatt-al-Arab Canal to claim territory. The Iran/Iraq war begins; it is to last for eight years.

In 1981 President Bani-Sadr is deposed. A bomb attack on the offices of the ruling Islamic Republic Party kills 70 politicians. A later bomb kills the President and Prime Minister. Hojatolislam Ali Khamenei becomes the new President. The Revolutionary Guards continue a campaign of terror, executions and arrests as the regime crushes all internal opposition. In 1982 Iranian students in foreign universities are banned from receiving money from Iran. Human rights abuses continue, Kurdish and Baha'i minorities are subject to widespread persecution. After signs of internal dissent in 1988, arrests and executions of political opponents escalate. At least 2,500 people are executed. Faced with an ailing economy and no prospect of winning the war with Iraq, President Khamenei agrees to a ceasefire, and to accept UN Resolution 598, calling for an end to fighting.

1990s: Ayatollah Khomeini dies in 1989 and Ayatollah Khameini becomes Iran's new spiritual leader. Another power struggle ends with the 'reformist' Hashemi Rafsanjani being elected President. There are further constitutional changes and the post of Prime Minister is abolished. The 'reformists' indicate a desire to improve relations with the West. During the 1991 Gulf War Iran maintains a neutral position. There are a few signs of improvements in human rights, such as an amnesty for draft evaders and war deserters. But arrests and executions of political activists continue. Former Prime Minister Bakhtiar is assassinated in Paris. Rafsanjani states that any returning refugees 'must adapt themselves to the country's revolutionary code of conduct'. In 1992 Rafsanjani is re-elected President. But there are disturbances in some of Iran's main cities due to dissatisfaction with Government policy, followed by mass arrests and executions. In 1993 the UN issues a resolution condemning human rights violations. President Rafsanjani stands down and following elections in 1997 he is replaced by Seyed Mohammad Khatami, who draws his power base from youth, women and the middle classes, who desire greater social freedom and more economic opportunity. Relations with western countries thaw. There are increased tensions between reformist and fundamentalist clerics and politicians culminating in the extrajudicial execution of several journalists in 1998. Gholamhossein Karbashi, Tehran's moderate and popular mayor, is suspended from duty, after corruption charges are levelled against him, and ultimately sentenced to five years imprisonment. Although human rights violations have decreased, journalists are still subject to harassment. The conditions faced by the Baha'i have not improved.

Iranian refugees in the UK – Statistics

Year	Asylum Applications	Refugee Status as percentage	ELR	Refusal
1993	365	36	46	22
1994	520	36	9	55
1995	615	43	7	50
1996	585	41	8	51
1997	585	45	7	48
1998	745	23	54	23
1999	1,320	37	13	50

These figures exclude dependants after 1985. Source: Home Office.

Most Iranian refugees live in north and west London, although most university towns have small Iranian communities. They encounter many of the same problems faced by other groups of refugees: unemployment, lack of recognition of qualifications and, for some, language problems. But Iranians who previously studied in the UK have generally faired better than other groups of refugees.

A visa requirement for Iranians was imposed in 1979, making it difficult for people to escape the country. Refugees who have been imprisoned in Iran are likely to have been tortured. The Medical Foundation for the Care of Victims of Torture has seen more Iranians than any other national group.

Iranian refugees come from different ethnic groups and have widely diverse political sympathies. Some of those who sought asylum in the early 1980s were supporters of the Shah. They may have already been in the UK, usually as students, and could not return. Other Iranians with monarchist sympathies fled immediately after the revolution. But at the same time many politically active Iranians, particularly on the left, welcomed the revolution and chose to return home. Most soon found themselves opposing the new regime once its abuse of human rights and fundamentalist policies became apparent. They then fled Iran. Those who had studied abroad often returned to exile in the countries and towns where they had studied. Other refugees, who had not been politically active at the time of the Shah's regime, increasingly found themselves in conflict with the post-revolutionary Government.

Iranian students are still coming to the UK, as asylum-seekers and for other reasons such as business or study. In 1986 a bomb killed an Iranian student who was known to be an opponent of the Iranian Government. This shocked the Iranian community. The bombing, the 1998 assassination of Iranian dissidents in Germany and Switzerland and the obvious political differences between different groups of Iranians engender distrust – some Iranians might to be suspicious of other groups of Iranians and/or students.

There are Iranian community organisations in London and Leeds, and a successful community school teaching Farsi to children in London. Minority groups such as the Baha'i and the Armenians generally use their own community organisations.

Bibliography

Cooper, R. (1991) *The Baha'is of Iran*, London: Minority Rights Group

Hiro, D. (1985) *Iran under the Ayatollahs*, London: Paladin

Refugee Council (1998) *Persian and English Words for School Use*, London: Refugee Council.

■ Refugees from Iraq (including Iraqi Kurdistan)

Over 23,000 Iraqi refugees, including Iraqi Kurds, have fled to the UK since the 1970s. Iraq had a population of 21 million in 1999 of whom 73 per cent live in urban areas. Since the end of the Gulf War in 1991 Iraq has been essentially divided: nearly four million Kurds live in autonomous Iraqi Kurdistan. The capital of Iraq is Baghdad. The administrative headquarters of Iraqi Kurdistan is Arbil.

Ethnic groups: About 70 per cent of the population are Arabs. Another 23 per cent are Kurdish, mostly living in Kurdistan. About two per cent of the population are Turkmen, another two per cent are Assyrian Christians. Iraq also has a small Armenian community. Most Iraqi refugees in the UK are Kurdish. The origins of the Kurdish people are uncertain, but some anthropologists believe that they are an amalgamation of Indo-European tribes who have lived in the Zagros mountains for over 4,000 years. Kurdish society has developed its own distinct culture and a strong sense of identity. In rural areas Iraqi Kurds have strong clan loyalties which still determine which political parties they support.

Within Iraqi Kurdistan other minority groups such as Jews and Assyrians have been absorbed into the predominantly Kurdish culture. The Assyrians are the other victims of the Iraqi Government's persecution, and many Assyrian villages and churches have been destroyed. They live in towns and villages in Iraqi Kurdistan, but unlike the Kurds their first language is Assyrian. They are generally more prosperous than their Kurdish neighbours, and many have relatives in the US or in Europe. During the Gulf War Assyrians were identified as being pro-western, whatever their real views were. There is also a Turkmen community of an estimated 350,000 to 900,000 people. They speak Turkmen, a language closely related to Turkish used also in Turkmeniya and Afghanistan. The Turkmen allege they have suffered persecution at the hands of the Iraqi Government. Relations between Turkmen and Kurds have often been tense, and no ethnic Turkmen have seats in the Kurdish parliament.

Languages: Arabic is the official language of Iraq, spoken as a second language by many Kurds and Assyrians. Arabic is a Semitic language, mostly closely related to Hebrew and Aramaic. Classical Arabic – the language of the Koran – is taught in *madrassah* and in schools. A modern simplified standard form of classical Arabic is used as a written language throughout the Arab world. Spoken Arabic varies from country to country, and the Iraqis have their own dialects.

Iraqi Kurds speak Kurdish as their first language. It is an Indo-European language, most closely related to Persian and Luri. There are two main Kurdish dialects: Kurmanji and Sorani. Kurmanji is spoken in Turkey and in Iraq northwards from Mosul to the Caucasus and has been scripted in Roman and Cyrillic scripts. Sorani is spoken in western Iraqi Kurdistan, and is written in a modified Arabic script. It is now the official Kurdish language used in Iraqi Kurdistan. It is also the dominant literary form because of the relative cultural freedoms granted to Iraqi Kurds. Unlike in Turkey and Iran, the Kurdish language was never banned in Iraq.

A minority Kurdish group called the Yazidis speak Kurmanji dialects. The Yazidis also adhere to their own religious beliefs, incorporating aspects of Islam, Zoroatrianism, Nestorian Christianity, Judaism and Manichaeism. Most Yazidis live in the Mosul region of Iraqi Kurdistan.

Assyrians speak Assyrian – sometimes incorrectly called Aramaic or Syriac – a Semitic language developed from Aramaic, the language used in the Middle East from about the 4th century BC when it was written in Hebrew script. Aramaic was the language of Jesus Christ. After the 7th century AD Aramaic was gradually replaced by Arabic and Turkish in most of the Middle East but the language has survived as Assyrian and Syriac. The latter is the liturgical language of the Chaldean, Nestorian and Maronite churches. Syriac is written in several different scripts. Assyrian is the first language of the Assyrian people. They live in northern Iraq, but also in Syria, Lebanon and Iran. Assyrian is written in the Nestorian script. The script has developed from cursive Hebrew, and is written from right to left. Kurdish Jews also speak Assyrian. Turkmen and Armenian are spoken by the respective minority groups.

Names: Iraqi Arabs use an Islamic naming system: a first personal name followed by their father's personal name, then their grandfather's. Women keep their own names on marriage. Many Iraqi Kurds use this naming system. Some Kurds may have a personal name and then use their grandfather's name as a family name. Other Kurds may have personal name, their father's name and then a family name reflecting a place or clan membership. In western countries many Kurds adopt their grandfather's name as a family name. Assyrian Christians may use a European naming system. Others have a first personal name, followed by their father's name and then their grandfather's name. The names used by Assyrian Christians are often the names of saints.

Religion: Shi'a Muslims make up 55 to 60 per cent of the total Iraqi population. The majority of Shi'a Muslims live in southern Iraq and in the poorer suburbs of Baghdad. Their numbers include a minority Shi'a Kurdish group called the Faili Kurds. Sunni Muslims make up 20 per cent of the Iraqi population, and mostly live in northern Iraq. Most Iraqi Kurds are also Sunni Muslims, although religion is not a major component of Kurdish identity.

The most important Shi'a shrine is at Kerbala in Iraq. Despite being in the majority, the Shi'a population has historically been underprivileged and politically weak. Few Shi'a hold senior government positions. Since the late 1970s the Iraqi Government has operated a carrot and stick policy towards the Shi'a, providing some economic assistance to southern Iraq and dispensing rewards to communities willing to cooperate. At the same time many religious Shi'a were suspected of having links with fellow Shi'a in Iran and ruthlessly oppressed.

The 1991 uprising in southern Iraq was started by dissident army personnel fleeing from Kuwait, not all Shi'a. For a brief period, repressed political forces – both Shi'a and secular – were active. Within a few weeks the uprising was ruthlessly crushed, suppressing both political and religious activity. Many clergy were arrested and Shi'a shrines desecrated. The Marsh Arabs of southern Iraq are Shi'a Muslims. They have seen their settlements bombed and their marshlands drained. Chemical weapons were probably used against the Marsh Arabs in 1993.

Assyrian Christians belong to two sects: Chaldeans and Nestorians. The Chaldeans recognise the Roman Catholic Pope as their patriarch but use the Eastern Rite when worshipping. The Nestorians are followers of Saint Nestor, a 5th century figure excommunicated for heresy by the Roman Catholic church. They have their own patriarch who lives in Chicago, USA. Both groups consider themselves ethnic Assyrians, and sometimes share the use of a church.

Education system: Until 1992 all primary and secondary education was under the control of the Ministry of Education. The medium of instruction was Arabic. Some pre-school education is available. Primary education starts at six and lasts for six years. Progress from class to class is dependent on passing examinations. At the end of primary schooling a Primary Baccalaureat examination can be taken.

Secondary education is divided into two three year cycles. During the intermediate cycle all students follow a common curriculum. They sit the Third Form Baccalaureat and those with the highest pass marks can progress to the second cycle but the rest can only attend vocational secondary schools. In the former students can choose between arts and science subjects, finishing school with the Sixth Form Baccalaureat, the basic qualification for university entrance. There are four types of vocational secondary school in Iraq: agricultural, industrial, veterinary and commercial. Courses last for three years (British Council, 1991). The literacy rate is 90 per cent for men and 88 per cent for women. Literacy is lower is rural Kurdistan and in southern Iraq.

In October 1991 the Iraqi Government withdrew all troops, funds and services from Iraqi Kurdistan (with the exception of the Kirkuk governorate). The Kurds started setting up their own administration, although they lacked funds and international recognition. Schools are functioning but lack basic equipment. The Kurdish administration has kept the basic structure of education but all teaching is now through the medium of Kurdish.

Economy: Iraq can be divided into three geographical regions. To the north are the mountains of Iraqi Kurdistan where the population is mostly rural and many are pastoralists. The plain of Mesopotamia runs through central Iraq, between the River Tigris and River Euphrates. This area is Iraq's food producing region; wheat and dates are the most important crops, and Iraq is the world's largest date producer. Iraq, nevertheless, has to import most of its basic foodstuffs. Southern Iraq is arid.

Until the Gulf War, Iraq was a middle-income country whose major source of income came from the production of crude oil. Iraqi oil sales are now restricted by UN resolutions, as is other trade with Iraq. Economic life has been severely affected by the embargo. Unemployment has risen and spare parts are in very short supply. Although food and medicine are exempt from sanctions, Iraq now lacks foreign exchange to purchase these goods and the UN embargo has hurt the poorest most of all. Hundreds of thousands of Iraqi children have died as a result of malnutrition and lack of basic medicines.

Causes of flight: Iraq: The territory which is now Iraq has been the cradle of many ancient civilisations: the Sumerians, Akkadians, Babylonians and Assyrians. The Greeks called the region 'Mesopotamia'. But the area paid dearly for its fertility and location and was conquered by many foreign powers. From the 16th century it was ruled by the Ottoman Empire. During the First World War the Arab population of the region rose up against their Turkish rulers. The British, keen to protect their oil interests, then occupied the country which was to become Iraq. After the First World War Iraq was placed under a League of Nations mandate administered by the British. Amir Faisal ibn Hussain, a member of the Hashemite family of Arabia, was nominated as monarch. Iraq gained full independence in 1931.

The 1940s and 1950s saw a rise in Arab nationalism throughout the Middle East, in particular the growth of Ba'athism, a political ideology developed in Syria in the 1940s. It emphasised Arab unity and promoted the idea of a single Arab nation. The Ba'athists advocated a secular socialist state which would redistribute wealth, but played down Marxist class conflict. Ba'athist parties gained great popular support in Iraq in the 1950s and were perceived as a threat to the monarchy. As a result all opposition parties were banned in 1953. In 1958 the monarchy was overthrown in a military coup which brought General Abdullah Karim Qasim to power. Initially he drew support from Ba'athists, communists and some Kurds. But over the next four years he lost his popularity, and was overthrown in 1963 by a coalition of Ba'athist and Iraqi nationalists. The Ba'athists were quickly driven from power and Iraq became ruled by a series of unstable governments. In 1968 the Ba'athist party staged a *coup d'etat.* Major General Ahmad Hassan al-Bakr became President, Prime Minister and Chairman of the Revolutionary Command Council (RCC). In 1979 Saddam Hussain, then Vice-Chairman of the RCC, replaced al-Bakr as President and Chairman.

Political power has been concentrated in the hands of the Ba'ath party. By establishing overlapping and competing security services and undermining the influence of alternative centres of power, Saddam Hussain has crushed any alternative political organisation. Since the 1970s Amnesty International has regularly documented extra-judicial executions, detentions, torture and large-scale disappearances. Up to 150,000 Kurdish people have disappeared. In the 1970s up to 100,000 people were deported to Iran, including a community of Shi'a Faili Kurds. At the beginning of the 1980s there was a second wave of deportations with up to 200,000 people, mostly Shi'a Muslims, being transferred to Iran after the Iraqi Government claimed they were Iranian.

In 1980 the Iraqi Government entered an expensive and bloody war with Iran following increased tensions between the two countries. In September 1980 Iraqi troops crossed into Iran to reclaim the Shatt-al-Arab Canal, which had been ceded to Iran in 1975. The war lasted eight years, and cost thousands of lives. Throughout the war the Iraqi Government received economic aid from Saudi Arabia and Kuwait, and was favoured by western powers who seemed oblivious to human rights violations. After the Iran-Iraq war ended the Iraqi Government launched a military campaign against the Kurds. In August 1990 Iraq marched into oil-rich Kuwait. To protect western interests the UN launched a military campaign against the Iraqi regime. Kuwait was liberated, but the campaign stopped short of toppling Saddam Hussain. Many Kurds and Iraqi Arabs saw it as the time to act. During March/April 1991 there were uprisings in Kurdistan and southern Iraq, but they were met with brutal repression by the army and security services, causing two million people to flee the country. In southern Iraq an estimated 150,000 people were arrested as a result of the uprising. Today human rights violations continue unabated. More than 3,000 people have been murdered in prison since 1997. Targets of human rights abuses include

- anyone suspected of supporting opposition politicians
- Kurds living outside Iraqi Kurdistan
- Marsh Arabs
- Shi'a Muslims, who face arbitary arrest, deportations, as a result of being suspected of disloyalty to the Iraqi Government
- Assyrians (suspected of siding with Kurdish opposition)

Since the Gulf War there have been moves among Iraqi opposition parties to develop a common platform. An alliance known as the Iraqi National Congress was formed in 1992 and is based in London.

The Kurds: The Kurds mostly live in the mountainous areas of eastern Turkey, northern Iraq, north west Iran and the southern Caucasus. In the years before the First World War Kurdistan was divided between the Ottoman and Persian Empires. The largely nomadic Kurdish population was afforded autonomy in return for policing this border. When the Ottoman Empire was broken up the Kurds had hopes of independence. The Treaty of Sevres signed in 1920 promised autonomy for both Armenians and Kurds. But it was vetoed by the Turkish Government, and in 1923 the Treaty of Lausanne divided Kurdistan between Turkey, Iran, Iraq, Syria and the Soviet Union. The reaction of the Kurds was to rebel. The early revolts were not nationalistic. But in 1958 a group of Kurds, led by Mullah Mustafa Barzani, returned from exile and founded the Kurdish Democratic Party (KDP). It called for Kurdish autonomy in a bi-national state. This demand was rejected by the Iraqi Government and Barzani returned to Kurdistan and launched a guerrilla war.

After nearly ten years of hostilities the Iraqi Government agreed to Kurdish autonomy in 1970. But mutual suspicion and Baghdad's reluctance to cede the oil-rich city of Kirkuk caused the agreement to break down. A much diluted autonomy agreement was offered to the Kurds in 1974. It was rejected and a fierce war followed in which the Kurds were supported by Iran. In 1975 Iran signed an agreement of cooperation with Iraq and withdrew its support for the Kurds in exchange for territorial concessions in the Persian Gulf. Kurdish resistance collapsed.

In 1975 the Patriotic Union of Kurdistan (PUK), led by Jalal Talabani, split from the KDP. Several smaller leftist parties also emerged together with an Islamic Party and an Assyrian party. The KDP began to revive its fortunes in the 1980s, and is now led by Masoud Barzani, son of Mullah Musafa Barzani. During the Iran-Iraq war (1980-88) Kurdish guerrillas – known as *peshmergas* – were again backed by Iran. From the mid-1980s the Iraqi Government began an operation to clear parts of Iraqi Kurdistan of their predominantly Kurdish population. An estimated 500,000 Kurds were deported from their homes on the Turkish and Iranian frontiers. Their villages were destroyed, making return impossible. The deliberate policy of clearing Kurdish villages culminated in the 1988 Anfal campaign. Up to 5,000 Kurdish villages were razed and many former inhabitants deported to towns in southern Iraq. Others were put in camps, or simply disappeared. An estimated 100,000 people disappeared, presumed murdered, in the Anfal campaign.

From 1987 the Iraq regime began to use chemical weapons against the Kurds. In March 1988 some 6,000 people were killed in a chemical weapons attack on the town of Halabja. The Iran-Iraq war came to an end on 20th August 1988. During the next two weeks the Iraqi army drove Kurdish guerrillas out of their strongholds, using saturation bombing and chemical weapons. Despite a UN Resolution condemning Iraq's use of chemical weapons, no member of the UN Security Council took any action against Iraq. By the end of 1988 340,000 Iraqi Kurdish refugees were living in Iran and another 90,000 in Turkey. Refugees also fled to European countries.

After the 1991 Gulf War there was a short-lived uprising in Kurdistan. It was followed by massive Iraqi reprisals. Nearly two million Kurdish refugees fled to Turkey and Iran. In April 1991 the Gulf War allies imposed a 'safe haven' covering north east Kurdistan and subsequently created a no-fly zone above the 36th parallel. This led to the return of many of the refugees, although Iraqi forces remained in the Kurdish areas outside the safe haven. Kurdish leaders held talks with the Iraqi Government in mid-1991, but these broke down, mainly over the issue of access to oil-rich Kirkuk. There were also skirmishes between Iraqi troops and *peshmergas*. In October 1991 the Iraqi Government withdrew all troops, funds and services from most of Kurdistan (apart from the governorate of Kirkuk). It imposed an embargo on goods crossing the *de facto* border. The Kurds have now set up their own administration and a Kurdish parliament, with the KDP and the PUK dividing most of the seats between them. The Kurdish administration is able to raise taxes but it lacks funds and international recognition and is under many strains. There have been continued clashes between supporters of the PUK and KDP and since 1995 Iraqi Kurdistan has effectively been divided into two areas – one owing loyalty to PUK, the other to the KDP. Iraqi Kurds have fled to the UK as a result of these clashes. Kurdish political leaders have been assassinated by fellow Kurds. Since 1996, the KDP has formed an alliance with the Iraqi Government, while the PUK is supported by the Iranian Government. Numerous attempts at reconciliation between the two Kurdish factions have failed.

In 1999 there were reports of fighting between Turkmen and Iraqi Kurds in Arbil. The continuation of the UN no-fly zone over northern Iraq, and the passage of basic supplies, is dependent on the Turkish Government which is violently opposed to a separate Kurdish state. The Turkish army has made numerous incursions into Iraqi Kurdistan, and Iraqi Kurds have become involved in efforts to crush Turkish Kurdish guerrillas. The Iranian army has also made incursions into Iraqi Kurdistan.

Iraqi and Iraqi Kurdish refugees in the UK – Statistics

Year	Applications for Asylum	Refugee Status as percentages	ELR	Refusal
1985	251	32	59	9
1986	210	15	57	28
1987	210	11	57	32
1988	163	9	74	17
1989	215	23	77	0
1990	985	32	63	5
1991	915	26	66	8
1992	700	13	84	3
1993	495	36	61	3
1994	550	59	34	7
1995	930	72	22	6
1996	965	71	20	9
1997	1,075	38	45	17
1998	1,295	47	45	8
1999	1,800	43	43	14

There are about 23,000 refugees from Iraq currently living in the UK. The largest group are Iraqi Kurds whose community numbers about 14,000 and mostly arrived in the UK after 1988. Since 1997, Iraqi Kurdish asylum applications have increased because of conflict between the two Kurdish factions in Iraqi Kurdistan. Iraqi Kurds now make up the majority of asylum applicants from Iraq. Most are single men aged between 15 and 25 years.

Most Iraqi Kurds live in Greater London or Kent. The dispersal of asylum-seekers from Kent and Greater London has meant that some are settled in other parts of the UK, in particular Liverpool, Glasgow, Yorkshire and the North East The Kurdish Cultural Centre is one of several community organisations working with Iraqi Kurdish refugees. It provides an advice and casework service for newly-arrived refugees and organises many cultural events, notably the *Nawroz* festivities – Kurdish New Year, celebrated in the Spring. Iraqi Kurdish children also have the opportunity to attend a supplementary school in London.

Most Iraqi Kurds are from middle class families, although some may have experienced inter-
ruptions to their education. Most arrive in the UK speaking little or no English so access to
English classes remains a major need. Although Iraqi Kurds and Turkish Kurds both have a distinct
Kurdish identity, there are important social and political differences between them. Different
community organisations represent the needs of the two communities.

The Iraqi Arab refugee community numbers about 5,000, although others have entered as business people or students. The community dates back to the 1950s and mostly lives in Greater
London although some live in university towns such as Manchester. The community is well-
educated: a survey carried out in 1998 indicated that 60 per cent of men had first or higher
degrees from a university. Many Iraqi Arab refugees have been active in opposition politics, and
some come from prosperous backgrounds. At least ten community organisations serve their
needs. There are a large number of secular and religious Arabic language community schools for
children to attend. Some of these schools are organised by Iraqi community groups.

The UK also hosts a small Assyrian community of about 4,000 people, mostly living in west
London, in Ealing, Kensington and Chelsea and Hammersmith. The Nestorian Patriarch stayed in
Kensington on his way to the USA. He established an Assyrian Christian church in the locality;
other refugees settled near the church and their compatriots. There is an active Assyrian community organisation which runs a supplementary school among many other activities. Very small
numbers of other Iraqi minority groups live in the UK, including Jews, Armenians and Turkmen.

Bibliography

Al-Rasheed, M. (1994) *The Myth of Return: Iraqi Arab and Assyrian Refugees in London*. Paper submitted to
the Fourth International IRAP Conference.

Chaliand, G. (1994) *A People without a Country: the Kurds and Kurdistan*, London: Zed Press

Graham Bown, S. (1999) *Sanctioning Saddam: the politics of intervention in Iraq*, London: St Martin's Press

Iraqi Community Association (1996) *Now We Are Here: a survey of the profile, structure, needs hopes and
aspirations of the Iraqi community in Britain 1995-96*, London: Iraqi Community Association

McDowall, D. (1997) *The Kurds*, London: Minority Rights Group.

■ Refugees from the Ivory Coast

The Ivorian community in the UK numbers about 4,000. Most Ivorian refugees have been
politically active in their home country, as students, trade unionists or members of political
parties. The Ivory Coast is a middle income country. Its population is 17 million and its political
and administrative capital is Yamassouko. The main economic centre and largest city, is the former
capital, Abijan.

French is the official language and the medium of education. Those who live in towns and cities
and younger people living in villages speak and use French in almost all circumstances. Only older
villagers use African languages widely, with over 50 languages and dialects spoken, the most used
being Bete, Baule and Mandekan dialects (the latter usually called Dyula and Malinke in the Ivory
Coast).

The Ivory Coast obtained independence from France in 1960. Felix Houphouet-Boigny and his
Parti Democratique de la Cote d'Ivoire – Rassemblement Democratique Africain (PDCI-RDA) governed
the country until 1990. Multi-party democracy was banned.

The Ivory Coast is the world's largest producer of cocoa and also produces significant amounts
of coffee. It also has a comparatively large industrial sector. As a result of this prosperity, it enjoyed
two decades of political stability before a marked economic downturn in the 1980s prompted
political unrest. In early 1990, students and workers demonstrated against government austerity
measures, which the country had been forced to adopt. Many academic institutions were closed,
political opposition arrested and troops were deployed on the streets of Abijan. As a result of
continuing unrest President Houphouet-Boigny was forced to accept multi-party democracy but
won the first contested election in 1990 with over 80 per cent of the vote. The Government
continued to experience considerable opposition, mostly from students. Political opponents faced
beatings and detention.

President Houphouet-Boigny died in 1993 and was replaced by Henri Konan Bedie. Further presidential elections took place in 1995, following weeks of violence and demonstrations. Most opposition parties boycotted the elections and Bedie was returned to office. A military coup in 1999 followed mutiny by soldiers angered by unpaid wages. The new Head of State, General Robert Guei, promised free and fair elections. These were held in October 2000, although the favoured candidate was excluded from the ballot. Guei was declared winner, amid much popular unrest which continues.

Almost all Ivorian refugees in the UK have been politically active. Many were student activists. A very large proportion have studied at universities or are from professional backgrounds. The largest communities live in south east London where there are several active community organisations and a bakery.

Sources include Amnesty International and the Library of Congress Country Studies available on www.loc.gov

■ Refugees from Kenya

Some 9,000 Kenyans have fled to the UK since 1993. Kenya had a population of 29 million in 1999. The capital is Nairobi.

Ethnic groups: Over 70 different ethnic groups live in Kenya, the largest of which are the Kikiyu, 21 per cent of the population. Other significant groups include the Luo (14 per cent), Luhya (13.2 per cent), Kamba (11 per cent), Kalenjin (10.9 per cent), Kisii (6.4 per cent), Meru (5 per cent), Mijikenda (4.8 per cent), Somali (2.3 per cent), Turkhana (1.9 per cent and Maasai (1.4 per cent). There are also significant Asian, Arab and European minorities. Complex inter-ethnic conflict has displaced thousands of Kenyans since 1991.

Languages: Swahili is the official language although spoken as a first language by a comparatively small number of Kenyans, most of whom live on the east coast, but is understood by much of the adult population. English is also widely understood throughout Kenya. Much of the population in south east Kenya will understand Luo. The African languages spoken in Kenya belong to three different language families. Kikuyu, Swahili, Kamba, Kisii and Meru are Bantu languages belonging to the Niger-Congo family. Luo, Kalenjin, Turkhana and Maasai are Chari-Nile languages. Somali is an Afro-Asiatic language.

Names: Many Kenyans use a 'European' naming system of a first name and a family name and Kenyans use both western Christian names and African names. Muslims from the east coast will usually use an Islamic naming system: a first personal name, followed by the father's personal name and the grandfather's personal name.

Religion: An estimated 69 per cent of Kenyans are Christian, belonging to Roman Catholic, Protestant and African-led churches. Another 25 per cent of Kenyans practice traditional religions and some six per cent are Muslims, the latter mostly living on the east coast.

Education system: Primary school starts at six and lasts eight years. Some children attend Harambee schools – self-help schools built by a village or community and maintained by fees and donations. Schooling is usually through the medium of English, although some Harambee schools use local languages in the first two years. The Kenya Certificate of Primary Education is taken at the end of primary school. A good pass is needed to progress to secondary education. After two years of secondary education students sit the Kenya Junior School Certificate to stay for a further two years, chosing options that will take them to the Kenya Certificate of Secondary Education.

Economy: Kenya is a land of diverse geography. Much of the north-east is semi-desert while eastern Kenya is savannah. Many whites own large farms in the Rift Valley area and produce cash crops for export. Western Kenya is a region of small, subsistence farms, known as *shamba*. Major cash crops are coffee, tea, sugar cane and vegetables. Kenya's economy is also heavily dependent on tourism.

A chronology of events: Kenya and other fertile parts of east Africa attracted the attention of

European colonists early in the 19th century. Their numbers encompassed missionaries, traders, including those from the East Africa Company and farmers. By 1895 much of coastal Kenya was a British protectorate, and the hinterland a British colony. To boost their control, the British encouraged settlement by Europeans who wished to farm. Farmland was expropriated from African small holders who were required to pay a poll tax. As they did not produce cash crops, African farmers were forced to sell their land to meet their tax burden. By the 1940s, European farmers had achieved considerable prosperity. Demand for independence began to grow. The first large African nationalist organisation was formed in **1947** and named the Kenya African Union. By 1947 KAU was led by Jomo Kenyatta. In the 1950s, the demand for independence grew more intense. The Land Freedom Army, called the 'Mau Mau' by the British press , was an armed, Kikuyu-led group. They conducted a small number of terrorist acts against white farmers. The British responded by calling a state of emergency, moving large numbers of Kenyans into 'protected villages', imprisoning Kenyans, including Jomo Kenyatta and executing over 1,500 Kenyans suspected of supporting the Mau Mau. Some 32 British civilians were killed by the Mau Mau while some 150,000 Kenyans were killed or starved to death in the 'protected' villages. The suppression of the Kenyan independence movement is one of the most shameful periods of British history.

Kenya won its independence in **1963**. In 1964 it declared itself a republic with Jomo Kenyatta as the first president. He soon became increasingly reclusive and autocratic. Political parties were banned, and from 1969 to 1991 Kenya was effectively a one party state. Kenyatta died in 1978 and was succeeded by his Vice-President, Daniel Arap Moi. At first he released political prisoners, but following an attempted *coup d'etat* in 1982, political opposition faced detention or worse (at least 200 political opponents were murdered in 1982). Opposition to Arap Moi grew in the **1980s**, as did human right abuses. Robert Ouko, the Minister of Foreign Affairs died in suspicious circumstances in 1990 and a fellow cabinet minister was arrested. In the aftermath of popular unrest in **1990**, over 1,000 political activists were arrested and some 20 people killed. In 1991 in the face of growing international pressure and the suspension of humanitarian aid, Arap Moi was forced to permit multi-party politics. But repression of political opposition continued throughout the early 1990s. Presidential and parliamentary elections were held in **1997**. There was no united opposition to Arap Moi and he was returned as President although opposition parliamentarians won 60 per cent of the vote. Political activists continue to face harassment, police brutality and arrest.

By 1991 Kenya was also experiencing serious inter-ethnic conflict. Throughout 1991 and 1992 there were clashes in the Rift Valley region involving the Kikuyu, Kalenjin and Maasai. Some human rights activists accused the Government of inciting the violence in order to undermine the move towards political pluralism. In the violence of 1991 and 1992, some 1,500 people were killed and 300,000 internally displaced. At the beginning of 2000 some 200,000 Kenyans were still internally displaced. Ethnic conflict flared up again in 1995 and 1998. The latter involved armed groups of Kikuyu and Kalenjin and resulted in about 120 deaths.

Kenyan refugees in the UK – Statistics

Year	Asylum Applications	Refugee Status	ELR	Refusal
1992	110	17	33	50
1993	630	5	50	45
1994	1,130	0	1	99
1995	1,395	<1	3	97
1996	1,170	1	3	97
1997	605	1	1	98
1998	885	1	1	98
1999	195	1	1	99

Source: Home Office

Almost all Kenyan asylum-seekers living in the UK claim political activity in their home country has endangered them. However, the majority of asylum applications are rejected by the Home Office – an issue of concern to human rights organisations.

Most Kenyan are well educated and speak excellent English. The majority remain in Greater London, particularly east London boroughs such as Hackney and Newham.

■ Refugees from Kosova

Since 1994 nearly 29,000 Kosovan refugees have fled to the UK, including 4,400 people who arrived as part of the 1999 Humanitarian Evacuation Programme. At the time of writing Kosova[1] was still part of the Federal Republic of Yugoslavia, although administered by NATO-led K-For forces. Its population was estimated to be 1.9 million in 1997.

Ethnic groups: In 1997 some 89 per cent of the population of Kosova were Albanian and nine per cent were Serb. Kosova also hosts small populations of minority groups, the largest of which are Roma. A 1991 estimate puts Kosova's Roma population at 43,000, but this is probably an underestimate. Since June 1999, almost all Kosovan Roma have been driven out of their homes by Albanian extremists – the Roma were accused of collaborating with Serbs. Today, Kosovan Roma have fled to Serbia or are living under K-For protection in displaced person's camps

Other minority groups include Turks, the Gorani, Muslim Slavs, Greeks and a small number of people of mixed marriage. Before 1998, the Gorani – about 12,000 people – lived in the Gora region of Kosova. They consider themselves to be Slavs, who practice Islam after conversion in the 18th century. Their first language is Serbian and they consider themselves a separate community to Kosova's Muslim Slavs. The latter speak Serbo-Croat and numbered about 35,000 before 1998. Many of their ancestors migrated from modern-day Bosnia or the Sanzhak and some describe themselves as Bosniak. Since 1999 both the Gorani and Muslim Slavs have experienced intimidation from ethnic Albanian extremists, mostly because of their home language.

Language: Albanian in the first language of the Albanian majority. Serbian, written in a Cyrillic script, is the first language of the Serb minority. Kosova's Roma are linguistically diverse: some speak various dialects of Romani as their first language, others speak Serbian or Albanian. Albanians call their language *Shqip*. It is also spoken in Albania and by ethnic Albanians in the Former Yugoslav Republic of Macedonia, Greece and Italy. Albanian is an Indo-European language, although not closely related to others. It has borrowed many words from Greek, Latin, Turkish and Slavic languages. It had two main dialect groups. Tosk is used in southern Albania and Gheg in northern Albania, Kosova and Macedonia. Each dialect family has numerous sub-dialects, not all of which are mutually intelligible. There will be spoken differences between Albanians from Kosova and those from Albania. Little Albanian literature dates before the 18th century. In 1916 the Roman script was adopted as the official script and a form of Gheg as standard Albanian. In 1945 Albanian was restandardised, with a form of Tosk adopted as the standard written form. The language uses 29 consonants and seven vowels.

Kosovan Serbs speak Serbian as their first language and use the Cyrillic script.

Names: Kosovan Albanians use a European naming system of first and family names, with some of the family names being ancient clan names. Albanian and Serbian names are very different so it is easy to identify a person's ethnic group by their name.

Religion: Some 95 per cent of Kosovan Albanians are Sunni Muslim and five per cent Roman Catholic. Like urban Bosnian Muslims, urban Kosovan Albanians are overwhelmingly secular and consume *haram* foods and alcohol (although few are willing to eat pork). Older Kosovan Albanians and those in rural areas are more likely to be observant. The main festivals for Kosovan Albanians are *Ramasan Bajram (Eid ul Fitr)* celebrated at the end of *Ramadan* and *Kurban Bajram (Eid ul Adha)*, the Feast of the Sacrifices, celebrated by the ritual slaughter and consumption of a sheep. New Year is also a major time of celebration: large meals, cakes and sweets.

---

1. The form Kosova (as opposed to the Serbian Kosovo) is used in this book.

The Serbian minority are nominally Serbian Orthodox. Urban Serbs, too, are secular. But allegiance to the Serbian Orthodox Church is crucial to the building of a Serbian nationalist identity and there has been renewed interest in religion since the mid-1980s. As the Serbian Orthodoxy's most ancient churches lie in Kosova, the latter is considered to be the religious and cultural heartland of Serbian people.

Kosova's Roma may owe religious allegiance to Christian churches or Islam.

Education system: The first Albanian medium school was founded in Tirana in 1886. In Kosova education through the medium of Albanian was forbidden until 1945. During the 1960s more and more Albanian medium schools opened their doors and in 1968 the University of Prishtina was opened, offering an Albanian language higher education. Between 1974 and 1987 Kosovan education was administered by regional government in Prishtina. After the death of Tito and the gradual resurgence of Serbian nationalism, Kosovan autonomy was threatened. Throughout the 1980s secondary school pupils who opposed the Yugoslav Government faced school expulsion and often worse. In 1990 thousands of Albanian schoolchildren required medical treatment after a suspected poisoning incident attributed to nerve gas.

In 1990, Albanian doctors, nurses, teachers and lecturers were sacked by the Government of the Federal Republic of Yugoslavia. Albanian medium schools were closed, teaching through the medium of Albanian was banned and a Serbian curriculum was imposed. A few schools reopened after international human rights bodies applied pressure to the Yugoslav Government but were soon closed again. The Albanian population responded by setting up a parallel education system, funded by an unofficial tax. In some parts of Kosova, Albanian teachers were allowed to take their classes in school buildings but received no state pay, equipment or other funding to do this. Elsewhere, schools operated out of cafes and empty houses. School was often part time, classes large and the curriculum limited to basic literacy and numeracy. In some regions the parallel system broke down at times and children received little schooling. The effects of this narrow curriculum on Kosovan refugee children at school in the UK can easily be seen. Children will be unfamiliar with technical and creative subjects or science laboratories. Induction courses will need to remedy this.

In Kosova, children start school at six or seven. Primary education lasts eight years. Secondary education lasts four years, until 19, with opportunities for specialisation. Before 1990 Kosovan students sat the Yugoslav *Matura* examination, now being replaced by an equivalent Kosovan examination. Serbian medium schools for Serbs, as well as 'Bosniak' schools for Muslim Slavs are also being organised. Schools have been damaged in the conflict. and there has been no teacher education since 1990. Older people and some rural women may also have limited literacy. The female literacy rate for rural Kosova is only 65 per cent.

Economy: Kosova is predominantly rural with the workforce mainly employed in agriculture. Parts of Kosova are fertile and can export fruit, vegetables and other agricultural products. There are precious metal reserves in northern Kosova, although not to the extent that Kosovars believe. During communist times there was little investment in agricultural production and general economic mismanagement. The little investment there was was directed towards heavy industry. Kosovan Serbs held a disproportionate number of industrial and state salaried jobs. Unemployment among Kosovan Albanians was the highest in Yugoslavia. The economy continued to suffer in the 1990s. The closure of the Kosova-Macedonian border prevented trade. As sanctions bit, both Serbian and Albanian criminals took control of the black market trade in petrol and other smuggled products. Very many families were affected by the sacking of Albanian teachers, lecturers and health service staff and further damage was done to farms and business during the conflict.

The economy is now dominated by the UNMIK administration. For Kosovars unemployment runs at about 70 per cent. Despite reconstruction, much of the infrastructure is still damaged. Power cuts are frequent and the distribution of water is restricted. Mines and other unexploded ordinance prevent many farmers from making a living.

A chronology of events: Like all regions that have experienced conflict, the history of Kosova/Kosova is contested, with Serbs and Albanians putting forward different historical arguments to justify their claim to the region. The Albanians base their claim to be the original inhabitants of Kosova on descent from the Illyrians who lived there and elsewhere in the Balkans before the Roman Empire. Some archaeologists believe that Albanians are the descendants of Thracians, but there is there is little archaeological or linguistic evidence to back either claim.

Slavic peoples appear to have migrated into the Balkans in the 5th and 6th century AD. Bulgarian kings controlled the region from about 850AD until the early 11th century and the region was the focus of conflict between Serbian kings and Byzantine Greeks until the final decades of the 12th century. The Orthodox Church expanded, many monasteries were built in Kosova during this period. Ottoman Turks became the dominant power. At the Battle of Kosovo Polje in 1389, an epic battle between the Serbian forces of Prince Lazar and the Ottoman army. Later Albanians and Bosnian Muslims fought alongside the Serbian army, while some Serbs fought with the Ottoman Turks. Nationalist folk poems and most versions of Serbian history relate this battle was an heroic defeat — some Serbian nationalists still mark the anniversary of Kosovo Polje. By 1459 all of Kosova and Serbia were incorporated into the Ottoman Empire. Serbian people began to migrate north.

The 1680s and 1690s saw Ottoman attempts at expansion in Europe and their ten-week siege of Vienna. Later they were defeated by a combined Austrian and Polish army that moved south into the Balkans. The Hapsburg army then extended its control over Kosova. Many of the Serbian inhabitants pledged their loyalty to the Austrian Emperor. But in early 1690, the Austrian army was forced to withdraw from Kosova, as a mixed Ottoman and Tartar army moved north, killing many in its wake. Serbian refugees fled. At the same time there was Albanian migration north, to more fertile farmland in Kosova.

In 1878 Serbia and Montenegro gained independence from the Ottoman Empire — but not Kosova. Albanian people were forcibly expelled from the newly independent Serbia and Montenegro with at least 200,000 settling in Kosova and Macedonia. In the same year the League of Prizren was founded at a meeting of Albanian clan leaders striving to free themselves of Ottoman rule. It marked the birth of modern Albanian nationalism.

Ottoman rule finally ended after the First Balkan War of 1912 when the combined forces of Serbia, Montenegro, Greece and Bulgaria drove out the Ottoman army. Kosova was incorporated into Serbia at considerable cost to its Albanian population. During the First World War, the Serbian army was driven out of much of Kosova by the Austro-Hungarian and Bulgarian armies, with some Albanian rebels taking revenge on retreating Serb troops. In 1918 Kosova became part of the new country of Yugoslavia, dominated by Serbia. Serb settlers were encouraged to move to Kosova, to help strengthen Serb control. Expressions of Albanian identity were heavily suppressed, and there is constant discontent among the Albanian population.

Recent history 1939-1979: During the Second World War most of Kosova is incorporated into Italian-controlled Albania although parts are occupied by the Nazis and their Bulgarian allies. Thousands of Serbs are driven out of Kosova. Opposition to Germany is led by Josep Broz Tito's communist partisans. He recruits the support of Kosovan Albanians by promising them unity with Albania after the war. This is never granted: in 1945 Kosova is incorporated into Serbia, the largest state in the Federal Republic of Yugoslavia. Until the mid-1960s any expression of Albanian separatism is repressed. But in 1974 Kosova is granted greater autonomy, with its police, health-care and education systems organised by regional government.

1990s: From 1987, limited self-rule is dismantled by Slobodan Milosevic, who whips up Serbian nationalism in order to climb to power and plays on the fears of the minority Serb population. In 1990 thousands of Albanian doctors, teachers and lecturers are sacked. Schools are closed and education through the medium of Albanian is banned. Human rights worsen; opponents of the Yugoslav government are arrested or beaten. During the Croatian and Bosnian wars, young Albanian men risked forcible conscription into frontline forces. Serbian refugees from Bosnia are settled in Kosova. The Albanian population at first opts for peaceful resistance to Serbian oppression. A parallel state is set up, of which the parallel education system is a part. Ibrahim Rugova is President of the parallel state but his position becomes increasingly challenged by radicals who support an armed struggle against Serbian rule. In 1997, the Kosova Liberation Army (UCK in Albanian) emerges as a fighting force.

By March 1998 civil war breaks out in parts of Kosova, causing at least 350,000 people to flee as refugees or internally displaced people. Unarmed peace monitors from the Organisation for Peace and Cooperation in Europe (OSCE) are placed in Kosova to prevent the conflict from escalating. In early 1999 peace talks between the Yugoslav Government, Kosova Albanian representatives and the Contact Group on the Former Yugoslavia are held in France. They call for Kosovan autonomy and the removal of most Yugoslav troops and police. Final status talks to determine the ultimate future of Kosova would be held after a three year period. Although the Albanian delegation agrees to the peace initiative, it is rejected by the Government of Yugoslavia. Human rights conditions deteriorate as the peace talks stall. The OSCE peace monitors are withdrawn and an ultimatum given to President Milosevic. In April 1999 NATO planes attack targets throughout Serbia and Kosova. Reprisals by Serbian paramilitaries, regular Serb soldiers and civilians drive some 750,000 Albanians to take refuge in Albania, Macedonia, Bosnia and Montenegro. At least as many others are internally displaced, hiding in mountains and forests, without food or shelter. Various governments accept Kosovars evacuated from camps in Macedonia. On 10 June 1999 NATO bombing stops and a peace accord is signed, providing for the withdrawal of the Yugoslav army from Kosova and the entry of K-FOR. Within days almost all refugees in Albania, Montenegro and Macedonia return. The withdrawal of Yugoslav troops is accompanied by the flight of Serbian and Roma refugees. By late 1999 only 4,000 Serbs remain, mostly in northern Kosova. Roma also flee, as many Albanians perceive them as siding with the Serbs. Those who stay are mostly confined to a heavily guarded displaced persons' camp in Kosova. In September 1999 the Kosova Liberation Army is officially disbanded and gives rise to the Party for a Progressive and Democratic Kosova (PPDK).

2000-2001: K-FOR soldiers continue to keep the peace, with the UN leading a civilian administration (UNMIK – the UN Interim Mission in Kosova). Although many refugees return, Kosova is far from safe. International police, to be attached to the UNMIK administration, have not materialised. The country is heavily mined and people are killed or injured every day in landmine and booby trap explosions. In parts of Kosova there is little law and order, with Serbs, Roma and moderate Albanians targeted by extremist and criminal elements. A particular focus for violence is Mitrovica, a city in northern Kosova where a Serb community is separated from an Albanian community by a river. Many houses in rural areas have been badly damaged. Kosova's long-term economic viability is doubtful. Some Albanians find themselves the victims of harassment or worse, including those accused of involvement with the former Serbian administration, those critical of the former KLA or the PPDK and those who expose crime and corruption. The persecution of Serbs, Roma and other ethnic groups continues.

Kosovan refugees in the UK

Few Albanians from Kosova lived in the UK before the persecution worsened in Yugoslavia in 1992, although there was a larger community from Albania itself. The Kosovan community in the UK now numbers about 29,000, including those who arrived in 1999 on the Humanitarian Evacuation Programme. Precise figures are difficult to determine, as the Home Office counts all asylum applications from the Federal Republic of Yugoslavia together. The Kosovan community includes at least 9,000 unaccompanied children and young people. Most asylum-seekers are young men, although family groups also arrive. Until 1999 most Kosovar asylum-seekers who received a decision were granted refugee status in the UK. In April-June 1999 when 4,400 Kosovans were admitted to the UK from refugee camps in Macedonia, policy changed. The 4,400 Kosovans who were entered under the Humanitarian Evacuation Programme were granted one year's Exceptional Leave to Remain (ELR). To bring this group in line with other Kosovans, the Home Office started awarding ELR to Kosovans who had not had their cases determined. In June 1999, as the

Humanitarian Evacuation Programme ended, Kosovan Albanians started to be refused asylum. Home Secretary Jack Straw has made public his intention that Kosovans should return when their ELR expires, including those who came on the Humanitarian Evacuation Programme, and many are being refused extensions of ELR. The Refugee Council is concerned that the return of large numbers of Kosovan refugees from western Europe will overwhelm the fragile peace in Kosova as well as putting greater strains on an already damaged infrastructure.

The largest Kosovan communities are in Greater London and Kent but many live elsewhere. As many Kosovans arrived as clandestine entrants, in the backs of lorries or at container ports, there are communities in areas where motorways pass through. The dispersal of asylum-seekers has led to growing Kosovan communities outside the South East.

The Kosovans who arrived in the UK on a Home Office-led Humanitarian Evacuation Programme (HEP). They were settled in 32 local authorities in Glasgow and northern England and initially housed in reception centres run usually by local authorities, although the Refugee Council, Refugee Action and the Red Cross also provided a small number. Their support was well resourced, as was support for those who wished to return home, who were given extensive advice before return, a paid flight and a cash allowance of £250 per person. One year after the start of the HEP, about a third decided to return to Kosova. A sense of safety, however, may not have been the primary motivating factor for return. Many Kosovans have spoken of the need to return to secure their property and jobs. The social care offered to unaccompanied Albanian children is a major issue of concern. Although assessed under the provisions of the Children Act 1989, local authorities opt to treat them as adult asylum-seekers. They are accommodated in bed and breakfast hotels for the homeless and receive food parcels or vouchers. Some have no allocated social worker, others lose their social worker upon the granting of refugee status or ELR. Lack of access to further education or cash has meant that many young Kosovan men have taken to congregating in public places to pass the time, attracting unfavourable media reports and hostility from the community. The tabloid media were generally sympathetic to Bosnian refugees, both in the UK and abroad but, in contrast, hostile to Albanian refugees in 1998, almost certainly as a result of negative media briefings from central and local government. They play upon the notion that asylum-seekers are competing for scarce resources at local government level.

There are a number of Kosovan community organsations inside and outside London and one youth project, set up by Albanian Youth Action. Nationally there are eleven Albanian language schools. There were three refugee community organisations outside London by the end of 2000.

Bibliography

Blake, C. and Ademi, X. (1998) 'Albanian Refugee Children' in *Multicultural Teaching*, Vol 17 No 1.

Malcolm, N. (1998) *Kosovo: a short history*, London: Papermac

Refugee Council (1998) *Albanian and English Words for School Use*, London: Refugee Council

Refugee Council (2000) *My Name came Up: Kosovo, war, exile and return*, London: Refugee Council

Vickers, M. (1998) *Between Serb and Albanian*, New York: Colombia University Press

Useful web sites in English include www.albanian.com, www.kosova.nu/, www.albania.co.uk. There are also numerous news and other web sites in Albanian. These are listed in *My Name Came Up*, cited above.

■ Refugees from Lebanon

About 5,500 Lebanese refugees have fled to the UK, most of them during 1989-1991. Lebanon has an estimated population of 4.2 million, of whom 82 per cent live in urban areas. The capital is Beirut.

Ethnic and religious groups

Lebanon's main communities are

Maronite Christians	900,000
Orthodox Christians	250,000
Greek Catholics	150,000
Shi'a Muslims	1,100,000
Sunni Muslims	750,000
Druze	200,000
Armenians	175,000
Other Christians	50,000
Palestinians	350,000
Kurds and Syrians	100,000

Most Kurds and Palestinians are not Lebanese citizens. The Druze practice a faith modified from Shi'a Islam in the 11th century, with Jethro a major prophet.

Languages: Arabic is the official language. The Lebanese speak their own Levantine dialect although newspapers and books are written in a simplified version of classical Arabic. Minority groups speak Armenian, Kurdish and Assyrian.

Names: Lebanese Christians have adopted a European naming system and so have many Muslims, having a first personal name, sometimes followed by their father's name, and then a family name.

Education system: There are four kinds of schools in Lebanon: state, private tuition-free, fee-paying and schools administered by UNRWA for Palestinian refugees. Arabic is the main medium of instruction, but some private schools use French or English. Primary education starts at six and lasts for five years. Students then spend three or four years in intermediate schools, which offer either a four-year academic course, three years in academic courses followed by a year preparing to enter vocational schools or teacher training institutes, or a three-year vocational course. All culminate in the *Brevet* certificate. Some then progress to upper secondary schools to follow academic courses leading to the Baccalaureate or a teaching diploma. There are also vocational courses in subjects such as commerce, nursing and electronics, finishing with a Baccalaureate Technique (British Council, 1998).

Private tuition-free (charitable) schools, private schools and UNRWA schools are organised in much the same way as state schools. The literacy rate is 86 per cent for men and 69 per cent for women and is lowest in rural areas.

Chronology of Events: Lebanon was ruled by the Ottoman Turks for more than 400 years, as part of the Ottoman Empire's Syrian Province with Lebanon's different communities generally living in peace, although clashes between Maronite Christians and Druze in 1860 and 1861 left 2,000 people dead. In 1920 the French took control of Syria and Lebanon after the Turks were defeated in the First World War and drew up new borders.

1940-1974: At independence in 1943 the 'National Pact' tries to satisfy all Lebanon's minority communities. Parliamentary seats are to be divided between Christians and Muslims in a ratio of six Christian seats to five Muslim. The president will be a Maronite Christian and the prime minister a Sunni Muslim. Other top administrative posts are to be evenly divided. By 1958 tensions grow between those who see Lebanon as an Arab nation, and those who want to be closely linked with European countries, leading to a brief civil war. From 1960 to 1974, poverty and the destabilising effect of Palestinian refugees exacerbate tensions. Parts of Lebanon are wealthy but Beirut and Tripoli are surrounded by slums and much of the countryside is impoverished. The poor are mostly Muslim and lack political representation. Their numbers are swelled by Palestinian refugees and Kurdish and Syrian migrant workers. The urban poor include educated young men who can find no work and turn to armed struggle to try and change Lebanon's political system. Some 350,000 Palestinian refugees living in the camps include guerrillas who start raiding northern Israel. The Lebanese Government, particularly Maronite Christian politicians, becomes increasingly hostile to the Palestinians, believing they are trying to create 'a state within a state'. Others, including some intellectuals, and the poor, mostly Muslim Lebanese, admire the Palestinian's courage and hope that they will be able to help change Lebanon.

1975-1989: In **1975** Phalangist Christian militia (right-wing political organisation) attack a bus of Palestinians in Beirut. The civil war begins, the Phalangists and other Christian groups fighting the National Movement, made up of several political organisations with mainly Muslim support. Muslims are forced to leave their homes in Christian neighbourhoods and vice versa. Syria intervenes to support the Christian Lebanese forces. In 1978 Israel invades southern Lebanon, displacing 200,000 people, but is forced to withdraw after UN and US pressure. It launches another invasion in **1982**, called 'Operation Peace for Galilee', intended to defeat the Palestinian fighters once and for all. Ssome 19,000 people are killed in fighting and Israeli air raids. Israeli forces then lay siege to Beirut. A multi-national peace-keeping force of British, French, Italian and US troops arrives to supervise the withdrawal of Palestinian guerrillas, and guard the refugees living in camps. Israel withdraws its troops, promising not to enter West Beirut. The peace-keepers leave as soon as the Palestinian guerrillas flee and Israeli troops enter Muslim West Beirut. With Israeli cooperation, Christian Lebanese forces enter Sabra and Chatilla refugee camps. Some 2,000 Palestinian refugees are murdered. In 1983 Israel is forced to withdraw to a 'security zone' in southern Lebanon after losing many troops, but it arms and trains Christian troops – the South Lebanese Army – who fight Palestinians and other militia, and who police a security zone in southern Lebanon.

The civil war worsens and thousands are killed. Christian and Muslim militia splinter. Christians fight Christians in East Beirut. Amal, a Shi'a Muslim group fights Palestinians and Hizbollah, an Islamic fundamentalist group. The Israelis continue to bomb southern Lebanon. In **1989** the increased violence prompts Syria to enter Lebanon. In October 1989 a peace agreement is signed, and the Syrians force the Lebanese to form a government of national reconciliation. There are attempts to disarm the militia.

1990s: In **1993** some 200,000 Lebanese flee their homes in southern Lebanon after suffering bombardments by the Israeli airforce, retaliating after Hizbollah guerrillas shell northern Israel. The bombing of south Lebanon continues to the present day. In 2000 the Israelis withdraw from the security zone in southern Lebanon, as part of a move towards peace in the Middle East. Members of the South Lebanese Army flee, to Israel and other countries.

Lebanese refugees in the UK: About 5,500 Lebanese refugees have fled to the UK, Peak years of application were 1990 and 1991. They are a diverse group and include Lebanese Christians and Muslims who fled during the civil war of 1975-1991, supporters of General Michel Aoun, other Christian militia and those associated with the South Lebanese Army who have fled since 1991 or after the Israeli withdrawal from its security zone in southern Lebanon, Palestinians who fled during the civil war or later and Armenians and other minority groups who fled during the civil war. Lebanese refugees have joined an existing Lebanese migrant community mostly living in the London Boroughs of Westminster, Kensington and Chelsea and Hammersmith and Fulham. The migrant community is more prosperous than the refugees; most Lebanese migrants are professionals or involved in commerce or the Arab media. Some Lebanese refugees and most stateless Palestinians arrive speaking little or no English. The latter group need most support. For many years the British Government awarded most Lebanese asylum-seekers Exceptional Leave to Remain. In December 1992 the Home Office announced that, with the end of the civil war, ELR was no longer justifiable.

Bibliography
McDowall, D. (1996) *Lebanon: a Conflict of Minorities*, London: Minority Rights Group

■ Refugees from Liberia

About 2,500 Liberian refugees have fled to the UK. Liberia has a population of three million. Its capital is Monrovia.

Liberia is a multi-ethnic country and inter-ethnic conflict was one of the causes of the civil war. Americo-Liberians, the descendants of freed African slaves from the USA, constitute about five per cent of the population but have dominated politics and control much of the country's wealth. Other large ethnic groups include the Kpelle, Basse and Gio/Mano. There is also a small Lebanese community, mostly living in Monrovia. The official language is English and the *lingua franca* is Liberian English, sometimes called Krio, Americo or Settler English. It is spoken by over one million people and derives from the creolised English of US slaves and influenced by the local languages of Liberia, so distinguishing it from the Krio of Sierra Leone.

Most refugees fled to the UK in 1994-1996 after the civil war of 1989-1996 killed 150,000. Virtually the whole population were displaced at one time or another during this war, but people gradually began to return after national elections installed Charles Taylor, a former rebel leader, as President. However, there are grave violations of human rights and sporadic violence, often perpetrated by ex-combatants. Most of the refugees in the UK are from the environs of Monrovia and include a small number of Lebanese. The largest communities are living in north east London. There are no Liberian community organisations although Liberians use some of the general support organisations working with west Africans.

■ Refugees from Nigeria

Nigeria had a population of 110 million in 1998. Its capital is Abuja, although Lagos is the largest city. Nigeria is a federal state.

Ethnic groups: Nigeria is very diverse country with over 250 different ethno-linguistic groups. The largest group – nearly 30 per cent of the population – are the predominantly Muslim Hausa-Fulani, living in northern Nigeria. The Yoruba, whose traditional homeland is south west Nigeria, make up nearly 18 per cent; the mainly Christian Igbo (or Ibo) about 12 per cent mostly living in south east Nigeria. Other significant ethnic groups include Kanuri, Ibibia, Tiv and Ijaw.

Languages: English is the official language and the medium of education after the third year of primary school. A creolised form of English is used as a *lingua franca* in many parts of Nigeria. The main African languages are Hausa, widely spoken in northern Nigeria (also in Niger), Yoruba (in the south west) and Ibo (in south east Nigeria). These are local languages of commerce and communication. Also widely spoken are Fulani, Kanuri, Efik, Ibibio, Tiv and Ijaw. All apart from Hausa belong to the Niger-Congo language family. Hausa is a member of the Afro-Asiatic language family. An adult Nigerian who has been to school will speak English and its creolised local form, a regional language such as Yoruba and often one of the 250 local languages.

Religion: Some 47 per cent of the population are Sunni Muslim, 35 per cent Christian and 18 per cent practice traditional beliefs. The northerners are mostly Muslim and the southerners mostly Christian. The range of Christian churches is wide and includes Roman Catholic, Anglican and Methodist churches, and various evangelical protestant churches, generally African led. There are religious tensions in Nigeria. A growing number of northern states are trying to introduce *shari'a* – Islamic law. All northern cites include minority Christians who are often fearful of *shari'a* and this has provoked Muslim-Christian violence.

Education system: Three different education systems operate in Nigeria: private religious schools, a traditional, rural 'apprentice' system and the modern state system. In northern Nigeria there is a long-standing Islamic education system. Children attend small *madrassah*, sometimes in the home of a *mallam* (a teacher), from the age of five or six. Here they learn Koranic Arabic, prayers and chapters of the Koran. Many then progress to the state education system. Other children may embark on further study in Islamic schools, perhaps moving to one of Nigeria's renowned centres of Islamic learning.

In rural areas children learn the skills of farming and crafts in a traditional system of apprentice-ship. About 70 per cent of Nigeria's children enroll in a state primary school. Compulsory education starts at six and lasts six years. In the three years of secondary school they study for the Junior School Certificate. To study further they attend either senior secondary school, technical college (for craft training) or teacher's college. At senior secondary school pupils study a range of eight or nine subjects for the Senior School Certificate. The drop-out rate in rural schools is high, especially among poor families. The literacy rate is 61 per cent for men and 19 per cent for women. Literacy rates are higher in southern Nigeria than in the north.

Economy: Nigeria is predominantly agricultural – most people survive as subsistence farmers. Cash crops include cocoa, rubber, cotton and peanuts. Northern Nigeria is much poorer than the south – one cause of tension. Another issue is that the economy is heavily dependent on the export of crude oil, which accounts for over 90 per cent of export earnings. Standards of living and the quality of government services fall when oil prices drop. The legacy of decades of economic mismanagement and corruption is an additional economic challenge.

A chronology of events: Archaeological evidence indicates that Nigeria was settled at least 3,000 years ago. During the last 1,000 years, villages began to group themselves into states, with subjects giving loyalty to a dynastic chieftain. Many artefacts survive from early states including the Yoruba kingdoms and the Edo Kingdom of Benin.

The region attracted the attention of European colonists from the 16th century. By the 18th century some of the Yoruba coastal city states were exporting slaves (forcibly taken in raids on the interior).

At the beginning of the 19th century the Yoruba were the dominant group in the south west, the Hausa in the north and the Igbo in the east. Britain steadily became the dominant colonial power in the region. In **1884**, after the Berlin Conference, Britain formed the Oil Rivers Protectorate, which included much of southern Nigeria. British control was confined to coastal Nigeria until 1900, but by **1914** northern and southern protectorates were unified and present day Nigeria was formed, a creation of British colonialism which arbitarily joined diverse peoples and regions.

Nigerian nationalism and the call for self-government began to emerge in the 1920s but was divided along ethnic and regional lines. Ethnic divisions intensified in the 1950s: northerners resented the power of the southern-dominated federal government and also resented the Igbo who had migrated north. Yoruba and Igbo competed for control of the political machinery. Regional and ethnic conflicts remained after independence was achieved in **1960**. Its first elected government was overthrown in a coup in 1966, with Chief Yabuku Gowon then installed as head of government.

By **1967** Nigeria had plunged into civil war. Ethnic Igbo living in northern Nigeria were attacked and at least 10,000 were killed. More than one million Igbo fled back to the Eastern region. In retaliation for the attacks on Igbo, northerners were murdered in south eastern cities such as Port Harcourt and others forced to flee their homes.

Following the attacks on Igbo, Lt-Col Ojukwu, the Eastern Region's military governor was pressed by Igbo army officers to gain independence from the federal government. Despite attempts to prevent it seceding, Ojukwu proclaimed an independent Republic of Biafra. Fighting started after the Nigerian army tried to assert its authority and regain territory. By 1968 some 250,000 soldiers of the federal government were fighting in Biafra. Food and medical supplies soon became scarce, despite the mobilisation of aid organisations. In January **1970**, Biafran resistance collapsed, after the fall of Owerri. By then up to three million Igbo people had been killed or died of starvation and disease and another three million displaced.

Gowon was overthrown in a coup in 1975 and the country was returned to civilian rule in 1979, until a military coup in **1983** installed Major General Mohammed Buhari as head of state. Military rule lasted until 1999, even though local state, assembly and presidential elections were held in 1993. The Presidential election of 1993 was widely thought to have ben won by Chief Moshood

Abiola. but the election results were annulled. General Sani Abacha overthrew a short-lived interim government, reinstating military rule and immediately banning new political parties. Abiola was arrested and held in custody until his death in 1998. Other political activists also faced arrest, such as writer Ken Saro-Wiwa. He and another eight Ogoni activists were executed in 1995. Human rights abuses continued, forcing political activists and journalists to flee the country until the death of Abacha in June 1998. General Abdulsalami Abubakar was then installed as head of state. Prominent political activists were released from detention and it was announced that Nigeria would return to elected civilian rule. Local, assembly and presidential elections were held in February **1999**, the latter won by General Olusegun Obasanjo, a former military ruler.

The arrest of political opposition has declined but torture is used by the police and prison conditions are life-threatening. There is growing tension in parts of northern Nigeria as a result of state governments declaring adherence to *shari'a*. Christians living in northern Nigeria and Muslims, mostly Hausa, living in southern cities, have been attacked and killed. Another tense area is the Niger Delta where minority groups such as the Ogoni and Ijaw resent their lack of access to benefits from the oil wealth.

Nigerian refugees in the UK – Asylum Statistics

Year	Applications	Refugee Status (as percentage)	ELR	Refusal
1992	615	0	1	99
1993	1,665	0	3	97
1994	4,340	0	0	100
1995	5,825	0	0	100
1996	2,900	<1	<1	100
1997	1,480	1	1	98
1998	1,380	5	3	92
1999	945	0	1	99

About 28,000 Nigerian asylum-seekers have arrived in the UK, mostly since 1992. It is not known how many have remained, as few are granted refugee status. Mostly from southern Nigeria, they are generally well-educated and speak fluent English. It has been a matter of concern that so few were allowed to remain in the UK, particularly in 1994 to 1998 when human rights violations were at their worst in Nigeria. Most have settled in Greater London and Manchester. There are many welfare organisations working with Nigerians, including one working specifically with refugees. There are also at least twelve community schools teaching languages such as Yoruba, Ewe and Igbo, as well as supplementing the mainstream school curriculum. Although most parents are English-speaking, a few of the children may enter school at five speaking a mixture of English and an African language and might need some additional support in their first few months of school.

Many schools do not identify Nigerian children from asylum-seeking or refugee families as such, assuming that they are part of the much larger settled Nigerian community. While this assumption usually presents no problems, teachers should be sensitive to possible political differences within the community. Additionally, some Nigerian children have had appalling past experiences. For example, a Nigerian client of the Refugee Council saw her husband murdered in front of her two young children, and all have been profoundly affected.

■ Refugees from the Palestine National Authority

Since the start of violence in the West Bank and Gaza in October 2000 a growing number of asylum-seekers have arrived in the UK. They include Arabic-speaking Palestinian Muslims and Christians, as well as Armenians. As well as escaping the violence, a small number of Palestinians have fled because they or their families have been accused of collaborating with the Israeli Security Service.

■ Eastern European Roma

Since 1994 over 11,000 eastern European Roma have sought asylum in the UK, mostly from Poland, the Czech Republic, Slovakia, Romania and the former Yugoslavia. Smaller numbers have fled Lithuania, Latvia, Belarus, Russia and Albania.

Roma populations and origins: Populations of Roma are difficult to estimate, as census data may not ask questions about ethnic origin. Additionally not all Roma may wish to declare themselves at a census. The forced settlement of Roma in eastern Europe has also made it difficult estimate population numbers. The following estimate is taken from D. Kenrick: *An Historical Atlas of the Gypsies (Romanies)*, Scarecrow Press, 1998.

Roma/Gypsy/Traveller Populations in European Countries

Albania	95,000
Austria	22,500
Belarus	12,500
Bosnia-Herzegovina	45,000
Bulgaria	750,000
Croatia	35,000
Czech Republic	275,000
France	310,000
Germany	120,000
Greece	180,000
Hungary	575,000
Ireland	23,000 (includes Travellers)
Italy	100,000
Kosova	43,000
Macedonia	240,000
Moldavia	22,500
Netherlands	37,500
Poland	55,000
Portugal	45,000
Romania	2,100,000
Russia	230,000
Serbia and Montenegro	382,000
Slovakia	500,000
Spain	725,000
Turkey	400,000
Ukraine	55,000
UK	105,000
Federal Republic of Yugoslavia	425,000

Note: *The terms Rom (singular, meaning a man) and Roma (plural) is used in this book to describe the ethnic minority group who identify themselves as Roma, may or may not speak the Romani (sometimes called Romanes) langauge and share traditions. Different groups of Roma, such as the Kalderash, and Manouche will also be referred to in the book. Names with a pejorative association such as 'gypsy' or 'tsigane', will not be used.*

About nine million people in Europe identify themselves as Roma. Other Roma communities live in the Middle East, USA, Australia and South Africa. Linguistic and anthropological evidence suggest that the Roma had their origins in North West India. Today certain Indian minority groups such as the Lambadi or Banjara appear to have linguistic and cultural similarities with European Roma.

During the 11th century there were one or several migrations of Roma from India to South West Asia, the Caucasus and Turkey. A secondary migratory wave in the 14th century, know in Romani as the *Aresajpe*, brought Roma to South East Europe. Historical records document a Roma presence in Crete in 1322 and in Prizren, Kosova, in 1348. During the next 400 years Roma migrated across Europe, often fleeing persecution and forced expulsion. Roma were first recorded in Scotland in1510. In 1530, Henry VII passed the first anti-Gypsy law in England. Ships' captains were fined £40 for transporting Roma and to be a 'foreign gypsy' in England became a crime punishable by death. A third migratory wave occurred in the 19th and early 20th century. After being freed from slavery in parts of eastern Europe, Roma migrated to North America.

Language: About 40 per cent of Eastern European Roma have maintained Romani as their first language. It is an Indo-European language with numerous dialects, not of all of which are mutually intelligible and some linguists argue that it is not a single language. Romani appears most closely related to Indian languages such as Gujerati. European Roma fall into three cultural-linguistic groups: Eastern Roma, the Sinto-Manouche and northern Roma. Eastern Roma, the largest group, live throughout eastern Europe. Certain Welsh Roma belong to this group, speaking a dialect of Romani closely related to eastern Roma dialects. There are over 50 dialects in this cultural-linguistic group, though not all are mutually intelligible. The Sinti and Manouche Roma of Germany, Italy and France form a second cultural-linguistic group. Traditionally they spoke dialects of Romani that differ considerably from those spoken in eastern Europe. Northern Roma include Anglo-Romani of England and the Ibero-Romani of Spain. Both groups traditionally spoke a language made up of a vestigial Romani vocabulary and the grammatical structure of the host country language: English or Spanish.

Written forms of Romani include a growing body of published literature, particularly poetry. The Linguistic Commission of the International Romani Union has been developing a standardised written form of the language, based on Romani spoken in the Balkans. Codification and standardisation are far from complete and standardised Romani does not reflect the dialectal variations of Baltic Roma groups for example. The relative absence of the written form makes Romani a threatened language. Throughout eastern Europe many Roma families now speak the majority language at home, particularly in the Czech Republic and Slovakia. Where Romani is still spoken at home, most children will speak two languages an early age. In countries of exile, literate Roma parents will use languages such as Czech, Slovak, Polish or Romanian as their first written language. In the UK translated advice materials should reflect this – although for Romanian Roma written material may be of limited use, given low literacy.

Polish Roma
Reliable estimates suggest that there are about 55,000 Roma in Poland from several different cultural and linguistic groups. The majority are Baltic Roma and speak Baltic Romani dialects. Baltic Roma also live in Russia, Belarus, Kazakhstan, Lithuania, Latvia and Estonia. The main Baltic Roma groups are: Xaladytka (also know as Russian Roma), Polish Lowland Roma (also known as Polish Feldytka) and Polska-Sasytka. Most Polish Roma asylum-seekers in the UK are Polish Lowland Roma. Many, especially from the towns and cities, have abandoned Romani as a home language, but those who still use it will speak the Polish Lowland Romani dialect. There have been attempts to standardise Baltic Romani and it has a growing literature. Many of the stories and poems published recently have drawn on the strong oral tradition. Traditionally, Polish Lowland Roma were traders, although their forced settlement and the industrialisation of Polish society changed this.

There are also non-Baltic Roma groups living in Poland. These include Polish Highland Roma (Galicians), Polish Kalderash, Polish Lovari as well as migrants from Romania. They speak non-Baltic dialects of Romani. A standardised form of the Kalderadi dialect is widely understood by many Roma (and is also understood by Roma in Romania and Yugoslavia). Small numbers of Polish Kalderash and Highland Roma have sought asylum in the UK. There is little social contact or intermarriage between the different Roma groups in Poland or in exile in the UK.

All have a strong customary and moral code. Important decisions will be taken by groups of adult men. Any discussion of sex is taboo. Many Roma girls are discouraged from attending school after puberty, reinforced by statements by the Polish Lowland *Sero Rom* (literally Chief Rom) that girls should not attend school after the age of 12 years. A real parental concern, both in Poland and the UK, is that girls will be abducted for marriage. Girls marry at a young age, sometimes under the age of 16, an issue that child protection teams and healthcare providers in the UK need to consider.

During the Nazi Holocaust, thousands of Polish Roma were deported to concentration and extermination camps. Today Polish Roma, as do Czech and Slovak Roma, face deep-seated prejudice. They are often denied access to public places such as bars and restaurants. Since the end of communism, there has been increased racial violence towards them. As in the Czech Republic and Slovakia, some of it has been perpetrated by far-right 'skin head' gangs but much is carried out by ordinary Poles on fellow citizens. The houses of Roma have been burned. According to the European Roma Rights Centre, police brutality is another issue, including beatings in detention, house searches and the unlawful confiscation of Roma property. As in other eastern European countries, Roma have little redress to police protection in the event of racist violence

Unemployment among Polish Roma is much higher than among ethnic Poles and they have suffered disproportionally from the closure of state-owned industries. Roma, too, are much more likely to be living in overcrowded or substandard housing. School attendance among children is poor. Although most (but not all) Roma children enrol in primary school, their attendance may be sporadic and some drop out. Girls of secondary school age may be actively discouraged from attending by parents and community elders. The high level of bullying and discriminatory treatment metered out to Roma pupils by fellow students and teachers also contributes to poor attendance. Roma parents will have had similar experiences at school so might not encourage their children to attend school.

Polish Roma are the largest eastern European Roma community in the UK, numbering about 5,500 since arriving in 1994. Over 95 per cent of asylum applications from Poland are by Roma. Statistics on asylum for Poland are

Year	Asylum Applications	Refugee status as percentages	ELR	Refusal
1994	360	0	1	99
1995	1210	0	1	99
1996	900	0	1	99
1997	565	1	1	98
1998	1,585	1 or 2 people		>99
1999	1,860	0	0	100

Source: Home Office

Few Polish Roma have been granted refugee status or Exceptional Leave to Remain. Home Office policy is that Polish Roma asylum-seekers face discrimination but not persecution in Poland.

Most Polish Roma live in Greater London. There are three refugee community organisations working with Polish Roma in London and also a community school where children can learn Romani. The Traveller Education Service of Kensington and Chelsea and Hammersmith and Fulham employs a Roma member of staff to work with Polish Roma children. School attendance continues to be an issue for Roma children in London. For Polish Roma, poor school attendance in the UK is caused by the cultural factors described above and the overwhelmingly negative educational experiences of the home country. Ensuring that some Polish Roma children have a positive school experience in the UK will help encourage poor attendees. Once some Roma children do well, others may want to follow. Given the negative media coverage of eastern European Roma asylum-seekers, as well as deep-seated prejudice towards all Roma/Travellers, the racist bullying of Roma children in schools is not surprising. Low educational expectations from teachers, high housing mobility and uncertainty about their future also affect the schooling of Polish Roma children.

Romanian Roma

Roma are the largest minority group in Romania, comprising about 2,100,000 people – about 10 per cent of the total population. Romanian Roma are a diverse minority group: some are assimilated while others form an identifiable minority group with separate lives. There is considerable linguistic diversity. Some Roma speak Romanian as their home language, particularly those from towns. Others speak Hungarian, while yet others speak Boyash (also written as Beyash or

Bayash) as the home language. Boyash is generally considered to be a dialect of Romanian. About 35 per cent speak one of the many Romani dialects at home. Most of the dialects are Vlax (or Vlach) Romani dialects and contain many loan words from Romanian. The Romanian Kalderadi dialect is also widely understood among Roma. Religious Roma are mostly Romanian Orthodox, but some belong to the Roman Catholic or Protestant churches.

The first historical evidence of Romanian Roma dates to 1387, in a document signed by Mircea the Great, a king of Wallachia. From the time of their earliest arrival in Romania, the Roma were targets of persecution. They were forcibly settled, and from the late 14th century were widely enslaved. The shackling of Roma slaves was commonplace and many Roma were little more than expendable chattels of Romanian and Moldavian landlords. Slavery was not abolished in Wallachia and Moldavia until 1856. It was this event that prompted the flight of many Romanian Roma to north America. The early 20th century saw the continued persecution of Romanian Roma. Latter in 1939, Marshall Anonescu, a fascist dictator came to power as Romania allied itself with Nazi Germany. During the Second World War over 26,000 Roma were deported to labour camps in the Ukraine where many died of cold, hunger and disease. Others were murdered in Romania. An estimated 30,000 between 1939 and 1945.

The post-war communist government refused to recognise Roma as a minority group and adopted a policy of forced settlement. In 1989, Nicolae Ceaucescu's communist government collapsed. Although Romania now enjoys some semblance of democracy, the situation for Roma has worsened. Far-right nationalists have been allowed to organise and express their opinions. Since 1989 Roma have been subject to worsening racial violence. Helsinki Watch, an international human rights organisation, estimates that over 300 Roma have been killed in racist violence since 1989 (see its World Report 2000 on www.hrw.org). Anti-Roma racism permeates all of Romanian society, readily turning to violence against individuals and whole communities, and Roma have virtually no recourse to police justice and police protection. Between 1990 and 1995 some 30 Roma communities were completely destroyed in mob violence and there is evidence of police involvement in it. Roma face other abuse from the police including arbitrary arrest, beating while in detention and 'raids' on settlements in which armed policemen arrive in Roma settlements early in the morning, often firing shots and forcibly entering homes.

Roma are the poorest ethnic group in Romania. Most live in overcrowded accommodation in rural settlements, housing estates or shanties without access to water, sanitation or electricity. As in other eastern European countries, they have been disproportionally affected by the collapse of nationalised industries. Discriminatory employment practices are almost universal. In 1992 the Social Studies Department of Bucharest University estimated that the unemployment rate among Romanian Roma was 50 per cent, as against 10.5 per cent overall. In the same year, some 63 per cent of Roma lived at or below subsistence level. Many Roma, lacking the necessary identity documents, cannot even claim basic state benefits. The high unemployment rate is also caused by the massive discrimination in the education system. As in Slovakia, most citizenship entitlements are granted only after the production of a local authority identity card. Since 1989 many Roma have migrated from their villages in search of employment (or been forced to flee after violence). Lacking identity documents from their new municipalities, they cannot enrol their children in school. Roma children who do attend school face racism and harassment from other pupils. There is evidence that schools where the majority of children are Roma are the least well resourced. Roma parents described their experiences to the Refugee Council in *Unwanted Journey: Why Central European Roma are Fleeing to the UK:*

'They call me 'Gypsy' and treat my children poorly. The teachers don't pay any attention to the children. They say 'You are a Gypsy and have no business sending your children here'.

'You can see the school there, at the edge of the settlement... it's closed, though it should be open right now.. the teachers just never turn up, or if they do it's only for a few hours'.

Few Roma complete schooling and fewer reach university. The 1992 survey by Bucharest University concluded that 27 per cent of Romanian Roma had never attended school, only 4.5 per cent had completed secondary education and 0.1 per cent had graduated from university (*cited in Refugee Council*, 1999).

As with other Roma communities, it is difficult to estimate the numbers of Romanian Roma in the UK, as Home Office asylum statistics do not record ethnic identity. However, the Refugee Council estimates that about 60 per cent of asylum applications from Romanian nationals are Roma. Asylum statistics for Romanians applying in the UK are

Year	Asylum applications	Refugee status	ELR	Refusal
1994	355	1	1	98
1995	770	1	2	97
1996	455	1	1	98
1997	605	1	1	98
1998	1,015	0	0	100
1999	1,985	1	0	99

Source: Home Office

As the above statistics show, almost all Romanian Roma are refused asylum in the UK. Home Office reasons are that although Roma face discrimination, their experiences in Romania do not amount to persecution. Romanian Roma have won refugee status on appeal when represented by a good lawyer, but many do not have good legal representation (if any), particularly outside London. Many arrived as illegal entrants, having paid agents to transport them across Europe. They may be discovered at ports such as Dover or left beside motorways in southern England. At present, the largest Romanian Roma communities are living in Kent and south east London.

Romanian Roma women may keep their traditional dress: floral skirts and jewellery. Their distinctive dress and that a few have supplemented their asylum support vouchers by begging or cleaning car windows has made them highly visible. At a time of increasing public hostility to refugees, their visibility in London has led to their being singled out. During March 2000, the national tabloid press hounded them with headlines such as '*Gipsy Palaces: beggars build mansions with OUR handouts*' (*The Sun*, 14.3.2000). After two weeks of such coverage, racial attacks on Romanian Roma increased.

More liberal commentators on refugee issues, including senior staff in children's organisations, also adopted an unhelpful position on Romanian Roma. Women seen begging with small children were accused of child neglect or drugging their children with medication such as infant paracetemol. 'Child protection issues' were highlighted in the liberal press. Yet no-one considered why Roma women might be begging with small children: that the asylum support system has rendered them short of cash. Moreover, some of the young children were still being breastfed and leaving children in the care of strangers is a cultural taboo for most Romanian Roma. At the time of writing there is no hard evidence to show that Roma women are drugging their children. No social services department has investigated child protection procedures against Roma families. Neither have any family centres or support projects been set up in London to try and support Roma women, develop their literacy and encourage them not to beg on the street.

Romanian Roma in the UK have shown great resilience. Adults have found work, albeit in the informal sector. But they are not gaining access to healthcare, education and other support services. Few know that they are entitled to free NHS treatment. Others find it difficult to register with a GP. More Romanian Roma children are out of school than other Roma groups in the UK. With a few notable exceptions, Romanian Roma do not use the generic refugee support services. For children in school, maintaining attendance can be a challenge. The negative experiences children (and their parents) have had in Romanian schools contributes to this, as does racism from their peers in the UK. Parents are unlikely to be literate, so communicating with the home can be difficult. Parents can be mistrustful of outsiders, including teachers. Teachers will have to spend time to win trust. A key factor that seems to ensure good school attendance is having an interpreter, bilingual classroom assistant or advocate who is trusted by the Romanian Roma community. One LEA has run a successful summer holiday scheme for Romanian Roma and employed the services of such a bi-cultural advocate and interpreter.

There are no community organisations working with the Romanian Roma but they have strong community organisation. Important decisions tend to be taken by 'councils' of men.

Czech Roma

Czech Roma are the third largest eastern European Roma group in the UK. Most have arrived since 1997. Almost all speak Czech as their home language, a western Slavonic language, most closely related to Slovak. (The languages are similar and mutually intelligible.) Only Roma from isolated rural areas will have maintained Romani as their home language. However, a standard form of Romani was developed in Czechoslovakia, based on the Carpathian Romani dialect spoken by Slovak Roma in today's Czech Republic and Slovakia. There is some published Romani in the Czech Republic (and Slovakia).

An estimated 275,000 Roma live in the Czech republic. Records of their presence go back to 1399 and they were the targets of violence and population expulsions. At the end of the 19th century, successive Hapsburg rulers forced Czech and Slovak Roma to give up their nomadic way of life and settle. Czechoslovakia achieved nationhood in 1918 but Roma continued to face extreme prejudice. After the Nazi invasion in 1938, Czechoslovakia was again divided. Bohemia and Moravia (today's Czech Republic) were annexed by Nazi Germany and a fascist puppet regime came to power in Slovakia. In Bohemia and Moravia, many Roma were imprisoned in concentration camps or transported to Auschwitz. An estimated 5,500 Roma men, women and children were murdered by the Nazis – some 93 per cent of the pre-war Roma population of Bohemia and Moravia.

Czechoslovakia became one country again in 1945. The post-war communist government followed a policy of forced settlement and assimilation and some 200,000 Slovak Roma were forcibly moved from their homes and resettled in western Czechoslovakia, many in homes left by the expelled Sudeten Germans. The forbears of almost all of today's Czech Roma lived in Slovakia before 1945. This has been used to deny some of them citizenship of their country and render them stateless. Some 20,000 former Slovak Roma who moved to the Czech lands after 1945 have been denied citizenship, for committing criminal or civil offences – including parking offences or failing to register a change of address.

The communist government collapsed in 1989 in the Velvet Revolution. The Czech Republic and Slovakia split in 1993. Since 1989 there has been a massive increase in racist violence against Czech Roma. Between 1990 and 1997, a respected Czech human rights organisation recorded 1,205 serious racist attacks on Roma, fifteen of them fatal. In 1998 Helena Bihariova, a 26 year old Roma woman and mother of four young children, was assaulted and thrown into the River Labe by a group of men. She drowned, despite the efforts of a witness who risked his own life trying to save her (cited in *Refugee Council*, 1999). No-one was convicted for her killing. The lack of recourse to police protection and an unwillingness to prosecute those who perpetrate racial attacks is a major human rights concern. Some attacks are perpetrated by 'skinhead' – gangs of young, male political extremists who openly identify with fascism. But many are carried out by ordinary Czechs who do not support far-right parties. Prejudice towards the Roma permeates almost all of Czech society.

Roma also face social exclusion. They are much more likely to live in overcrowded, substandard accommodation, some without running water or electricity. Some 70-80 per cent are unemployed – few Czech Roma have educational qualifications, because most Roma children have been effectively confined to special schools for children with learning difficulties. In 1999, the Czech Ministry of Education reported that about 80 per cent of Roma children were being educated in special schools usually without any assessment of their needs. Such schools offer a limited curriculum that seldom extend pupils. Czech law restricts secondary education opportunities for any pupil who attends a special school to 'remedial' technical schools offering low-level vocational training. This prevents Roma children from sitting the *Maturita* examination and qualifying for further or higher education or success in the job market. The effects of such a limited curriculum will be evident among Czech Roma refugee children in the UK: many aspects of UK schooling with be new to them.

Human rights organisations have challenged this educational discrimination. At the time of writing, the Czech government has committed itself to ending the practice of confining Roma children to special schools. The Ministry of Education plans to set up special nursery classes in mainstream education for Roma children where they will be helped with their learning of formal Czech, before being integrated into mainstream education. How this will work out in practice remains uncertain. There are concerns that this approach does not tackle the racism faced by those 20 per cent of Czech Roma children already educated in the mainstream: children may suffer negative teacher perceptions, harassment from fellow pupils and demands from non-Roma parents that they be removed from the school.

About 2,000 Czech Roma now live in the UK. Others removed after asylum has been refused. Some have returned, although their return could hardly be described as voluntary. Many who return to the Czech Republic later seek asylum in another country. The treatment of Czech asylum applications by the Home Office remains a cause for concern. To date no Czech Roma has been granted refugee status or ELR after an initial asylum application. Those who appeal have had some success if legally represented. The Home Office does acknowledge the problems faced by Czech Roma, but does not agree that these amount to persecution. It also disputes that skinheads are 'agents of persecution' according to the 1951 UN Convention Relation to the Status of Refugees. As the Horvath case illustrates (see Slovakia below), both the Home Office and the British judiciary are of the opinion that Czech and Slovak Roma have recourse to police protection. The treatment of Czech Roma in the UK contrasts with that of Canada, where some 85.9 per cent of Czech Roma asylum applications in 1998 resulted in grants of refugee status or temporary protection.

Another concern is how the media portray Czech and Slovak Roma in the UK. Those arriving in late 1997 and early 1998 were subjected to a barrage of extremely hostile media coverage, with headlines such as 'Arrival of the Giro Czechs' . Perhaps the worst was a local Kent paper, the Dover Express in October 1998: 'We want to wash this dross down the drain'. Its sister paper ran wholly unfounded stories linking asylum-seekers with prostitution. The coverage was so extreme that the Kent police warned the editor of Dover Express that he faced being charged with incitement to racial hatred and indeed there have been numerous racial attacks on Roma asylum-seekers in Kent.

The largest UK Czech Roma community is in Kent, as many have come through the port of Dover. Others are living in Greater London, Southend and in the North East where they have been moved by the dispersal programme. In London there are two community organisations working specifically with Czech and Slovak Roma. Some education authorities have implemented interesting projects to support Roma children, such as a summer school in Slough. Kent Adult Education Institute has organised a pioneering parent and toddler group in Margate. Parents attend English classes and bring their pre-school children with them. Its programme for under fives includes visits to primary schools.

A major issue in the UK is providing adequate interpreting services. It can be hard to find Polish, Czech, Slovak and Romanian interpreters in most towns. Almost all the interpreters are non-Roma, and some bring with them their own prejudices towards Roma.

Slovak Roma
An estimated 500,000 Roma of a total population of 5.1 million live in Slovakia. Most Roma live in eastern and southern Slovakia, many in isolated villages or run-down urban housing developments. More of the Slovak Roma have retained Romani as their home language than in the Czech Republic.

Slovakia split from the Czech Republic in 1993 and for five years its Prime Minister was the authoritarian and racist Vladimir Meciar. His public stance and much government policy was hostile towards Roma and other minority groups. Slovak was enshrined as the sole official language (including in the education system). Official documents, such as the '1996 Resolution of the Government of the Slovak Republic to the Proposal of the Activities and Measures in order to solve the *problems of citizens in need of social care'*, are full of references to their 'low work ethics' and make other pejorative statements. Meciar's coalition partner in government was the Slovak National Party, an ultranationalist and racist party whose members frequently express anti-Roma views. As in the Czech Republic, there is almost universal prejudice towards Roma, coupled with rising levels of racial violence. In March 1998, for example, three young Roma children in Presov were badly beaten by six skinheads. Human rights organisations record a great deal of police harassment, including beatings in detention and the use of electric cattle prods, knives and guns during 'raids' on Roma settlements. Not surprisingly, Roma are often reluctant to report racial attacks to the police.

Over 80 per cent of Roma are unemployed. Many who had work before 1989 have lost their jobs as Slovakia has progressed to a free market economy and state industries have closed. They face discrimination when attempting to find work and they, too, lack qualifications because they are forced to attend special schools. Housing conditions faced by most Roma families are appalling. Between 1997 and 1999 some 1,210 asylum applications from the Slovak Republic were lodged in the UK. Not one was initially successful, although about 30 per cent succeeded on appeal. However, in 2000, a landmark asylum appeal (Horvath) judged that Slovak Roma have recourse to police protection.

Like the Czech Roma, most live in Kent, Greater London, Southend and the North East. In London, they are supported by two refugee community organisations working with Czech Roma.

Roma from the former Yugoslavia
About 1000 Roma from the former Yugoslavia have arrived in the UK since 1992. They include
• Bosnian Roma admitted to the UK as part of the Bosnian Programme (1992-95) and settled in Derby and Edinburgh
• Bosnian Roma who made their own way to the UK during or after the war and applied for asylum
• Serbian Roma – both Muslim and Christian – who fled racism
• Croatian Roma, mostly from near the Hungarian border, persecuted for belonging to the Serbian Orthodox church
• Kosovan Roma who have arrived since 1999, escaping attacks by Albanian extremists who accuse them of siding with the Serbs during the Kosova conflict.

Numbers are small and it is a diverse community. Some are Muslim, others Serbian Orthodox. Some speak Romani as their home language, others Serbo-Croat or Albanian. Apart from the Roma who came to Derby and Edinburgh, no community groups are working with them. A large proportion of adults have limited literacy in their home language. This group has also attracted negative media coverage in the UK as a result of a small number of Roma children being convicted of theft in central London.

Bibliography

European Roma Rights Centre (1996) *Sudden Rage at Dawn: Violence Against Roma in Romania*, Budapest: European Roma Rights Centre

European Roma Rights Centre (1997) *Time of the Skinheads: denial and exclusion of Roma in Slovakia*, Budapest: European Roma Rights Centre

European Roma Rights Centre (1999) *Roma in Poland*, Budapest: European Roma Rights Centre. Available on www.errc.org

Fonseca, I. (1996) *Bury Me Standing; the Gypsies and their Journey*, London: Vintage

Fraser, A. (1995) *The Gypsies*, Oxford, Blackwells

Kenrick, D. (1995) and Puxon, G. (1995) *Gypsies under the Swastika*, Hatfield, UK: University of Hertfordshire Press

Kenrick, D. (1998) *An Historical Dictionary of the Gypsies (Romanies)*, Maryland: Scarecrow Press

Liegeois, J-P (1998) *School Provision for Ethnic Minorities; the Gypsy Paradigm*, Hatfield, UK: University of Hertfordshire Press

Refugee Council (1999) *Unwanted Journey: Why Central European Roma are Fleeing to the UK*, London: Refugee Council.

Useful web sites
www.errc.org
European Roma Rights Centre

http://patrin.com
The Patrin web site gives extensive information about Roma issues, as well as links to other web sites.

Readers may also find the *Interface* journal useful. It is published by the Gypsy Research Centre of the Universite Rene Descartes, Paris and can be obtained by faxing 33 (0) 1 42 86 20 65.

■ Refugees from Sierra Leone

Since 1992 over 10,000 Sierra Leonean refugees have fled to the UK. Sierra Leone had a population of 5 million in 1998 with 65 per cent living in rural areas. The capital is Freetown.

Ethnic groups: The Temne (30 per cent of the population) and Mende (30 per cent) are the two largest ethnic groups. Ethnic identity is not a factor in conflict, although there is some employment discrimination along ethnic lines. In the countryside Sierra Leoneans have strong allegiance to extended family and chieftaincies. About 10 per cent of the population identify themselves as Krio and are the descendants of freed African slaves returned by the British in the 19th century. There is also a Lebanese minority group living in Freetown. The Lebanese and the Krio dominate commercial life, causing some resentment among other ethnic groups.

Languages: English is the official language and the medium of education. Newspapers and books are mostly published in English and all literate Sierra Leoneans write good English. The dominant spoken language is Krio, an English-based Creole originally spoken by former slaves living the environs of Freetown. Krio is the first language of 10 per cent of the population, but understood by about 95 per cent. It draws on an English vocabulary, but has its own grammar.

Older Sierra Leonean refugee children arriving in the UK will generally write good English. They may need time and help with spoken English, as they will be used to speaking Krio. Mende is widely spoken in southern Sierra Leone and Temne in central and northern Sierra Leone. Other African languages include Limba, Vai, Kissi and Gola. Mende, Temne and others belong to the Niger-Congo language family. The Lebanese minority speak Arabic.

Names: The Muslim majority use Islamic names and often its naming system: personal name, father's name and grandfather's name. Most Krio have English first names and family names. Others will use English or African first names and African family names.

Religion: Nearly 60 per cent of the population are Muslim, mostly in the north. Another 30 per cent follow traditional beliefs. Some 10 per cent are Christian, mostly in the Freetown area.

Education system: School starts at five or six and primary education lasts six years and culminates in the National Primary School Examination. Secondary education lasts for up to seven years. Children can attend a junior secondary school from 12-15 years and at 15 sit for the Basic Education Certificate. Some progress to senior secondary school for three years. Alternatively children may follow a more UK-based secondary education pathway, working towards the West African School Certificate or GCE O-Level or the Cambridge Overseas School Certificate at 16 years. At the end of sixth form, students sit for the West African Higher School Certificate, GCE A-Levels or the Cambridge Overseas School Certificate.

English is the medium of education. As in all poor countries, class sizes in state schools are high and students have little access to books and equipment. (The few private or religious schools are better equipped.) Only primary education is free (although parents have to pay for books) so most of the poor are forced to leave to school to work. The male literacy rate is about 45 per cent with female literacy 18 per cent. The war has forced the closure of many schools.

Economy: Sierra Leone is one of the world's poorest countries, despite its many natural resources such as gold, diamonds, iron ore and tropical timber. Before the civil war, longstanding corruption and economic mismanagement meant that only an elite benefited from the country's wealth. Most people survive by subsistence farming or trading in the informal sector. The war has caused severe disruption to the economy. The country's infrastructure is undeveloped and basic services do not meet people's needs. Sierra Leone has the world's highest infant mortality and the world's lowest life expectancy.

A chronology of events: During the 15th and 16th century Sudanic people from central Africa migrated to the area now comprising Sierra Leone and integrated with the local population. When European colonists arrived, people were ruled by chieftains. By the end of the 18th century, slaves who had been freed or had escaped were being transported to the Freetown area by the British. In 1808, coastal Sierra Leone became a British colony, which grew as the British transported more freed slaves.

Late 19th Century: From 1850-1900, Sierra Leone grows in prosperity, exporting palm oil and minerals. The Krio population do well and soon become dominant in commerce and politics in all the UK's West African colonies. The British bring the interior under their control, setting the boundaries of modern Sierra Leone in 1896. Resistance to British rule grows, particularly among Temne and Mende peoples to the unpopular tax system. People are forced to pay a tax on their homes so, as subsistence farmers who have no money, they have to sell their land. This land is then subsumed in plantations that give employment to the new landless.

1930s-1970s – The Krio support a growing independence movement, later joined by other ethnic groups. In 1951, people gain more democratic rights, voting for their own government for the first time, although still a British colony. In 1961, Sierra Leone becomes an independent state within the Commonwealth. Its first Prime Minister is Milton Margai of the Sierra Leone People's Party, succeeded in 1964 by his half-brother. But the economic situation deteriorates and Government supporters are accused of corruption and diamond smuggling. Dr Siaka Stevens, a trade unionist and leader of the All People's Congress wins the election of 1967. He promises to improve the lot of the poor, but is prevented from taking power by a military coup. Junior army officers seize power in another military coup and Siaka Stevens is invited to form a civilian government.

In 1971, Sierra Leone declares itself a republic, with Siaka Stevens as the first President. The economic situation deteriorates, there is much political unrest and widespread violence during the 1977 election. In 1978, the All People's Congress become the sole legal party.

1980s – Sierra Leone's foreign debt increases. Food prices rise and many government salaries are unpaid, causing demonstrations and riots in Freetown and other urban areas. There are continued Government scandals over misuse of public money, corruption and diamond smuggling. The violence becomes so intense in 1982 that over 4,000 refugees flee to Liberia. In 1985 Siaka Stevens is replaced by Major-General Joseph Saidu Momoh, a Cabinet Minister and Commander of the Armed Forces. Momoh expands the armed forces and uses them to suppress opposition. His popularity declines because he cannot make economic improvements. There is continued unrest and an attempted coup in 1987, followed by declaration of a state of emergency. The media is censored and some legal rights are suspended. A number of opposition politicians are executed in 1989.

1990s – Civil war begins in neighbouring Liberia. Sierra Leone sends troops to Liberia as part of the West African Peace Keeping Force (ECOWAS). The conflict spills over into Sierra Leone. Rebels belonging to the National Patriotic Front of Liberia advance into eastern Sierra Leone, partly to gain revenge for Sierra Leone's support for the ECOWAS force. Over 200,000 people flee as refugees; by the end of 1991 another 150,000 people are internally displaced. Liberian refugees are attacked by the Sierra Leonean army who blame them for causing conflict in Sierra Leone. More and more Sierra Leoneans are dragged into the fighting. A new rebel group begins to emerge: the Revolutionary United Front, led by Foday Sankoh.

In 1992 President Momoh is overthrown in a coup led by junior army officers. Captain Valentine Strasser becomes President at the age of 25. Although elections are promised, opponents of the new Government face detention without trial, torture or extrajudicial execution. Despite promises to end the war, violence spreads throughout Sierra Leone. Both rebel soldiers and the regular army are accused of murder. Looting is widespread as it is often the only means by which rebel soldiers, the army and civilians can sustain themselves. 'Rebels' – RUF soldiers, current or ex-Sierra Leonean army soldiers or common criminals – attack villages, creating panic. People flee their homes which are looted and owners who resist are killed. Gold and diamonds are smuggled out of the country and used to finance the war. Much fighting involves child soldiers as young as ten. By the end of 1992, the only safe area is in Freetown.

As fighting intensifies 200,000 people flee as refugees, with a further 900,000 internally displaced by 1994. In 1995 the government invites Executive Outcomes, a private South African security force, to help secure key diamond mines. A West African Peace Keeping Force (ECOMOG) also operates in the country. In 1996, Strasser is deposed in a coup and replaced by Julius Maada Bio, another army officer. Free elections are promised and Ahmed Tejan Kabbah is elected President. Peace is agreed in the Abijan Accord. But in May 1997 the democratically elected Government is overthrown by the Armed Forces Revolutionary Council, which plays on fears that the Government of President Kabbah favours the Mende. The AFRC is led by Major Johnny Paul Koroma.

Widespread human rights violations follow the coup. The new AFRC Government is joined by the Revolution United Front. ECOMOG forces bombard Freetown in an attempt to restore the Government of Ahmed Tejan Kabbah. They liberate Freetown and go on to take most major towns. President Kabbah is restored to power but fighting continues in many parts of the country. By 1999 rebel soldiers enter Freetown. Later, reinforced ECOMOG troops launch a counter-offensive and retake the capital. Fighting continues in much of the country and appalling human rights violations and destruction are perpetrated by the rebels. Many civilians have limbs amputated; children are abducted: girls raped and boys conscripted. However, President Kabbah remains in power and in July 1999 a peace agreement is signed between the Government and the Revolutionary United Front. The promised peace remains fragile. Over 200,00 people have been killed since 1992. Most of the eastern part of Freetown has been completely destroyed.

Sierra Leonean refugees in the UK – Statistics

Year	Asylum Applications	Refugee Status as percentages	ELR	Refusal
1992	325	5	0	95
1993	1,050	1	3	94
1994	1,810	1	1	98
1995	855	1	2	97
1996	395	1	1	98
1997	815	1	3	96
1998	565	2	13	92
1999	1,125	83	13	4

The Sierra Leonean refugee community in the UK numbers over 10,000. It includes about 500 Lebanese, most from Freetown. Small numbers of refugees associated with opposition politics have arrived since the 1960s. A few have joined family living in the UK, which has had a small community since the early 20th century. (A number of Sierra Leonean men fought in the British armed forces in World War Two and later settled in the UK.)

Greater numbers of refugees came after the 1992 coup when security deteriorated. The first to arrive were those associated with opposition parties, journalists, trade unionists and human rights activists, many of them with their families. Soon they were joined by young single men, many fleeing forced conscription, from all parts of the country.

Very few were granted refugee status or ELR between 1993 and 1997. Asylum-seekers whose applications had failed were removed to Sierra Leone, much to the concern of human rights and refugee organisations. The Refugee Council believes that the security situation and the clear dangers faced by some groups meant that almost all Sierra Leoneans should have been granted refugee status or ELR.

In December 1998 the Home Office stopped enforced removals of asylum-seekers to Sierra Leone and suspended all decisions on their cases. In July 1999, it announced that all Sierra Leonean asylum-seekers would be granted one year's ELR to be reviewed after one year.

Most refugees live in south and east London and a few in Manchester and other cities. There is a well-established Sierra Leonean community group is based in Greenwich, with an organised youth club. Several smaller community organisations also work with Sierra Leonean refugees. The Lebanese community makes use of Arab and Lebanese community organisations. Many refugees have managed to find work in the UK but a significant number of young single men face social exclusion. Their education may have been severely interrupted because of war. Usually able to write English, they may need specific help in improving their spoken English and job search skills. Sadly, all too few further education course are targeted at Anglophone refugees.

Bibliography

Human Rights Watch (1999) *Getting away with Murder, Mutilation, Rape: new testimonies from Sierra Leone*, New York: Human Rights Watch

Save the Children (2000) *War Brought Us Here*, London: Save the Children

www.sierra-leone.org is a very useful web site, proving bibliographies and links to many other sources of information on Sierra Leone.

■ Refugees from Somalia

Since the mid-1980s over 120,000 Somali refugees have arrived in the UK, joining existing communities in London, Cardiff, Liverpool and in other industrial areas. Before 1991 the capital was Mogadishu. The country has now split into Somalia, the Republic of Somaliland and the Puntland State of Somalia, the latter two administrations being unrecognised by the UN as states. The population is about 11 million of whom 24 per cent live in urban areas. At least 500,000 people died in the famine of 1992/93, including half of all children under five.

Ethnic groups: The Somalis form one of the most homogenous populations in Africa and over 80 per cent identify themselves as ethnic Somalis. But in other ways they are immensely divided. Despite their strong sense of linguistic and cultural unity, clan affiliation has proved to be an increasingly divisive factor, culminating in the present crisis. There are four major clan families plus minority clans

- the Dir, living in north west Somalia
- the Daarood, a pastoral clan living in the north, east and southern regions
- the Issaq, a pastoral clan living in the north to which the majority of Somali refugees in the UK
- the Hawiye, a pastoral clan whose members predominate in parts of the south and eastern coasts and around Mogadishu

The Digil and and Rahanwayn are 'minority' clans living mostly in the south. Each clan family is divided up into many clans and sub-clans. For example the Daarood clan family contains clans such as the Ogaadeen, Majeerteen and Mareehan. Clans may range in size from an few hundred members to several thousand. Somalis will identify more with their clans than with the larger clan families. Clans are divided into branches down to the level of extended families. The office of clan leader is usually hereditary, but clan elders, called Sultan, are normally figureheads who make many of the political decisions. The clan system is patrilineal; a person's clan, branch and family loyalties are determined by his or her father. Most families take their genealogy very seriously, as it locates them within Somali society. Political parties and militia also draw their support along clan lines and the dominant clans have excluded other clans and minorities from sharing power. In the UK clan affiliations are less important among the older established migrant Somali communities but are still very imortant among newly-arrived refugees. Many community groups draw their membership from one particular clan family so Somali community organisations can seem sectarian.

There are also two minority clans – the Digil and agro-pastoral Rahanweyn. Although they speak dialects of Somali, some anthropologists (as well as many Somalis) believe them to be of mixed ethnic origin, leading to prejudice and discrimination on the part of the major clans. There are also a small number of Somali occupational caste groups including the Tomal (blacksmiths), Migdan (barbers and shoe-makers) and Yibir (peddlers who claim Jewish ancestry). Like the Digil and Rahanwayn, these occupational caste groups have been the targets of widespread prejudice and discrimination.

Over 20 per cent of the population belong to ethnic minority groups, the largest of whom are the Bantu, living around the Juba river. Largely of sub-Saharan African appearance, the Bantu are believed to be either the indigenous inhabitants of this area or the descendants of slaves brought to southern Somalia. Many Bantu have lost their land to armed militia and are internally displaced. They speak their own languages and usually a little Somali.

Over 40 per cent of the inhabitants of pre-1991 Mogadishu belonged to ethnic minority groups, the most significant being the Bravanese, who also live in Brava and other southern coastal towns. They trace their ancestry back to Yemen and coastal Kenya and most have paler skins than their ethnic Somali compatriots. The Bravanese speak a dialect of Swahili called Chimini or Brava. Bravanese children with little education in Somalia will not speak Somali although adult Bravanese usually do.

Other southern minority groups include the Benadiris (who claim mixed Yemeni and east African origin) and the Banjuni (a maritime community living in Kismayo and some of the coastal islands and speak Kibanjuni, another Swahili dialect). The reer Hamar are an urban Arabic-speaking group and the Tunni a Brava-speaking group living in rural southern Somalia. Both Bravanese and Benadiris have been targets of violence and continued harassment since the start of the civil war. Although some Bravanese did achieve high office in government, as a community they were some-what isolated from the mainstream of Somali life, often deemed foreigners by Somali nationalists. Many were comparatively wealthy and resented so became subject to militia violence. Since the start of the civil war, most Bravanese have been robbed, the town of Brava has been all but destroyed and many Bravanese have been forced into exile. Today, the Bravanese refugee community in the UK numbers about 4,000.

Languages: Somali is the first language spoken by the great majority of the population plus another 1.5 million people in Ethiopia, 300,000 in Kenya and about 125,000 in Djibouti. Somali belongs to the Cushitic group of languages within the Afro-Asiatic language family. It is most closely related to Ethiopian and Eritrean languages such as Oromo, Beja and Saho.

Somali also uses words borrowed from Arabic or of Arabic origin. Somali became the national and official language of Somalia in 1973, after being transcribed into a written form in the early 1970s. Previously Arabic and English were used in written communication, and English was the language of administration. After much debate, it was decided to use a Roman script for the Somali language, although the ordering of the alphabet is similar to Arabic. There are 21 consonants, five short vowels, five long vowels and five diphthongs; the letters 'p', 'v' and 'z' are not used. Letters are also pronounced differently, for example 'x' is pronounced 'h'. Somali children who are literate in their own language may initially find the different ordering and pronunciation in English confusing. There are many dialects and regional accents, not always mutually intelligible, although most Somalis understand northern dialects which form the basis for standard Somali. Written Somali shows considerable variations in spelling as this is not fully standardised. Somali has a rich oral and poetic tradition. Storytelling is important to cultural identity. The implementation of the written form of the language had a profound effect on its development. A new vocabulary had to be created to cover aspects of life such as science, technology and social sciences. Many of the new words have been borrowed from English.

Arabic is also widely understood in Somalia. There are strong cultural and trading links with Yemen and Saudi Arabia and a significant number of Somalis work in the Gulf States. Many boys and girls attend madrassah and learn classical Arabic and the Koran. English and Italian were introduced as colonial languages in the 19th century. Swahili dialects such as Chimini (Brava) are also spoken among minority communities in the southern coastal towns.

Names: Somalis use Islamic names and naming system, taking three names: a first name, followed by their father's and grandfather's name. A woman usually keeps her name on marriage. Nicknames are frequently used.

Religion: Almost all Somalis are Sunni Muslims of the Shafi'i sect. In the UK, Somalis tend to worship separately because most Muslims are from the Indian sub-continent so the sermons preached in mosques are usually in Bengali or Urdu and Somalis can feel sidelined. Most Somalis are observant and try and live according to Koranic law. They celebrate all the main festivals and have the same Muslim dietary restrictions. Unlawful foods include all pig meat, all meat from flesh-eating animals and any meat containing blood. Alcohol is forbidden. Both women and men are expected to dress modestly. Schools should be sensitive to the religious needs of observant Muslims by

- providing a place to wash and to pray
- acknowledging that children who fast during Ramadan may feel tired or lack concentration
- providing halal food
- ensuring that PE kit is modest and that private cubicles are provided for showering after games
- meeting with parents to discuss their concerns about sex education while ensuing that Somali children have a right to sex education.

Education system: In pre-colonial Somalia few people received a formal education. Most Somalis were nomadic; storytelling provided the main means of teaching children the cultural and moral values of Somali society, although some children in coastal towns attended *madrassah*. After British and Italian Somaliland were colonised there was an expansion of urban education, designed to provide an educated middle class to service the administrative and trading interests of the respective colonial powers. In British Somaliland the educational system was modelled on the UK and the medium of instruction was English. In Italian Somaliland the medium of instruction was Italian. At independence and unification of the two former colonies, there were two educational systems but by 1965 the Somali government had unified them. The languages of instruction were English and Arabic in the north, Italian and English in the south.

Education policy changed in line with the new socialist ideology after 1969. Schools were nationalised and the newly scripted Somali language became the official language. During the literacy campaign of the early 1970s, schools and colleges were closed and school students, college students and teachers were sent out to teach the new alphabet. By 1980 Somalia had a literacy rate of 60 per cent – no mean achievement in a country where about 60 per cent of the population are nomadic. Today, as a result of war, literacy has fallen below 20 per cent. In 1975 Somali replaced English, Arabic and Italian as the language of instruction.

Until the civil war, schooling lasted for twelve years: from age 6-18. Until 1991 children in urban areas could well have attended *madrassah* for about a year before starting state education at six. In theory, education was compulsory up to the age of 14. State education was divided into three levels: elementary, intermediate and secondary, each of four years. Children were tested every term and through an annual examination to progress to the next year. As in many poor countries, classes included students of many different ages. Girls and boys were taught together, although many more boys than girls attended school. Most Somali schools only operated in the morning. During the first eight years, Somali, Arabic, religious studies, mathematics, history, geography, sciences, social science, art, physical education and home economics were taught, plus English during the last four years, ending with the Secondary School Leaving Certificate examination.

In this poor country, funds for education have always been limited. Even before the current crisis school buildings were in poor condition, books in short supply and class sizes large, with up to 60 children in a class. Teaching methods were formal, with an emphasis on learning facts. Somali children will have no experience of laboratory practicals, or group and collaborative learning methods. In Somalia, parents had very little involvement with schools so refugee parents in the UK may be reticent about visiting schools or becoming involved in their activities.

Siad Barre's assault on northern towns, followed by the collapse of the Somali government has gravely affected education. In the north – now the Republic of Somaliland – most urban schools were destroyed in 1988 and for over three years many children from northern Somalia were unable to attend school. There have been attempts to restore primary education in the towns but many teachers are still working without wages (or even books). Today these primary schools exist alongside *madrassah*, the latter providing the main schooling. In southern Somalia education has been completely destroyed by the fighting. Teachers have fled and the schools bombed or burnt. Although a few primary schools have reopened in Mogadishu, the only form of education for many children is in the *madrassah*. Some families have made informal arrangements for their children in home schools. Teachers of Somali refugee children can expect them to have had severely interrupted education, or none at all.

Economy: Most of Somalia is semi-desert, except for the Juba Plain in the south, where export and subsistence crops are grown. Despite recent urbanisation Somalia is essentially a pastoral society, with about 60 per cent of the people grazing camels, sheep, goats and cattle. About 80 per cent of Somalia's exports come from livestock, others include fresh fruit such as bananas, and fish. The major market is Saudi Arabia, and other Gulf States. Much livestock is provided for the pilgrims attending the *Haj*. Somalia's trading links with the Arabian Peninsula stretch back thousands of years. Towns are the centre for livestock trading. Town-dwelling Somalis maintain strong links with their relatives in the countryside. Urban Somalis often have joint shares in livestock with their rural kin, and children are frequently sent to spend holidays with relatives who live in the interior.

In the 20th century foreign remittances have become increasingly important economically. Somalis were recruited into the British armed forces during the Second World War and later into the British merchant navy. Today many work in the Gulf States.

A chronology of events: Archaeologists first identified Somali people living in the Horn of Africa in 2000-1500BC. Somalia was known by the Egyptians as 'the Land of Punt' – frankincense – and close trading relationships were developed between Egypt and Red Sea villages and towns. By 900AD, Somali nomads were living in present-day Somalia and parts of present-day Ethiopia, Djibouti and Kenya. Islam replaced animism as the religion and Somalia gradually emerged as a centre of trade.

1850-1930: In the 19th century Somalia begins to attract the attention of colonial powers, as it is of strategic importance at the mouth of the Red Sea. The Berlin Conference in 1884 divides up the African continent between the European imperial powers. The northern part of Somalia becomes a British colony – British Somaliland – while the Italians take control of the south. In 1897 the Anglo-Abyssinian Treaty allocates the Ogaden region of British Somaliland to the Ethiopians. During the early years of the 20th century Sheikh Mohammed Abdilleh Hassan, called the 'Mad Mullah' by the British, leads rebellions against the Ethiopians, British and Italians. Although unsuccessful, he is credited with beginning modern Somali nationalism.

1939-1960: In the Second World War the UK uses British Somaliland as a base to fight the Italians in Eritrea, Abyssinia and Italian Somaliland. Many Somalis join the British armed forces and Italian Somaliland is captured. In 1950 Somalia is again divided. The Italians return to the south with UN backing, and the British continue to administer British Somaliland, where nationalists, led by the Somali Youth Club, begin to demand independence and national unity.

1960-1968: In 1960 British and Italian Somaliland gain independence and unite to form one country. But there are many problems: the country is extremely poor and north and south have experienced different colonial and administrative systems. There are deep clan and political divisions; nevertheless the Somali Republic is a democracy and human rights are respected. Many Somalis are also living outside the new nation, in Ethiopia, Djibouti and Kenya.

1969-1990: In 1969 the democratically elected Somali Government loses public support. President Abdirashid Ali Shermaarke is assassinated and army officers seize power in a military coup. Major General Mohammed Siad Barre becomes president of the newly named Somali Democratic Republic, and the country is ruled by an unelected body called the Supreme Revolutionary Council. But the Government affirms that the country will be returned to democracy, and will introduce new policies to improve the lives of ordinary people. The next five years see the literacy campaign and ambitious rural development projects. In **1970** the Government announces its commitment to socialism, and looks to the Soviet Union for support. Financial and military aid is given, and the country soon has one of the largest armies in Africa. But there are also severe food shortages. In 1970 the Government oprganises an efficient relief operation and few people die of starvation. In 1977 war breaks out with Ethiopia over the disputed territory of the Ogaden, which President Barre wanted to bring into 'Greater Somalia'. The Somali army joins the Ogaden-based guerrillas of the Western Somali Liberation Front. The Soviet-Somali alliance ends, as the new Ethiopian regime develops its own ties with the Soviet Union. The USA steps in and gives military aid to the Somali Government. Neither super-power contributes much to the economic development of the country. Ethiopia wins back control of the Ogaden in 1978, but the guerrilla war continues until 1988.

Present Barre begins to experience the first opposition to his rule in the late 1970s. Oil price rises hit Somalia badly, and the country falls deep in debt. The IMF steps in, forcing the Somali Government to cut public spending and adopt a structural adjustment policy. Food subsidies are cut, causing hardship among the urban population. Prompted by rising popular discontent, members of the Majeerteen clan back a *coup d'etat*. This fails, but President Barre launches reprisal attacks on the Majeerteen, destroying their water sources. Over 2,000 clan members die or are killed with other Government opponents.

Three opposition parties have started to organise by 1982 including the Somali National Movement (SNM). All soon commit themselves to armed struggle to overthrow President Barre. Civil war has begun. President Barre unleashes terror against clans associated with opposition parties. Northern Somalia is worst affected, with members of the Issaq clan facing repressive measures ranging from imprisonment to execution of those suspected of supporting the SNM. In retaliation for attacks on the Issaq clan the SNM launches a military offensive in **1988** in northern towns. The Government responds with extreme force destroying the northern towns of Burao and Hargeisa by shelling and aerial bombardment. Over 72,000 people are killed in Hargeisa, and 400,000 flee as refugees, some subsequently seeking asylum in the UK.

Persecution then shifts to the Hawiye clan in central Somalia, the powerbase of the United Somali Congress (USC). Throughout 1989 civilians are imprisoned and killed although the USC is better able to challenge Siad Barre's misrule and oppression.

1991-2001: In early 1991 the USC marches into Mogadishu and Siad Barre is forced to flee. But the USC splits into two groups, one led by General Aidid and the other by interim President Ali Mahdi Mohamed. Each is backed by a sub-group of the Hawiye clan and both factions are heavily armed by Soviet and US weaponry left in the country. In other parts of the country political parties and factions fail to unite, and inter-clan conflict worsens. Nearly one million people are forced into exile or are internally displaced. By the end of 1991 Somalia is facing severe food shortages as a result of drought and the war's disruption of the agrarian economy. UN relief agencies are criticised for their slow response. In May 1991 the SNM declares independence in the north. There is a fragile peace in the new Republic of Somaliland. But it is an unrecognised state and does not qualify for international aid, desperately needed for the reconstruction of the country.

In 1992 the International Committee of the Red Cross warns that 4,000,000 Somalis are at risk of starvation. Diplomatic solutions to the conflicts fail. Fighting prevents food aid from being distributed. Aid agencies are forced to hire militia to protect food convoys and their employees. Some 500,000 Somalis die of starvation in 1992, including half of all children under five. By the end of the year one million people are displaced, and a further one million are refugees in

Ethiopia, Kenya, Yemen and European countries. Non-governmental organisations become increasingly frustrated with the UN's slow reaction to the worsening crisis. US troops land in Mogadishu, in 'Operation Restore Hope' in 1992, evoking mixed international responses. Some aid agencies fear that without the full cooperation of the Somalis, it will end in disaster. Others accept that the need to stop people dying justifies military intervention. Food security is assured, but attempts to disarm the militias are of limited success. In 1993 a UN peacekeeping force takes over from the US in Mogadishu. But no transitional government or united leadership has emerged, and the country remains divided. In southern Somalia much fighting focuses on the conflicts between Ali Mahdi, General Hersi Morgan and General Aideed and his son.

In 1994-96 US troops are withdrawn. Heavy fighting continues in Mogadishu between Aideed and Ali Mahdi's militia. In the breakaway Republic of Somaliland there is also clan fighting, causing over 30,000 people to flee Hargeisa. Many seek sanctuary in Ethiopia. Fighting continues in the southern towns. In 1996 the Ethiopian government hosts peace talks between 26 Somali factions, but Hussein Aideed refuses to take part. There is a brief ceasefire in Mogadishu at the end of the year. Further peace talks are held in Cairo in 1997, resulting in the signing of the Cairo declaration. Fighting lessens in Mogadishu.

In 1998 a unified civilian administration is set up in Mogadishu. Former militia men are demobilised and trained as police officers. But fighting breaks out in Kismayo, Baidoa and other southern towns. The autonomous 'Puntland State of Somalia' is proclaimed in Garaowe by various political groups, mostly dominated by the Daarood clan and, although unrecognised, receives support from the Ethiopian government. Right from the start there is tension between the adminstration in Puntland and that in Somaliland. In 2000 further peace talks are held in Djibouti.

Somali refugees in the UK – Statistics

Year	Asylum Applications	Refugee Status as percentages	ELR	Refusal
1989	1,850	75	24	1
1990	2,250	73	20	7
1991	1,995	16	71	13
1992	1,575	1	86	13
1993	1,465	1	92	7
1994	1,840	1	91	8
1995	3,465	1	92	7
1996	1,780	1	93	6
1997	2,730	43	44	13
1998	4,685	83	13	4
1999	7,485	42	18	39

The figures exclude dependants. Source: Home Office

There are about 120,000 Somalis in the UK. Almost a century ago sailors from British Somaliland settled in the ports of London, Cardiff and Liverpool, and in industrial cities such as Sheffield, Middlesborough, Manchester and Birmingham. Since the assault on the northern Somali towns in 1988, the community has grown. The first arrivals were primarily Issaq, from towns such as Hargeisa, many joining family already living in the UK. In 1990 members of the Hawiye clan from central Somalia started fleeing to the UK. Since 1991 the majority of refugees are from southern Somalia, including many Bravanese.

There are class differences among the Somali refugees. The early refugees were predominately urban, middle class and well-educated, but more recent arrivals include men and women who have received little or no education in Somalia. A recent study in one London local authority found that about 50 per cent of recently arrived adult women from Somalia were not literate. Some travel to the UK via Kenya, Ethiopia or Yemen. Recently Somalis who have sought asylum in the Netherlands or Germany have started arriving, to join family and because the UK has a lower rate of refusing Somali asylum applications.

The Somali community in Greater London, is concentrated in Hackney and Tower Hamlets in the east and Ealing and Brent in west London. Most Bravanese live in east London and Manchester. Somalis live in all London boroughs, and almost every London secondary school has received Somali refugees, as have many primary schools. Outside London there are significant Somali communities in Manchester, Liverpool, Sheffield, Middlesborough, Cardiff and Bristol and smaller ones in many of the new areas for the dispersal of asylum-seekers.

There are Somali community organisations in many parts of the UK but some represent only particular clan and political alignments and in some London authorities there could be four or five different Somali community groups, many unfunded. To outsiders this factionalism can appear bewildering and teachers cannot always tell what group to contact. Many community organisations are running community schools for children where they learn Somali and Koranic Arabic.

The Refugee Council believes that Somalis are one of the most vulnerable refugee communities in the UK. Many Somali refugees are now living in deprived conditions and there is a disproportionate number of single female heads of household. The main concerns of the Somali community are family separation, poor housing, racial harassment, unemployment, specific healthcare issues and underachievement in schools.

Family separation – The exodus of Somalis has followed many different routes and family members are often left or lost during different stages of a family's journey. Some children have parents or siblings (as well as other family) left in Somalia. Many Somalis have spent periods of time in refugee camps, in Yemen, Kenya and Ethiopia and limited money means that some relatives are left behind in camps until a family can secure the finance and papers needed to bring relatives to the UK. Other Somali children have close relatives working in the Gulf States or living in exile in Sweden, Germany, the Netherlands and other western countries.

Poor housing – Almost all London-based Somali refugee families spend much time in bed and breakfast hotels. They are also over-represented in hard-to-let local authority accommodation. Extended family often join relatives who have housing: an estimated that 88 per cent of Somali families in East London live in overcrowded conditions (*London Borough of Tower Hamlets Survey 1992*).

Racial harassment is a common experience: on one east London housing estate there were 123 racial attacks on Somalis in a one year ranging from spitting and verbal abuse to serious incidents such as assault and arson. Two London local authorities have funded work specifically to support Somalis facing racial harassment.

Unemployment among Somali refugees remains very high: over 85 per cent of refugees of 35-50 years were unemployed according to one survey (*London Borough of Tower Hamlets Survey 1992*).

Specific health issues – Somali refugees also have unique health problems caused by recent events in Somalia, life in refugee camps in East Africa, and poverty and stress in the UK. The assault on Hargeisa in 1988 left 72,000 people dead and a further 290,000 civilians injured. Some refugees still bear their war injuries and others psychological scars. Over 400,000 refugees fled from the northern towns to camps in Somalia and neighbouring countries. Conditions in the refugee camps were harsh, access to food and clean water was problematic. Most refugees from these camps suffered from malnutrition and gastro-intestinal infections. Female genital mutilation and the abuse of *qat*, a leaf chewed for its amphetamine-like qualities (described in Chapter Four) are also specific health issues. Many Somali refugee organisations also feel that the NHS has not responded to the needs of their community. Surveys have found that the refugees have difficulty in gaining access to healthcare, because of language barriers or not knowing about the services that are available.

Educational underachievement is a concern of both parents and schools. A research project conducted in the London Borough of Camden in 2000 showed 3.1 per cent of Somali children attaining Grades A-C at GCSE, compared with 47.7 per cent of all children in the LEA. One determinant of attainment in secondary schools is prior educational experience: many children who have come directly from southern Somalia might have little or none. It is not unusual for a Somali child to enrol in an UK secondary school with little or no previous schooling.

Disproportionate numbers of Somali boys are being excluded from school. That some have witnessed continued violence in their home country is undoubtedly a contributory factor in disturbed behaviour that can lead to exclusion from school. Continued racial harassment can provoke a child fight back, resulting (perhaps wrongly) in exclusion from school. The Refugee Council is also concerned that some teachers have a stereotype of a violent and/or disturbed Somali male and this can lead to inappropriate interventions by schools.

Bibliography

Banafunzi, B. (1996) The Education of the Bravanese Community' in Vol 1 *Race, Ethnicity and Education*

Bolloten and Spafford, T. (1996) *Brava: an educational resource pack*, London: Newham English Language Service

Daycare Trust (1995) *Reaching First Base: guidelines of good practice on meeting the needs of refugee children from the Horn of Africa*, London: Daycare Trust

Dorkenoo, E. and Ellworthy, S. (1994) *Female Genital Mutilation: proposals for change*, London: Minority Rights Group

Griffith, D. (1997) 'Somali refugees in Tower Hamlets: clanship and new identity' in *New Community*, vol23 no 1 pp5-24

Haringey, London Borough of (1998) *Refugees and Asylum-Seekers in Haringey*, London: LB Haringey

Kahin, M. (1997) *Educating Somali Children in Britain*, Stoke on Trent: Trentham Books

Refugee Council (1998) Somali and English Words for School Use, London: Refugee Council

Save the Children (1994) *The Somali Community in Cardiff*, Cardiff: Save the Children (Wales Division)

Tower Hamlets, London Borough of (1992) *Somali Refugee Survey*, unpublished research report

Warner, R. (1991) *Voices from Somalia*, London: Minority Rights Group.

A useful publisher is Haan Associates. It publishes social and political backgrounds to Somalia as well as bilingual school books. The web site is www.haan.demon.co.uk

■ Refugees from the Former Soviet Union

There has been a major increase in asylum applications from the former Soviet Union, from 30 asylum applications in 1993 to 4,105 in 1999. The main countries of origin for applications in 1999 were

Armenia	95
Azerbaijan	50
Belarus	600
Estonia	455
Georgia	70
Latvia	515
Lithuania	615
Moldova	180
Russia	685
Ukraine	775

Country backgrounds: Belarus

Belarus' population was 10.7 million in 1999 and its capital is Minsk. Some 78 per cent of the population are Belarussians, 13.2 per cent are Russians, 4.1 per cent Poles, 2.9 per cent Ukrainian. Other significant minority groups are Jews, Roma, Lithuanians, Latvians and Tartars. Russian is the official language and the medium of education. Belarussian is spoken by some people and has to be studied in school, but is less dominant.

Belarus declared its independence in 1991, following the collapse of the Soviet Union, and was for three years a member of the Commonwealth of Independent States, retaining close links with Russia. In 1994 Belarus became a fully independent state with an elected president. The first winner of a hastily organised presidential election was Alyaksandr Lukashyenka, who supported close ties with Russia. Throughout the 1990s he accumulated more and more political powers. In 1999 Lukashyenka refused to hold fresh elections and extended his mandate until 2001. Opposition groups staged a number of peaceful protests. Amnesty International states there were several hundred arrests after these protests and numerous allegations of police ill-treatment. Other opposition figures were arrested and imprisoned in 1999, in the appalling prison conditions of Belarus. Amnesty International also reported the 'disappearance' (presumably murder) of three leading opposition figures.

Today political opposition faces increased repression, as do human rights activists, independent journalists and those who expose organised crime and government corruption. (Like Russia and the Ukraine, Belarus has experienced the growth of organised crime). These human rights violations have forced Belarussians into exile. A few Belarussian Roma have also fled, after experiencing violence, police brutality and lack of police protection.

Lithuania
Lithuania's population was 3.7 million in 1999 and its capital is Vilnius. The UK has had a Lithuanian refugee population since the end of the 19th century. Between 1870 and 1914 Jews from Lithuania (then part of the Russian Empire), as well as other parts of eastern Europe, sought refuge in the UK.

Between the two world wars Lithuania was an independent state, although part of its territory, including today's capital, was incorporated into Poland. From 1926 until 1940, Lithuania's government was extremely authoritarian and nationalist. Small numbers of Lithuanians, many of them Jewish, fled during this period. In 1939, the part of today's Lithuania then in Poland was occupied by the Nazis. In 1941 Soviet troops entered northern and eastern Lithuania. In 1945, following the defeat of the Nazis, the boundaries of Lithuania were redrawn. Vilna became part of Lithuania and the whole of the region was incorporated into the Soviet Union.

The Second World War and its aftermath saw the flight of many Lithuanian refugees. Jews and other opponents of the Nazis fled from western Lithuania. After Soviet troops entered eastern Lithuania, those who had collaborated with the Nazis were forced to flee. From 1945 onwards, small numbers of other opponents of Soviet communism aldso fled Lithuania, including people seeking political and religious freedom. The period 1945-1970 saw about 7,000 Lithuanian refugees enter the UK, in three migratory movements. Some 5,732 Lithuanian men and women came between 1946 and 1951 as part of the European Volunteer Worker Scheme. They had been selected from refugee camps in Europe and billeted to industries experiencing labour shortages. From 1951 to 1956, Lithuanians arrived on the '2000' scheme taking refugees stranded in camps in Europe. A third migratory movement was the post-1945 'border jumpers' who left Lithuania because of political and religious persecution.

In 1980 about 7,000 people of Lithuanian descent were living in the UK, excluding Lithuanian Jews. There were active community organisations many parts of the UK where Lithuanian refugees had settled. These were often nationalistic and conservative and did not work with minority groups such as Jews and Russians. The 1980s saw growing anti-Soviet dissent in Lithuania. In 1990, as communist regimes collapsed across eastern Europe, Lithuania declared its independence, precipitating a Soviet economic embargo. In 1991 Soviet troops moved in and seized a broadcasting centre, killing eleven peaceful protestors, but later that year Soviet policy changed and the USSR State Council recognised Lithuania as an independent state.

The number of Lithuanian asylum-seekers has increased in the late 1990s. Some UK asylum claims are undoubtedly unfounded, and are a pretext for seeking work. But there are groups who may be endangered. Organised crime has flourished, as has police involvement in it. Lithuanians who fall foul of criminal gangs or expose police corruption are almost certainly endangered people: Home Office country information cities police reprisals as a legitimate cause of concern. Lithuania has a small Roma population of about 4,000 and a small number of Roma have sought asylum in the UK.

Latvia

Latvia had a population of 2.3 million in 1999. Its capital is Riga. Some 56 per cent of the population are ethnic Latvian, and 30 per cent ethnic Russian. There are also small populations of Poles, Belarussians, Ukrainians, Lithuanians, Jews, Roma and Armenians. Asylum applications have risen in the UK in the late 1990s. Some may be unfounded, but some Latvian asylum-seekers may have a well-founded fear of persecution. As with many parts of the former Soviet Union, organised crime has flourished, as has police involvement in it. Latvians who fall foul of criminal gangs or expose police corruption are almost certainly endangered people. There have also been reports of police brutality and harassment of ethnic Russians and Roma in Latvia.

Russia

Russia had a population of 150 million in 1999. Its capital is Moscow. Some 82.6 per cent of the population are ethnic Russian. There are over 100 other minority groups, the largest of which are Tartars, Ukrainians, Chuvash and Bashkirs. The official language is Russian, although over 100 other languages are spoken.

Russians and other citizens of the former Soviet Union fled as refugees, during the Tsarist period, during the civil war of 1917-1921, as a result of Stalin's oppression, during the era of the Second World War and because of post-war communist oppression. By 1980 about 3,000 ethnic Russian refugees lived in the UK, as well as other ethnic groups from the former Soviet Union.

In 1988 President Gorbachev instituted political reforms. In 1991 the collapse of the Soviet Union accelerated. Yeltsin was elected president and the Baltic states and the Ukraine declared independence. The Soviet Union later ceased to exist as a political entity. Organised crime and corruption has flourished and the UK Home Office country assessment states that 9,000 criminal gangs may control up to 40 per cent of the Russian economy. Many criminals are given cover by a corrupt police, judiciary and civil service. Those who expose criminal gangs or government corruption risk assassination.

Economic reforms accompanied political change and Russia has moved towards a market economy. State-owned industries have been closed and many people lost jobs. Today about 35 per cent of all Russians live below the poverty line. Millions are suffering severe malnutrition, particularly in the Arctic and Far Eastern regions. Other Russians rely on cultivating the smallholdings they own in the countryside. This economic collapse has forced some internally displaced Russians to flee as refugees as they have no internal flight options within Russia – unemployment and poverty means that they cannot move and find work elsewhere in their country.

Vladimir Putin was appointed Prime Minister in 1999. Later when President Yeltsin resigned, Putin was named as acting President, his position was confirmed in elections in March 2000. There was full-scale war in Chechnya in 1994-1996 and again in 1999, the latter killing at least 10,000 people and displacing another 600,000. There are at least 75,000 unregistered and displaced Caucasians living in Moscow alone. There has also been violence in Dagestan, Ingushetia and in the Prigorodnyi region of the North Ossetia. Much of the northern Caucasus remains lawless and under the control of criminals, and kidnapping and extortion is a major problem. These conditions have contributed to a negative stereotype of those from the Caucasus as criminals or Islamic extremists and has in turn led to racial abuse and violent attacks on people from the Caucasus, particularly in Moscow. Following a spate of bombings in Moscow in 1999, some 2,000 people from the Caucasus were arrested in the city and 500 deported. The treatment of Caucasians in Moscow is a concern to human rights organisations. Prison conditions are appalling and every year 10,000-20,000 people die in detention, as a result of beatings, cold, starvation and disease. So people flee from Russia. Although not all have a strong claim to asylum, endangered groups who have come to the UK include

- Chechens, Russians, Jews, Armenians and others who have fled the conflict in Chechnya
- others who have fled violence an unrest in the Caucasus
- Caucasian groups who were initially displaced and became victims of racism in parts of Russia such as Moscow

- conscientious objectors to military service
- those who expose organised crime or corruption
- some human rights activists
- those who have fled localised police harassment.

A major cause for concern is that the Home Office has made very few decisions on Russian asylum applications and that almost all those decisions have been refusals. There is considerable linguistic diversity among the refugees. Most ethnic Russian asylum-seekers are living in Greater London, where organisations such as the Eastern European Advice Centre are able to provide advice and assistance. There is at least one Russian home language school in London.

Ukraine

Ukraine had a population of 50.5 million in 1999. Its capital is Kiev. Ukraine has always been a multi-ethnic state. Today some 73 per cent of the population are ethnic Ukrainians and 22 per cent are ethnic Russians. Other significant minority groups are Jews (500,000 people) Belarussians (440,000), Moldovans, Bulgarians (234,000), Poles (220,000), Hungarians (165,000), Ruthenians (700,000), Crimean Tartars (300,000), Romanians (138,000) and Roma (55,000). Ukrainian is the official language. It is an eastern Slavonic language most closely related to Belarussian and Russian. Ruthenian, spoken in parts of western Ukraine formerly in Czechoslovakia, is considered by most linguistics to be a dialect of Ukrainian, although those who advocate a distinct Ruthenian identity would dispute this.

In 1667 most of today's Ukraine was incorporated into the Russian Empire. The Ukraine itself was divided; the western Ukraine was formed part of Russian Poland, while territory east of the Dniepr was part of Russia. After the 1917, the eastern Ukraine experienced a brief period of independence but in 1921, however, the Treaty of Riga, signed between Poland and the Soviet Union, split the western Ukraine between Poland, Czechoslovakia and Romania. The eastern Ukraine was incorporated into the Soviet Union.

The 1920s, 30s and early 40s were a period of immense hardship. Stalin collectivised Ukrainian agriculture and murdered many Ukrainian peasants. The agricultural reforms led to major drops in food production and over seven million died during the 1920s from starvation and murder. All Ukrainian cultural and religious expression was brutally repressed. Whole populations were deported, among them the Crimean Tatars. The Nazi-Soviet Pact of 1939 incorporated the eastern Ukraine into the Soviet Union. Many Ukrainians, as well as those from the minority Polish population, faced arrest. Nearly one million Poles were deported eastwards to labour camps in Siberia (many of this group later came to the UK as refugees). The Nazis invaded the Ukraine in 1941 and were initially welcomed by some ethnic Ukrainians. But fighting and the Nazi extermination of Jews caused the death of over six million Ukrainian nationals, including about 90 per cent of the country's Jewish population. At the end of the Second World War many Ukrainians found themselves in Europe's refugee camps. There were further boundary changes in 1945. The western Ukraine was ceded to the Soviet Union. From 1945 to the end of the 1980s all religious, cultural and political dissent was repressed in the Ukraine.

In 1980 there were about 35,000 ethnic Ukrainians and their descendants living in the UK. Nearly 21,000 ethnic Ukrainians arrived between 1946 and 1951 as part of the European Volunteer Worker Scheme; almost all had previously lived in refugee camps in Europe. Another 8,320 Ukrainian ex-prisoners of war were also accepted under this scheme – people who had fought with the Nazis and surrendered to the British in 1945. Another 5,000 Ukrainians came to the UK between 1945 and 1980. Most ethnic Ukrainians settled in the north west, Yorkshire and the west Midlands. Here community groups and Ukrainian churches were organised. In 1989 dissent began to grow among intellectuals in the Ukraine. Ukrainian workers formed their own independent union. The collapse of the Soviet Union soon followed and in 1991 the Ukraine was declared an independent state. Subsequent elections have indicated a political divide. The eastern Ukraine, where most ethnic Russians live, returns left-wing candidates but in the west, Ukrainian nationalists have assumed power.

The main human rights concerns centre around police corruption and violence, beatings and torture in detention, harassment of independent media, harassment of some academics, racist violence towards the Roma, including by the police. Perhaps the most serious human rights violation concerns the violence that attends the growth of organised crime. An estimated 100,000 Ukrainian women may have been trafficked to work as prostitutes.

The numbers of Ukrainian asylum-seekers arriving in the UK increased in the late 1990s. Some may not have strong claims to asylum, but two groups do have a well-founded fear of persecution, the Roma (although the number of Ukrainian Roma seeking asylum in the UK is very small) and those who expose organised crime, government corruption and the trafficking of people. Those fleeing organised crime usually wish to keep a low profile and may avoid mixing with fellow nationals. The Home Office's own country assessment of the Ukraine states:

Covering corruption and organised crime within the Ukrainian media has resulted in assassination attempts against journalists, in particular in Crimea, a region most heavily affected by organised crime, where the intermingling of officials and organised crime figures is stronger than anywhere else in Ukraine, and where the security service has openly displayed its hostility to Russian journalists, who are accused of biased reporting. Others at risk include businessmen, tax inspectors and politicians who refuse to co-operate with organised crime figures. The areas most affected, in addition to Crimea, are Donetsk and Dnipropetrovsk.

Bibliography

Home Office (2000) *Russia: Country Assessment,* London: Immigration and Nationality Directorate

Home Office (2000) *Ukraine: Country Assessment, London: Immigration and Nationality Directorate*, Home Office

Krag, H. and Fuchs, L. (1994) *The Northern Caucasus*, London: Minority Rights Group.

■ Refugees from Sri Lanka

Over 46,000 Sri Lankan Tamil refugees have arrived in the UK since 1983. Sri Lanka had a population of 19 million in 1999 of whom 21 per cent live in urban areas. The capital is Colombo.

Ethnic groups: About 74 per cent of the population are Sinhalese, believed to have migrated from India in waves after the 5th century BC. Eighteen per cent are Tamils, first arriving at much the same time. Most of these Tamils live in northern and eastern Sri Lanka. About one million 'plantation Tamils' live in the central tea-producing areas, descendants of indentured labour brought by the British in the 19th century to work on plantations. Most Tamil refugees in the UK are from northern and eastern Sri Lanka. In prehistoric times Sri Lanka was joined by land to India and inhabited by the Veddahs: today small numbers of Veddahs still live in the south.

Muslims make up about seven per cent of the population, and are sometimes called Moors, because they were wrongly believed to be descendants of Moroccan Arabs. There are also small numbers of 'Burghers' – people of Dutch and Portuguese descent.

Languages: The Sinhalese population speaks Sinhala as its first language. Sinhala, unlike Tamil, is an Indo-European language descended from Sanskrit. This suggests that the Sinhalese originally migrated from North India. But the Sinhala alphabet, with its rounded letters, more closely resembles the alphabets of the Dravidian languages of South India.

The Tamil and Muslim populations speak Tamil, which belongs to the Dravidian language family. Other closely related languages are Kannada and Malayalam, both spoken in south India. About 60 million people speak Tamil throughout the world: 50 million in south India, four million in Sri Lanka, and others in Malaysia, Singapore, Fiji, Trinidad, Guyana and parts of East Africa. Tamil has standard written forms, but different dialects are spoken in Sri Lanka and in south India. The alphabet has 247 letters. There are 12 vowel sounds and 18 consonants. Each vowel sound then modifies a consonant, giving an extra 216 letters; there is also a special letter for the 'f' sound.

Language issues are an integral part of the conflict in Sri Lanka. Under British rule, English was the language of government, and the medium of instruction in schools and higher education. Up until 1948 an educated Tamil would speak Tamil and then English. From independence until 1956 English was still the language of government but in 1956 Sinhala became the sole official language, and the language of government, sparking protest. In 1989 Tamil became an official language, but the language of government is still Sinhala.

Names: Tamil names are complicated, because Tamil refugees may use two different naming systems. A man's name might be **R. Sivanandan** or **M. V. Vijayapalan**, where 'Sivanandan' and 'Vijayapalan' are neither first names nor family names. They would be called Sivanandan or Vijayapalan, and a polite form of address would be Mr Sivanandan and Mr Vijayapalan. The initials 'R' and 'V' refer to the man's father's name. A few Tamils also have family names, particularly if they have well known and respected forebears whose name they might wish to remember. Vijayapalan's family name is Malavarayan, and is written down as the first initial. When a woman marries she will take her husband's name as an initial before her name. Many Tamils also have nicknames or pet names; these are sometimes abbreviated – such as 'Vijay' or 'Siva'.

In both the UK and Sri Lanka some Tamils use the European naming system. As Home Office, school and medical records are not designed to cope with different naming systems, many Tamils in the UK feel obliged to use the European system. Additionally if they have a well known forebear they might want to keep that name, as their family name. For example Gopal Sivalingham and Parvathi Sivalingham are brother and sister, whose parents have adopted Sivalingham as their family name. Sri Lankan Christians use a European naming system, and usually have an English first name. (Burghers have family names of Dutch or Portuguese origin.) Sri Lankan Muslims use the Islamic naming system. The Sinhalese use a first name and a family name, as in North India and Europe.

Religion: Most Sinhalese are Buddhists and most Sri Lankan Tamils are Hindu. Tamil houses may have a shrine to a particular god or goddess, and Tamils are generally more religiously observant than most people in the UK. Many Tamils also visit Hindu temples; each temple is dedicated to one particular god or goddess. The main Tamil festivals are

*   Pongal – the harvest festival, celebrated on 14 January
*   Navarathiri – celebrated for nine days in October in honour of the goddesses Parawathy, Lakshmi and Saraswathy
*   Divali – the Hindu festival of lights, celebrated in November. In Tamil this festival is known as Deepavali.

Tamils will also celebrate the temple festivals of their own temple.

Sri Lankan Tamils are not strict vegetarians, and usually eat meat and fish, although few eat beef. Many Tamils do not eat meat on Fridays or religious holidays. Like all Hindu societies, Tamils belong to different castes. Allegiance to caste is still an important factor in social relations in Sri Lanka's villages, but less so in the towns or the UK. Caste allegiance does not impinge on refugee community groups but is still considered when arranging a marriage. A few Sri Lankan Tamils are Christians. The UK has also received Tamil-speaking Muslim refugees, but these two groups are in the minority.

Education system: Education is held in high esteem by Tamils, in both Sri Lanka and the UK. Tamil refugee children are usually highly motivated.

In Sri Lanka education is compulsory from five to 14 years, and free from kindergarten to university level in state institutions. There are also fee-paying schools. The Sri Lankan education system is probably the best in South Asia, and the literacy level is very high: 81 per cent for women and 91 per cent for men. Almost all Sri Lankan children attend primary schools. However, access to higher education is a major grievance of the Tamil community. In the 1960s proportionally more Tamils than Sinhalese entered universities. Sinhala nationalists responded by putting pressure on the Government to restrict the numbers of Tamil students in higher education. From 1970 higher marks were demanded from Tamil students in A-Level examinations in order to enter university. This caused enormous discontent among Tamil students, many of whom became politically active.

Education has been disrupted by the civil war, and by the siege of the Jaffna Peninsula. The children of displaced people are seldom enrolled in school. In many parts of northern and eastern Sri Lanka the army has intimidated and arrested students during school hours. Papers for O-Level and A-Level examinations have arrived late or not at all. Many Tamil school students are now travelling to Colombo to take examinations. The Jaffna Peninsula was under total blockade between 1990 and 1995. The Sri Lankan Air Force has bombed schools and other civilian targets, and children were killed. The Government prevented many essential goods from reaching the Jaffna Peninsula, including basic foodstuffs, medicines and paper. Despite the destruction of some schools, and the absence of exercise books, desks and other equipment, schools generally stayed open, although Sri Lankan Government examinations were not taken.

Until the early 1960s English was the medium of instruction but now it is Sinhala and Tamil and Sinhalese and Tamil students are usually educated in separate institutions. English is taught as a second language from the fourth year at primary school, but is not compulsory for O-Level or university entrance. Tamil refugee children will require language support, although most will be familiar with the Roman alphabet. Their parents are likely to speak English and, if encouraged, can help their children learn the language.

Sri Lankan education was reorganised in 1985. Schooling is at four levels: six years of primary education starting at six, two years in junior and three years in senior secondary school, and two years on pre-university courses. Students sit the Sri Lankan GCE O-Levels in eight subjects and must pass six including mathematics, and Sinhala or Tamil. A credit or distinction in a Sri Lankan O-Level subject is considered the equivalent of a GCSE pass at grades A, B or C. The pre-university course culminates in Sri Lankan GCE A-Levels in four subjects, and universities require passes in at least three. These are considered equivalent to English A-Levels.

Economy: About 45 per cent of the population are employed on plantations or small farms in agriculture or in fishing or forestry. Rice is the main subsistence crop and tea the main export. Other plantation crops include rubber, coconut and fruit. Precious and semi-precious stones are another important export, as is clothing. The tourist industry has been devastated by the civil war. Economic activity has been limited in war-torn northern and eastern Sri Lanka, save for the cultivation of subsistence crops. Farmers cannot obtain diesel and fertilisers and merchants have no produce to sell.

A chronology of events: During the 11th and 12th century AD there was a Tamil kingdom in northern Sri Lanka followed in the 14th century by the Sinhalese Kingdoms of Kotte and of Kandy. In 1505 the Portuguese arrived, trading in spices, and capturing the Kotte and Tamil kingdoms. In **1656** the Dutch colonised Portuguese Ceylon, and introduced plantation crops: coffee, sugar cane, spices and tobacco – but they, too, fail to capture the Kandyan kingdom in central Ceylon. In 1796 the Tamil and Kotte Kingdoms were handed over to the British East India Company. Plantation agriculture and the spice trade are expanded.

19th century: In 1802 Ceylon becomes a British colony. In 1815 the Kandyan Kingdom is brought under British rule. The former Tamil and Sinhalese kingdoms, previously ruled separately, are brought under one administration in 1833. In 1840 the British pass the 'Waste Lands Ordinance' which allows them to claim any land where ownership cannot be proved. As few farmers hold title deeds, the colonial administration claims much land which they sell cheaply to plantation owners. Coffee, coconuts and rubber are grown on the plantations and over 200,000 Indian Tamils are brought as indentured labour to work on them. In 1870 the coffee crop is killed by a fungal disease and tea replaces coffee as Ceylon's main export. Tamils begin to obtain jobs in the British colonial administration. By 1911 there are more Plantation Tamils than Ceylonese Tamils. They work mainly on the tea plantations and are poorer than Ceylonese Tamils.

Independence: In 1944 the Soulbury Commission arrives from London to prepare Ceylon for independence. Tamil politicians request legal safeguards to protect minorities. Mr D. S. Senanrayake, President of the Ceylon National Congress, promised that the rights of Tamils and other minority groups will be protected. When Ceylon gains independence in **1948** the new government promptly passes the Citizenship Act making all Plantation Tamils stateless and another new law removes the right of stateless Tamils to vote. In 1956 Sinhala becomes Ceylon's official language, replacing English as the language of government. Many Tamils protest, fearing exclusion from government employment. Twelve Tamil MPs and their supporters stage a peaceful protest outside Parliament. A Sinhalese crowd stones the protestors while the police take no action. Rioting spreads to many parts of Colombo, and over 150 Tamils die. Protests about the language issue continue in an atmosphere of great tension. In 1958 Sinhalese crowds attack Tamils, and over 1,000 people are killed. Some 12,000 Tamils are rescued from Colombo by British and French ships. In 1964 an agreement is signed between India and Ceylon that will allow 525,000 Plantation Tamils Indian citizenship and repatriation over 15 years. Some 300,000 Plantation Tamils are to be given Ceylonese citizenship and allowed to stay. In 1974 by a further treaty gives the remaining Plantation Tamils Indian and Ceylonese citizenship, but the process is very slow.

1972-2001: In **1972** Ceylon becomes Sri Lanka, and Buddhism is declared the religion of the state. There are no longer any legal safeguards to protect the rights of minorities. Tamil leaders meet in 1976 and call for a separate state for Tamils – widely supported by the Tamil people. Tamil Eelam, the proposed state, would comprise northern and eastern Sri Lanka. Young Tamils form a group which later becomes the Liberation Tigers of Tamil Eelam (LTTE) and soon resorts to armed struggle.

Separatism and War: Over 500 Tamils are killed in communal violence in 1977 while the police and army do nothing. In 1978 Tamil is made a national language, but this means little.

Communal violence flares up in 1981 and in 1983 a week of rioting leaves 2,500 Tamils dead, 150,000 people in refugee camps, and 23,000 homes and businesses destroyed. Many Tamils leave Colombo for good, fleeing to northern and eastern Sri Lanka where they are not in a minority. Others flee to India, North America and Europe. Talks arranged by India in 1985 break down. The LTTE murder 146 Sinhalese Buddhist pilgrims, triggering intense violence between the Sinhalese and Tamil communities. The Government is condemned by Amnesty International for the torture of Tamil prisoners, and for extrajudicial executions. Fighting breaks out between some Tamil guerrilla groups. By 1987 at least 85,000 Tamils have fled to southern India where many live in poverty. The LTTE leadership is forced out of India, and returns to Sri Lanka, establishing a parallel government in Jaffna. The Sri Lankan Government retaliates with an armed offensive which stops just short of Jaffna and an economic blockade of the Jaffna Peninsula.

India arranges further peace-keeping talks. Among the provisions is the return of refugees and the dispatch of an Indian Peace Keeping Force (IPKF) to northern Sri Lanka. But by October 1987 fighting breaks out between the LTTE and the IPKF. The latter is accused of human rights violations, in particular extrajudicial executions. In the southern the Janata Vimukti Peramuna (JVP), a Sinhalese political party espousing a mixture of Marxist and Sinhala nationalist policies, begins guerrilla activity. Violence perpetrated in the struggle between the JVP and the Sri Lankan army leaves at least 1,000 people dead. Foreign diplomats estimate that 40,000 Sri Lankans disappeared in 1987.

After a violent start to 1989 the LTTE and the Sri Lankan Government begin peace talks and the IPKF agrees to leave. In **1990** the LTTE attacks 17 police stations and executes 110 police officers. The Sri Lankan army retaliates, and the war enters a new stage. Within two weeks over 1,000 people are killed and 200,000 left homeless. The Sri Lankan Government operates an economic blockade of the Jaffna Peninsula, which is held by the LTTE. Food, medicines and many other essential goods are banned from sale in northern Sri Lanka and electricity is cut off. Malnutrition is severe. In 1991 the LTTE assassinates Rajiv Gandhi, former Prime Minister of India. Tamil refugees in India are forcibly returned. The blockade and bombing of the Jaffna Peninsula continues. By 1991 over 1,000,000 people are internally displaced in Sri Lanka. Some 220,000 refugees have fled to southern India, and 400,000 Tamils have sought asylum in Europe and North America. Later the Governments of India and Sri Lanka announce they are collaborating on a plan to encourage the early return of refugees living in India. Aid agencies oppose this, as they believe Sri Lanka to be unsafe. In 1993 India returns 25,000 refugees to Sri Lanka. UNHCR has no access to these returnees, so cannot ascertain whether they returned voluntarily or were coerced.

Those who return find their houses destroyed or looted and they receive very little resettlement assistance to enable them to rebuild their homes. Sri Lanka's President is assassinated in Colombo, allegedly by the LTTE. Switzerland and Norway announce plans to return Tamil refugees to Colombo.

Peace talks between the Sri Lankan Government and the LTTE in 1994 break down within a year. Government troops capture Jaffna and the blockade ends. In 1999 the LTTE recapture territory in northern Sri Lanka. Some 800,000 Tamils are internally displaced in Sri Lanka and about 530,000 are refugees, mostly in India, Europe and North America.

Tamil refugees in the UK – Statistics

Year	Asylum Applications as percentages	Refugee Status	ELR	Refusals
1984	548	1	23	76
1985	1,893	1	97	2
1986	1,275	0.5	99	0.5
1987	992	1	91	8
1988	402	2	79	18
1989	1,790	1	95	4
1990	3,330	3	96	1
1991	3,765	3	94	3
1992	2,085	1	94	5
1993	1,965	0.5	98	1.5
1994	1,070	1	10	89
1995	1,335	1	7	92
1996	2,145		1	99
1997	1,830	3	1	96
1998	3,505	3	0	97
1999	5,130	1	0	99

Figures exclude dependants after 1985. Source Home Office.

Since 1983 few Tamil refugees have been given refugee status in Europe (except France). In the UK Tamil refugees were given ELR until mid-1993, when the Home Office abruptly changed its policy and refused almost all Tamils on the grounds that they should have sought asylum in India.

Until 1992 very few Tamil refugees were returned from European countries. There was one well-publicised deportation case in 1988: five Tamils who had been refused refugee status in the UK were returned to Sri Lanka, where three were arrested by the IPKF, and another by the Sri Lankan police. Three were beaten in custody and submitted an appeal, asserting they had been unfairly denied refugee status. The immigration adjudicator ordered that the five be returned to the UK for reconsideration of their asylum case. In 1992 the Swiss Government announced plans to return some groups of Tamils who had been refused asylum in that country. Sri Lanka was to be divided up into four regions: Greater Colombo, southern Sri Lanka, central Sri Lanka and northern and eastern Sri Lanka. The Swiss Government declared that some Tamils could be returned to Colombo. (Human rights organisations believe Colombo to be presently unsafe for Tamils returnees). Other European governments seem likely to follow the Swiss policy, and return Tamils.

Tamil refugees can be divided into two social groups: young single men who have been politically active in Sri Lanka, and an older age group, usually with a family. Many young Tamil men have been held in police or army custody and may have been tortured. They may have missed large parts of their school or university education. Young Tamil men have been more successful than most groups of refugees in finding work, although most jobs are badly paid and in small retail outlets and petrol stations, offering little opportunity for promotion and preventing their studying. Refugees who came to the UK with qualifications and work experience have generally done better in commerce or the professions.

Most Tamil refugees live in Greater London, particularly in South London -Croydon, Merton and Sutton – and East London. Many young Tamil men have opted not to be dispersed by the Home Office and are staying with friends and relatives in Greater London – often in overcrowded conditions. There a several active community organisations, most of which represent a broad range of political opinion. Some Tamil community activists have built bridges with the UK Sinhalese community. There are at least ten Tamil community schools for children. Hindu temples are another focus of community activity. Four radio stations broadcast Sri Lankan and UK news and music.

Bibliography

Medical Foundation (2000) *Caught in the Middle: a study of Tamil torture survivors coming to the UK from Sri Lanka*, London: Medical Foundation

Nissan, E. (1996) *Sri Lanka: a bitter harvest*, London: Minority Rights Group

Refugee Council (1998) *Why Do They Have to Fight: refugee children's stories from Bosnia, Somalia, Sri Lanka and Kurdistan*, London: Refugee Council

Refugee Council (1999) *Sri Lankan refugees in the Indian State of Tamil Nadu*, unpublished report.

Tamil Information Centre (1998) *Tamil Education in the UK*, London: Tamil Information Centre

The Refugee Council publishes the monthly *Sri Lanka Monitor* which can be obtained on www.gn.apc.org/brcslproject. Another useful web site is that of the Internal Displacement Project on www.idpproject.org

■ Refugees from Sudan

About 6,500 Sudanese refugees live in the UK. A few arrived in the 1980s but most have fled since the military coup of 1989. Sudan had a population of 28 million in 1998. Before the civil war intensified in 1987 about 80 per cent of Sudanese lived in rural areas. Fighting has driven many southern Sudanese to take refuge in shanty towns surrounding the major cities. The capital is Khartoum.

Ethnic groups: Sudan is an ethnically diverse country. Some 40 per cent of the population identify themselves as Arabs, although the claim of Arab descent is more a matter of cultural allegiance than ethnic origin. Since the Arab conquest in the 7th century there has been much intermixing of Arabs, Nubians and other African peoples.

Sudanese Arabs live in northern Sudan. Non-Arab groups living there make up another 20 per cent of the population. They include the Nile Nubians, who consider themselves the descendants of the ancient Kingdom of Nubia, living in the Nile Valley, north of Khartoum. Under the influence of Ethiopia, the Nubians embraced Christianity in the 6th century, later converting to Islam. They speak a dialect of Nubian, an eastern Sudanic language most closely related to Nilotic languages such as Dinka and Nuer. Many other smaller ethnic groups live in northern Sudan including the Beja, Nuba, Ingessana, Fur and Massalete. The non-Arab peoples of northern Sudan speak many different languages. So great is the mixing of ethnic groups that languages from three major linguistic families (Hamito-Semitic, Chari-Nile and Niger-Congo) are spoken in northern Sudan, plus a number of independent languages.

Much has recently been written about the Nuba – a diverse group of peoples living in the Nuba mountains of southern Kordofan – numbering about one million people. They are culturally different from their Arab neighbours and many speak a dialect of Nubian, although they look like southern Sudanese. Their relationship with the Nile Nubians is a matter of anthropological debate. Some retain their traditional beliefs, others have converted to Islam or Christianity.

Cattle-herding Arabs, known as Baggara Arabs, also live in the Nuba mountains, competing for land and wells. Since the civil war began, the Sudanese People's Liberation Army (SPLA) has tried to recruit support among the Nuba mountain groups, murdering Nuba leaders who refused to cooperate.

The Sudanese Government's response to Nuba insurgency has been to arm Baggara Arabs, who then raid Nuba villages. Thousands of Nuba have been killed in what amounts to 'ethnic cleansing'. The Sudanese Government has also arrested and killed large numbers of educated Nuba. Since

October 1990 the Nuba mountains have been sealed off, and in 1992 a *jihad* (a Holy War) was declared against the Nuba. The Army and armed militia moved into Nuba villages, destroying them, and moving people to relocation camps. Other Nuba peoples were murdered: up to 6,000 were killed near the village of Heiban in 1992.

About 320,000 Eritrean refugees live towns and camps in western Sudan and in Khartoum.

Southern Sudanese form about 30 per cent of the population. As in the North there has been much intermixing of different ethnic groups. The southern Sudanese can be divided into two groups: those living in the central grasslands and in south east Sudan, and the peoples living in the forests along the border with the Central African Republic, the Democratic Republic of Congo and Uganda. The Dinka, Nuer and Shilluk belong to the first group. All speak Nilotic languages. The peoples of the south west Sudan are linguistically more diverse, and include ethnic groups such as the Azande and Bari.

Almost all ethnic groups are represented among the Sudanese refugees who have fled to the UK.

Languages: Arabic is the official language of Sudan, spoken by about half the population, mostly in northern Sudan. It is the medium of instruction in schools. Almost all Sudanese refugees in the UK will speak Arabic whether they are from the north or south.

Arabic is a Semitic language. Sudanese people speak dialects of eastern Arabic. Modern Standard Arabic is taught in schools. Young children who have not been to school will not be able to understand Modern Standard Arabic and so cannot converse with children from other Arabic speaking countries. Further information about the Arabic language is given on page 186.

Other main languages are dialects of Nubian, spoken in northern Sudan and in Kordofan. Beja, a Hamito-Semitic language related to Somali, is spoken in eastern Sudan. Dinka, Nuer, Shilluk, Zande and Bari are the languages most frequently spoken in southern Sudan. English is widely spoken in Government and academic circles.

Names: Several different naming systems are used. Muslims in northern Sudan use Islamic names. A person has a first name, followed by the father's first name, then usually the paternal grandfather's name. Women keep their names after they marry.

Among the Copts, and in western and southern Sudan the same system of a first name, father's name and grandfather's name may be used but the names themselves are Sudanese or Christian, not Islamic. Some Sudanese Christians also have a baptismal name, which they use every day but which may appear on official papers. Copts and some southern Sudanese may also use a European naming system of a first personal name plus family name.

Southern Sudanese may use different naming systems, for example a person may have a first personal name, followed by a name indicating the circumstances of their birth. They may also have a family name, or use their father's name as a last name. Other southern Sudanese have adopted a western naming system of Christian name followed by family name.

Some southern Sudanese use a naming system similar to that used in Uganda. A child will have a first name, then a name that relates to the circumstance in which he or she is born, followed by the father's name. Women tend to keep their names when they marry.

Religion: About 70 per cent of the population are Sunni Muslims, 18 per cent animists, 8 per cent Roman Catholic, 0.5 per cent Protestant and 0.5 per cent Coptic Christian.

Islam has a strong Sufi element – most Sudanese Muslims claim allegiance to the Khatmiya or the Tiganiya Sufi order. These sects preach a Sudanese version of Islam, characterised by austerity, mysticism, a direct relation with God, and tolerance of other religions.

In recent years other Islamic sects and groupings have flourished, including Islamic fundamentalist organisations. The economic crises of the 1970s and 1980s have undoubtedly led to a rise in religious fundamentalism. In 1983 *shari'a* – Islamic laws – were introduced by President Nimeiri. These were extended in 1991 and 1992, although *shari'a* does not apply to southern Sudan. Human rights activists have expressed concern about *shari'a*: penalties such as stoning and amputation are cruel and degrading. Non-Muslims no longer share the same rights of citizenship as Muslims.

Most Sudanese Christians live in southern Sudan. Exceptions are the Coptic Christians - about 200,000 people, living mostly in Khartoum, Omdurman, Dongola, Atbara, Wad Medani, Port Sudan and El Obeid. They speak Arabic, although Coptic is still used as a liturgical language. Since 1989 the Sudanese Government has enacted policies which are intended to drive them out of the country. Hundreds of Copts have been dismissed from their jobs, simply because they are Christian. About 2,500 Sudanese Copts have fled to the UK.

Education system: Primary education is free in Sudan, and lasts for eight years. Most children enrol when they are about six years old. Children from poorer families may enter school later. At the end of every year all pupils are tested. Failure at annual tests means that children repeat the year, so classes may contain children of many different ages. Sometimes parents of Sudanese (and other African refugee children) may not understand how age-determined the UK education system can be.

At the end of primary education pupils have to pass an examination to gain access to the three years of secondary schooling. There are several types of secondary schools including academic schools, commercial schools, agricultural schools, industrial schools and home economics schools for girls.

The first two years of academic schools offer a common curriculum. In the third year students specialise in arts or science subjects. Arabic, mathematics, religion and English are compulsory subjects. At the end of three years students sit for the Sudan Secondary School Certificate, considered comparable to a GCSE pass at grades A to C, on a subject-for-subject basis.

The medium of instruction in northern Sudan is Arabic. English is a compulsory subject from the end of primary schooling. In Government-held regions in southern Sudan, the medium of instruction is also Arabic. In areas outside Government control it can be either Arabic or the local language (where scripted) in primary schools. Secondary schools teach through the medium of Arabic or English.

The education system has been in turmoil since the late 1970s. The al-Bashir regime has sought the Islamisation of education so Arabic has been imposed as a medium of education in southern Sudan. Large numbers of *madrassah* have been set up in northern Sudan, as an alternative to state education. The war has resulted in many southern schools being destroyed. Many teachers have left Sudan, as refugees or migrant workers. Cuts in public spending forced upon Sudan by the International Monetary Fund have severely restricted educational expenditure. Sudanese schools are consequently badly equipped, classes large and teaching is formal. A student will have little experience of laboratory practicals or subjects such as drama.

The literacy rate is 36 per cent for men, and 6 per cent for women. In urban areas the literacy rate is much higher, but only 12 per cent of all Sudanese girls are enrolled at secondary schools.

Economy: Sudan can be divided into four geographical regions: the northern deserts, the Nile Valley, the savannah of central and South East Sudan and the rainforests bordering the Democratic Republic of Congo. Most people live along the Nile.

Sudan is a predominantly agricultural economy – some 62 per cent of all Sudanese work on the land. The main export crops are cattle, cotton, sesame, and gum arabic. The Sudanese economy has been affected by the war in the south. High levels of military expenditure have prevented economic investment. Commercial activity in the south has ground to a halt with a barter system being the only form of trade.

A chronology of events: Sudan, called Kush by the Egyptians and Nubia by the Greeks, has come under the influence of many different cultures.

Until the 16th century there were Christian kingdoms clustered along the Nile. At the start of the modern period these collapsed and gave way to a series of Islamic states. In 1889 an Anglo-Egyptian army defeated the Sudanese army of Mohamed Ahmad al Mahadi (a self-claimed Muslim redeemer) at the Battle of Omdurman and the two countries established joint rule over Sudan.

1920s: The British moved to separate the Arab and Muslim north from the African south. The two parts of Sudan are ruled separately, and colonial policies are enacted that accentuate the differences.

1930s and 1940s: The northern Sudanese begin a campaign of independence. Many southern Sudanese, fearing they would be dominated by the north, are less intent on immediate independence.

1956: Sudan becomes independent. Even before independence there is fighting between the Sudanese army and rebel soldiers in the South. Their rebellion forms the basis of a larger separatist movement that fights Sudan's first civil war, lasting until 1972. During this time the Sudanese Government spends large sums of money on weapons and army pay and there is little investment in Sudan's infrastructure. Thousands of people are killed and many more flee as refugees to Ethiopia, Zaire, the Central African Republic and Uganda.

1969: A *coup d'etat* brings Colonel Nimeiri to power.

1970s: The world market price of cotton – a major Sudanese export – begins to fall in the 1970s. Following the rise in oil prices Sudan faces a huge balance of payments deficit and economic crisis. The International Monetary Fund (IMF) is eventually called in. It recommends a series of austerity measures, such as te abolition of food subsidies, and other cuts in public spending. By the end of the 1970s food prices begin to rise. Many Sudanese join protests against the IMF programme. Others turn to Islamic fundamentalism. President Nimeiri is eventually forced into coalition with the fundamentalist Muslim Brothers.

1980s: President Nimeiri imposes *shari'a* on Sudan. He also divides the south into three adminis-trative regions. Both decisions cause much discontent and civil war breaks out again between the Government and southern forces. By 1984 drought from the early 1980s turns to widespread famine. The IMF forces the Government to raise food prices in 1985. There are widespread demonstrations and Nimeiri is overthrown in a military coup. The transitional government promise to hold elections and to review *shari'a*. There is a further attempted coup later in 1985. A coalition government is formed after the 1986 elections, led by Sadiq al Mahadi. Civil war continues in southern Sudan and several southern cities are kept under siege by the SPLA.

The civil war intensifies in 1988 and over 250,000 people starve to death in southern towns because both the Government and the SPLA prevent food aid reaching the starving. Refugees flee to Ethiopia and Uganda. All peace negotiations fail. Over 1,000,000 people flee to Khartoum to escape fighting and famine. Most of the internally displaced live in slums around the edge of the city. In the south thousands of boys are seen walking towards Ethiopia having fled villages in the Bahr el Gazal region, to escape attacks by Government soldiers. As well as peace, many boys want the chance to go to school. There are also attacks on Dinka people perpetrated by Arab militias, armed by the Government. *Shari'a* is frozen in 1988 pending a constitutional conference.

In 1989 another *coup d'etat* installs Brigadier Omar al Bashir as President. He has much support from fundamentalist elements in Sudanese society. A state of emergency is declared. The coup puts pay to any peace agreement between the Government and SPLA. Human rights violations worsen, including mass detentions, extrajudicial executions, the banning of political parties and trade unions, media censorship and the abolition of an independent secular judiciary.

1990s: There is widespread famine in southern Sudan. The Nuba mountains are also sealed off by Government forces. *Shari'a* is again imposed on Sudan, apart from three southern states. More than 5,000 people are murdered in and around the town of Bor in a feud between two factions of the SPLA (one faction largely supported by the Dinka the other by the Nuer). The southern political and armed opposition becomes increasingly split.

The Sudanese Government expels more than 400,000 displaced people from their homes in Khartoum's squatter camps in 1992. They are transferred to the desert, without adequate food, water or shelter. A military offensive forces the SPLA from many of their positions.

In 1993 the Government declares their war in the south to be a *jihad* – a holy war. The famine in southern Sudan worsens. Over 400,000 people flee to Ethiopia, Kenya, Uganda, Zaire and the Central African Republic. As many as four million people are internally displaced. Later southern Sudanese camps for displaced people are bombed by Government forces. Sudanese Government forces also attack targets in Uganda. Opposition forces hold a meeting in Eritrea to develop a political strategy once the al-Bashir regime is ousted.

Uncontested presidential elections held in 1996 return General al-Bashir for another five year term of office. Fighting breaks out again between two southern guerrilla factions. Opposition politicians continue to be arrested. By 1997 fighting escalates in southern Sudan, although several southern guerrilla groups sign a peace agreement. The SPLA, led by John Garang, continues to fight. Soon famine threatens much of south west Sudan. A ceasefire is declared to assist in the distribution of food aid. At the end of 1999 some 420,000 Sudanese are refugees, mostly in neighbouring countries and another four million are internally displaced.

Sudanese refugees in the UK – Statistics

Year	Asylum Applications	Refugee Status as percentages	ELR	Refusals
1989	110	90	0	10
1990	340	50	25	25
1991	1,150	40	20	40
1992	560	38	29	33
1993	300	50	45	5
1994	330	15	10	75
1995	345	13	8	79
1996	280	34	6	60
1997	230	22	5	73
1998	250	46	2	52
1999	280	43	3	54

Source: Home Office.

Before 1989 most Sudanese refugees who fled to the UK came from southern Sudan and their numbers were very small. Following the 1989 *coup d'etat* greater numbers arrived and today the Sudanese refugee community numbers about 6,500.

Sudanese refugees are a diverse group. They include southern Sudanese, Copts, people associated with Nimeiri's regime, politicians from different political parties, trade unionists, politically active university students and other opposition forces. Christians face particular harassment in northern Sudan causing some to flee . What draws most Sudanese refugees together is their opposition to the current Government and its fundamentalist policies.

The largest communities are in London, Brighton, Manchester and Birmingham. About 4,000 Sudanese refugees live in London. Over 2,000 Sudanese live in Brighton – they are the largest refugee group in the area. They are 70 per Coptic Christian, and 30 per cent Muslim, mostly from northern Sudan. Most come from middle class backgrounds with high aspirations of returning to Sudan when it becomes safe. A matter of concern is that the Home Office does not acknowledge that the experiences of Sudanese Copts amounts to persecution, so refuses most asylum applications.

Sudanese refugees share many of the problems of other refugee groups. A recent survey indicted that 65 per cent of adult Sudanese refugees lacked fluent English, most notably northern Sudanese women, and cannot gain access to services. Many Sudanese have complained that they have suffered racial harassment in their homes. (A Sudanese man was murdered in Brighton in November 1993, in a racially motivated attack.)

Sudanese community organisations have been formed in Brighton, London and Manchester, some working specifically with south Sudanese or Coptic Christians. Two women's groups have been active in campaigning against female genital mutilation (some 90 per cent of northern Sudanese women are infibulated; in southern Sudan circumcision and excision is widespread in some ethnic groups).

There is a community school teaching Arabic in central London.

Bibliography

Peters, C. (ed) (1995) *Sudan*, Oxford, Oxfam

Refugee Council (1998) *Arabic and English Words for School Use*, London: refugee Council

Warner (1995) *Voices from Sudan*, London: Minority Rights Group

Wilkes, S. (1994) *One Day We Had To Run*, London: Evans Brothers.
(this is a children's book containing stories, paintings and background information about refugee children from Sudan, Ethiopia and Somalia.

The website of the Internally Displaced Project offers useful information on the Sudam at www.idpproject.org.

■ Refugees from Turkey

Over 38,000 Turkish refugees have arrived in the UK since 1988, most of them Kurds. Turkey had a population of 64 million in 1999, of whom 48 per cent lived in urban areas. The capital is Ankara.

Ethnic groups: About 80 per cent of the population are ethnic Turks, the descendants of people who migrated from central Asia. Another 19 per cent are Kurds, living mostly in eastern Turkey. Other minority groups include Circassians, Georgians, Armenians and Sephardic Jews who migrated from Spain and Portugal in the 15th century. The origins of the Kurdish population are uncertain, but they have lived in the region for at least 4,000 years. Most anthropologists believe them to be an amalgamation of Indo-European tribes who lived in the Zagros mountains. Even in modern urban Turkey Kurdish people have a distinct cultural identity. In rural areas Kurds have strong clan loyalties.

Languages: Turkish is the official language. It belongs to the Altaic language family and its structure is different from most European languages. Written in the Roman alphabet, modified by accents, it uses 21 consonants and eight vowels. Almost all male Kurds speak some Turkish but village women may not, if they have not attended school. Most Kurdish people will speak some Kurdish although few will be literate in it. It is central to their ethnic identity. Kurdish is an Indo-European language, most closely related to Persian. There are two main dialects: Kurmanji and Sorani. Kurmanji is spoken in Turkey and in parts of Iraq from Mosul northwards to the Caucasus. It is written in a Roman script (Sorani is written in Arabic script). Zaza is another dialect spoken in the western parts of Turkish Kurdistan as well as in Iran. Some Alevi Kurds living in the UK speak Zaza. From 1935 until 1991 the speaking of Kurdish was illegal. It is now legal for colloquial use, but not in a political speech or any form of the media.

Names: Most Turkish Kurds use a European naming system, and have a first name followed by a family name.

Religion: Over 60 per cent of Turkish Kurds are nominally Sunni Muslims, but there are also Shi'a groups. Another third practice Aleviism, a heterodox form of Islam also practised in Syria. Aleviism draws on Shi'a Islam, as well as Zoroastrian and other pre-Islamic religions of the Middle East. The Alevis follow the teachings of mystics so there are no *imams*. They observe few fundamental tenets of Islam such as fasting during Ramadan or the cleansing rituals before prayer, so they are considered heretics by many Islamic fundamentalists. In south east Turkey around Dersim (known as Tunceli in Turkish) both Kurds and ethnic Turks are Alevis. There are other Alevi enclaves in south east Turkey. Many Turkish Kurdish refugees in the UK and Germany are Alevis – the result of political and ethnic rather than religious persecution. Islamic fundamentalists have, however, targeted Alevis, burning 37 Alevi intellectuals to death in 1993. Allegiance to Aleviism weakened in the 20th century as Turkish and Kurdish society became more secular, although there have been recent attempts to revive its doctrines. But for all Kurds their distinct identity is ethnic and national, rather than religious.

Education system: Education is compulsory between the ages of six and 11. Primary education usually lasts five years, although some schools run an eight year programme. The primary curriculum covers Turkish, maths, science, social studies, religious education, art, music and physical education. Children must pass class examinations in every subject to progress to the following year. Middle schooling lasts for three years, ending with a Basic Education Diploma. A foreign language is taught, usually English or German.

There are several types of secondary schools, and programmes can last for three or four years, culminating in the leaving certificate – *Lise Diplomasi*. There are general high schools, science high schools which place more emphasis on sciences and mathematics, vocational and commercial high schools which prepare students for work in agriculture, industry or commerce and technical high schools preparing students for employment or university. Anatolian high schools are selective, and teach some courses in a foreign language. Competition for places is fierce and students normally progress to university

All state education is carried out through the medium of Turkish. The drop-out rate is high, young people often leaving to work on family farms or because they are disenchanted with an education system that fails to acknowledge their ethnic identity. And many villages have no accessible school, so illiteracy is much higher than the national average. There is only one university in Kurdistan, and it is often difficult for Kurds to obtain higher education outside the region. About 86 per cent of Turkish men and 62 per cent of Turkish women are literate but in Kurdistan the literacy rate is only 48 per cent. Only 18 per cent of Turkish Kurds start secondary education and only 9 per cent complete it. Many Turkish Kurdish refugees in the UK, particularly women, may have limited literacy.

Economy: Turkey is a middle income country whose main exports are textiles, fruit, iron and steel and petroleum products. Some 45 per cent of the workforce are employed in agriculture. Most Turkish Kurds work on the land although Kurdistan is a mountainous region, and snow covers the southern districts for about half the year cutting off some villages. Summer temperatures can reach 35°C. Most Turkish Kurds are landless peasants or small farmers. Kurdish provinces are the poorest in Turkey, and income per head is half the national average and unemployment double. There is a less developed infrastructure, and the standard of healthcare is lower. This is reflected in life expectancy and infant mortality statistics: 150 deaths per 1,000 live births compared with 70 deaths in Turkey.

Chronology of events: Before the First World War Kurdistan was divided between the Ottoman and Persian Empires. The largely nomadic Kurdish population was afforded autonomy in return for policing this border. Kurdish national identity began to develop in the 19th century and there were several revolts against Ottoman rule. At the same time there were organised deportations of Kurds: whole villages were transferred to areas deemed less susceptible to insurgency. This policy continues today. The Kurds suffered at the hands of Turkish nationalists. In **1908** the 'Young Turks', a nationalist grouping, led a revolution and the the Sultan was replaced by a more democratic government. Non-Turkish minorities such as the Armenians and Kurds became victim to repressive legislation. The new government denied that Kurds were a different ethnic group and deemed them 'mountain Turks'. When the Ottoman Empire was broken up the Kurds hoped for independence. The Treaty of Sevres signed in 1920 promised autonomy for both Armenians and Kurds. But it was vetoed by the Turkish Government, and in **1923** the Treaty of Lausanne divided Kurdistan between Turkey, Iran, Iraq, Syria and the Soviet Union. The Kurdish reaction was rebellion, in 1923 and 1927, both of which were put down harshly. At least 100,000 Kurds were killed, and anti-Kurdish legislation banned the Kurdish language, Kurdish-medium schools, associations and publications. In 1932 there were large-scale deportations of Kurds to Turkish areas.

During the **1960s** and **1970s** Kurdish political parties were formed, almost all calling for political independence. The best known is the Partiya Karkeren Kurdistan (PKK) which until recently was committed to armed struggle against the Turkish state. The PKK has been accused of human rights abuses against Kurds and Turks. From 1978 onwards there have been increased human rights violations in Kurdistan. In 1978 there was a massacre of Kurds at Maras, organised by the neo-fascist Grey Wolves. Martial law was proclaimed in Kurdish provinces in 1979, followed by a state of emergency in 1987. Large numbers of soldiers are stationed in Kurdistan. Since 1980 some 250,000 Kurdish men have been detained and tortured in prisons. About 4,000 civilians have been killed every year since 1980. The Turkish army enters villages it suspects of being sympathetic to the PKK. In acts of intimidation men are randomly detained and tortured, others executed. Throughout the late 1990s the Turkish army made regular incursions into Iraq, to drive out PKK guerrillas who maintained bases there.

In February 1999, Abdullah Ocalan, the PKK's leader, was abducted in Kenya by Turkish agents and returned to Turkey where he was tried for treason and sentenced to death (not yet carried out). His return led to Kurdish protests, as well as arrests of prominent Kurds. After Ocalan was found guilty, he called publicly for an end to PKK guerrilla activity. His statement was confirmed by the PKK which announced it would pursue only democratic methods in order to achieve Kurdish autonomy and independence.

Refugees in the UK – Statistics

Year	Asylum Applications	Refugee Status as percentages	ELR	Refusals
1988	337	10	27	63
1989	2,415	20	73	7
1990	1,590	27	67	6
1991	2,110	24	54	22
1992	1,865	17	58	25
1993	1,480	18	45	33
19994	1,145	8	5	87
1995	995	5	4	91
1996	1,405	4	2	94
1997	1,445	5	2	93
1998	2,015	4	3	94
199	2,045	22	3	75

Source: Home Office

Turkish nationals are one of the largest groups to arrive in the UK as refugees in recent years, about 38,000 since 1980 and mostly Kurds. Most have arrived since 1989 following local elections in south east Turkey where right-wing and Islamic parties made many gains. Among the election winners was a man suspected of organising a massacre of Kurds. For many Kurdish people in the Maras region this was the last straw, and some sought asylum in western countries. A number of ethnic Turks have also fled as refugees because of their political activities or because they were human rights activists or journalists.

In June 1989 the UK imposed a visa requirement on Turkish nationals, to try and prevent more refugees arriving. Many Kurds were detained on arrival. The Refugee Council is concerned that the vast majority of Turkish Kurdish asylum-seekers are now refused asylum. There are a significant number of cases of Kurds who can show strong evidence of being tortured being refused asylum but the Home Office claims that Kurds are safe in western Turkey.

Most Turkish Kurds have remained in Greater London, the largest communities being in the London Boroughs of Islington, Hackney and Haringey. Over 90 per cent of Turkish Kurds arrive in the UK speaking little or no English. Although colleges have organised some excellent English language programmes for them, demand far outstrips provision. As many as 20 per cent of adult Kurds have received little or no education, particularly women from the far south east of Turkey. Teachers need to be aware of this when sending written information to a child's home. Highly-skilled or well-educated Kurds have difficulty finding work. Most have to settle for jobs in the clothing trade, retailing or the hotel and catering industry. The Kurdistan Worker's Association estimates that 60 per cent of Kurdish refugees are single men, and 10 per cent single women.

Many male refugees have left family behind and family reunion can be difficult to achieve causing great distress to many people. Turkish Kurds have mounted several family reunion campaigns.

Most Kurdish refugees hold strong political beliefs. Political differences may mean that some Kurdish parents may wish to have little to do with one another, even though their children attend the same school. There are several community organisations working with Turkish Kurds, representing different political views. Not all Turkish Kurdish refugees feel safe in asserting their ethnic identity, particularly in places with a large ethnic Turkish community. In some London schools, children may be unwilling to say they are Kurdish. There are seven community schools teaching Kurdish (as well as Turkish) to children from Turkish Kurdistan.

Bibliography

Laizer, S. (1991) *Into Kurdistan*, London: Zed Press

McDowall, D. (1997) *The Kurds*, London: Minority Rights Group

Refugee Council (1998) *Kurdish, Turkish and English Words for School Use*, London: Refugee Council

Warner, R. (1993) *Voices from Kurdistan*, London: Minority Rights Group.

■ Refugees from Uganda

Over 13,000 Uganda refugees have fled to the UK since the early 1980s, joining a larger Ugandan Asian community who arrived in 1972. Uganda had a population of 21 million in 1999 with 90 per cent of people living in rural areas. The capital is Kampala.

Ethnic groups: There are over 30 ethnic groups, which can be divided into peoples of three different language families: Bantu, Nilotic and Central Sudanic. The ethnic groups who speak Bantu languages mostly live in southern and western Uganda. They include the Baganda, Banyankole, Batutsi, Bahutu, Banyoro and Batoro. The Batutsi and the Bahutu came to Uganda in the last 100 years, becoming citizens when Belgium and the UK redrew colonial boundaries. Others were encouraged by the British to move from densely populated Rwanda to Uganda, to increase Uganda's labour force. Those speaking Nilotic languages live mostly in northern Uganda and include the Acholi, Langi and Karamojong. The ethnic groups who speak Central Sudanic languages live in north west Uganda. There are also minorities of Indian and European origin.

Uganda's recent history has been characterised by conflict, with ethnic as well as religious and economic dimensions. Prior to colonisation the ethnic groups from southern Uganda who spoke Bantu languages were mostly settled farmers, and lived in well-organised kingdoms with a developed commercial life. The Nilotic-speaking groups from northern Uganda were a mixture of pastoralists and settled farmers and lived more loosely structured societies. British colonisers regarded southern Uganda as more developed, and made it the centre of their administration. They placed greater educational and infrastructural resources there, and preferred southern Ugandans for important administrative posts. Northern Ugandans were favoured for jobs in the police force and army. The British allowed ethnic rivalry between northerners and southerners to develop, as part of a deliberate divide and rule policy. These divisions remain today.

Languages: The official language is English, widely spoken and understood. The most important African language is Luganda, spoken by over three million people around Kampala. Luganda is a Bantu language. Other important Bantu languages include Swahili, Nkole, Chiga, Gisu, Toro and Nyoro. Swahili is rarely the first langauge of Ugandans, but it is often used as a means of communication between different groups. Nilotic languages include Acholi, Lango, Alur and Karamojong. Central Sudanic languages include Lugbara and Madi. Many of the African languages are scripted using Roman letters.

Names: Ugandan Muslims follow an Islamic naming system: a first personal name, followed by the father's name and the grandfather's name. Ugandan Christians and animists use an African naming system – a first personal name, which is often European in origin, a second name that relates to the circumstances of their birth and finally their father's name or a family name. In Uganda women usually keep their own family name after marriage. In European countries, and sometimes in urban Uganda, women take their husband's family name after marriage.

Religion: Over 60 per cent of the population are Christian, another 25 per cent follow traditional beliefs, and about 15 per cent are Muslim. There is a religious element to conflict in Uganda. British and French missionaries arrived in Uganda at the same time. In the late 19th century there were many conversions to Anglican and Roman Catholic churches and rivalry between them. Today many political parties draw their support from members of particular religious groups.

Education system: Private nursery schools are available in some parts of Uganda but most children start school at six or later. Primary education lasts seven years. The medium of instruction is English and pupils study mathematics, science, English, the major local language, religious education, arts and crafts, music, physical education and social studies, culminating in the Primary Leaving Examination. Since 1997 primary education is provided free for the first four children in a family and school enrolment has increased to 93 per cent.

Lower secondary education runs for four years, ending with the Uganda Certificate of Education, equivalent of GCSE. After two years of upper secondary education, students can sit for the Uganda Advanced Certificate of Education. Technical schools offer an alternative to secondary schooling, providing a three year full-time course. As in other poor African countries, class sizes in state schools are large. There is not strict progression from class to class according to age, as in the UK. Children who miss schooling or fail examinations may stay down a school year.

Economy: Uganda is a fertile country. Many people are subsistence farmers, cultivating small plots of rice and maize. Cash crops such as coffee, cotton, tea and tobacco are grown on small farms as well as plantations. Most people in rural southern Uganda are settled farmers whereas in northern Uganda many are pastoral nomads or semi-nomads, living alongside pockets of settled agriculturalists. Northern Uganda is less prosperous, and this north/south divide is a source of tension. Fishing is an important occupation and Uganda also has copper reserves.

A chronology of events: Before colonisation Uganda was made up of many small kingdoms, some with a well-developed commercial life. During the mid 19th century Uganda attracted the attention of European explorers who found a fertile and beautiful country. To counter the spread of Islam and secure Uganda for their own use, European Governments dispatched missionaries to convert the local population. There was much rivalry between the French Roman Catholic and Anglican missions. The Berlin Conference grants the territory to the British, who draw up the borders. People from many ethnic groups were now ruled as one colony. By the 1950s Ugandan nationalist parties begin to agitate for independence. Milton Obote leads the United People's Congress which draws its support from Protestants and northern Ugandans. Other parties represent Roman Catholics and southerners.

1962-1971: In 1962 Uganda wins independence, with Milton Obote Prime Minister. The first human rights abuses are reported in 1966. Disagreements about Government policy, and accusations of corruption lead Obote to dismiss the *Kabaka* (the king), install himself as President and make Uganda a one-party state. Colonel Idi Amin leads an armed services attack on the *Kabaka's* palace and gains popular support and political power in a period marked by political and economic problems.

1971-1980: In 1971 Amin uses Obote's absence from Uganda to seize power in a *coup d'etat*. He publicly lifts the state of emergency and frees some political prisoners, at the same time as imprisoning and killing many of his own opponents. Within three months he suspends all democratic rights, makes himself president for life, and gives the army unlimited powers to arrest all opponents. Over 60,000 Ugandan Asians are expelled from Uganda as part of his plan to 'Africanise' the country. They are central to the economy, and further economic chaos follows their expulsion. The British Government agrees to accept 29,000 Ugandan Asian refugees; others resettle in India and Kenya. Human rights abuses increase. During Amin's rule up to 500,000 people are murdered, mainly Acholi and Langi. Other victims include the Anglican Archbishop of Uganda. Thousands of people become refugees. To distract attention from the terrors and collapsing economy Amin orders the invasion of neighbouring Tanzania in 1978. The Ugandan National Liberation Army, a composite group of exiled civilians, joins the Tanzanian army and invades Uganda. They depose Amin and install a coalition government, which cannot agree. Two years of short-lived governments follow.

In 1980 the United People's Congress, led by Milton Obote, comes to power after rigged elections. Obote becomes president for the second time, and uses his power to suppress all opposition. Nearly 300,000 people are killed by the army. In the Luwero triangle, an area north of Kampala, up to 200,000 people are murdered. Thousands are illegally detained. Bahutu and Batutsi minorities are forcibly driven out of Uganda. Some 450,000 people flee as refugees to Sudan and Zaire. The National Resistance Army (NRA), founded by Yoweri Museveni, works to overthrow Milton Obote. This guerrilla army slowly gains control of large parts of the country and in 1985 Milton Obote is overthrown in a military coup led by two high-ranking Acholi officers, one of whom, Tito Okello, becomes Uganda's new president. Some political prisoners are released, but army killing continues.

In 1986 the NRA takes Kampala, and Okello is overthrown. Yoweri Museveni, a Muslim from southern Uganda, becomes the new president and strives to restore respect for human rights. Almost all army looting and killing stops in southern and western Uganda. Nearly 400,000 refugees return home from neighbouring countries. But there are still many human rights concerns. There is still habitual indiscipline in the army, and reports of NRA killings in northern Uganda of those suspected of supporting opposition groups, particularly Acholi. Also at risk are ex-soldiers in Obote's army, members of the Ugandan People's Congress and human rights activists. By 1989, more Ugandan refugees begin to flee to the UK and other European countries. Others are internally displaced or flee to Zaire. Counter-insurgency operations against remnants of Obote's army target the Acholi. In southern Uganda the security and human rights situation improves.

In 1994 refugees from Rwanda flee to camps in Uganda. Rwandan rebels begin entering isolated parts of western Uganda and rebel activity continues. In 1998 Ugandan troops are sent to the Democratic Republic of Congo, ostensibly to counter Allied Democratic Forces rebels who reportedly had bases in the DR Congo. The Congolese government claims, however, that the Ugandans are there to support an uprising against them.

In 2000 some 70,000 Ugandans are internally displaced by rebel activity in northern and western Uganda. The main rebel groups are

- The Lords Resistance Army (LRA) in northern Uganda. The LRA has perpetrated appalling human rights abuses against the local Acholi population, to punish them for failing to support them. Abuses include the murder of whole villages, maiming people, laying mines on roads and abducting children and forcing them to fight with the LRA. The LRA is backed by the Sudanese government, and in return the LRA fights Sudanese rebels in southern Sudan.

- The Allied Democratic Forces (ADF) operating in western Uganda and led by Islamic fundamentalists. The organisation is responsible for hundreds of deaths.

- The West Nile Bank Front operates from time to time in north west Uganda.

- The National Army for the Liberation of Uganda is committed to overthrowing the government of Uganda.

Human right conditions in Uganda have improved and the Acholi are no longer the targets of human rights abuses by government soldiers but there are still local incidents of police and army brutality. In June 2000 a referendum was held to decide if Uganda should move to a multi-party democracy. A pluralist political system was rejected by the Uganda people in favour of the 'no-party' system of President Museveni. Over a thousand members of the Movement for the Restoration of the Ten Commandments were murdered. In a country torn by war and with a life expectancy of 45 years, religious sects thrive.

Ugandan refugees in the UK: Over 29,000 Ugandan Asians arrived in Britain in 1972. They were not refugees in the legal sense, as they had been given British travel documents. They arrive with few belongings, and after initial periods in reception centres, were settled in many parts the UK. Today they are a successful community, their children achieve well in school and h gone on to succeed in commerce and academic life.

Statistics for recent arrivals

Year	Applications for Asylum	Refugee Status	ELR	Refusal
1988	414	6	88	6
1989	1235	6	92	2
1990	2125	3	89	8
1991	1450	6	50	45
1992	295	1	78	21
1993	595	<1	72	27
1994	360	3	9	88
1995	365	1	10	89
1996	215	1	7	92
1997	220	1	16	83
1998	210	3	35	62
1999	420	5	20	75

Ugandan refugees in the UK have fled for a range of reasons, some because they were associated with opposition parties; the many changes of government means that Uganda refugees have different political opinions. The largest group are Acholi, who fled during period 1989-1991. Until 1994 most Ugandan refugees were granted ELR. The Home Office is now refusing an increasing number of asylum-seekers, and there are isolated reports of ELR not being extended. The UNHCR has organised a voluntary repatriation programme and this has led the Home Office to consider Uganda a safe country. Although Uganda is safer than in the past three decades, the Refugee Council believes that certain people may be at risk if returned such as those associated with the Obote and Okello governments.

Most Ugandan refugees have settled in Greater London, where they face many of the same problems as other refugees, although most adult Ugandan refugees are likely to speak fluent English on arrival. Many are well educated and parents can by asked to help their children learn English. There are at least seven Ugandan community associations in Greater London, representing people of different political opinions. A Ugandan community school in east London teaches children African languages including Luganda and Luo. Several HIV/AIDS support projects are also working with Ugandan community groups. In 1990 an estimated 20 per cent of the Ugandan population were HIV positive but a successful and widespread public information campaign reduced this to about 12 per cent – a major success for a poor country. But a small number of Ugandan refugee families living in the UK are affected by HIV and AIDS.

Bibliography

Amnesty International (2000) 'Uganda' in *Annual Report*, London: Amnesty International.

Bell, J. (1993) *Ugandan Refugees: a study of housing conditions and the circumstances of children*. London: Community Development Foundation

Hooper, E. and Pirouet, L. (1989) *Uganda*, London: Minority Rights Group

Warner, R. (1995) *Voices from Uganda*, London: Minority Rights Group.

■ Refugees from Viet Nam

Over 1,400,000 refugees fled Viet Nam between 1975 and 1990. The UK has accepted 24,000. Although many Vietnamese children in schools have been born in the UK, the Vietnamese are included in this book because so many of the children are underachieving in schools. Viet Nam has a population of 65 million of whom 81 per cent live in urban areas. The capital is Hanoi.

Ethnic Groups: Some 98 per cent of the population are ethnic Vietnamese; the rest are ethnic Chinese, Cambodian or belong to indigenous minority groups. Until 1978 Viet Nam had an ethnic Chinese community of 2 per cent, who were artisans or merchants in towns, but after a border dispute between Viet Nam and China in 1978 they faced restrictions on movement, and some ad their businesses confiscated. Many fled as a result.

Languages: Vietnamese is spoken by almost everyone. It does not appear to be closely related he major languages of South East Asia but has borrowed about half of its vocabulary from

Chinese. It has a standard written form and many regional dialects. It is a tonal language – levels of pitch convey different meanings. The language is written in Roman script, modified by accents that alter the tone or inflection on each syllable.

Most ethnic Chinese in Vietnam spoke Cantonese. It is written in characters known as ideographs, which have no relation to the sound of the word but represent the word. All written Chinese languages use the same ideographs. This means that a text written by a Cantonese speaker can be read by a Mandarin Chinese speaker, even though the two cannot communicate verbally. Chinese ideographs are highly complex: some can take 30 strokes to draw. A Chinese child will learn about 2,000 ideographs by age ten. A newspaper or novel may contain 5,000-6,000. Cantonese is also a tonal language. Khmer is spoken by about 400,000 people living near the Cambodian border. The indigenous minority groups speak various languages, including Muong, Nung, Miao and Yao. Civil servants and some older people also speak French.

Most ethnic Chinese refugees from Viet Nam in Britain speak Cantonese as their first language, and also good Vietnamese. Most will be literate in Cantonese and also Vietnamese. A small minority do not speak Cantonese but another Chinese dialect such as Fukienese, Wu or Hakka Chinese. Ethnic Vietnamese refugees speak Vietnamese, and many are literate in it. Some who have married into Chinese families will speak Cantonese or other Chinese dialects.

Names: The naming system used by Vietnamese and ethnic Chinese is different from the European. Names have three parts. The family name is always written first, followed by the middle name and then the personal name.

Family Name	Middle Name	Personal Name	
Tran	Van	Tai	(M)
Hoang	Khin	Chan	(M)
Nguyen	Thi	Hoa	(F)
Ly	Nhi	Mui	(F)

Children use the same family name as their father. Women do not change their names on marriage but are often addressed formally by their husband's family name. There are about 25 common Vietnamese family names, and about 100 common Chinese family names. Some, such as Tran and Vuong, can be either Vietnamese or Chinese. The middle name is a second personal name. It may add meaning to the first personal name, for example Minh Chau: Beautiful Pearl. Among the Vietnamese the middle name or female title indicates the person's sex, such as Van for a boy or Thi for a girl. Among the Chinese community the middle name can also be used as a generational name: in some families all brothers, sisters and paternal cousins have the same name. The personal name comes last. Not all are specifically male or female.

In the UK some refugees have reversed the order of their names to fit in with European filing systems. It is worth asking people for their family names, middle names and personal names. The mother's family name should also be recorded by schools, as it will be different from the father's. Both Vietnamese and ethnic Chinese refugees may have nicknames. Usually the personal name is used to address a Vietnamese informally; for an ethnic Chinese the middle name and personal name are used. To address a Vietnamese man formally, the title and personal name should be used: Mr Tai, and for a married woman, her title and her husband's personal name: Mrs Tai. For an ethnic Chinese man, formal address uses his title and family name: Mr Tran, and for a married woman, her title and her husband's family name: Mrs Tran.

Religion: Religious belief is an integral part of Vietnamese culture. Although most Vietnamese do not have specific religious affiliations, their lives will have been influenced by Buddhist, Taoist, Confucian and traditional belief systems. Buddhists believe in reincarnation, and the possibility of achieving Nirvana – release from the endless cycle of rebirth. Some Buddhists – but few Vietnamese refugees – may be vegetarian, although some abstain from eating meat for two days every month, on the full and new moon.

Taoism (pronounced dowism) and Confucianism are sets of philosophical ideas. Taoists believe that humankind has a fixed place in the natural order of the universe and try to achieve a state of harmony with the natural world in daily life. Confucians have a strict code of conduct and aim towards a state of perfection in the present world. Many Vietnamese homes have a small shrine devoted to the memory of family ancestors. Some Vietnamese maintain ancient customs and may believe in a spirit world of dead ancestors. Respect for ancestors and one's parents is also central to Confucian philosophy. Buddhism, Taoism and Confucianism are not mutually exclusive. Asked about her religion, a Vietnamese may well say she is Buddhist and Confucian. About 20 per cent of Vietnamese refugees in Britain are practising Roman Catholics.

Education System: Before the reunification of Vietnam in 1975 there were four almost separate educational systems: Vietnamese, Franco-Vietnamese, French and Chinese. On reunification in 1975 the education system was reorganised along the lines of the North Vietnamese educational system and Chinese schools were gradually closed. Education is now compulsory for children aged six to 15. Teaching methods are formal and disciplined and the curriculum academic. To some Vietnamese parents British schools may seem chaotic. Parents may expect their children to pursue academic rather than vocational courses at school and it is essential to explain that vocational courses, play, drama, sports and arts and crafts are part of school life in the UK.

Economy: Over 70 per cent of Viet Nam's labour force is employed in agriculture, fishing or forestry. Rice is the main crop, and an important export. Others include rubber, coffee, tea, cotton, soybeans, clothing and footwear, coal and minerals. There are substantial oil, coal and mineral reserves in the north. The Gross National Product is estimated to be about $150 per head, making Viet Nam one of the poorest countries in the world. Its foreign debt is enormous, with the main creditors being the governments of Japan, Iraq and Algeria. World Bank and IMF loans were blocked by the USA, and until recently there was little foreign investment. Concerns were expressed about the effects of the end of aid from the Soviet Union which for a long time propped up the Vietnamese economy. But apart from shortages of some agricultural spare parts these fears have not been realised and the industrial economy is expanding at a rapid rate.

But there are greater challenges in the countryside. The central provinces of Nghe Tinh and Binh Tri Thien are particularly isolated and impoverished. The land bears the scars of the intense aerial bombardments of 1968-73. Deforestation, soil erosion and flooding have worsened in recent years. Roads are poor, spare parts and fuel always in short supply and power cuts hamper small-scale industry. Halting environmental degradation and improving the economic infrastructure will be central to improving the quality of life in rural areas. These needs will only be met with substantial amounts of bilateral and multilateral aid. The majority of Vietnamese refugees in the UK have come from the small towns and fishing villages of North Viet Nam. The continued poverty of this area makes it unlikely that they will ever return in large numbers, although more are now visiting their homeland.

Chronology of events: Viet Nam's early history was dominated by rivalries with Cambodian, Chinese and Thai dynasties. In 1802 Viet Nam was united under the Nguyen dynasty, but unity and independence did not last long as by 1887 France controlled all of present day Viet Nam, Laos and Cambodia. In 1940 the Japanese invaded French Indochina. Ho Chi Minh, a communist, formed the Viet Minh, a broad-based independence movement. He led a guerrilla war against the Japanese from a cave in northern Viet Nam. By the time the Japanese surrendered in 1945, the Viet Minh controlled most of the north. The victorious Allies agreed that Britain would administer the south, and China the north. But the Viet Minh marched into Hanoi before the Chinese arrived, and the Democratic Republic of Viet Nam was proclaimed in September 1945. Not even the Soviet Union recognised the new country. The British and French ruthlessly suppressed the Viet Minh, reconquering southern Viet Nam. By March 1946 the French had installed a colonial government there, headed by Bao Dai.

Lacking international recognition, the communist Viet Minh Government was forced into fighting a guerrilla war. Initially backed by China, this lasted from 1946 to 1954, and some 172,000 French soldiers were killed. The French were backed by the US, who feared a communist takeover in South East Asia. In 1954, after massive military defeat by the Viet Minh, the French were drawn to the negotiating table. The Geneva Accords temporarily divided Viet Nam in two, along the 17th parallel. The Viet Minh were to govern the north, while the head of government in South Viet Nam was to be Ngo Dinh Diem, a nationalist leader. Elections were scheduled for 1956, but were prevented by the South Vietnamese Government. The Diem regime tortured and killed thousands of its opponents, including Buddhist monks. Opponents of the government formed the National Liberation Front, a communist-supported guerrilla army.

The US Government provided aid to the South Vietnamese, including military aid. By 1961 US troops were fighting in Viet Nam and by 1965 had 200,000 US troops in South Viet Nam and began its carpet bombing of the region. Between 1968 and 1973 nearly two million people were killed. Cambodia and Laos were also heavily bombed. In the early 1970s resistance to conscription and the gathering anti-war movement forced US President Nixon to disengage from Viet Nam. The US signed the Paris Agreement in 1973, and withdrew its troops. But the North and South Vietnamese armies continued fighting. In 1975 the North Vietnamese reached Saigon, the South Vietnamese Government collapsed and the country was again united. Since then the country has been economically isolated. Not one US dollar of reparation has been paid to a war-damaged country. Until 1993 the US Government vetoed all proposals for International Monetary Fund and World Bank loans, even though the Vietnamese Government achieved the political and economic preconditions that were ostensibly preventing multilateral loans and grants.

The first refugees to leave Viet Nam were mostly ethnic Vietnamese southerners, who fled soon after the fall of Saigon in 1975 – about 130,000 people. Most were officials in the former South Vietnamese Government, or had had close contact with the US during the war and most settled in the US. The second exodus began in 1977, when 880,000 fled, many by boat. Between 1977 and 1990 over 155,000 Vietnamese asylum-seekers died at sea, from dehydration, drowning or murder by pirates. People fled both north and south Viet Nam. Some were opponents of the new regime, who had been imprisoned in re-education camps. Others were north Vietnamese who did not want to be moved to farm the new economic zones.

After 1978, subjected to anti-Chinese racism, the ethnic Chinese also fled. Some 260,000 fled to China and settled there; others travelled to Malaysia, Singapore, Indonesia, the Philippines and Hong Kong. By 1979 the exodus of people from Viet Nam was so great that the UN was forced to convene an international conference in Geneva. It was here that the British Government agreed to accept 10,000 refugees from the camps in Hong Kong and more were accepted later. Up until 1988 all Vietnamese were automatically given refugee status on leaving the country, giving a green light to all those who wanted to flee. British and Hong Kong authorities came under much criticism for conditions in the Hong Kong camps and detention centres, most of them built in former factories. Families were stacked in containers on top of each other, and such overcrowded conditions were very stressful. The last detention centres in Hong Kong closed in 1999. Refugees who fled to other South East Asian countries were resettled in US, France, Canada, Australia, Germany, Britain and other European countries. The US has the largest community, all from South Viet Nam.

Vietnamese Refugees in the UK – Statistics
Arrivals in UK from Hong Kong 1979-1992: 14,666
Arrivals from other SE Asian countries: 4,420
Arrivals from the Viet Nam Orderly Departure Programme: 4,475
Total UK Vietnamese population: 24,000

About 65 per cent of Britain's Vietnamese community is from northern Viet Nam, because most have been resettled via camps in Hong Kong. The boat journey to Hong Kong is fairly straightforward, although not without hazards. Until 1979 Britain received very few Vietnamese refugees, mainly those rescued at sea by British registered ships. The 10,000 refugees from Hong Kong accepted as part of the First Vietnamese Settlement Programme came between 1979 and 1984. Three NGOs – The Save the Children Fund, the Ockenden Venture, and the British Council for Aid to Refugees – administered reception centres. Refugees stayed there for three to six months, then were sent to local authority accommodation throughout Britain, where they received some initial support, but were soon left in isolation. In 1984 the Government agreed to take another quota of refugees as part of the Second Vietnamese Programme, mainly people who had relatives in the UK and were thus entitled to family reunion. They came from Hong Kong, or were allowed to leave Viet Nam as part of the 'Orderly Departure Programme'. They spent time in reception centres, then sent to areas where there were existing Vietnamese communities. Funding was provided to set up community groups. In 1988 a third Resettlement Programme was agreed by the Home Office, lasting until 1992. Three different groups of people were allowed to resettle in Britain: those entitled to family reunion, those who met certain selection criteria plus a small quota of vulnerable refugees and unaccompanied children. The selection criteria were criticised for being too rigid. This and slow administrative procedures meant that by the end of the Programme the quota of 2,000 had not been reached. Refugee Action, a national NGO run largely by Vietnamese, administered the reception centres for this Programme.

The reception arrangements made for Vietnamese programme refugees have come under much criticism, particularly as regards the dispersal of refugees on the First Programme. In 1985 the Government's Home Affairs Select Committee on Race and Immigration examined the resettlement programmes and it concluded that the policy was unsuccessful. This has been born out by the refugees' secondary migration: 50 per cent of all Vietnamese refugees had moved from their resettlement areas by 1989, most to major conurbations, particularly London, Birmingham and Manchester. Today about 14,000 Vietnamese live in London, mostly in the London Boroughs of Southwark, Lewisham and Greenwich, another 4,000 live in Birmingham and another 2,500 in Manchester. Most wanted to live near other Vietnamese and where they thought the chances of employment would be better. The provision of English in reception centres has also been criticised, as many refugees left them speaking little English, and could find no classes in the areas to which they were sent. This has been a major barrier to employment. Today the Vietnamese are still one of the most disadvantaged refugee groups. Throughout the early 1980s the majority of those available for work were unemployed and this still applies to 40-50 per cent of single and married male Vietnamese, well above the national average. Language barriers have also meant that many Vietnamese have not had equal access to services, which is a particular problem for elderly refugees.

Bibliography

Courtland Robinson, W. (1998) *Terms of Refuge: the Indo-Chinese Exodus and the International Response*, London: Zed Press

Duke, K and Marshall, T. (1995) *Vietnamese refugees since 1982*, London: HMSO

Mares, P. (1982) *The Vietnamese in Britain: a handbook for health workers*, Cambridge: National Extension College

Refugee Council (1991) *Vietnamese Refugee Reception and Resettlement 1979-88*, London: Refugee Council

Robinson, V. and Hale, S. (1989) *The Geography of Vietnamese Secondary Migration in the UK*, Research Paper 10, Warwick: Centre for Research in Ethnic Relations.

■ Refugees from the former Yugoslavia (excluding Kosova)

Since June 1991 and the beginning of the conflict in former Yugoslavia over 45,000 asylum-seekers and evacuees from the former Yugoslavia have arrived in the UK. About 29,000 refugees are from Kosova (Kosovo in Serbian) and are described separately on page 228. Other refugees have fled Bosnia, Croatia and Serbia.

The **Federal Republic of Yugoslavia,** comprising
Serbia (excluding Kosova) 8.5 million, capital Belgrade
Montenegro 680,000, capital Podgorica

Croatia 4.8 million, capital Zagreb
Bosnia and Herzegovina 3.1 million, capital Sarajevo
Former Yugoslav Republic of Macedonia 2 million, capital Skopje[1]

1. Populations are estimates, because of considerable refugee numbers, particularly in Serbia.

Ethnic Groups: Yugoslavia means 'the country of the southern Slavs', and most people are Slavs. Serbs, Croats and Bosnians are closely related ethnically and linguistically, although there are many differences in their backgrounds. Figures on ethnicity in Croatia, Bosnia and Herzegovina and the Federal Republic of Yugoslavia vary according to their source.

Serbia and Montenegro: The Serbs form the largest ethnic group in Serbia, where they constitute about 75 per cent of the population including Serbian refugees who were expelled from the Krajina (now part of Croatia) or fled eastern Slavonia (also part of Croatia). Serbian refugees have also fled Bosnia and Herzegovina and more recently Kosova. Minority groups living in Serbia include Roma (4 per cent of the population), Hungarians (3.5 per cent), Slav Muslims (3 per cent), Croats (1 per cent), Albanians (0.8 per cent). The Roma include refugees from Kosova and Bosnia. As in other eastern European countries, prejudice against Roma is widespread. Roma have suffered at the hands of 'skinhead' gangs – in one incident in 1999 grenades were thrown into a Roma settlement in south east Serbia. The Roma also experience widespread police harassment.

There are concerns about the rights of Serbia's Hungarian minority, who mostly live in the northern province of Voyvodina and make up about 17 per cent of the population. Most Croats who have chosen to remain in Serbia also live there. Until 1992, Voyvodina retained some political autonomy, originally granted by Tito. The regional assembly and the right to organise education, health and the police service ended in 1992. Since then some Hungarian secondary schools have been closed down. Both Hungarians and Croats living in Voyvodina suffer continued harassment, particularly from the Serbian refugee population and there is widespread discrimination in the allocation of public sector jobs.

Serbian speaking Muslims mostly live in the Sandzak on the border with Bosnia-Herzegovina where they make up about 54 per cent of the population. The Sandzak could easily be dragged into further conflict in the Balkans. There are continued reports of police harassment of Sandzak Muslims, who also face discrimination in access to public sector employment.

Some 70,000 ethnic Albanians remain in Serbia. Most live in the Presevo Valley in south east Serbia. Ethnic Albanian militia are active in the area, as are the Serbian police, army and militia. Albanian refugees have started to cross the border into Kosova.

A final casualty of the break-up of Yugoslavia are the five per cent of people who identify themselves as Yugoslavs. Since 20 per cent of all marriages took place across the ethnic divide, many are the children of mixed marriages. Unable to identify with the nationalist wave, they feel they have lost their country. Today they face harassment and may be very isolated.

Montenegro: Some 62 per cent of the population identify themselves as Montenegrins, 9.3 per cent are Serbs, 14.5 per cent Slav Muslims and 6.5 per cent Albanians. Other groups include Croats, Roma and those of mixed ethnic heritage. Montenegro's population has been swelled by refugees from Kosova, Bosnia and other parts of the former Yugoslavia.

The Montenegrins speak Serbo-Croat, which they generally call Montenegrin. Ethnic identity lies at the heart of the conflict. Montenegrin nationalists who support independence consider the Montenegrin people to be a distinct cultural and ethnic group whereas those who favour their state remaining within the Federal Republic of Yugoslavia consider themselves ethnically and politically close to the Serbs. Despite this, Montenegro has considerably better inter-ethnic relations than the rest of the former Yugoslavia. The present government has committed itself to policies of ethnic inclusion and has Albanian and Slav Muslim ministers. In January 2000 the government began a pilot programme to devolve greater local government powers to certain ethnic Albanian communities.

Croatia: Some 78 per cent of the population of Croatia are Croat, 8 per cent are Slovenian, about 5 per cent Serb, 0.9 per cent Muslim, 0.8 per cent Hungarian. Other groups include Roma, Italians and those of mixed ethnic heritage. Prior to 1991, Croatian Serbs comprised about 12 per cent of the population with most living in eastern Croatia. During the war, Serbs fled their homes or were forcibly evicted in actions such as 'Operation Storm' that drove almost all Serbs from the Krajina.

Three groups experience violations of their human rights: the families of mixed ethnic heritage, the Roma and the Serbs, who face harassment and lack police protection, particularly in Eastern Slavonia, where two were murdered in 1999, apparently by Croatian extremists although no one has yet been charged. Serbs who have been internally displaced within Croatia, or have returned to their homes from exile in the Federal Republic of Yugoslavia often have difficulty regaining their property. Tens of thousands of Croatian Serb refugees still living in the Federal Republic of Yugoslavia have expressed their wish to return home but cannot establish their right to citizenship. The Roma face prejudice, racial harassment and discrimination. Although official statistics put the community at 6,000, it seems likely that there are 30-40,000 Roma living in Croatia, some of whom have fled as refugees from other parts of the former Yugoslavia. They cannot obtain citizenship and suffer police ill-treatment and racial attacks, particularly those living in northern Croatia and belonging to the Serbian Orthodox Church. Few Roma children complete their education: the European Roma Rights centre estimated that some 90 per cent of Roma children have never been to school or have dropped out. Harassment and prejudice from fellow students is undoubtedly a contributory factor. Of the few Croatian Roma children in the UK, most have had little or no prior education.

Bosnia and Herzegovina: About 18 per cent of the population of Bosnia-Herzegovina are Croats. Bosnian Muslims 'Bosniaks' constitute about 40 per cent of the population. They were converted to Islam during Turkish rule and although they have a relaxed attitude to their religion, it is an integral part of their identity. Another 30 per cent of the population are Serbs. In 1995 Bosnia and Herzegovina were split along ethnic lines into two federated states: Republika Srpska and the Muslim-Croat Federation. The latter was facing strains during early 2001.

Macedonia: About 67 per cent of the population are ethnic Macedonians and another 25 per cent Albanian, although the latter figure is disputed by nationalists on both sides. Other minority groups are Serbs, Roma, ethnic Turks and Serbian speaking Muslims. There has been much debate about the ethnic origins of Macedonian people. They speak a language with Serb and Bulgarian roots and nationalist Serbs regard them as Serbs. Greek nationalists believe them to be Greeks who happen to speak a Slavic language. The Bulgarian Government asserts that Macedonians are a Bulgarian people. Both Greece and Bulgaria have a minority Macedonian population within their borders. Macedonia still has the potential for inter-ethnic conflict that could drag in other Balkan states and in early 2001 was on the brink of civil war.

Languages: Serbo-Croat, Slovenian and Macedonian were the official languages of former Yugoslavia, Serbo-Croat being the language of government. All are southern Slavonic languages. Until 1992 Serbo-Croat was generally considered one language, but since the collapse of former Yugoslavia, it is now customary to call it either Serbian, Croatian or Bosnian, although the 'new' languages are much alike. As time goes by, greater differences will emerge. Already there are some differences in spelling. It is easy to identify a person's origin by their accent, dialect and use of words. Most dialects are mutually intelligible but some words for particular things differ, for example Serbs use the word *igra* for dance, while Croatians use *ples*. Serbian has tended to borrow international terms from other languages, while Croatian uses its own words – for example *biblioteka* is Serbian for library and *knjizica* Croatian. Serbian, spoken in Serbia and Montenegro, is usually written in the Cyrillic script. Bosnian and Croatian use the Roman alphabet.

Albanian is spoken by over one million people in Kosova, Macedonia and small minorities in Serbia (see page 228) and Hungarian by about 340,000 people in Voyvodina. The Hungarians call their language Magyar. It is not Indo-European, but a Finno-Ugric language, related to Finnish, Estonian and a number of languages spoken in Siberia. Hungarian is written phonetically in a modified Roman alphabet. Yugoslav Roma may speak Serbo-Croat, Romani or sometimes Albanian as their first language.

Names: All ethnic groups in Yugoslavia use a European naming system of a personal name followed by a family name. Women adopt their husband's family name on marriage. As in many countries, a person's name can indicate their ethnic origin: some names are distinctly Muslim,

Hungarian or Albanian. Muslims are likely to be given personal names which are Islamic in origin: Alija, Ramiz and Amira are typical.

Religion: Most Serbs and some Montenegrins and Macedonians nominally belong to the Serbian Orthodox Church, although they may not be religiously observant. Under the Communist regime this church was receptive to government policies. Today the clergy are closely identified with nationalist sentiments and allegiance to the Orthodox Church is part of 'Serbian' identity. It has its own archbishops and hierarchies. The Macedonian Christians have their own Orthodox church and archbishops. In Montenegro, a group of pro-independence priests have broken away from the Serbian Orthodox church and proclaimed their own Montenegrin church. Most ethnic Croats (and Slovenes) are nominally Roman Catholic.

Most Muslims are now living in Bosnia-Herzegovina, although Serbo-Croat-speaking Muslims also live in the Sandzak region of Serbia and in Montenegro, Macedonia and Kosova. Almost all ethnic Albanians are Muslim, as are some Roma. Most Balkan Muslims converted to Islam in the 15th century under Ottoman rule and are Sunni Muslim. Religious observance differs between communities – less than 15 per cent of Bosnian Muslims describe themselves as religious, compared with 45 per cent of ethnic Albanians. But for all Muslims, observant or not, religion forms part of their identity.

Education System: From 1945-1991 the education system in Yugoslavia was decentralised. Basic policy was laid down by the federal government, but each republic had considerable freedom in deciding how policies would be implemented. After the collapse of Yugoslavia, the new states assumed responsibility for education. But in Serbia, the Government removed the rights of the regional government on Kosova and Voyvodina to determine education policy (see page 228). The education systems in Serbia, Bosnia and Croatia still share a similar structure. There are limited places in creches and kindergartens. Primary education lasts for eight years. Most children start school at the age of seven, a few schools at six. Primary education is compulsory, but children are allowed to leave school at 15. Children begin to learn foreign languages at 12, choosing between French, German, English or Russian. Secondary education lasts four years, up to the age of 19 and specialisation operates throughout, with vocational subjects on offer. At the end of four years students sit for the *matura* examination, administered by their different governments. The medium of education is Serbian in Serbia, Croatian in Croatia and Bosnian in Bosnia.

Before 1990 there were about 200 Hungarian language schools in Voyvodina but then some were closed and others were moved to locations away from the Hungarian population. School textbooks imported from Hungary are now banned. There are several Romani medium schools in Serbia, and some Croatian schools organise Romani classes. Illiteracy is still a problem among older people in rural areas and among the Roma.

A chronology of events: There is no simple explanation for the conflicts that have engulfed the former Yugoslavia since 1990. They have their roots in history, in long-standing disputes between the different ethnic groups in the region and in the bloody events of 1941-45. The seeds of today's conflict were sown as communist regimes collapsed throughout eastern Europe, leaving a void that was filled by nationalism. Aspiring leaders in different Yugoslav republics whipped up nationalist sentiment as a means to keep power. Economic factors also played a part: the prosperous republics of northern Yugoslavia sought to divorce themselves from the poorer south. There is also tension between the richer urban areas and the poorer and more conservative countryside. Nationalist leaders have found it easier to gain support from the rural population, as there is less concern for a person's ethnic origins in towns. Some commentators also believe that the old communist system's desperate struggle for survival contributed to the war: the large Yugoslav army was brought into action to maintain a united country and ensure survival of the system and itself. Yugoslavia's armaments industry, concentrated in Bosnia and Serbia, has ensured that regular and irregular Serbian soldiers have easy access to weapons. The wars can also be viewed as a number of different conflicts, varying between regions and between militia.

For many centuries Yugoslavia was divided between two great empires which cut across Europe. To the north, Slovenia and Croatia were part of the Western Roman Empire and subsequently the Austro-Hungarian Empire. In the south, Serbia was incorporated into the Eastern Roman Empire and later the Ottoman Empire. Yugoslavia was not a united state until the end of the First World War, when it was proclaimed under the name of the Kingdom of Serbs, Croats and Slovenes. It was a marriage of convenience rather than a love affair, and from the start there was serious tension between the different ethnic groups. Croats and Slovenes were fearful of Serbian domination, and there were continual disputes between the three groups. It was these conflicts which promoted the Serbian head of state, King Alexander Karadjordjevic, to dissolve the democratic constitution in 1929. Five years later he was murdered during a visit to Marseilles, on the orders of Croatian fascists.

The conflict between Serbs and Croats reached a climax during the Second World War. The Nazis invaded Yugoslavia in 1941 and created a puppet state in Croatia, with the support of the Ustashe-Croatian fascists. This state included parts of Bosnia-Herzegovina and Serbia. Hundreds of thousands of Serbs, Croatian democrats, Jews and Roma were murdered by the Ustashe. They were opposed by the Serbian nationalist Chetniks, and Josep Broz Tito's communist partisans. The Chetniks and communist partisans also fought each other with great brutality. Over 1,700,000 people – one tenth of Yugoslavia's population – were killed between 1941 and 1945, most of them by fellow Yugoslavs. This period of history is subject to claim and counter-claim by nationalist historians. Whatever the truth, memories of the Second World War play in today's hostilities.

Tito emerged victorious in **1945** and ruled the country until his death in **1980.** He chose to sweep ethnic conflict under the carpet and attempted to unite the population under the slogan 'Unity and Fraternity'. He created a socialist government that stood outside the Soviet bloc and a relatively liberal society with some privatised enterprise that was more prosperous than other eastern European nations. But Tito did not succeed in ironing out the great regional differences in the country. Slovenia was, and still remains, a prosperous central European country, while the south is largely a peasant society. Obsessed with the threat of Soviet invasion, Tito built up the largest army in Europe – virtually all adult men will have done military service – and a huge armaments industry. Both have contributed to the intensity of today's war. Under Tito Yugoslavia was divided up into six republics and two autonomous provinces (Kosova and Voyvodina). There was legislation to protect minority rights. It is ironic that the towns of Bosnia-Herzegovina were regarded as cosmopolitan and tolerant. Tito played off different ethnic groups to create a stable balance of power. While the Serbs dominated the army and the Communist Party apparatus, Tito gave constituent republics extensive autonomy, particularly in the 1974 constitutional reforms. But on his death autonomy slowly transformed into disintegration.

A common socialist ideal and an extensive party apparatus held Yugoslavia together until **1990**. But with the collapse of eastern European communism, the last thin threads snapped and Kosova Albanians took to the streets demanding greater autonomy. These demonstrations were brutally suppressed. Yugoslavia's disintegration gathered momentum in 1990 when Slovenia held multi-party elections. Other republics then held elections, and everywhere nationalist parties were victorious. Even in Serbia and Montenegro, where former communists won, they did so by appealing to nationalist sentiments. Slobodan Milosevic, the Serbian President, made his career by his campaign against Kosova Albanians and his calls for a Greater Serbia.

The new Governments of Slovenia and Croatia wished to turn Yugoslavia into a looser confederation of states and so secure greater autonomy for themselves. The republics of Serbia and Montenegro wanted to retain a central government and a central army. The Governments of Macedonia and Bosnia-Herzegovina initially supported a federal Yugoslavia, but nationalist fervour forced a change of policy. In 1991 Croatia and Slovenia declared their independence. The Yugoslav People's Army was brought into action, firstly in Slovenia. After a ten-day war, Slovenia won its independence and the conflict shifted to Croatia, where a Serb minority rebelled against the moves towards Croatian independence, fearing Croatian nationalism and the revival of many of the Ustashe symbols. Milosevic and other nationalists stirred up these fears. In the bloodshed, thousands were killed and towns such as Osijek, Dubrovnik and Vukovar suffered extensive damage. The Croatian war created thousands of refugees, both Croatian and Serbian. Croatian territory was initially occupied by the army of the Federal Republic of Yugoslavia, causing Croats to flee. Later Serbs fled or were driven from their homes in the Krajina and Eastern Slavonia. The UN brokered a ceasefire and 14,000 peace-keeping soldiers were stationed in Croatia. Under the UN Peace Plan, Croatia regained its occupied areas, although few Croatian Serbs have felt able to return.

Bosnia 1992-1995 – After the ceasefire in Croatia the conflict moved further south and became more bloody. In Bosnia-Herzegovina Muslims made up 40 per cent of the population, Serbs 30 per cent and Croats about 18 per cent. By 1992 Bosnia-Herzegovina had a hung parliament representing different ethnic groups, and a Bosnian Muslim President. It tried to maintain a multi-ethnic state, initially within Yugoslavia. But in February 1992 nationalist pressures caused the Government of Bosnia-Herzegovina to declare independence. Bosnian Serbs then proclaimed their own state and soon Serbian forces attacked Sarajevo and other Bosnian cities. Regular soldiers, formerly of the Yugoslav People's Army, and irregular Serbian militia gained control of 70 per cent of Bosnia-Herzegovina. Bosnian Croats had seized control of most of western Herzegovina and central Bosnia, and also proclaimed their own state. The Slav Muslims had no mother republic or powerful supporters. The international arms embargo initially rendered them militarily inferior. Although the largest ethnic group, they have been driven out of large parts of Bosnia-Herzegovina during campaigns of 'ethnic cleansing'. Both Serbs and Croats were accused of using methods reminiscent of the Nazis to drive people from their homes and their actions were described as 'ethnic cleansing'. Some 150,000 people were killed between 1992 and 1995. In June 2000, 17,000 Bosnians of all backgrounds remain 'missing'.

After several failed attempts, a peace agreement was signed in Dayton, Ohio in 1995. This provided for the retention of Bosnia-Herzegovina as one sovereign republic, but divided it into two autonomous entities: the Republika Srpska and the Muslim/Croat Federation of Bosnia-Herzegovina. There is a three-member rotating presidency, as well as Presidents of the two auto-nomous regions. Despite the end of armed conflict, many people are still displaced – Bosnian Muslims and Croats feel unable to return to their homes in the Republika Srpska nor do Serbs to their homes in the Muslim/Croat Federation. In June 2000 there were still 300,000 Bosnians living as refugees and another 830,000 internally displaced people.

The Federal Republic of Yugoslavia 1992-2000 – By 1992 the republics of Serbia and Montenegro were all that remained of Yugoslavia and the two republics became the Federal Republic of Yugoslavia. Slobodan Milosevic was the President of Serbia (which by 1992 incor-porated Kosova and Voyvodina) with Dobrica Cosic as President of the Federal Republic of Yugoslavia. In 1992 Montenegro's President was Momir Bulatovic, who was supportive of the policies of Slobodan Milosevic. During 1995, the Yugoslav government passed a decree granting advantageous loans to Serbs who wished to settle in Kosova. Human rights abuses mounted in this region (see page 228). Political opposition and the free press faced continued harassment in Serbia throughout the 1990s but there was always an active, if disunited, opposition. Most opposi-tion parties supported Vojislav Kostunica, the victorious Presidential candidate, who beat Milosevic in the elections of late 2000. Despite a democratic change in Yugoslavia, there are still many human rights concerns, as well as unanswered questions about the future of Montenegro and Kosova. There is a breakdown of law and order in the Presevo valley region, bordering on Kosova. There many of the majority Albanian community wish for union with Kosova; Kosovan paramilitaries have also infiltrated the Presevo valley.

In 1996 UN sanctions against Yugoslavia were temporarily lifted but imposed again in 1998. The Serbian economy is in ruins. Tourism had been a major source of foreign exchange, but tourist areas were lost to Croatia in 1992. UN sanctions and the demands of war damaged the economy; the war also created profiteers who smuggled arms and fuel. During the Kosova conflict, NATO bombers targeted Serbian power stations, oil refineries and other key infrastructure, doing further economic damage. The corruption and mismanagement of the Milosevic regime have added to Serbia's economic plight. Unemployment is running at about 60 per cent of the adult male population, there is hyper-inflation and the average family's purchasing power halved in the year 1999-2000. The wars in Croatia, Bosnia and, most recently, Kosova, have resulted in large numbers of Serbian refugees fleeing to Serbia. At least 400,000 internally displaced people are living in the Federal Republic of Yugoslavia, some 150,000 of them from the Krajina region of Croatia and many of the rest from Kosova.

There are still many reports of human rights abuse. Those at risk of harassment or arrest include

* ethnic Hungarian political activists
* independent journalists and human rights activists
* Roma
* Sanzhak Muslims
* ethnic Albanians from the Presevo valley region of Serbia (at least 10 per cent of the 70,000 strong population have fled since 1999).

Macedonia 2001: Most of Macedonia's Albanian population live in western Macedonia or in Skopje, the capital. They are mostly educated through the medium of Albanian, in separate state schools to their Macedonian-speaking peers. Gheg dialects of Albanian are spoken in Macedonia.

Macedonia achieved peaceful independence in 1991, followed the break-up of Yugoslavia. Peace monitors were placed in Macedonia during the Bosnian war and the country remained calm until 2001. Albanian political parties were represented in coalition governments, although many Albanians complained of discrimination meted out by the majority ethnic Macedonian population. That discrimination comprises under-investment in Albanian medium schools, other public services and in the workplace. In early 2001 extremist Albanian guerrillas infiltrated Macedonia from neighbouring Kosova. Fighting broke out between the Macedonian armed forces and Albanian guerrillas, a conflict that neither side appeared to be able to win. The fighting caused several thousand refugees to flee, but also increased ethnic tensions between ethnic Macedonians and Albanians. The latter rift could lead to greater conflict in this tense country.

Montenegro – In 1997, Milo Djukanovic was returned in Presidential elections in Montenegro. He favours closer links with western governments and looser ties with Serbia and has made moves to deepen the country's commitment to democracy. Today Montenegro is a multi-party democracy where minority groups enjoy greater rights and safety than anywhere else in Yugoslavia. Montenegrin demands for autonomy came to a head during the 1999 Kosova conflict, as its government did not support the actions of Slobodan Milosevic. For a while it seemed likely that it would be dragged into the Kosova conflict, after the army of the Federal Republic of Yugoslavia (loyal to Milosevic) moved in more troops. Today, there are still 40,000 Yugoslav soldiers in Montenegro, with equal numbers of police and independent militia who are loyal to Milo Djukanovic. The president has renewed his calls for looser ties with Serbia and stated that he will hold a referendum on independence if the Federal Government does not accede to his demands. The potential for bloodshed in Montenegro remains high and the economy still faces difficulties. In 1999, the government introduced the Deutschmark as its parallel currency, in a bid to wrest greater economic autonomy from Serbia. Milosevic responded by introducing its own economic sanctions, preventing all goods from crossing the Serbia/Montenegrin border. Today, Montenegro is dependent on aid from western governments. The change of Government in Serbia means that Montenegro has lost its western supporters.

Former-Yugoslav Refugees in the UK – Refugees have been fleeing former Yugoslavia since 1991. About 29,000 are Kosovan Albanians and are described on page 228. Another 9,000 are from Bosnia, 3,000 from Croatia, 4,000 from Serbia and Montenegro. The latter have joined an existing Serb community of about 35,000 (mostly living in London, Yorkshire and the East Midlands), many of whom came to the UK after the Second World War. The first refugees were mostly Croats displaced by fighting and many returned home after the UN-brokered ceasefire. Refugees remaining in the UK include

- Bosnians who arrived by themselves and have applied for political asylum
- Bosnians brought to the UK by voluntary organisations on convoys, most of whom have applied for political asylum
- former prison camp detainees, plus medical evacuees who have been admitted as part of a British Government programme administered by the Refugee Council and other charities between 1992 and 1995
- Croatian Serbs, people from mixed marriages and Croatian Roma
- Serbian peace activists and political opposition
- A small number of men who did not wish to service in the Yugoslav People's Army during the Bosnian or Kosovan conflict
- Roma from Serbia

Refugees from former Yugoslavia encounter most of the problems faced by other groups. It has become increasingly difficult to reach the UK: in 1992 Britain imposed a visa requirement on nationals from Serbia, Montenegro, Macedonia and Bosnia-Herzegovina. One group of Bosnian refugees was admitted to the UK as part of a government programme. In 1992 the British Government granted temporary protection to 1,000 former prison camp detainees, plus their dependants. They were given temporary leave to enter Britain, to be accommodated by the Refugee Council, Refugee Action, the Scottish Refugee Council and the British Red Cross, who set up reception centres in London, Cambridge, Rugby, Dewsbury and Edinburgh. The refugees spent several months in reception centres before being moved into housing association accommodation adequate for the refugees to stay near each other. Once they moved into permanent accommodation there were staff to assist them. About 30 per cent of those who arrived on the Bosnian Progamme or came as asylum-seekers have returned to Bosnia, although not always to their previous homes. In 2000, numbers of asylum-seekers from Serbia increased. There are Serbian and Bosnian community organisations in many parts of the UK, many of the former set up by Serbian churches. There are five Bosnian community organisations in south east London, plus a bilingual theatre group and a community school.

Bibliography

European Roma Rights Centre (1998) *The ERRC in Croatia*, Budapest: European Roma Rights Centre

Glenny, M. (1992) *The Fall of Yugoslavia*, London: Penguin

Glenny, M. (1999) *The Balkans, 1804-1999: Nationalism, War and the Great Powers*, London: Granta Books.

Malcolm, N. (1994) *Bosnia: a short history*, London: Papermac

Poulton, H. (1994) *The Balkans*, London: Minority Rights Group

Silber, L. and Little, A. (1995) *The Death of Yugoslavia*, London: Penguin.

■ Refugees from Zimbabwe

A small number of Zimbabwean refugees have fled to the UK since the mid-1980s, comprising political opposition and those fleeing Matabeleland where there have been human rights abuses perpetrated by police, army and government supporters. The Zimbabwean government, a one-party state from 1979 until 2000, views Matabeleland as the heartland of political opposition and 3,000 people there may have been murdered in extrajudicial executions. In the early 1980s an Amnesty International report of 1997 suggests that there have also been more than 7,000 beatings or use of torture in Matabeleland and 10,000 arbitrary arrests.

The Ndebele call themselves amaNdebele and their language is Ndebele. Matabele and Matabeleland are anglicisations. While most Zimbabwean refugees in the UK speak Ndebele as their first language they usually speak excellent English, the official language of Zimbabwe, and also Shona, the most widely spoken African language.

At the time of writing, the newly elected Zimbabwean government continues to support the seizure of white-owned farms. The Zimbabwean economy is in ruins, with food likely to be in short supply in the autumn of 2000. If there is a worsening of the security situation, the British government has plans to evacuate British passport-holders to the UK.

Sources: Amnesty International archive sources on Zimbabwe.

Terminology

Asylum-seeker – a person who has fled from his or her home country in search of safety, and has applied for political asylum in another country.

Bilingual student – a student who has access to, or needs to use two or more languages at home and school. It does not imply fluency in the languages and includes students who are beginning to learn English.

EAL – English as an Additional Language.

ELR – Exceptional Leave to Remain. This is an immigration status granted at the discretion of the Home Secretary, for 'humanitarian or administrative reasons'. Many asylum-seekers are now granted ELR instead of full refugee status. ELR does not afford the same rights as refugee status. In this book people with ELR are referred to as refugees, apart from where it is important to distinguish between those with full refugee status and ELR – for example when describing rights to grants for higher education.

EMAG – the Ethnic Minority Achievement Grant. This is monies available from the Department of Education and Employment in England to fund EAL and refugee support, *inter alia*. (EMAG was known as EMTAG between 1999 and 2000, when the Traveller Education Fund was temporarily merged with it).

Internally displaced persons – people who have fled their homes in refugee-like circumstances but has not crossed an international border. Statistics for internally displaced people can be difficult to estimate.

LEA – local education authority.

NASS – National Asylum Support Service, the section of the Immigration and Nationality Directorate of the Home Office that now administers support for asylum-seekers.

Refugee – a person who has been given full refugee status, according to the provisions of the 1951 UN Convention and 1967 UN Protocol Relating to the Status of Refugees, after having been judged to have fled from his or her home country, or be unable to return to it 'owing to a well-founded fear of being persecuted for reasons of race, religion, nationality, membership of a particular social group or political opinion'.

UNHCR – The United Nations High Commissioner for Refugees. This is the UN organisation responsible for giving legal protection to asylum-seekers and refugees and coordinating settlement and relief.

Bibliography

Abdelrazak, M. (2000) *Towards More Effective Supplementary and Mother Tongue Schools*, London: Resource Unit for Supplementary and Mother Tongue Schools

Acimovic, S. (2000) A Refugee Health Strategy, unpublished paper, from the Refugee Council

Ajdukovic, M. and Ajdukovic, D. (1992) 'Psychological well-being of refugee children', *Child Abuse and Neglect*, Vol. 17, p 843 – 854

Al-Rasheed, M. (1994) *The Myth of Return: Iraqi Arab and Assyrian Refugees in London*. Paper submitted to the Fourth International IRAP Conference

Amnesty International (1997) *Women in Afghanistan*, London: Amnesty International

Amnesty International (UK) (1999) *Most Vulnerable of All: the treatment of unaccompanied children in the UK*, London: Amnesty International (UK)

Amnesty International (2000) 'Cameroon' in *Annual Report*, London: Amnesty International.

Amnesty International (2000) 'Uganda' in *Annual Report*, London: Amnesty International.

Arshad, R., Closs, A. and Stead, J. (1999) *Doing our Best: Scottish School Education, Refugee Pupils and Parents – a strategy for social inclusion*, Edinburgh: Centre for Education in Racial Equality in Scotland

Asikainen, E. (1996) 'The Construction of Identity among Bosnian Refugees in Finland' in *Journal of Refugee Studies*, Vol 9

Association of Chief Police Officers (2000) The Policing of Asylum Seeker and Refugee Communities, unpublished report

Audit Commission (2000) *Another Country: implementing dispersal under the Immigration and Asylum Act 1999*, London: Audit Commission

Ayotte, W. (1998) *Supporting Unaccompanied Children in the Asylum Process*, London: Save the Children

Baker, P. and Mohieldeen, Y. (2000) 'Using School Language data to estimate the total number of speakers of London's top 40 languages' in Baker, P and Eversley, J. *Multilingual Capital*, London: Corporation of London.

Baker, R. (1983) 'Refugees – an overview of an international problem' in Baker, R. (ed) *The Psychosocial Problems of Refugees*, London: Refugee Council.

Banafunzi, B. (1996) The Education of the Bravanese Community' in Vol 1 *Race Ethnicity and Education*, Oxford: Carfax Publishing

Barnet, London Borough of (1998) *New to Schooling: guidelines for schools*, London, Barnet Multicultural and English Language Support Service

Bastiani, J. (ed) (1997) *Home-School Work in Multicultural Settings*, London: David Fulton

Bell, A. (1996) *Only for Three Months: The Basque Children in Exile*, Norwich: Mousehole Press

Bell, J. (1993) *Ugandan Refugees: a study of housing conditions and the circumstances of children*. London: Community Development Foundation

Berghahn, M. (1984) *German Jewish Refugees in Britain*, London: Macmillan

Biddlecombe, P. (1994) *French Lessons in Africa*, London: Abacus

Blackwell, D. and Melzak, S. (2000) *Far from the battle but still at war: troubled refugee children in school*, London: The Child Psychotherapy Trust

Blake, C and Ademi, X. (1998) 'Albanian Refugee Children' in *Multicultural Teaching*, Vol 17 No 1

Bloch, A and Levy, C. (eds) (2000) *Refugees, Citizenship and Social Policy in Europe*, London: Macmillan

Bolloten, B. and Spafford, T. (1996) *Brava: an educational resource pack*, London: Newham English Language Service

Bolloten, B. and Spafford, T. (1998) 'Supporting Refugee Children in East London Primary Schools', in Rutter, J. and Jones, C. (eds.) *Refugee Education: Mapping the Field*, Stoke on Trent: Trentham Books

Bourne, J. and Blair, M. (1998) *Making the Difference: teaching and learning stratgies in successful multi-ethnic schools,* London: DfEE

Brittain, V. (1998) *The Death of Dignity: Angola's Civil War,* London: Africa World Press

British Council (1998) *International Guide to Qualifications and Education,* London: Routledge

Brown, B. (1998) *Unlearning Discrimination in the Early Years,* Stoke on Trent; Trentham Books

Camden Education (1996) *Refugee Education Policy,* London: Camden Education

Camden Education and Camden and Islington Health Authority (1999) *Meeting the Needs of Refugee Children: a checklist for all staff who work with refugee children in schools,* London: Camden Education

Carey-Wood, J. Duke, K., Karn, V. and Marshall, T. (1995) *The Settlement of Refugees in Britain, Home Office Study 141,* London: HMSO

Case C. and Dalley, T. (1992) *The Handbook of Art Therapy,* London: Routledge

Cattanach, A. (1995) *Play Therapy: Where the Sky Meets the Underworld,* London: Jessica Kingsley

Chaliand, G. (1994) *A People without a Country: the Kurds and Kurdistan,* London: Zed Press

Chan, C. and Christie, K. (1995) 'Past, Present and Future: the Indochinese Refugee Experience Twenty Years Later' in *Journal of Refugee Studies* Vol 8 No 1 pp 75-94

Children of the Storm (1998) *Invisible Students: practical and peer-led approaches to enhancing the educational and emotional support for refugee children in schools,* London: Children of the Storm

Chin Ung Ho (2000) *The Chinese of South-East Asia,* London: Minority Rights Group

City Of Westminster (1998) Consultation Document of Integrated Nursery Settings in Westminster, unpublished local authority document

Commission for Racial Equality (1986) *Teaching English as a Second Language: Report of a formal investigation in Calderdale LEA,* London: CRE

Commission for Racial Equality (1988) *Learning in Terror: survey of racial harassment in schools and colleges,* London: CRE

Commission for Racial Equality (1996) *From Cradle to School: a practical guide to racial equality in the early years,* London: CRE

Commission for Racial Equality (2000) *Learning for All: standards for racial equality in schools,* London: CRE

Commission for Racial Equality (2001) *Strengthening the Race Relations Act,* London: CRE

Committee of Inquiry into the Education of Children from Ethnic Minority Groups (1985) *Education for All: The Report of the Committee of Inquiry into the Education of Children from Ethnic Minority Groups (Swann Report),* London: HMSO

Cooper, R. (1991) *The Baha'is of Iran,* London: Minority Rights Group

Cummins, J. (1981) 'The role of primary language development in promoting educational success for language minority students' in California State Department of Education (Ed) *Schooling and language minority students: a theoretical framework,* Los Angeles: California State University

Cummins, J. (1996) *Negotiating Identities: Education for Improvement in a Diverse Society,* Ontario, USA: California Association for Bilingual Education

Courtland Robinson, W. (1998) *Terms of Refuge: the Indo-Chinese Exodus and the International Response,* London: Zed Press

Dalby, A. (1999) *Dictionary of Languages,* London: Bloomsbury

Danish Refugee Council (2000) *The Legal and Social Conditions for Refugees in Europe,* Copenhagen, Danish Refugee Council

Darke, D. (1999) *The leaves have lost their trees: the long term effect of a refugee childhood on ten German Jewish children,* York: William Sessions

Daycare Trust (1995) *Reaching First Base: guidelines of good practice on meeting the needs of refugee children from the Horn of Africa,* London: Daycare Trust

Department for Education (1991) *Partnership Teaching,* London, HMSO

Department for Education and Employment (1994) *The Education of Children Being Looked After by Local Authorities,* London: Department for Education and Employment

Department for Education and Employment (2000) *National Literacy Strategy: Supporting Pupils Learning English as an Additional Language,* London: DfEE

Department of Health (2000) *Guidance on The Education of Children Being Looked After by Local Authorities, Circular LAC (2000) 13*, London: Department of Health and DfEE

Department of Health/OFSTED (1995) *The Education of Children who are Looked After by Local Authorities*, London: HMSO.

Department of Health Social Services Inspectorate (1995) *Unaccompanied Asylum-seeking Children: a practice guide*, London: HMSO.

Department of Health Social Services Inspectorate (1995) *Unaccompanied Asylum-seeking Children: a training pack*, London: HMSO

Derman-Sparks, L. (1989) *The Anti-Bias Curriculum: tools for empowering young children*, Washington DC: National Association for the Education of Young Children

Doktor, D. (1998) *Arts Therapists, Refugees and Migrants; reaching across borders,* London: Jessica Kingsley

Dorkenoo, E. and Ellworthy, S. (1994) *Female Genital Mutilation: proposals for change*, London: Minority Rights Group

Duke, K and Marshall, T. (1995) *Vietnamese refugees since 1982*, London: HMSO

Early Years Trainers Anti Racist Network (1994) *Children without Prejudice*: a video pack, Liverpool: EYTARN

Economic and Social Research Council (2000) 'Extraordinary childhoods: the social lives of refugee children' ESCR Research Briefing 5

Edwards, V. (1998) *The Power of Babel: teaching and learning in multilingual classrooms*, Stoke on Trent: Trentham Books

Elbedour, S., ten Bensel, R. and Bastien D. (1993) 'Ecological integrated model of children of war' in *Child Abuse and Neglect*, Vol 17, p 805-819

Eth, S. and Pynoos, R. (Eds) *Post Traumatic Stress Disorder in Children*, Washington: American Psychiatric Press

Ethnic Communities Oral History Project (1992) *The Ship of Hope*, London: Ethnic Communities Oral History Project

European Roma Rights Centre (1996) *Sudden Rage at Dawn: Violence Against Roma in Romania*, Budapest: European Roma Rights Centre

European Roma Rights Centre (1997) *Time of the Skinheads: denial and exclusion of Roma in Slovakia*, Budapest: European Roma Rights Centre.

European Roma Rights Centre (1998) *The ERRC in Croatia*, Budapest: European Roma Rights Centre

European Roma Rights Centre (1999) *Roma in Poland*, Budapest: European Roma Rights Centre. Available on www.errc.org

Fekete, L. (2000) *The Dispersal of Xenophobia*, London: Institute of Race Relations

Fonseca, I. (1996) *Bury Me Standing; the Gypsies and their Journey,* London: Vintage

Fraser, A. (1995) *The Gypsies*, Oxford, Blackwell

Gershon, K. (ed) (1989) *We Came as Children*, London and Basingstoke: Papermac/Macmillan

Gibbons, P. (1991) *Learning to Learn in a Second Language*, Newtown, Australia: Primary English Teaching Association

Gillborn, D. and Gipps. C. (1996) *Recent Research on the Achievement of Ethnic Minority Pupils*, London: Office for Standards in Education

Gillborn, D. and Youdell, D. (2000) *Rationing Education: policy, practice, reform and equity*, Buckingham: Open University Press

Gilroy, P. (1990) 'The End of Anti-Racism' in *New Community,* Vol 17 (1): 71-83

Glenny, M. (1992) *The Fall of Yugoslavia*, London: Penguin

Glenny, M. (1999) *The Balkans, 1804-1999: Nationalism, War and the Great Powers*, London: Granta Books

Gloucestershire County Council (2000) A Policy for the Education of Refugees and Asylum-Seekers (unpublished policy report)

Goodwin-Gill, G. (1996) *The Refugee in International Law,* Oxford: Clarendon Press

Graham Bown, S. (1999) *Sanctioning Saddam: the politics of intervention in Iraq*, London: St Martin's Press

Grant, W. (1985) 'Insider and Outsider Pressure Groups,' *Social Studies Review*, September 1985

Gravelle, M (1996) *Supporting Bilingual Learners in Schools*, Stoke on Trent: Trentham Books

Gravelle, M. (ed) (2000) *Planning for Bilingual Learners*, Stoke on Trent: Trentham Books

Griffith, D. (1997) 'Somali refugees in Tower Hamlets: clanship and new identity' in *New Community*, vol23 no 1 p 5-24

Hall, D. (1995) *Assessing the Needs of Bilingual Pupils*, London: David Fulton

Hall, S. (1992) 'The Question of Cultural Identity' in (eds) Hall, S., Held, D. and McGrew, T. *Modernity and its Futures*, Cambridge, Polity Press

Haringey, London Borough of (1998) *Refugees and Asylum-Seekers in Haringey*, London: LB Haringey

Harris, A. and Hewitt, M. (1990) *Talking Time*, London: Learning by Design

Hathaway, J. (eds) (1997) *Reconceiving International Refugee Law*, The Hague: Kluwer Law International

Health of Londoners Project (1999) *Refugee Health in London,* London: East London and City Health Authority

Healthy Islington 2000 (1994) The Islington Zairean Refugee Survey Report. London: Healthy Islington 2000 (unpublished report)

Hewitt, R. (1996) *Routes of Racism: the social basis of racist action*, Stoke on Trent: Trentham Books

Hiro, D. (1985) *Iran under the Ayatollahs*, London: Paladin

Hirson, J. (1999) New to Schooling: a survey of practice, Unpublished research report available from the Refugee Council

Holmes, C. (1988) *John Bull's Island: Immigration and British Society 1871-1971*, London: Macmillan

Home Office (1984) *Race relations and Immigration Sub-Committee Session 1984-85: Refugees*, London: HMSO

Home Office Research and Statistics Department (1993) *Asylum Statistics, UK 1985-92*, London: Government Statistical Service

Home Office (2000) *Asylum Statistics 1999,* London: HMSO

Home Office (2000) *Algeria:* Country Assessment, London: Home Office Immigration and Nationality Directorate

Home Office (2000) *Russia: Country Assessment*, London: Immigration and Nationality Directorate, Home Office

Home Office (2000) *Ukraine: Country Assessment,* London: Immigration and Nationality Directorate, Home Office

Home Office (2000) *Full and Equal Citizens: a strategy for the integration of refugees in the UK*, London: Home Office

Hooper, E. and Pirouet, L. (1989) *Uganda*, London: Minority Rights Group

Human Rights Watch (1999) *Getting away with Murder, Mutilation, Rape: new testimonies from Sierra Leone*, New York: Human Rights Watch

Hyder, T. (1998) 'Supporting Refugee Children in the Early Years' in Rutter, J and Jones, C. (eds) *Refugee Education: Mapping the Field*, Stoke on Trent: Trentham Books

Iraqi Community Association (1996) *Now We Are Here: a survey of the profile, structure, needs hopes and aspirations of the Iraqi community in Britain 1995-96*, London: Iraqi Community Association

Isaacs, S. (ed) (1941) *The Cambridge Evacuation Survey*, London: Methuen

Jackson, S. (1988) *The Education of Children in Care*, Bristol Papers No 1: University of Bristol (School of Applied Social Services)

Jaine, S. (2000) 'Teaching English as an Additional Language: time for a productive sythesis' in Shaw, S. (ed) *Intercultural Education in European Classrooms*, Stoke on Trent: Trentham Books

Jamba, S. (1995) *Patriots*, London: Penguin

Joint Council for the Welfare of Immigrants (1999) *The Immigration and Nationality Law Handbook*, London: JCWI

Kahin, M. (1997) *Educating Somali Children in Britain*, Stoke on Trent: Trentham Books

Kalmanowitz, D. and Lloyd, B. (1997) *The portable studio: art therapy and political conflict*, London: Health Education Authority

Katzner, K. (1986) *The Languages of the World*, London: Routledge

Kay, D. (1987) *Chileans in Exile: Private Struggles, Public Lives,* London: Macmillan

Kay, D. and Miles, R. (1988) 'Refugees or Migrant Workers? The Case of the European Volunteer Workers in Britain (1946-1951)' in *Journal of Refugee Studies* Vol 1 No 3/4 p 214-236

Kaye, R. (1992) 'British Refugee Policy and 1992: the Breakdown of a Policy Community', *Journal of Refugee Studies*, Vol 5 No 1 p 47-65

Keneally, T. (1989) *Towards Asmara*, London: Paladin

Kenrick, D. (1995) and Puxon, G. (1995) *Gypsies under the Swastika*, Hatfield, UK: University of Hertfordshire Press

Kenrick, D. (1998) *An Historical Dictionary of the Gypsies (Romanies)*, Maryland: Scarecrow Press

Klein, G. (1993) *Education Towards Race Equality*, London: Cassell

Knox, K. (1997) *Credit to the Nation: a study of refugees in the UK,* London: Refugee Council

Krag, H. and Fuchs, L. (1994) *The Northern Caucasus*, London: Minority Rights Group

Kunz, Egon (1985) *The Hungarians in Australia*, Melbourne: Australian Ethnic Heritage Series

Kushner, T. and Knox, K. (1999) *Refugees in an Age of Genocide*. London: Frank Cass

Laizer, S. (1991) *Into Kurdistan*, London: Zed Press

Lambert, W. and Peal E. (1962) 'The relation of bilingualism to intelligence' in *Psychological Monographs,* 76

Lancashire County Council (1999) *National Literacy Strategy Guidelines for Primary Schools*, Preston: Lancashire County Council

Landau, R. (1992) *The Nazi Holocaust*, London: I B Tauris

Lane, J. (1998) *Planning for Excellence; Implementing the DfEE Guidance for the Equal Opportunity Strategy in Early Years Development Plans, and introducing a Framework for Equality*, Liverpool: Early Years Trainers Anti-Racist Network.

Language and Curriculum Access Service Enfield (1999) *Refugee Education Handbook*, London: Language and Curriculum Access Service Publications

Legarreta, D. (1984) *The Guernica Generation: Basque Refugee Children of the Spanish Civil War*, Reno, Nevada: University of Nevada Press

Liebman, M. (1986) *Art Therapy for Groups: a handbook of themes, games and exercises*, London: Routledge

Liegeois, J-P (1998) *School Provision for Ethnic Minorities; the Gypsy Paradigm*, Hatfield, UK: University of Hertfordshire Press

Linguistic Minorities Project (1983) *The Other Languages of England*, London: Routledge and Kegan Paul

Lodge, C. (1998) 'Working with Refugee Children: One School's Experience' in Rutter, J. and Jones, C. *Refugee Education: Mapping the Field*, Stoke on Trent: Trentham Books

Lynch, E. and Hanson, M. (1992) *Developing Cross-cultural Competence: a guide for working with young children*, London: Jessica Kingsley

McCallin, M. (ed) (1993) *The Psychological Well-Being of Refugee Children*, Geneva: International Catholic Child Bureau

Macdonald. I. (1989) *Murder in the Playground: the Burnage Report*, London: Longsight Press

McDonald, J. (1995) *Entitled to learn? A report on young refugees experiences of access and progression in the UK education system*, London: World University Service

McDonald, J. (1998) 'Refugee Students' Experiences of the UK Educational System' in Rutter, J. and Jones, C. (eds) *Refugee Education: Mapping the Field*, Stoke-on-Trent: Trentham Books

McDowall, D. (1996) *Lebanon: a Conflict of Minorities*, London: Minority Rights Group

McDowall, D. (1997) *The Kurds*, London: Minority Rights Group

McMahon, L. (1992) *The Handbook of Play Therapy*, London: Routledge

Macpherson, W. *et al* (1999) *The Stephen Lawrence Inquiry: the report of the Inquiry by Sir William Macpherson of Cluny*, London: HMSO

McWilliam, N. (1998) *What's in a Word? Vocabulary Development in Multilingual Classrooms*, Stoke on Trent: Trentham Books

Machiodi, C. (1990) *Breaking the Silence: art therapy with children from violent homes*, New York: Brunner/Mazel Publishers

Maksoud, M. (1992) 'Assessing War Trauma in Children: a case study of Lebanese children' in *Journal of Refugee Studies*, Vol 5 (1)

Malcolm, N. (1994) *Bosnia: a short history*, London: Papermac

Malcolm, N. (1998) *Kosovo: a short history,* London: Papermac

Malkki, L. (1995) *Purity and Exile*, Chicago: University of Chicago Press

Marcus, H. (1995) *A History of Ethiopia*, Berkeley, CA: University of California Press

Mares, P. (1982) *The Vietnamese in Britian: a handbook for health workers*, Cambridge: National Extension College

Marrus, M. (1985) *The Unwanted: European Refugees in the Twentieth Century*, Oxford: OUP

Marsden, P. (1998) *The Taliban: War Religion and the New Order in Afghanistan*, London: Zed Books

Marshall, T. (1991) *Cultural Aspects of Job-Seeking*, London: Refugee Council

Marshall, T. (1992) *Careers Guidance with Refugees*, London: Refugee Council

Marshall Lang, D. and Walker, C. (1991) *The Armenians*, London, Minority Rights Group

Medical Foundation (2000) *Caught in the Middle: a study of Tamil torture survivors coming to the UK from Sri Lanka*, London: Medical Foundation

Melzak, S. and Warner, R. (1992) *Integrating Refugee Children in Schools*, London: Minority Rights Group

Melzak, S. (1994) What do you do when your parents are crying? Unpublished paper, Medical Foundation

Minority Rights Group (1992) *Afghanistan: a nation of minorities*, London: Minority Rights Group

Minority Rights Group (1998) *Burundi,* London: Minority Rights Group

Munoz, N. (1999) *Other People's Children: an exploration of the needs of and the provision for 16 and 17 year old unaccompanied asylum-seekers*, London: Children of the Storm and Guildhall University

National Association for Language Development in the Curriculum (1998) *Provision in Literacy Hours for Pupils Learning English as an Additional Language*, London: NALDIC

Nicolson, F. and Twomey, P. (2000) *Refugee Rights and Realities*, Cambridge: Cambridge University Press

Nissan, E. (1996) *Sri Lanka: a bitter harvest*, London: Minority Rights Group

Northamptonshire County Council (1990) *Dealing with Harassment and Racist Incidents in Schools,* Northampton: Northamptonshire County Council Education and Libraries

Norton, R. and Cohen, B. (2000) *Out of Exile: Developing Youth Work with Young Refugees,* London: National Youth Agency

Nylund, B., Legrand, J.-C. and Holtsberg, P. (1999) 'The role of art in psychosocial care and protection for displaced children' in *Forced Migration Review*, Vol 6 December 1999

OFSTED (2000) *Evaluating Inclusion: guidance for inspectors and schools*, London: OFSTED

OFSTED (2000) *Framework 2000: Inspecting Schools*, London: OFSTED

Pankhurst, R. and Pankhurst B. (1998) *The Ethiopians,* Oxford: Blackwells

Peters, C. (ed) (1995) *Sudan*, Oxford, Oxfam

Peters, J. (1985) *A Family From Flanders*, London: Collins

Praxis (1998) Unpublished research on childcare provision in refugee community organsiations, London: Praxis

Pool, D. (1997) *Eritrea: Towards Unity in Diversity*, London: Minority Rights Group

Poulton, H. (1994) *The Balkans*, London: Minority Rights Group

Power, S., Whitty, G. and Youdell. D. (1998) 'Refugees, Asylum-seekers and the Housing Crisis: no place to learn' in (eds) Rutter, J. and Jones, C. (1998) *Refugee Education: Mapping the Field,* Stoke on Trent: Trentham Books

Qualifications and Curriculum Authority (2000) *A Language in Common,* London: QCA

Rainey, Kelly, Campbell, Roafe (1997) Refugees – from a small issue to an important cause, unpublished report to the Refugee Council

Refugee Council Publications

(1989) *Asylum Statistics 1980-1988*

(1991) *At Risk: Refugees and the Convention forty years on*

(1991) *Vietnamese Refugee Reception and Resettlement 1979-88*

(1997) *Asylum Statistics 1986-96*

(1997) *Caught in the Crossfire: Colombian asylum seekers in the UK*

(1997) *The Development of a Refugee Settlement Policy in the UK*

(1998) *Asylum Statistics 1987-97*

(1998) *Refugee Community Schools Directory*

(1998) *The Cost of Survival*

(1999) Sri Lankan refugees in the Indian State of Tamil Nadu (unpublished report)

(1999) *Unwanted Journey: Why Central European Roma are Fleeing to the UK*

(2000) *Immigration and Asylum Act 1999: a briefing*

(2000) *My Name came Up: Kosovo, war, exile and return*

(2000) *Helping Refugee Children in Schools*

Refugee Council and Save the Children (2001) *In Safe Hands: a video training pack for those working with young refugee children*, London: Refugee Council and Save the Children

Resource Unit for Supplementary and Mother Tongue Schools (2000) *Directory of Supplementary and Mother Tongue Classes 1999-2000*, London: Resource Unit for Supplementary and Mother Tongue Schools

Ressler, E., Boothby, N. and Steinbock, D. (1988) *Unaccompanied Children*, New York and Oxford: OUP

Ricardson, R. (1999) *Enriching Literacy: text, talk and tales in today's classroom*, Stoke on Trent: Tretham Books

Richman, N. (1993) *Communicating with Children – Helping children in Distress*, London: Save the Children

Richman, N. (1995) They Don't Recognise our Dignity: a study of young refugees in the London Borough of Hackney, unpublished report from City and Hackney Community NHS Trust

Richman, N. (1998) *In the Midst of the Whirlwind: a manual for helping refugee children*, Stoke on Trent: Trentham Books

Robinson, V. and Hale, S. (1989) *The Geography of Vietnamese Secondary Migration in the UK*, Research Paper 10, Warwick: Centre for Research in Ethnic Relations

Ruthven, M. (1984) *Islam in the World,* London: Penguin

Rutter, J and Hyder, T. (1998) *Refugee Children in the early years: issues for policy makers and providers*, London: Refugee Council and Save the Children

Rutter, M. (1985) 'Resilience in the Face of Adversity – Protective Factors and Resistance to Psychiatric Disorder', in British Journal of Psychiatry, 147, p 598-611

Save the Children (1994) *The Somali Community in Cardiff*, Cardiff: Save the Children (Wales Division)

Save the Children (1997) *Let's Spell It Out: Peer Research by the Horn of Africa Youth Scheme,* London: Save the Children

Save the Children (1999) *Seeking Asylum in the UK: a leaflet for adults supporting unaccompanied children with legal representation and the asylum process*, London: Save the Children

Save the Children (2000) *War Brought Us Here*, London: Save the Children.

Searchlight (1995) *When Hate Comes to Town: community responses to racism and fascism*, London: Searchlight Educational Trust

Sellen, D. *et al* (2000) *Young Refugee Children's Diets and Family Coping Strategies in East London*, London: London School of Hygiene and Tropical Medicine

Shackman, J. (1997) *A right to be understood: a training pack for interpreters*, Cambridge: National Extension College

Shelter (1995) *No Place to Learn: Homelessness and Education*, London: Shelter

Silber, L. and Little, A. (1995) *The Death of Yugoslavia*, London: Penguin

Siraj-Blatchford, I. (1994) *The Early Years: laying the foundation for racial equality*, Stoke on Trent: Trentham Books

Skutnabb-Kangas, T. (1984) *Bilingualism or not: the education of minorities*, Clevedon: England: Multilingual Matters

Skutnabb-Kangas, T. and Cummins, J. (eds) (1998) *Minority Education*, Clevedon, UK: Multilingual Matters

Skutnabb-Kangas, T. and Philipsson, R. (1994) *Linguistic human rights*, Berlin: Mouton de Gruyter

Srinavasan, S (1995) 'An Overview of Research into Refugee Groups in Britain During the 1900s' in Delle Donne, M. (ed) *Avenues to Integration: refugees in contemporary Europe*, Naples: Ipermedium.

Stone, M. (1997) *The Agony of Algeria*, New York: Colombia University Press

Sword, K. (ed) (1989) *The Formation of the Polish Community in UK*, London: School of Slavonic Studies, University of London

Tamil Information Centre (1998) *Tamil Education in the UK*, London: Tamil Information Centre

Tolfree, D. (1996) *Restoring Playfulness: different approaches to assisting children who are psychologically affected by war or displacement*, Stockholm: Radda Barnen

Tronvoll, K. (2000) *Ethiopia: A New Start*, London: Minority Rights Group

Troyna, B. (1992) 'Can You See The Join? An historical analysis of multicultural and anti-racist education policies' in (eds) Blair, M., Gill, D. and Mayor, B. (1992) *Racism and Education: Structures and Strategies*, London: Sage

Turner, B. (1990) *And the Policeman Smiled*, London: Bloomsbury

Tvedten, I., Wright, S. and Bowman, L. (eds) (1997) *Angola: the Struggle for Peace and Reconstruction*, Boulder, Colorado: Westview Press

UNHCR (1994) *Refugee Children: Guidelines on Protection and Care*, Geneva: UNHCR

UNHCR (2000) *The State of the World's Refugees*, Geneva: UNHCR

United Nations (1989) *Convention on the Rights of the Child*, New York and Geneva: United Nations

US Committee for Refugees (2000) *Refugee Report 1999*, Washington DC: US Committee for Refugees

Utting, W. (1991) *Children in the Public Care*, London: HMSO

Valtonen, K. (1994) 'The Adaption of Vietnamese Refugees in Finland' in *Journal of Refugee Studies*, Vol 7 No 1

Vevstad, V. (1998) *Refugee Protection: a European Challenge*, Oslo: Norwegian Refugee Council

Vickers, M. (1998) *Between Serb and Albanian*, New York: Colombia University Press

Vickers, M. (1999) *The Albanians: a modern history*, London: IB Tauris.

Vincent, C. and Warren, S. (1998) Supporting Refugee Children: a focus on home-school liaison. Unpublished report of a research project conducted by the University of Warwick.

Vygotsky, L. (1992) *The Mind in Society: the development of higher psychological processes*, Cambridge, USA: Harvard University Press

Wicks, B. (1989) *The Day They Took the Children*, London: Bloomsbury

Whiteman, K. (1988) *Chad*, London: Minority Rights Group

Williamson, L. (1998) 'Unaccompanied – but not unsupported' in Rutter, J. and Jones, C. (ed.) *Refugee Education: Mapping the Field*, Stoke on Trent: Trentham Books.

Williamson, L. (2000) 'Unaccompanied refugee children: legal framework and local application in Britain' in Bloch, A. and Levy, C. (ed) *Refugees, Citizenship and Social Policy in Europe*, London: Macmillan

World University Service (UK) (1974) *Reception and Resettlement of Refugees from Chile*, London: WUS (UK)

World University Service (2000) *Refugee Education Handbook*, London: World University Service.

Young Minds (1994) *War and Refugee Children: the effects of war on child mental health*, London: The National Association for Child and Family Mental Health

Yule, W. (1998) 'The Psychological Adaption of Refugee Children' in Rutter, J. and Jones, C. (eds) *Refugee Education: Mapping the Field*, Stoke on Trent: Trentham Books

Zetter, R. (1991) 'Labelling Refugees: forming and transforming a bureaucratic identity' in *Journal of Refugee Studies*, Vol 4 (1).

Useful Web Sites

General- www.idpproject.org – Information about internal displacement in Colombia, the Democratic Republic of Congo, Sierra Leone, Sudan *inter alia*.

General – www.loc.gov – The US Library of Congress has a detailed country backgrounds for countries that include Algeria and Colombia

General – www.drc.dk – The Danish Refugee Council

General – www.ecre.org – A legal web site of the European Council for Refugees and Exiles

General – www.refugeecouncil.org.uk – Refugee Council

General – www.unhcr.ch – UNHCR

General – www.refugees.org – the US Committee for Refugees

Education – www.refugeeproj.free-online.co.uk

Education – www.refugeecamp.org

Ethiopia – www.ethiouk.co.uk – the Ethiopian Community Organisation in the UK

Human rights – www.amnesty.org – Amnesty International

Kosova – Useful web sites in English include www.albanian.com, www.kosova.nu/, www.albania.co.uk. There are also numerous news and other web sites in Albanian. These are listed in *My Name Came Up*, cited above.

Indonesia – www.gn.apc.org/tapol – TAPOL, the Indonesia human rights organisations.

Race – www.irr.org.uk – The Institute of Race Relations, including the excellent School Against Deportations site (irr.org.uk/sad).

Roma – www.errc.org – European Roma Rights Centre,

Roma – http://patrin.com – The Patrin web site, with extensive information about Roma issues, as well as links to other web sites.

Sierra Leone – www.sierra-leone.org is a very useful web site, proving bibliographies and links to many other sources of information on Sierra Leone.

Somalia – A useful resource is Haan Associates, publishing social and political backgrounds to Somalia as well as bilingual school books. The web site is www.haan.demon.co.uk

Sri Lanka – The Refugee Council publishes the monthly Sri Lanka Monitor which can be obtained on www.gn.apc.org/brcslproject.

A refugee education discussion group has been formed in the UK. To subscribe to refed contact http://refed.listbot.com.

Children's books and teaching material about refugees

Ashley, B. (1999) *Little Soldier*, London: Orchard Books

Hicyilmaz, G. (2000) *Girl in Red*, London: Orion Books

Naidoo, B. (2000) *The Other Side of Truth*, London: Penguin

Jewish Council for Racial Equality (1999) *Let's Make a Difference: teaching anti-racism in primary schools*, London: JCORE

Laird, E. (1991) *Kiss the Dust*, London: Heinemann

Refugee Council (1998) *Why Do They Have to Fight: refugee children's stories from Bosnia, Somalia, Sri Lanka and Kurdistan*, London: Refugee Council

Rutter, J. (1998) *Refugees: a primary school resource*, London: Refugee Council

Rutter (1996) *Refugees: We Left Because We Had To*, London: Refugee Council

Serraillier, I. (1956) *The Silver Sword*, London: Puffin

Taylor, M. (1999) *Faraway Home,* Dublin: O'Brien Press

UNHCR (1998) *To Feel At Home: Refugee Integration in Europe*, Geneva: UNHCR

By Rachel Warner and published by the Minority Rights Group, London:

Voices from Angola

Voices from Eritrea

Voices from Kurdistan

Voices from Somalia

Voices from Uganda

Voices from Zaire

Wilkes, S. (1994) *One Day We Had To Run*, London: Evans Brothers

Publishers and Suppliers of Bilingual Books

Haan Associates
PO Box 607
London SW16 1EB
0208 769 8282
0208 677 5568 (fax)
orders@haan.demon.co.uk (e-mail)
Haan publishes information and teaching
resources about Somalia.

Hounslow Language Service
Education Centre
Martindale Road
Hounslow TW4 7HE
0208 570 2393

Learning by Design
Tower Hamlets Professional Development
Centre
English Street
London E3 4TA
0208 983 1944
info@learningdesign.org
www.learningdesign.org.uk

Letterbox Library
Unit 2D, Leroy House
436 Essex Road
London N1 3QP
0207 226 1633
Distributes anti-discriminatory books for
children.

Magi Publications
189 Munster Road
London SW6
0207 385 6333

Mantra Publishers
5 Alexandra Grove
London N12 8NU
0208 445 5123
E-mail: orders@mantrapublishing.com
www.mantrapublishing.com

Milet Publishing
19 North End Parade
London W14 0SL
www.milet.com

Mirage Theatre
Park walk School
Park Walk
Kings Road
London SW10 0AY
Tel: 0207 349 9969
Produces bilingual story tapes for young
children.

The Refugee Council publishes bilingual
school books in many refugee languages – see
Useful Organisations

Roy Yates Books
Rudgewick
Horsham
West Sussex RH12 3DE
01403 822299
Roy Yates distributes a wide range of bilingual
books.

Useful Organisations

The Refugee Council
3 Bondway
London SW8 1SJ
0207 820 3000
0207 582 9929 (fax)
www.refugeecouncil.org.uk

The Refugee Council is the largest charity working with refugees in the UK. It gives practical help to asylum-seekers and refugees and promotes their rights in the UK and abroad. There are offices in London, Leeds, Birmingham and Ipswich. The Refugee Council's work to support young refugees includes

- helping local authorities and schools develop services to support refugee children including those who are unaccompanied

- providing in-service training about refugees and educational provision for refugee children

- publishing a wide range of leaflets and books, including advice leaflets for refugees, as well as educational information for teachers, bilingual teaching material for newly-arrived refugees and development education material about refugees

- answering individual inquiries requesting information and advice

- putting people in contact with refugee community organisations and other refugee agencies in their locality

- visiting schools and youth groups to speak to young people

- coordinating teachers' networks on refugee education

- coordinating the Panel of Advisers for Unaccompanied Refugee Children.

Advisory Centre for Education
1b Aberdeen Studios
22 Highbury Grove
London N5 2EA
0207 354 8321
ACE offers free advice to parents of children in maintained schools, and produces a wide range of publications on all aspects of education.

Africa Education Trust
38 King Street
London WC2E 8JS
0207 836 5075
AET offers advice and a limited number of scholarships for refugees from Africa.

Amnesty International (UK)
99-119 Rosebery Avenue
London EC1R 4RE
0207 814 6200
Amnesty International is a worldwide human rights organisation. In the UK AI presents information about the risks that individual refugees may face in their countries of origin, and may provide statements of support for asylum applicants. AI also produces a wide range of published material and is engaged in human rights education.

Artists in Exile
0207 794 1416

Asylum Aid
28 Commercial Street
London E1 6LS
www.asylumaid.org.uk

Commission for Racial Equality
Elliot House
10 Allington Street
London SW1H 5EH
0207 828 7022
www.cre.gov.uk

British Red Cross Society
9 Grosvenor Crescent
London SW1X 7EJ
0207 235 5454
The British Red Cross operates a tracing and family message service to enable peope separated by conflict or disaster to make contact with other members of their family. It also deals with family reunion cases and has a refugee project based in London.

Centre for Young Children's Rights
356 Holloway Road
London N7 6PA
0207 700 8127
A Save the Children project which addresses equality issues in early years provision. It provides in-service training and has a resource centre containing activity packs, toys and other resources.

Development Education Association
3rd Floor
29-31 Cowper Street
London EC1R 4AP
0207 490 8108
The DEA has a list of local development education centres.

Early Years Trainers Anti-Racist Network (EYTARN)
PO Box 28
Wallasey L45 9NP
0151 639 6136

English as an Additional Language Association for Wales
c/o Mark Sims
Education Department
County Hall
Atlantic Whard
Cardiff CF15UW
01222 872777

Immigration Law Practitioner's Association
Lindsey House
40 Charterhouse Street
London EC1M 6JH
0207 251 8383

INK
31 Hallwelle Road
London NW11 0DH

Joint Council for the Welfare of Immigrants
115 Old Street, London EC1V 9JR
0207 251 8708
JCWI produces information materials on legal matters and advises individuals.

Law Centres Federation
Duchess House
18 Warren Street
London W1P 5DB
0207 387 8570
Law centres give free advice, and this organisation will give information about their location.

Medical Foundation for the Care of Victims of Torture
Star House
104 Grafton Raod
London NW5 5ET
0207 813 9999 (Children's Section)
The Medical Foundation provides support for survivors of torture and their families. It employs a wide range of staff including psychotherapists, social workers and doctors. It offers specialist services for children.

Minority Rights Group
379 Brixton Road
London SW9 7DE
0207 978 9498

National Association of Language Development in the Curriculum (NALDIC)
c/o South West Herts LCSC
Hollywell School Site
Tolpits Lane
Watford WD1 8NT
www.naldic.org.uk

North of England Refugee Service
19 Bigg Market
Newcastle upon Tyne NE1 1UN
0191 222 0406
Offices in Middlesborough, Newcastle and Sunderland.

Northern Refugee Centre
10 Carver Street
Sheffield S1 4FS
0114 275 3114

Oxfam
274 Banbury Road
Oxford OX2 7DZ
0865 311311

Refugee Action
3rd Floor
Old Fire Station
150 Waterloo Road
London SE1 8SB
0207 654 7700
Refugee Action provides advice and support for asylum-seekers and refugees. It has offices in Bristol, Exeter, Derby, Leicester, Liverpool, Manchester, Nottingham, Oxford and Southampton.

Refugee Arrivals Project
Room 1116, 1st Floor
Queen's Building
Heathrow Airport
Hounslow, Middlesex TW6 1DN
0208 759 5740
The Refugee Arrival's Project offers advice for asylum-seekers at all the London airports.

Refugee Housing
CWU House
Crescent Lane
London SW4 9RS
0207 501 2200

Refugee Legal Centre
Sussex House
39 Bermondsey Street
London SE1 3XF
0207-827-9090
Out of hours emergency number 0831-598057
The Refugee Legal Centre provides free legal advice and representation for asylum-seekers including those in detention or appealing.

Refugee Support Centre
47 South Lambeth Road
London SW8 1RH
0207 820 3606
The Refugee Support Centre offers a free, confidential counselling service for asylum-seekers and refugees who are experiencing emotional distress.

Refugee Studies Centre
Queen Elizabeth House
St Giles
Oxford OX1 3LA
01865 270722
RSP is an academic research institute.

The Resource Unit for Supplementary and Mother Tongue Schools
15 Great St Thomas Apostle
Mansion House
London EC4V 2BB
0207 329 0815
This organisation supports supplementary and mother tongue schools and can put people in contact with local supplementary schools.

Save the Children
17 Grove Lane
London SE5
0207 703 5400
www.scfuk.org.uk

Scottish Refugee Council
1st Floor Wellgate House
200 Cowgate
Edinburgh EH1 1NQ
0131 225 9994
There are also offices in Glasgow.

STAR – Student Action for Refugees
3 Bondway
London SW8 1SJ
Tel: 0207 820 3006
www.star-network.org.uk

Office of the United Nations High Commissioner for Refugees
Millbank Tower
Millbank
London SW1P 4QP
0207 828 9191
Free resources for schools

Welsh Refugee Council
Unit 8
Williams Court
Trade Street
Cardiff CF10 5DQ
02920 666250

World University Service
14 Dufferin Street
London EC1Y 8PD
0207 426 5800

Index

Acholi 273-274, 276
admission to school 89-96,
157
Legislation 89-90
adolescent refugees 161-168
adverse factors 122-124
Afar 208, 211
Afghanistan 181-184
refugees 8, 10, 14, 102,
151, 181-185
AIDS 62-63
Aimaq 181
Airline Liaison Officer 22
Albania 185-186
Albanian
language 186, 228-230,
246, 282,286
refugees 119, 151, 186,
230, 232, 282
Roma 238
in Serbia 280, 286
Aleviism 270-271
Aliens Act 1905 13
Aliens Order 1920 15
Algeria 186-190
Algerian refugees 10, 14, 190-
191
Amharic 208, 211, 212, 214
Amsterdam, Treaty of 23, 30-
31
Angola 191-193
refugees 5, 10, 14, 102,
191-194
antiracist education 71-72
Arabic 186-187, 208, 211,
215, 220, 233, 246, 255,
265-267
Aramaic 220-221
Armenian language 195
Armenian refugees 10, 13,
194, 215-217, 219,-221,
233, 237, 256
art therapy 55, 85, 130-131
Assyrian refugees 215, 220-
221, 225, 234

Asylum and Immigration Act
1996 21, 22, 24, 39, 41
Asylum and Immigration
(Appeals) Act 1993 21,
22, 24, 39
Asylum appeals 22, 27, 38-41
certified asylum appeals
27, 39-40
Asylum procedures 23, 25,
33-39, 151, 158
Asylum-seekers 7, 33
Entitlements 42-45
In country 23, 33-34, 36
Port 23, 33-36
Autobiographical writing 113,
130-131
Azeri refugees 10, 215, 256

Baha'i 216-217, 219
Bakongo 194
Baluchi 181, 215
Bari 266
Barya 208
Basque children 14-15
Basse 235
Baule 225
befriending and buddying 93
Beja 208, 265-266
Belarus 256-257
Roma 238, 257
Belgian refugees 13-15
Benadiris 251
Berber 186-188
Bete 226
Bhutanese refugees 10
Bidoons 12
Biharis 12
Bilen 208
bilingual classroom assistants
98-100
Bolivian refugees 196
Bosnia 280, 281-285
refugees 10, 14, 21, 22,
33, 287, 288
Roma 238, 245

Boyash 240-241
Bravanese 250, 254
Buddhists 261,277
Bulgarian refugees 196
bullying 83
Bulu 198
Burmese refugees 10
Burundi 196-198
Burundi refugees 5, 10, 197-
198

Calderdale Judgement 93
Camden, London borough of
95
Cameroon refugees 198
careers advice 157, 162, 165-
167
Chadian refugees 10, 198-199
Chaouia 187
Chechnya 5, 11, 260
Chiga 273
Children Act 1989 23, 27, 28,
41, 53, 74, 150, 151, 152-
156
Chilean refugees 14, 18-19,
33
Chinese
Indonesia 215
language 278
refugees 151, 199
Vietnam 276
Citizenship education 83,
141-144
Colombian refugees 5, 10, 14,
21, 199-202
Community schools 17, 109-
110, 115-119
Confucianism 277
Congo-Brazzaville 10, 207
Congolese refugees (Zaire)
5, 10, 14, 60, 102, 202-
207
Connexions 166-167
consortia, asylum 46-47, 53,
90

Coptic Church 266-268
Croatia 280-285
    language 280-282
    refugees 10, 286-287
    Roma 245, 287
Cyprus 14
Czech
    Language 244-245
    refugees 14, 18
    Roma 238, 243-244

Dari 181, 215
Department for Education
    and Employment 52, 89
Department of Health 52,
    152, 153
Detention 23, 27, 28
Dinka 265-266, 268
directed lettings 110, 117
dispersal policy 16, 18-20, 46-
    48, 281
drama 131
Druze 233
Duala 198
Dublin Convention 23, 26,
    29-31, 35
Dyula 225

Early years education and
    care 44, 54, 75, 128, 168-
    180
East Timor 10
Ecuadorian refugees 196
Education Act 1996 28, 74, 90
Education Action Zones 78,
    79
Education (Fees and Awards)
    Regulations 1994 44-45
Education Reform Act 1988
    110
educational psychologists 75,
    127, 132
Enfield, London borough of
    132, 143, 179
English as an additional
    language (EAL) 79-80,
    82, 92-93, 95, 97-107,
    163-164, 177
    Assessment 102, 104,
    113, 164
English curriculum 141
English language qualifications
    95, 106-107

English speaking refugees
    198, 226, 228, 235, 246,
    275
Eritrea 207-211
Eritrean refugees 10, 14, 19,
    60, 151, 207-211
Estonia 256
Ethiopia 211-214
Ethiopian refugees 10, 14, 60,
    151, 211-214
Ethnic Minority Achievement
    Grant 77, 78-79, 94, 96,
    97-98, 110
ethnic monitoring 76-77
European asylum policy 29-
    31
European Commission 24, 29
European Convention on
    Human Rights 4
Exceptional Leave to Remain
    (ELR) 25, 34, 37-38, 42-
    45, 233
Excellence in Cities Grant
    78, 79

Faili Kurds 221, 222
family learning 85, 146-147
family reunion 38, 43
Farsi 181, 215, 217
'Fast track procedures' 22,
    27, 35, 36, 38
Female genital mutilation 59-
    61, 255, 270
Foreign and Commonwealth
    Office 52
fostering 154
free school meals 28, 74, 75,
    81, 82
French 186, 196, 198, 203,
    207, 225, 278
Fulani 198
further education 44-45, 161,
    164-166
Further and Higher
    Education Act 1994 166

Gender issues 19
Geography curriculum 141
Georgian refugees 10, 256
Ghanaian refugees 10, 14, 22
Gio/Mano 235
Gisu 273
Globalisation theory 72-73

Gola 246
Gorani 238
Greenwich, London borough
    of 117, 138-139
Guinea-Bissau 10

Haitian refugees 10
'hard cases' 47
Hausa 235-237
Hazara 181-185
HC1 and HC2 57
Healthcare 43, 57-63, 91, 95
higher education 44-45
history curriculum 141, 158
HIV/AIDS 62-63, 276
homework clubs 83, 85, 95
home language teaching
    (mother tongue) 109-
    119, 177
housing legislation 24, 43, 53,
    171
Human Rights Act 1998 4
Huguenots 13-14, 70
humanities curriculum 142
Hungarian
    language 240
    refugees 14, 17
    in Serbia 281, 282, 283
Hutu 196-198, 203, 272

Ibibio 235
Igbo 235-237
Ijaw 235
illegal entry to UK 7-8, 26, 33
Immigration Act 1971 20, 25,
    39
Immigration advice,
    regulation of 27
Immigration Appeals
    Authority 39, 52
Immigration and Asylum Act
    1999 21, 22, 24, 26-28,
    35, 39, 46, 74, 151
Immigration and Nationality
    Directorate 33, 35-36,
    52
Immigration (Carriers
    Liability) Act 1987 21-
    22, 26
Immigration officers, powers
    of 28
Immigration Rules 25, 151

Immigration Services
    Commissioner 27
income support 21, 23, 43
Indian refugees 10, 214
Indonesian refugees 10, 215
induction courses 94-95, 103,
    163
induction in schools 82, 89-
    96, 103
integrated nurseries 170
Interim Support Scheme 44,
    47, 74
internal displacement 4-5, 6-
    7, 10-12
interpreting 53, 55-57, 91,
    242, 244
interrupted education 74, 82,
    102-103, 156, 164, 255
Iranian
    Jews 216
    Kurds 215, 217
    refugees 10, 14, 19, 118,
    215-219
Iraq
    Jews 225
    Kurds 220-225
    refugees 10, 14, 151,
    220-225
Irish Travellers 238
Ismaeli Muslims 182, 185
Ivory Coast 225-226

Jehovah's Witnesses 203, 205,
    208, 212
Jewish refugees 13-15, 17, 70,
    215, 225, 257

Kabyle 187
Kalenjin 226
Kamba 226
Kanuri 235
Kashmir 214
Kenyan refugees 10, 14, 226-
    227
key skills 163
Kikongo 191-192, 202, 203,
    207
Kikuyu 226
Kimbanguist Church 191, 203
Kimbundu 191-192
Kindertransporte 15
Kingwana 203
Kinyarwanda 196

Kirundi 196
Kisii 226
Kosova 5, 228-233, 280
    refugees 8, 10, 14, 33,
    102, 119, 149-150, 156,
    231-232, 285
    Roma 225, 238, 245
Kpelle 235
Krio 235, 247
Kurdish language 215, 220,
    266
Kurds
    Iranian 215
    Iraqi 220-225
    Lebanese 233
    refugees 7, 8, 10, 14, 21,
    102
    Turkey 270-273
Kurmanji 220, 270

language centres 92-93
Latvia 256, 258
    Roma 238
league tables, school 90
Lebanon 6-7, 10, 233-234
Lebanese refugees 234, 246
legal help 41
Lewisham, London borough
    of 96
Liberia 235
libraries 55, 75, 113
life story work 130-131
Limba 246
Literacy Hour 82, 101-102,
    141
Lithuania 256-258
    Roma 238, 258
Local Government Act 1966
    70
Lord Chancellor's Office 52
Luba 203
Luganda 269, 276
Luhya 226
Lunda-Chokwe 191
Luo 226, 276

Maastricht, Treaty of 30
Macedonia 22, 280-287
Macpherson Report 136, 139
Madrassah 116. 220, 267
Madurese refugees 215
Malinke 225
Mandekan 225

Manyamulenge 203
Maronite Christians 233-234
Mauritanian refugees 10
media portrayal of refugees
    20, 24, 136, 232, 242
Mende 247
Meru 226
Mexico 12
Moldova 256, 259
Montenegro 22, 281-287

National Assistance Act 1948
    23, 27, 46
National Asylum Support
    Service (NASS) 24, 28,
    41, 46-49, 77, 78, 91,
    152, 156
National Childcare Strategy
    169
Ndebele 287
Nestorian Church 220
Newham, London borough of
    85-86, 147
Nigeria 235-237
    refugees 12, 14, 237
Nkole 273
Northern Ireland 90
Nubians 265-266
Nuer 265-266

OFSTED 74, 81, 170
Ogoni 238
Oromo 211, 212, 214
Organisation of African Unity
    4
Ovimbundu 191-192
Ovishambo 191

Pakistani refugees 14
Palestinian refugees 12, 233-
    234, 237
parental involvement 83, 127,
    145-147, 177, 179
partnership teaching 99
Persian 181, 215
Peruvian refugees 12
Philippines 12
play 129-130, 173, 175-177
Poland 240-241
    refugees 13-17, 115
    Roma 238, 239-240
Portuguese 191, 194

programme refugees 18-19, 33, 53, 229, 233, 245, 278
Prohibition of Female Circumcision Act 1985 61
protective factors 122-124
psychological adaption 5-7, 122-124, 175
risk/adverse factors 122-124
protective/mediating factors 122-124
psychological needs 82, 121-134, 175
Punjab 214
Punjabi 181, 214
Pushto 181

Race Relations Act 1976 52, 55, 74, 90, 93
Race Relations (Amendment) Act 2000 52, 74
racism 13, 15, 19, 24, 48, 73, 83, 135-144, 178, 256
reception centres 9, 15-18, 19, 48
Red Cross 157
refugee camps 8-9, 16, 58
refugee community organisations 53, 64, 147-148
Refugee Council 17
refugee status 4, 25, 34, 37-38, 42-45
refugee support teachers 75, 79-80
relationship web 124-125
religious education 141
removals 26, 40-41, 151
repatriation, voluntary 19
risk factors 122-124
Roma refugees 17, 75, 102, 238-245
Albanian Roma 186, 238
Belarussian 238
Bosnian 245
Bulgarian Roma 196
Croatian 245, 281, 287
Czech 238, 243-244
Kosovan 228, 231, 245
Latvian 238
Lithuanian 238
Polish 238, 239-240

Romanian 238, 240-243
Russian 238
Serbian 245, 275, 280, 287
Slovak 238, 243, 244-245
Yugoslav Roma 245, 283-287
Romani 238-239
Romania
refugees 13-14
Roma 238, 240-243
Rundi 196
Russia 256, 258
refugees 12, 13-14, 256, 258
Roma 238
Ruthenian 259
Rwanda language 196
Rwandan refugees 12

safe third countries 27, 35
Saho 208, 211
Salusbury Primary School and Salusbury World 83-84
Sara 198
Schengen Group 29-31
Scotland 24, 27, 28, 46, 78, 90, 98
Section 11 70, 78, 110

Serbia 280-286
refugees 286-287
Serbo-Croat 245, 282
setting and streaming 163-164
sex education 61-63
Shi'a Muslims 182, 216, 221-223, 231, 270
Shilluk 266
Shona 287
sickle cell disease and trait 58-59
Sidamo 211
Sierra Leone 246-249
refugees 12, 14, 21, 102, 247-248
Sikh refugees 181-182, 185, 214
Sinhala 260, 262
Slovakia
Roma 238, 243, 245
Solomon Islands 12
Somalia 12, 249-254

language 208, 211, 226, 250-251
refugees 7,8, 12, 14, 60-61, 94-95, 102, 151, 253-256
South Camden Community School 94
Sorani 220
Spanish 199
special educational needs 102
Special Immigration Adjudicator 22
Sri Lanka 5, 260-265
refugees 3, 12, 14, 22, 151, 264-265
Standard Acknowledgment Letter 34-36
statelessness 12
Statement of Evidence Form 34, 36, 151
Steering Group on Immigration and Asylum 29-31
Stephen Lawrence Inquiry 136, 139
study skills 163
Sudan 265-270
refugees 12, 14, 60-61, 269
Sunni Muslims 182, 187, 209, 211, 215-217, 221, 228, 233, 235, 251, 266, 270, 283
Sure Start 78, 170
Swahili 196, 203, 226, 273
Swann Report 70
Syriac 220-221

Tajik refugees 12, 181
Tamazight 187
Tamils 260-265
Tamil refugees 3, 12, 14, 22, 151, 264-266
Taoism 277
Tartars 12, 256, 258, 259
temporary protection 31, 33
thalassaemia 58-59
Tibetan refugees 12
Tigray 210, 211, 214
Tigre 208, 211
Tigrinya 208, 211, 212
Tiv 235
Tocoist Church 191
torture 6

trafficking 3, 7-8, 31, 232, 242
traumatic experiences 121-
122, 123
travel documents 38, 42
Tshiluba 203
Turkey 12, 14, 22, 270-273
Kurds 270-273
language 270
Turkmen 181, 215, 220, 221,
224
Tutsi 196-198, 203
Twa 196, 203

Uganda 273-276
Asians 18
refugees 12, 14, 21, 22,
60, 275-276
Ukraine 12, 241, 259,-260
unaccompanied refugee
children 14, 15, 17, 28,
33, 40, 44, 75, 149-160,
211, 214, 231, 232
Panel of Advisers 151,
158, 159
UN Convention on Refugees
4-5, 25, 31, 37, 38
UN Convention on Rights of
the Child 150
UN High Commissioner for
Refugees 3, 18, 25, 150
Uzbek 181

Vai 246
Vietnam 276-280
Chinese 276-277, 279
refugees 7, 8, 12, 14, 19,
33, 278-280
visa policy 21-22, 26
voucher support 46-48

Wales 78, 90, 98, 239
West Papua 215
Western Sahara 12
withdrawal of school
students 92-93, 98-99

Yaoude 198
Yazidis 220
year 11 arrivals 83, 90
Yoruba 235-237
youth work 75, 116, 119, 162,
164, 167-168
Yugoslavia 22, 228-233, 280-
287
Roma 245, 283-287

Zaza 270
Zande 266
Zimbabwe 287
Zoroastrians 216, 270